SPREADSHEET MENU OPTIONS

Worksheet

Global
Format
  Fixed
  Integer
  $
  Comma
  Percent
  Date
  Time
  Scientific
  General
  + /-
Alignment
  Values
  Labels
Width
  Enter width
Protection
  Allow Changes
  Disallow Changes
Recalculation {F5}
  Automatic
  Manual
  Iteration
  Step
Transpose
  From range
    To range

Range
Format
  Fixed
  Integer
  $
  Comma
  Percent
  Date
  Time
  Scientific
  General
  + /-
  Reset
Alignment
  Left {Ctrl-[}
  Right {Ctrl-]}
  Centered {Alt-F4} {F9 Del + }
  1 = Reset
Protect
Unprotect
Erase {F9 Del B}
Data-Fill
  Initialize
  Modify
Name
  Create
  Delete
  Modify

Labels
Reset
Sort
  Execute
  View-Options
  Sort-Range
  Column
  Row
  1 = Primary key
  2 = Secondary key
Insert
  Column
    Enter number of columns
  Row {F9 Ins L} {F3}
    Enter number of rows
Delete
  Column
  Row {Alt-F3} {F9 Del L}
Width
  Set
    Enter column width
  Reset: Current
  Reset: Hidden
Copy {F8}
  From range
    To range

Move {Alt-F8}
  From range
    To range
Titles
  Both
  Horizontal
  Vertical
  Clear
Audit
  List
    Status
    Formulas
    Range-Names
  Highlight
    Dependent Cells
    Referenced Cells
    Consolidated Formulas
  Map
    Set
    Clear
Erase
  No
  Yes
Vcopy
  From range
    To range

MCM

This Window
  Split
    Horizontal {F9 W H}
    Vertical {F9 W V}
    Synchronize scrolling {F9 W S}
    Unsynchronize scrolling {F9 W U}
    Clear {F9 W X}
  Close
    No
    Yes {Alt-End} {F9 W C}
  Modify Size or Location {F9 W L}
    M (move)
    S (shrink)
    E (expand)
  Previous-Size {F9 W P}
  Zoom {F9 W Z}
Other Windows
  Go to 1...8 {F9 W [n] G}
  Display Status {F9 W ?}
  Open {Alt-Home} {F9 W O}
Files
  Spreadsheet-Files {F9-D}
  Other
Screen
  Mono
  CO80
  BW80
  Graphics

Print {Alt-F2}

Execute
  Disk-File
    Enter file name
  Printer
View-Options
Setup
Range
Header
  Specify Header
    Enter header
  Delete Header
Footer
  Specify Footer
    Enter footer
  Delete Footer
Borders
  Row-Borders
    Set row border
    Clear row border
  Col-Borders
    Set column border
    Clear column border
  ID-Borders
    Select ID border
    Clear ID border
List-Formulas
  Yes
    Recalculation Order
    Cell Order
  No

Graph

Select
  Select name
    Options
    Display
    Print
    L = Plot
    E = Perspective{tm}
Create
  Enter name
    Options
    Display
    Print
    L = Plot
    E = Perspective{tm}
Delete
  Select name
  1 = Copy
    Select name
    Enter new name

Save {F9 S E}

Accept Options
Change Options

Combine

Copy
  From: Disk-File
  From: Window
Add
  From: Disk-File
  From: Window
Subtract
  From: Disk-File
  From: Window

DBMS

Link

Quit

No
Yes

Mastering Enable/OA

Mastering Enable/OA™

Christopher Van Buren
Robert Bixby

San Francisco □ Paris □ Düsseldorf □ Soest

Acquisitions Editor: Dianne King
Developmental Editor: Cheryl Holzaepfel
Copy Editors: Kathy Hummel and Tanya Kucak
Technical Editor: Michael Gross
Editorial Assistant: Kathleen D. Lattinville
Word Processors: Deborah Maizels and Chris Mockel
Book Designer: Julie Bilski
Chapter Art: Charlotte Carter
Screen Graphics: Delia Brown
Proofreader: Lisa Jaffe
Indexer: Julie Kawabata
Cover Designer: Thomas Ingalls + Associates
Cover Photographer: Mark Johann

To my nephews and nieces—Josh, Luke, and Aaron Hardy; Erin Lee; Heather, Bonnie, and Chris Nash; and Tom and Jennifer Rose.

CVB

Acknowledgments

The authors would like to thank the following people for their involvement in this book:

Thanks to friend and fellow author Gordon McComb for loaning essential equipment for this book; to Star Micronics for the use of the fine Laserprinter 8, which produced endless pages of text and high-quality graphics without a problem; to our agent, Bill Gladstone, and Waterside Productions; and to Cheryl Holzaepfel, our editor at SYBEX, for her patience and human touch with the manuscript and with the authors. Also at SYBEX, thanks go to Michael Gross, our technical editor, who worked hard to insure the technical integrity of this book through the perils of working with two authors; and to Deborah Maizels and Chris Mockel from the word processing department, who were given more than their share of additions and edits.

Finally, thanks to Kathy, Jennifer, and Steven for the time and understanding to produce the book; and thanks to Trudy for listening, being interested, and offering suggestions.

Contents at a Glance

Table of Contents

PART 2   SPREADSHEETS AND GRAPHS

7   Creating a Spreadsheet   139

12 Using Perspective for Graphs   **277**

PART 4   *TELECOMMUNICATIONS*

PART 5 CUSTOMIZING ENABLE

Introduction

Welcome to *Mastering Enable/OA*. This book will show you how to become proficient with the Enable/OA software package on your IBM or IBM-compatible XT, AT, or OS/2 computer. Using detailed steps and practical examples, the book will teach you how to get work done with Enable as quickly as possible and increase your productivity. *Mastering Enable/OA* will show you how to write letters and memos quickly, create lengthy documents with headings, footnotes, and page numbers, create custom databases and database reports, and construct automated financial worksheets such as budgets, projections, and expense reports.

If you're not interested in all of these applications, don't worry. The book is designed to let you concentrate on the tasks you'll require most.

ABOUT THIS BOOK

Mastering Enable/OA focuses on the most important and useful tasks and provides step-by-step instructions on how to accomplish them. As you follow the steps in each section of the book, you'll create examples and build on them as you use Enable. As you progress through each of the book's six parts, the explanations will become more advanced, assuming that you know more about the program from previous lessons. For example, where an early lesson may take you through each step in setting up a spreadsheet, a later lesson may assume that you know most basic steps and ask that you perform the necessary steps to make your screen look like an accompanying illustration.

As you use this tutorial, keep in mind that the lessons build on each other. However, each main part of the book begins a new example (or set of examples) and takes you from the beginning well into the intermediate level of use in one of the four main modules of the program. So you *can* begin with any of the main parts if you like.

To create the examples, you'll follow numbered steps for each task:

1. First step here.

2. This is the second step.

At times, the book explains ways to accomplish tasks that are not part of the example. These steps are *not* numbered:

- First step here.

- This is the next step.

Do not perform these steps as part of the example; or, if you do, be sure to return the document to its original state.

A QUICK TOUR THROUGH THE CHAPTERS

Part 1 guides you through the word processing module of Enable. Chapters 1–3 introduce you to basic word processing features via the creation and printing of a business memo. Chapters 4–6 show you some of the more advanced features of word processing, including Enable's powerful spell checker and thesaurus, and some special techniques for working with long documents.

Part 2 covers spreadsheets and graphs. In Chapters 7–9 you'll create, edit, format, and print a spreadsheet showing business expenses. Then, in Chapter 10, you'll learn to use functions to make calculations on the spreadsheet data. Chapter 11 shows you how to create graphs (including 3D graphs) from spreadsheet data, and Chapter 12 introduces you to Perspective, Enable's special graphing program.

In Part 3 you'll learn about databases. You'll start in Chapter 13 with the basics, then in Chapter 14 you'll create three more complex databases. Chapter 15 uses these databases to explain how to sort information and create reports from database information, and how to link databases. In Chapter 16 you'll learn another dimension of database management—Enable's database procedural programming language.

The telecommunications module is covered in Part 4. Chapters 17 and 18 take you from Quick-Connect, Enable's fast and simple telecommunications setup, to time-saving custom setups.

In Part 5 you'll learn how to customize Enable to meet your own needs. Chapters 19 and 20 get you started with general and spreadsheet macros. Then, in Chapter 21, you'll use macros to create some custom menus. Chapter 22 explores profiles, Enable's feature for customizing the many settings you use in all four of the modules.

Part 6 shows you how to bring all of the modules together. Chapters 23 and 24 explain how to integrate modules and share information among them.

Installation procedures are covered in the Appendix.

WHERE TO START

If you have not installed Enable for your system, begin with the Appendix. This will take you through the installation procedure. Once Enable is installed properly, begin with the next section in this Introduction, "An Overview of Computers," if you are unfamiliar with hardware and software. Otherwise, go to the section "An Introduction to Enable/OA" for an overview of each of the Enable modules. You then can start reading this book at any of the first four parts. If you like, go ahead and skip from one part to another. But be sure to save your work so you can return to the same place without repeating steps.

AN OVERVIEW OF COMPUTERS

If this is your first time with a PC computer, take this opportunity to review some basics about the computer and keyboard. The *operating system*, or *DOS*, is the fundamental piece of software that controls the hardware. Regardless of the program or application, you must have DOS running on the system. There are several kinds of DOS available, the most common being PC-DOS or MS-DOS. Enable and other software products rely on DOS for the "behind the scenes" work going on inside the computer.

Computer memory and storage comes in several different forms, or media. The most important are magnetic media (including hard and floppy disks) and chips (or random access memory, known as RAM). The computer's internal RAM chips control the amount of information you can have "in the computer" at one time. If you have added RAM to your computer, you have either expanded memory or extended memory. Consult your hardware manuals and RAM enhancements for details. However, one thing is important to know at this point: Enable uses expanded memory for document storage. The more expanded RAM you have, the larger your documents and programs can be.

RAM is a temporary storage place for information because it exists only as long as the computer power is on. When the computer is shut off, RAM—and everything in it—goes away. RAM is used despite this limitation because it lets you store and retrieve information very fast.

Much slower than RAM is magnetic media, which includes the floppy and hard disks you use with the system. While these are slower than RAM, they store information permanently (or until you specifically remove it). Therefore, disks work hand in hand with RAM to form the basis of an efficient system. Information can be stored temporarily in RAM while you're working, but saved permanently onto disk when finished. In general, the more you have of either kind of memory the better.

Since Enable and most other programs take care of using RAM efficiently, your only task is to learn how to create and store information using the program. The tool for accomplishing this is the keyboard. Figure I.1 shows three styles of keyboards used with IBM and compatible machines. All are similar, but the location of some of the special keys varies from keyboard to keyboard.

The computer keyboard is similar to a typewriter keyboard, but has a number of additional keys. These special keys include the *function keys*. These are labeled F1 through F10 (or F12 on the extended keyboard), and are located either to the left or at the top of the keyboard. These are assigned special purposes by the software package you are using. Enable uses them for frequently needed commands. Used alone and in combination with the Shift key, the Ctrl key, or the Alt key, the function keys provide over 30 possible functions for a program. The effects of pressing these keys in Enable are described throughout this book.

Remember also that the Ctrl and Alt keys are special keys that work in combination with other keys. By holding down Ctrl or Alt and pressing other keys, you can accomplish many special functions. Such

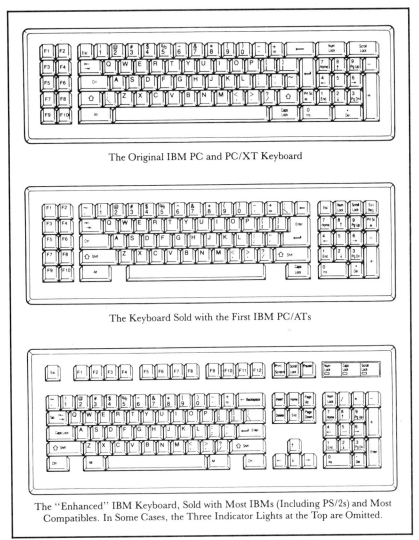

The Original IBM PC and PC/XT Keyboard

The Keyboard Sold with the First IBM PC/ATs

The "Enhanced" IBM Keyboard, Sold with Most IBMs (Including PS/2s) and Most
Compatibles. In Some Cases, the Three Indicator Lights at the Top are Omitted.

Figure I.1: Keyboards for IBM and compatible computers

combinations appear in this book like this: Alt-F3. This means, "Hold
down the Alt key and press the F3 key. Then release both keys."

You'll also notice that in addition to the number keys at the top of
the keyboard, there is a separate numeric keypad at the right side
of the keyboard. The numeric keypad has two purposes. It contains a
10-key pad for numeric entry, and it has directional, or Arrow, keys
(←, →, ↑, and ↓) for moving the cursor around the screen.

Notice that some keys on the numeric keypad have numerals as well as special commands. Normally, the numbers are not effective if the command keys are active. To use these keys for numeric input, press the Num Lock key. This disables the command keys and activates the number keys on this keypad. Press Num Lock again to return to the command keys. The enhanced keyboard has an alternate set of these command keys. If you have this type of keyboard, you might keep the Num Lock active (that is numbers active) since the command keys are available elsewhere. Remember that you have an alternate set of number keys in the usual "typewriter" position at the top of the standard keys.

AN INTRODUCTION TO ENABLE/OA

Enable/OA is an integrated program. An *integrated* program combines several types of application programs that are often purchased separately. Rather than purchasing a separate word processor, database, and spreadsheet—possibly made by three separate software companies—you can turn to an integrated product that combines all the features you need in one package. The individual programs combined in the integrated product are called *modules*. Enable/OA is one of the premier integrated products on the market. It combines four applications: word processing, database management, spreadsheet management, and telecommunications. In addition, the word processing module includes a spell checker for correcting words with an 80,000-word dictionary. The spreadsheet includes graphing capabilities for creating charts and graphs from numeric data—including 3D graphs.

The advantages offered by an integrated product are numerous. First, it makes the purchasing decision easier when you don't have to compare products individually. Support of the product comes from a single company, rather than several companies. Generally, purchasing one integrated product costs less than the combined total of separate products.

But the most important advantage is the "common interface" shared by each of the modules in the integrated product. The modules work generally the same way, using the same sorts of commands and options. A general command used in the word processor often performs the same function in the database and spreadsheet, and the style of choosing commands and menu options is the same throughout the modules. Separate products may each have a unique way of presenting features and functions, requiring many times the effort to learn them all.

Finally, integrated products can share data between the modules. Data stored in the database module can be sent directly to the word processor for use in letters, reports, and so on. Spreadsheet data used for numeric analysis can be presented in a report or even sent to the database.

Enable/OA uses a powerful method of integrating the modules. Each document you create or revise in Enable is displayed in a *window*. A window is simply a view into a word processor, spreadsheet, database, or telecommunications document. You can open up to eight windows simultaneously in Enable, and you can move between these windows at any time. When you move from one window to another, the work you leave remains intact until you return. In fact, you can even leave the window while the computer is still processing information in it (such as making calculations or arranging data). This is called *multitasking* and it's a powerful Enable feature. Besides being able to move between these windows, Enable lets you transfer information between them.

In the past, integrated products were considered less powerful than "stand-alone" applications because the modules are squeezed into one package. Memory limitations forced the products to offer fewer features. Often, integrated products performed slower than their stand-alone counterparts. But as PCs became more powerful, so did integrated products. Enable/OA offers four modules that, separately, rival many stand-alone products. And Enable/OA is fast and efficient.

ENABLE'S MENUS AND COMMANDS

The key to using Enable efficiently is learning the commands and menu options that are most important to your work. It is not necessary to learn all of Enable's commands and options, but it's important to feel comfortable with the ones you use most. This book focuses on the most important options and commands throughout the program.

Enable has four ways of presenting options: menus, keystroke commands, expert commands, and setup screens. Each has a different style of operating and each has its advantages. Often, an action can be accomplished using two or more of these methods— you can choose the style you like best. When there is more than one way of accomplishing a task, this book will describe the alternatives.

MENUS   Menus are used in each of the modules to hold options for operating the program. These options relate to the menu title. To view the menus in a module, press the F10 key. The menu titles then appear on the first line across the top of the screen. This line of menu titles is, therefore, called the Top Line menu. (You also can use the slash key (/) to bring up the Top Line menu in the spreadsheet module.)

You can select a menu using two methods. You can highlight any of the menus by pressing Tab, Shift-Tab, ←, or → until the desired menu is highlighted. The second line of the screen then displays a brief description of the currently highlighted menu. When the desired menu is highlighted, press ← to view its options; a second menu appears with a list of options. You can also select a menu from the Top Line menu by typing the first character of the menu's name. To see the Layout menu options, for example, simply type L. This is a quick way of choosing menu options, eliminating the need to press the Arrow or Tab keys and the ← key. You can use the Esc key to back out of any menu option selections.

To select one of the options, press Tab, Shift-Tab, ↑, or ↓ to highlight the desired option, then press ←. Again, pressing the number or letter associated with the option also selects it and does not require the use of the ← key. Some options, when selected, will present more options from which to choose. Others may present setup screens. Still others may complete the desired operation without further options.

SETUP SCREENS   A *setup screen* often appears at the end of a series of menu options. Setup screens present settings, or choices. For example a setup screen appears after selecting various print options, giving you options for settings such as number of copies to print, line spacing, and paper type.

If you have already installed Enable for your system, you are probably familiar with setup screens, since the installation procedure uses them extensively.

KEYSTROKE COMMANDS Keystroke commands accomplish tasks the fastest because they use the fewest keystrokes. They also provide no options—they immediately carry out a task without further questions. Some keystroke commands use the function keys. These function keys have different results in the different modules. Other keystroke commands are Alt key combinations—you invoke the command by holding down the Alt key and pressing another key. Similarly, the Ctrl and Shift keys used with other keys to accomplish tasks. When using key combinations, just remember to hold down the first key while you press the second key, then release both keys.

Keystroke commands often perform the same actions as menu commands, but much faster. But many keystroke commands do not have menu equivalents.

EXPERT COMMANDS Expert commands appear at the bottom of the screen and are similar to menu options in that selecting one command often presents a subset of more commands. These commands do not use menus to present themselves, so you cannot select them using Arrow keys or Tab keys, but only by typing the letter (or key) associated with the desired option.

Theoretically, this style of selecting options is faster than using menus because the keys remind you of their effects. In other words, the expert commands are mnemonic: To delete a line in the word processor, for example, consists of the expert commands Del and L (line). Remembering this combination is easier than using the equivalent menu option.

Expert commands are often alternatives to menu commands. That is, you can accomplish a task using either. However, there are some menu commands that have no expert equivalents and vice-versa.

Each module has a different set of expert commands that can be accessed by pressing the F9 key. However, the word processor and spreadsheet have an extra set of expert commands that contain commands for moving around in the spreadsheet or word processor.

THE WORD PROCESSOR

Enable's word processor provides features for creating letters, reports, even complete books. You can store these documents on disk and edit them later. Using various print features, you can create professional printouts from the word processor.

Like most word processors, Enable lets you insert and delete text anywhere in your document. You also can copy and move text anywhere in the document. Enable can automatically place customized headers and footers on the pages as you print, and can automatically number the pages using various numbering styles. For larger documents, Enable can automatically create a table of contents and an index.

One of the special features included in Enable's word processor is the ability to check the spelling of words. Enable includes a dictionary that compares each word in your document to its listing, telling you of discrepancies, or just correcting them automatically. A built-in thesaurus offers you synonyms when you need them.

When you first start a word processor document, the screen is mostly blank, ready for you to type information. To "process" the words that you type into the word processor, you use a series of special commands. These commands appear as choices in menus that you can access with the F10 key.

There are 11 menus available in the word processor. *EditOpts* contains options for changing the information in the document. This includes editing headers, footers, footnotes, spacing, page breaks, and rulers. These options are for editing only; the *Layout* menu includes options for changing the layout of data on the page, such as adding headers, footers, page breaks, and spacing.

The *Copy* menu includes options for copying or moving text from place to place within a document or between documents.

Delete contains several options for deleting various information on the page. It also includes an "Undo" feature for changing your mind.

The *Find* menu contains options for finding and replacing information within the document. You can specify what information to find and, if desired, Enable will automatically replace it with your specified information.

MCM includes many features common to all modules. MCM options are used to add or move windows, manipulate files, change the screen from color to black and white, and so on.

Print prints the current document after presenting a number of print options. These options let you select the printer type, add a title page, print in draft mode, and more. You can also change the page size, margins, and other attributes.

Save saves the document under the current name, or lets you change the name and location of the document before saving. After saving, you can return to the document or continue with some other document.

DBMS lets you add database information to your word processing documents.

Dictionary lets you check the spelling of words in your document as well as examine the on-line thesaurus for selected words.

Quit leaves the current file without saving. Be sure to save before using this option.

THE DATABASE

A *database* is simply a collection of similar data, such as a collection of names and addresses. You have probably used a number of common databases like a library card catalog, a recipe card file, or a Rolodex™ address file. For example, picture a Rolodex card file filled with cards. On each card is a name, address, and phone number. The Rolodex is a database because it's a collection of data set up in a way that is meaningful, and because all records in the database (the cards in the Rolodex) are somehow related to each other. When you look up an address, change a phone number, add a few new cards, or toss out an old one, you are managing the Rolodex database. This is where the term *database management* system comes from.

Database management consists of a few main tasks:

- *Storing data*   Enable stores your data in files on disk. Each file represents a different database of records. You can modify any file at any time, and there is no limit to the number of records allowed in a single database.

- *Retrieving data* Enable lets you locate any information in any database and presents that information on the screen in an understandable format.

- *Sorting data* Enable arranges data into a useful order. Usually data is sorted alphabetically, numerically, or chronologically, depending on the need. You can select one or more pieces of information in the database on which to sort the data.

- *Adding and removing data* Enable adds and removes data from a database at your request.

- *Reporting information* Enable formats data into reports to be used for analysis and decision making.

Like the word processor, the database offers its features in the form of menu options. The database main menu is accessed with the F10 key and includes a host of menus containing various options.

You can create and maintain as many separate databases as you like in Enable; each database may have hundreds or even thousands of records in it. Each individual database is stored as a separate file on disk with the .DBF extension.

THE SPREADSHEET

A *spreadsheet* is an electronic version of a columnar pad used for accounting and numeric calculations. Some typical uses of spreadsheets include budgets, sales analysis, projections, payroll calculations, tax calculations, expense reports, and accounting tasks including A/P, A/R, and general ledger. Like a columnar pad, the spreadsheet includes columns for holding information under specific headings. Also, it includes columns and rows that keep line entries together. To help you keep track, Enable uses letters to identify the columns (column A, column B, and so on) and numbers to identify rows (row 1, row 2). The intersection of a column and a row is called a *cell*. Everything you enter into the spreadsheet is entered into cells. You can move from cell to cell entering numbers and headings as you like.

As you might guess, the end purpose of creating a spreadsheet is to perform various mathematical calculations on the data, such as adding the values down columns and across rows. This is where an electronic spreadsheet is so useful. By entering *formulas* into the spreadsheet, it will automatically calculate your desired results. That is, it will automatically add rows, sum columns, calculate percentages, produce averages, and much more. All you need to know is how to enter a formula and reference the cells you want to calculate. Each time you change one of the numbers in a row or column, the formulas recalculate their values using the new numbers.

The Enable spreadsheet offers some special features, including the ability to link spreadsheets, a complete spreadsheet macro language (called the *procedural* language) for automating tasks, and the ability to create graphs from data in a spreadsheet. Graphing includes two-dimensional and three-dimensional graphs.

Like other modules, the spreadsheet uses menus to store these options for you. There are nine menus in the spreadsheet. The *Worksheet* menu contains options for altering the worksheet. This includes copying information, deleting, setting titles, and changing specific settings. The *MCM* menu contains options common to all modules. This includes manipulating windows and files, and changing the size and shape of the screen window. *Print* contains options for printing the current spreadsheet. This includes selection of the print range, addition of headers and footers, and more. *Graph* includes options for creating and changing graphs, such as setting data ranges, choosing graph types, and setting graph titles and legend items. The *Save* menu saves the current spreadsheet document on disk under the specified name. *Combine* includes options for combining two or more spreadsheets. *DBMS* contains options for using database information in a spreadsheet. The *Link* menu includes options for linking spreadsheets. (Linking is the ability to have data from one spreadsheet appear in another.) *Quit* returns to the Main menu without saving the spreadsheet.

TELECOMMUNICATIONS

The ability to transfer data across phone lines is fast becoming a necessity for computer users. Telecommunicating requires only a modem and telecommunications software in your PC. If you have a modem, Enable has the telecommunications software. Using this module, you can receive and send information from your modem, access on-line services, and perform other file transfer tasks. Many of these tasks you can perform unattended (that is, Enable takes care of it while you work...or sleep).

Telecommunicating is very simple and involves only a few essential commands and options. Like the other modules in Enable, the telecommunications module contains a set of menus containing the various options.

MAKING ENABLE EASIER TO USE

Although Enable is not difficult to use, it is a large program with a lot of commands and options. Remembering its features and the commands that invoke them can be a challenge. Plus, it's common to need to repeat certain tasks over and over. When these tasks require several steps to perform, they can become tedious. Fortunately, Enable comes with several features to make it work efficiently for your specific needs. The tools used to enhance Enable include macros, custom menus, and profiles.

MACROS

A macro is a prerecorded set of keystrokes that you can play back by pressing the macro's "play" button. The play button is really just the key used to name the macro. Each macro has a unique name, which is usually a letter on the keyboard. By pressing Alt-F9 and then the letter associated with the desired macro, you can play back the keystrokes stored. You can store any series of keystrokes in a macro; when you run (or play) the macro, it's as if you pressed the keys yourself. But macros issue keystrokes much faster than you can, which saves you time and effort.

A simple macro might type your name and address. Since this is something you might do frequently, a macro is useful for automating the task. More complex macros can be used to combine commands and options into single-key macro commands. For example, you can use a macro to perform a series of commands that change the way your document prints. You can even create macros that make decisions based on your input in the program.

CUSTOM MENUS

You may create your own menus and add them to the existing Enable menus within any module. Custom menus can be used to invoke a series of simple commands, such as moving to another module, entering data, or choosing Enable commands. You decide what options go into your menu and what each option does.

You might be thinking that menus sound a lot like macros. The two are, in fact, similar. The main difference is that macros do not appear on the screen like a menu, but are selected by entering special keystrokes. Menus, on the other hand, appear on the screen and contain several options. Another difference is that macros are actually more powerful than menus because you can enter more complex and lengthy procedures into them.

PROFILES

As you use Enable, you'll probably want to tailor it to your specific needs. When you enter the word processor, for example, Enable assumes standard settings for page margins, tab stops, and many other features. You can change these standards, or *defaults,* at any time using the Enable Profiles feature. Each module has a series of these defaults that you might want to change, including page setup options, margin settings, printer specifications, and other settings. Since these settings can be changed independently for each document, a profile should be used only when you consistently and repeatedly reset the defaults to your own standards. Then, each time you start a new document, your custom settings are active. You will still be able to change these new defaults (your custom settings) within the document if desired.

PART

1

Word Processing

Getting Started with the Word Processor

THIS CHAPTER INTRODUCES YOU TO THE ENABLE word processor module. It shows you how to start a new document, type text on the screen, change your work, and save your document for future use. You will use a simple example of creating a memo for interoffice communication. This memo will be used in the next chapter as you learn more editing features. Before you begin, make sure that you have Enable properly installed for your system. If you are using a hard disk, Enable should be copied to it. Installation and setup instructions are located in the Appendix.

STARTING ENABLE

If you are using a floppy-disk system, insert the Enable Utility Disk in drive A and a blank data disk in drive B. Make sure that the default directory is set to drive A (the DOS prompt should indicate the drive A, as in A:\>). Now enter the startup command:

Enable ↵

If you are using a hard-disk system, set the default directory to the Enable directory by entering the following at the C prompt:

cd C:\EN300 ⬅

This should make your DOS prompt look something like this: C:\EN300>. Now enter the startup command:

Enable ⬅

Enable's sign-on screen is now in view, and looks like the screen in Figure 1.1. Here is your opportunity to enter the current date and time, and to select a profile for this session of Enable. As described in the Introduction, a *profile* is a custom setup for Enable that activates various settings throughout the program. Until you know more about the various modules in Enable, creating profiles will be of little value. Therefore, you'll be using the default (system-supplied) profile throughout this chapter. Useful profile options will be presented in margin notes for future reference.

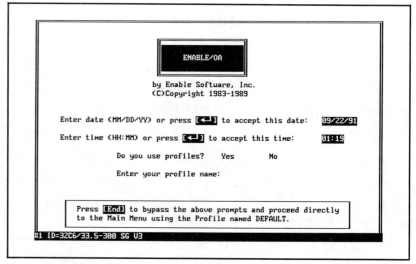

Figure 1.1: Enable's sign-on screen

With the sign-on screen in view, follow these steps to proceed to the Main menu. (If you want to go back and reenter any of the options on the screen, just press ↑.)

1. Enter the current date in the format *09/22/91*. Be sure to include either slash characters, spaces, or hyphens between the parts of the date. Press ⏎ to proceed to the next option. If the date shown is already correct, or if you don't care about setting the correct date, you can simply press ⏎ to move to the next option.

2. Enter the current time in the format *15:45* (24-hour format). Be sure to use the colon between the parts of the time. Press ⏎ to proceed to the next option. To use the time currently shown, just press ⏎.

3. At the prompt "Do you use profiles?" press → once to highlight *No*, then press ⏎. This will cause Enable to select the default profile for this session. You will now be at the Main menu (Figure 1.2).

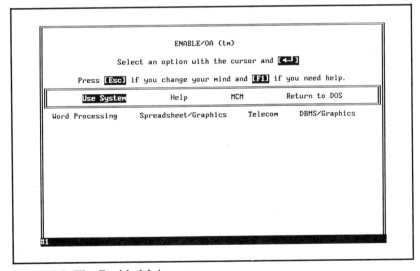

Figure 1.2: The Enable Main menu

LOOKING AT THE MAIN MENU

From the Main menu, you can go into any of the four Enable modules and begin new documents. You can also retrieve existing documents and make changes to them. There are four options on the Main menu.

The *Use System* option is used to enter any of the four modules. After selecting this option you will be able to select the Word Processing, Spreadsheet/Graphics, or DBMS/Graphics module and then choose either a new or existing document, or select the Telecom module. Use System will be the most used of the four Main menu options.

The *Help* option presents the Enable Help screens, which include information about the tutorials that come with the program. If you are using a hard drive, you can access the tutorials from a floppy disk or from the hard disk, depending on the way you installed the program. See the installation process in the Appendix for more information.

The *MCM* option takes you to the Master Control Module, a special part of Enable that controls system-wide features. The Master Control Module, sometimes considered a fifth module in Enable, houses special features, such as custom menu generation, macro creation, and special display options. Since the MCM features are fairly advanced, you won't be using this module until later in the book.

The *Return to DOS* option quits Enable and returns you to the active directory in DOS.

STARTING A NEW DOCUMENT

Begin a new word processing document from the Enable Main menu using these steps. (If you make a mistake, you can start over by pressing Esc.)

1. The Main menu option *Use System* should be highlighted; if it's not, press → until *Use System* is highlighted, then press ←. This produces a new line of menu items listing the four Enable modules.

2. The *Word Processing* option should be highlighted, since it's first in the list. If this option is not highlighted, press → until

it is. Now press ◄─┘ to select the option. Another line of options appears.

3. Press ◄─┘ to select the *Create* option, which is already highlighted. This tells Enable that you want to create a new document. Enable now asks you to name the new document. The screen should look like Figure 1.3.

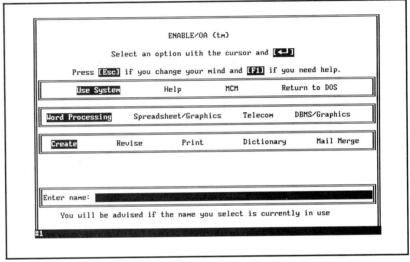

Figure 1.3: Getting to the word processor with a new document

Naming a new document before entering the word processor is really just a formality, since you can change the name later when (and if) you save the document. Just remember that word processor file names can have a maximum of eight characters. These characters can be any combination of letters and numbers, as well as the special characters & $ # @ % ! ' ( ) - { } _ ^ and ˜ . Do not include spaces or periods in file names. Enable does not distinguish between upper- and lowercase letters in filenames. Some examples of acceptable file names include JanLTRs, Let(new), Chapter1, 101A, and STOCK-RPT. You can also add an extension to the name consisting of a period and up to three characters (as in *JAN.LTR*); however, since Enable applies its own extensions to your documents, do not add them unless you have some specific purpose for doing so.

4. Enter the name **DEMOMEMO** and press ◄─┘.

You are now in the word processor with a new, blank document called DEMOMEMO. The screen should look like Figure 1.4. Notice that Enable displays a ruler at the top of the screen. This is called the *initial ruler*. More on this later.

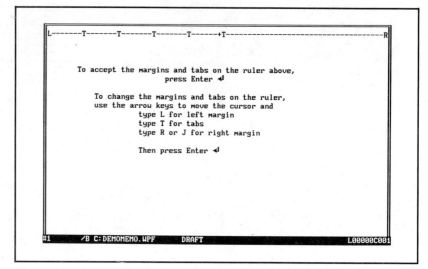

Figure 1.4: The first word processor screen showing ruler instructions

At this time, you have the option of accepting the initial ruler as is, or changing the settings. This is by no means a permanent choice. You can always go back and change the ruler later. The default ruler settings are sufficient for our memo, so at this point, accept the default ruler:

5. Press ← to accept the default settings. You see the screen shown in Figure 1.5.

EXAMINING THE WORD PROCESSOR SCREEN

Before you begin typing your memo, take a moment to examine the screen. Refer to Figure 1.5 as you read through this section.

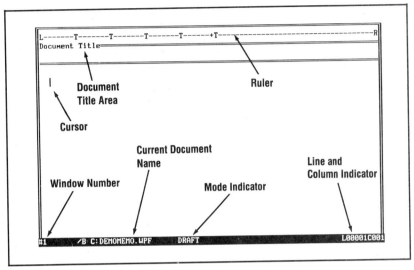

Figure 1.5: The word processor screen

THE STATUS LINE

Notice the line of information at the bottom of the screen. This status line can be useful as you create or edit documents. At the far left you see the *window number*. You can have several documents on the screen at one time, each in its own window. The double box surrounding the entire document is the current window and, since it is the only window in use, is window #1. If you were to open a new window without closing the current one, the window numbers would indicate the order in which they were opened. Windows are covered in detail in Part 6 of this book.

To the right of the window number is the *current document name*. This is the name you entered for the document when first creating it. Along with the basic file name (DEMOMEMO) is the current drive (in this case, it is C:), the current path, and the extension name, which is automatically applied by Enable (in this case, .WPF).

There are two ways of viewing a word processor document: in Draft mode and in Final mode. The *mode indicator* in the middle of the status line shows that you are currently in Draft mode. This means that many of the formatting and layout elements of the document that would otherwise be invisible on the printout will be displayed.

The *line and column indicator* at the right shows the exact position of the cursor at all times. The five-digit number following the "L" indicates the line on which the cursor is located, and the three-digit number following the "C" indicates the column in which the cursor is located. As you type or move the cursor, you'll notice the numbers change to reflect the current position.

THE CURSOR

The flashing line on the screen is the cursor. This indicates the exact position where your typing will appear. As you type, the cursor follows along. You can move the cursor at any time to type elsewhere on the page. This is discussed under "Basic Cursor Movement" later in this chapter.

THE RULER

The ruler indicates the current margins and tab stops of the document. Typing will begin at the column indicated by the "L" and end at the column indicated by the "R." The tab stops, indicated by "T," show where the cursor will stop when you press the Tab key. The center of the left and right margins is marked with a plus sign (+).

DOCUMENT TITLE AREA

The document title area at the top of the screen is used to hold title page information. The double-line borders surrounding this area will not appear on the printout; they are to show you the entire title area. If you use this area, Enable will place the information on a separate page at the front of the document.

TYPING TEXT

See the Introduction for an explanation of the keys on your keyboard and their functions.

You are now ready to type your memo. Remember that the text will appear at the location of the cursor. If you make an error as you type, just use the Backspace and Delete (Del) keys to correct your error. When you reach the end of a line, do not use the Return

(Enter) key (◀—┘) to move to the next line. Enable will stop accepting text when you reach the end of a line and will "beep" to inform you that you have reached the limit for that line. Later you'll see how to avoid these limitations, but for now, just become familiar with the basics of entering text.

Since this memo does not need a title page, let's begin by removing the document title area.

1. Press ↑ three times to place the cursor on the top line of the title area.

2. Press Alt-F3 to remove the title area.

That's it. The title area will no longer be in the way. Now begin typing the memo.

3. Type the following (remember, don't press ◀—┘ at the end of the line):

   Here is the information you requested regarding completion of the ARIS project.

Notice that the cursor stops at the end of the line, before you finish typing the word "project." This is because Enable's automatic *word wrap* feature (called *Automatic Reformat*) is off. With this feature off, you have to press ◀—┘ at the end of each line. This is not the preferred way to use a word processor. With word wrap on, Enable would automatically wrap the text to the next line when a line is full.

Let's back up, turn on the Automatic Format feature, and retype the end of this line.

4. Press the Backspace key five times, until most of the word "project" is removed. Press the space bar once. The screen should look like Figure 1.6.

5. Turn the Automatic Reformat feature on by pressing the following four keys (upper- or lowercase letters are acceptable, but do not type the spaces): F9 O A R.

This is the expert command for activating the Automatic Reformat feature. *Expert commands* are simple keystroke versions of menu commands. (Menu commands are accessed with the F10 key.)

Enable provides an on-screen quick reference of the function keys and their effects. If you remember this one function key, you'll always be able to determine the rest: Alt-F1. When you press Alt-F1, Enable displays a list of the function keys and their effects.

Unless you use a profile to make the Automatic Reformat feature active at all times, you will have to turn it on each time you enter the word processor with a new or existing document.

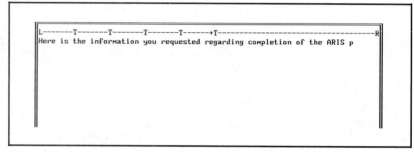

Figure 1.6: Ready to retype the end of the line

6. Now retype the word **project.** (Include the period.) Notice that Enable wraps the word to the beginning of the next line because it does not fit on the first line.

7. Now press the space bar twice and type in the rest of this document, as shown here. (Press ◄┘ twice at the end of the last sentence.)

> **As you know, we have over 20 people working on this project, including two coordinators. The project began March 1, 1989 and is scheduled to conclude August 15, 1991. ◄┘ ◄┘**

Notice that each line now wraps to the next line when it reaches the right margin (the right margin is shown on the ruler by the *R*).

Leave the memo on your screen. In the next section you use it to learn how to move the cursor around in the document.

BASIC CURSOR MOVEMENT

A good deal of word processing skill comes with the ability to position the cursor where you want it—quickly. Enable has over 50 commands for moving the cursor in various ways. You will find some more useful than others for your particular needs. Table 1.1 describes the basic cursor movement commands.

Table 1.1: Basic Enable Cursor Movement Commands

COMMAND	MOVES CURSOR:
↑	Up one line
↓	Down one line
←	Left one character
→	Right one character
Ctrl-→	Right one word
Ctrl-←	Left one word
PgUp	Up by 1/2 screen length (This is useful when your document fills more than one screen.)
PgDn	Down by 1/2 screen length
Home	To the top of the screen
End	To the bottom of the screen
Ctrl-Home	To the top of the document (When the document is less than one screen long, this will have the same effect as the Home key.)
Ctrl-End	To the bottom of the document
Tab	To the next tab stop
Shift-Tab	To the previous tab stop
Ctrl-W	To the next word (similar to Ctrl-→)
Ctrl-C	To the next character (similar to →)
Ctrl-L	To the next line (similar to ↓)
Ctrl-S	To the end of the current sentence (marked by a period)
Ctrl-G	To the bottom of the current page
Ctrl-P	To the next paragraph (marked by a carriage return)

Experiment with these commands on the sample document. You can hold down the keys for most of these commands for rapid repetition. For example, holding down → quickly moves the cursor to the right, space by space, until you release the key. Notice that you can move all the way up to the ruler at the top of the document and down beyond the bottom of the screen. If you move far enough down, you'll see a double line, which indicates the bottom of the document. If you continue to press ↓ after reaching the bottom marker, you'll actually push the marker farther down, making the document longer.

SAVING THE DOCUMENT

Now that you have created a new document in the word processor, the next step is to save it for future use. This means storing it on disk as a word processor file. If you want to take a break and leave the Enable program, go to the section "Quitting Enable." Otherwise follow the steps below to save the document and remain in Enable.

1. Press F10 to display the Top Line menu.

2. Press **S** to display the Save menu options.

3. Press the Tab key once to select the *Change Options* option, then press ⏎. The screen should look like Figure 1.7.

Enable displays a list of formats in which you can save this document. If you plan to use this document with a program other than Enable, you can select one of the other formats shown. In this case, we'll be using this document with Enable only.

4. Press ⏎ to select the Enable format.

5. Enable now asks if you want to save the entire file, the marked text, or the specified block. Press ⏎ to select the *Entire File* option. The screen now looks like Figure 1.8.

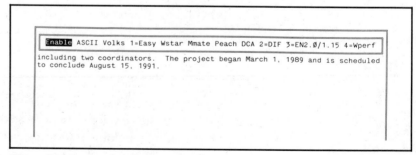

```
Enable ASCII Volks 1=Easy Wstar Mmate Peach DCA 2=DIF 3=EN2.Ø/1.15 4=Wperf
```
including two coordinators.   The project began March 1, 1989 and is scheduled
to conclude August 15, 1991.

Figure 1.7: Saving the document with new options

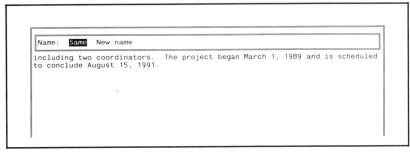

Figure 1.8: Naming the file

You can now specify a new name for the document or keep the one you entered when starting this document. The current name is displayed at the bottom of the screen. Preceding the name is the drive and directory location of the file. In this case, the entire name is C:DEMOMEMO.WPF. When you save this document, it will be placed in the default directory of drive C. Since you created a special directory for data files when you installed Enable in the Appendix, let's change the name of this file to include the correct directory location.

6. Press Tab once to move to the *New name* option, then press ←⤶.

The *New name* option can be used to change the file name per se, and to change the path, leaving the filename unchanged (as in step 7). It also can be used to change both the path and the filename.

You can now enter the new name for the file. Be sure to include the drive and directory location if it's different than the one shown at the bottom of the screen.

7. For hard-drive systems, enter the following:

    C:\DATA\DEMOMEMO.WPF

   If you use a floppy-drive system enter this:

    B:DEMOMEMO.WPF

8. Press ←⤶ when finished. Enable saves the document under the specified name in the specified directory.

You now choose what to do next by selecting one of the five options shown on your screen. Select *Edit* to return to the same document for further editing. Select *Revise another* to select and open another document, leaving this one open. Choose *Create another* to create a new document, leaving this one open. *Window close* closes this document and returns you to the Main menu or the previous open document if more than one is open. The *DOS* option quits the program and returns you to the DOS prompt.

9. Press ◄━┛ to select the *Edit* option. You are now back in the document with a copy saved on disk. Keep the document on your screen—you'll use it in the next chapter.

Notice that Enable has not updated the name shown at the bottom of the screen to reflect the new name you entered. This is a quirk in the program. Next time you use this process to save the document, you'll have to repeat all the steps because Enable does not remember the new name. To get Enable to display the correct name, you must type in the file name (including the entire path) when you create the word processor document. If the correct name is displayed at the bottom of the screen, you can follow these steps to save:

- Press F10 to display the Top Line menu.

- Press **S** to display the Save menu options.

- Press ◄━┛ to select the *Accept Options* option.

USING THE QUICK SAVE FEATURE

Enable provides another way to save your document that is much faster than the steps listed above. This method uses expert commands instead of menu options to save the file. This is how it works. First press F9 to activate the expert commands, then choose **S** (for Save). Choose one of the six options shown:

- Press Home to save the document and close the window. You then return to the Main menu if no other document is open.

- Press **C** (Create) to save the document and open a new one with the name you provide. The existing document window will be closed.

- Press End to save the document and quit Enable, returning to DOS.

- Press **E** (*Edit*) to save the document and return to it for further editing.

- Press **R** (*Revise another*) to save the document and open a different document (that is, another existing document) whose name you provide.

- Press **N** (*Name*) to save the document after you are prompted to input a new name.

QUITTING ENABLE

If you decide to take a break in the middle of an exercise, you can use the command F9 S End to save the document and quit the program.

You may want to quit without saving to destroy anything you might have done since the last time you saved the document. This is simple:

- Press F10 for the Top Line menu.

- Press **Q** (Quit).

- Press **Y** (Yes) to confirm your action. This will close the document without saving and take you to the Main menu.

- Press **R** (Return to DOS) to quit the program entirely.

Basic Editing Techniques

NOW THAT YOU'VE CREATED YOUR FIRST DOCUMENT, you're ready to explore Enable's editing capabilities. Using various commands and options, you can change text on the screen, move text to other locations (even to other documents entirely), remove unwanted material, and insert new material into existing text.

INSERTING NEW TEXT

One of the benefits of a word processor is that you can insert information into the middle of existing text. Enable will simply reformat the rest of the document to allow for the new information.

Enable offers two ways to enter text—Edit (or Overstrike) mode and Insert mode. In Edit mode, the new text you type in replaces existing text. This mode is most useful when you need to add new text without retaining existing text. In this mode, the cursor is a flashing line. When you enter text in Insert mode, the new text pushes the existing text aside as you type. This mode is useful if you need to add text to existing text. The cursor is a flashing block in Insert mode. You can switch between these modes by pressing the Ins key.

In this section you'll use both modes to insert text. You'll enter a heading for your memorandum in Edit mode, then you'll add a sentence in the middle of the document and create two paragraphs out of one in Insert mode.

If your DEMOMEMO document isn't on the screen, follow these steps to retrieve it now:

- Start Enable and go to the Main menu (see "Starting Enable" in Chapter 1).

- Press ◄┘ to select the *Use System* option.

- Press ◄┘ to select the *Word Processor* option.

- Press Tab once, then press ◄┘ to select the *Revise* option.

- Enter the name **C:\DATA\DEMOMEMO** then press ◄┘ to bring up the sample document.

The document will be on the screen and you can begin the following exercise.

1. Press the Home key to move the cursor to the top line of the text.

2. Press ↑ once to move the cursor above the text (to the ruler line).

3. Press F3 seven times to insert seven lines. The text moves down to make room.

4. Press ↑ six times to move back to the top of the document.

5. Type **MEMORANDUM**, then press ◄┘ two times. Notice that pressing ◄┘ does not insert a new line, but moves the cursor to the beginning of the next line. Pressing it twice will skip a line.

6. Type **TO: Mary Klein**, then press ◄┘.

7. Type **FR:** [*your name*], then press ◄┘.

8. Type **SUBJ: ARIS schedule**, then press ◄┘.

9. Type **DATE: 7/22/90**, then press ←┘ twice. The cursor should now be back to the "H" in "Here," and the screen should look like Figure 2.1.

The next text you enter will be in the Insert mode. When in Insert mode, you can type information anywhere on the screen, and text to the right of the cursor will move over and down to make room for the inserted information.

10. Press Ctrl-S twice to move the cursor to the end of the second sentence in the memo.

11. Press the Ins key. This changes the cursor from a blinking underline character to a blinking block. The block indicates that you are in Insert mode.

At this point, make sure that the Automatic Reformat feature is active. If you have started this chapter by retrieving the DEMO-MEMO document from the Main menu, you will have to use the command F9 O A R to reactivate the Automatic Reformat.

When repeating key commands that involve the Ctrl or Alt keys, you can hold down the Ctrl or Alt key and, while holding it down, press the combination key as many times as you like. This may be easier than pressing both keys again and again.

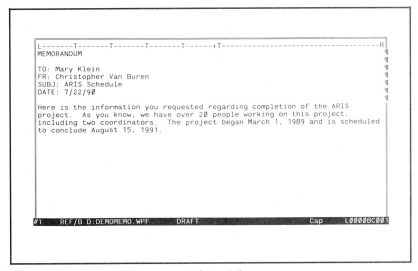

Figure 2.1: The sample document after adding text

12. Press the space bar twice to prepare for a new sentence, then enter the following (don't press ←):

   We are currently on schedule for the first phase of the project, which ends later this year.

When in the Insert mode, using the Backspace key can accumulate stray characters to the right of the cursor. This is because the cursor pushes everything to the right when inserting. Earlier, you used the Backspace key in the Edit mode and found that stray characters did not accumulate because you could type over the characters to the right of the cursor. Do you have to put up with this when using the Insert mode? Not at all. You can just press the Del key to remove the stray characters.

13. Press Del repeatedly until any unwanted characters are gone. Your screen should now look like Figure 2.2.

Now let's break the paragraph into two paragraphs.

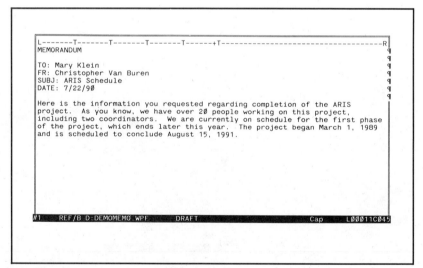

Figure 2.2: The document with inserted text and with deleted stray characters

14. Make sure that the cursor is on the space directly left of the "T" in "The" of the last sentence (just right of the flashing cursor). Then press Ctrl-◄┘ two times. This creates a new paragraph out of the last sentence of the memo or, in other words, inserts a paragraph marker.

Enable lets you type over any text on the screen any time you want. For example, suppose you remember that the ARIS project suffered a delay for the first month and did not actually start until April 1, 1989. Now you want to go back and change the date from March to April. Here's how.

1. The cursor should be at the beginning of the second paragraph (on the "T" in the word "The"). If it's not, press ◄┘ until the cursor is in position.

2. The cursor should also be in Edit mode (blinking underscore). If it's not, press Ins once to change it.

3. Press Ctrl-W three times to move to the beginning of the word "March."

4. Type the word **April**.

Transposing two characters is such a common typographical error that Enable has a special editing feature for correcting it. Place the cursor at the character just after the two transposed characters, then press Ctrl-T. The two characters preceding the cursor will be transposed.

Notice that the new word completely replaces the old. Now you may be thinking, that's great when the new word is exactly the same size as the old one, but what if it's larger or smaller? Let's take a look at replacing one word with a larger one. We can do this without learning any new commands. In this case, replace the word April with January using the following process:

5. Press ◄ five times to move to the beginning of the word "April."

6. Type the first five characters—**Janua**. This will replace the word "April."

7. Press the Ins key to change to the Insert mode.

8. Type the rest of the word—**ry**—using the insert cursor. The document looks like Figure 2.3.

Keep the document on the screen—you'll use it in the next exercise.

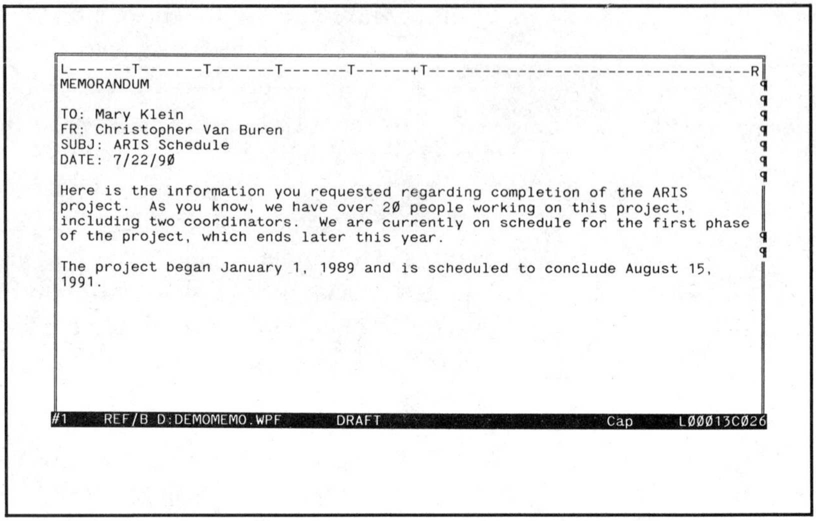

```
L-------T-------T-------T-------T------+T---------------------------------R
MEMORANDUM                                                                q
                                                                          q
TO: Mary Klein                                                            q
FR: Christopher Van Buren                                                 q
SUBJ: ARIS Schedule                                                       q
DATE: 7/22/90                                                             q
                                                                          q
Here is the information you requested regarding completion of the ARIS
project.  As you know, we have over 20 people working on this project,
including two coordinators.  We are currently on schedule for the first phase
of the project, which ends later this year.                               q
                                                                          q
The project began January 1, 1989 and is scheduled to conclude August 15,
1991.                                                                     q



#1    REF/B D:DEMOMEMO.WPF        DRAFT                    Cap    L0013C026
```

Figure 2.3: Replacing text with a larger word

DELETING TEXT

You just replaced a word in the middle of the document with a larger word, using a combination of the Edit and Insert modes. Now you'll see how to delete characters and words and replace them with any other text. Three different ways to accomplish this are shown below. Try them all for practice. The first method deletes a word at a time.

1. Press ← seven times to return to the beginning of the word "January."

2. Press F4 to delete the word that the cursor is on. The cursor can be on any one of the letters in the word for this command to work, but if the cursor is not on the first character, it may be misplaced for step 3.

3. Make sure the cursor is in Insert mode (blinking block) by pressing the Ins key, then enter the new word **February** (include a space after the word).

Try this method to delete one character at a time.

1. Press ← nine times to return to the beginning of the word "February."

2. Make sure the cursor is in Edit mode (flashing underscore) by pressing the Ins key, then type **March**.

3. Press the Del key three times to remove the remainder of the unwanted word.

Or try this method.

1. Press ← five times to return to the beginning of the word "March."

2. Press Ins to use the Insert mode, then type **April**.

3. Press Del five times to remove the unwanted word.

The three methods shown above use Delete commands in various ways to help you replace text. Of course, you can use Delete commands to completely remove text. Enable provides numerous Delete commands for this purpose. Table 2.1 lists the most common ones.

Table 2.1: Common Enable Delete Commands

COMMAND	DELETES:
Del	One character directly at the cursor position and moves text over (to the left) to fill the space. The cursor remains in the same line and column position.
Backspace	One character directly at the cursor position and moves the cursor to the left one space. Does not close up the empty space.
F4	The word in which the cursor is currently located
F9 Del ←	From the cursor position to the first space to the left
F9 Del →	From the cursor position to the first space to the right
F9 Del S	From the cursor position to the end of the sentence (until a period is located)

Table 2.1: Common Enable Delete Commands (continued)

COMMAND	DELETES:
F9 Del P	From cursor to the end of the paragraph (until a carriage return marker is located)
F9 Del ↓	From cursor position to the end of the current line
Alt-F3	The line in which the cursor is positioned. Fills the empty space by bringing up any lines following the deleted line. (This is the opposite of inserting a line with F3.)
F9 Del L	Expert version of the Alt-F3 command (same result)

Before you experiment with these commands on the sample document, be sure to save the document. This is described in the previous chapter, but the steps are repeated in brief here:

1. Press F10 S C (F10 invokes the menu, S for Save options, C for Change).

2. Press ◄─┘ to select the *Enable* option.

3. Press ◄─┘ to select the *Entire File* option.

4. Press Tab once to move to the *New name* option, then press ◄─┘.

5. Enter the name:

   C:\DATA\DEMOMEMO.WPF

   Press ◄─┘ when finished.

6. Press ◄─┘ to select the *Edit* option.

After saving the document, go ahead and experiment with the various Delete commands listed in Table 2.1. When finished, follow these steps to close the document without saving it, then retrieve the version of the document you just saved.

1. Enter the command F10 Q Y. This will close the document without saving it and take you to the Main menu.

2. To retrieve the previously saved version of the document select the *Use System* option, then the *Word Processing* option, then the *Revise* option.

3. Enter the name of the document, including the directory name, **C:\DATA\DEMOMEMO**, and press ⏎.

> If you quit Enable and return to DOS, you will have to turn the Automatic Reformat feature back on (F9 O A R). If you return to the Main menu without quitting, Automatic Reformat will still be on when you return to the document.

You see the DEMOMEMO document as you last saved it, before experimenting with the Delete commands (Figure 2.4). You may notice an extra ruler at the top of the document; this will be explained in the next chapter. Keep the document on your screen.

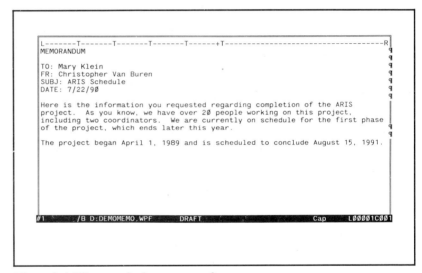

```
L-------T-------T-------T-------T------+T--------------------------------R
MEMORANDUM                                                               q
                                                                         q
TO: Mary Klein                                                           q
FR: Christopher Van Buren                                                q
SUBJ: ARIS Schedule                                                      q
DATE: 7/22/90                                                            q
                                                                         q
Here is the information you requested regarding completion of the ARIS
project.  As you know, we have over 20 people working on this project,
including two coordinators.  We are currently on schedule for the first phase
of the project, which ends later this year.                              q
                                                                         q
The project began April 1, 1989 and is scheduled to conclude August 15, 1991.
```

```
#1        /B D:DEMOMEMO.WPF        DRAFT                    Cap      L0001C001
```

Figure 2.4: The sample document so far

COPYING AND MOVING TEXT

When you think of word processing, perhaps you think of the ability to move large blocks of text around the page. Copying and moving blocks of text are two of the most common tasks in word processing. Enable provides several ways to copy and move information.

USING BLOCKS TO MOVE TEXT

The newly added sentence, "We are currently on schedule...." might sound better at the end of the memo. Thankfully, Enable lets you move text within a document using a few simple commands so you don't have to retype the text. You'll move this sentence to the end of the document using Enable's Block feature.

1. Press Home to move the cursor to the top of the document.

2. Press Ctrl-S two times to move to the beginning of the desired sentence.

3. Press F7. This marks the current location of the cursor with a highlighted block.

4. Press Ctrl-S to move to the end of this sentence.

5. Press F7 again. This highlights the entire sentence from the first position to the last. This is called a *block*.

6. Press Ctrl-S again to move to the end of the document.

7. Press Alt-F8 to move the highlighted block to the current position of the cursor. Your screen should look like Figure 2.5.

To remove the current block highlight, simply press Alt-F7. The cursor can be anywhere in the document when you use this command, and the currently highlighted block will be unhighlighted.

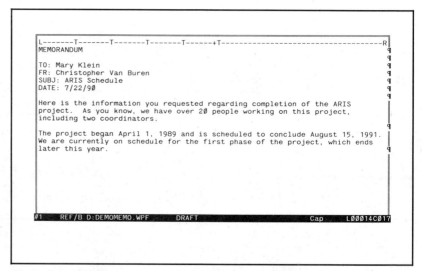

Figure 2.5: Sample document after moving the sentence

The command Alt-F8 moves the currently highlighted block to the current location of the cursor. This is the fastest way to accomplish the task. However, you also can use an expert command to move blocked text. In this case, you would highlight the block as described above, then enter F9 B M (B for Block, M for Move) instead of Alt-F8.

A third alternative is to use the following menu options after highlighting the block:

- Press F10.

- Press **C** to select the *Copy* option.

- Press **2** to select the *Move* option.

- Press ⏎ to select the *Accept Options* option.

You have just seen three ways to move a block of text from one position to another. You might notice some extra space in front of the moved sentence. This appears because Enable has not properly reformatted the moved sentence with the rest of the paragraph. An extra carriage return marker is now in the middle of the paragraph. Look at the right edge of your screen. You'll see a number of carriage return markers. Paragraphs should have these markers only at the end, but your document has one after the line that ends "1991." Remove the unwanted carriage return marker using the following steps:

1. Using the Arrow keys, position the cursor anywhere in the line beginning "The project began...." This should be line 12 of the document.

2. Enter the command F9 Del ⏎. This will cause the carriage return marker on the line to be removed and the paragraph to be reformatted.

If you have many unwanted markers in a paragraph, or if you want to create one paragraph out of many, you can use this method:

- Press F7 at the beginning and the end of the text you want to reformat to highlight the entire block of text.

- Press F9 O A P to reformat the block as a single paragraph.

- Press Alt-F7 to remove the highlight.

If you want to insert a paragraph marker, making two paragraphs from one, move to the breaking spot, then press Ctrl-← twice.

THREE WAYS TO COPY TEXT

Just as there are three ways to move text, there are three ways to copy it. Copying is just like moving text, except that the original remains in place and a duplicate is moved to the location of the cursor. Copied text is inserted into the document at the location of the cursor, and any text to the right of the cursor always moves over to make room, regardless of whether you are in Insert or Edit mode.

Using the keyboard command:

- First, move the cursor to the beginning of the text that you want to copy and press F7. Then, move the cursor to the end of the text and press F7 again. This will highlight the block.

- Move the cursor to the position where you would like to place the copy.

- Press F8 to copy the highlighted block.

You can copy the block over and over again using the F8 key.

Using the expert command:

- Highlight the desired block of text.

- Move the cursor to the position where you would like to place the new copy.

- Press F9 B C (B for Block, C for Copy).

Pressing the F9 key twice repeats the previous expert command.

Using the Top Line menu:

- Highlight the desired block of text.

- Move the cursor to the position where you would like to place the new copy.

- Press F10 to activate the Top Line menu.

- Press **C** for the Copy menu.

- Press ← to select the *Copy* option.

- Press ← to choose the *Accept Options* option.

MARKING TEXT

You've just seen how to create a highlighted block of text in the word processor. However, there is one limitation to establishing a block like this: the text in the block must be contiguous. When you mark the beginning and end of the block with the F7 key, everything between is highlighted. If you highlight a different block, the current block highlight is removed and replaced by the new one. This means you cannot highlight two separate chunks of text as one block.

Suppose you want to copy the first and last sentence in a paragraph that contains several sentences? You would have to highlight the first sentence, making it a block, then use the Copy command, then perform the same task again on the last sentence. It would be faster if you could highlight both sentences at once and use the Copy command only once. Enable does let you highlight text this way; the result is called *marked* text rather than a block. To mark text, you would follow these steps:

- Press Alt-M (M for Mark).

- Use any cursor movement command to move the cursor to the beginning of the text you would like to mark.

- Use the Ctrl-W, Ctrl-C, Ctrl-G, Ctrl-P, and Ctrl-S keys to move the cursor, highlighting the text you want to move. (Refer to Table 1.1 for an explanation of these commands.)

- When you highlight all the text in this first segment, repeat the two previous steps to highlight any other text segments you want marked.

- Press Alt-M when finished. Figure 2.6 shows what the marked text would look like.

COPYING AND MOVING MARKED TEXT

Marked text can be used with the Copy and Move commands discussed earlier. However, you must use the menu commands with the *Marked text* option. The expert commands do not even offer an option for working with marked text and are, therefore, not available for moving or copying marked text (only blocks).

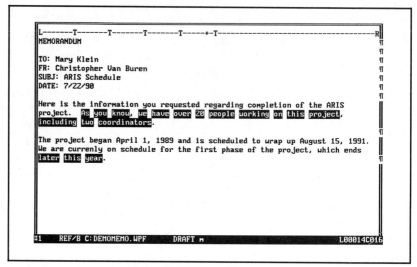

```
L-------T-------T-------T-------T-----+-T-------------------------------R
MEMORANDUM                                                             ¶
                                                                       ¶
TO: Mary Klein                                                         ¶
FR: Christopher Van Buren                                              ¶
SUBJ: ARIS Schedule                                                    ¶
DATE: 7/22/90                                                          ¶
                                                                       ¶
Here is the information you requested regarding completion of the ARIS
project.  As you know, we have over 20 people working on this project,
including two coordinators.
                                                                       ¶
The project began April 1, 1989 and is scheduled to wrap up August 15, 1991.
We are currenly on schedule for the first phase of the project, which ends
later this year.                                                       ¶

#1   REF/B C:DEMOMEMO.WPF       DRAFT M                     L00014C016
```

Figure 2.6: Highlighting noncontiguous text

Here's how to copy marked text:

- Press F10.
- Choose the *Copy* option.
- Choose the *Copy* option.
- Choose the *Change Options* option.
- Choose the *Marked text* option.
- Choose the *This Window* option.

Here's how to move marked text:

- Press F10.
- Choose the *Copy* option.
- Choose the *Move* option.
- Choose the *Change Options* option.
- Choose the *Marked text* option.
- Choose the *This Window* option.

UNMARKING TEXT

To unmark text that was marked with the Alt-M command (described at the beginning of this section), use the same procedure for marking the text, but substitute Alt-N for Alt-M. The Alt-N command returns marked text to normal. Be sure to turn the marked text command off first by pressing Alt-M. This should remove the "M" from the status line at the bottom of the screen.

Printing Your Document

THIS CHAPTER EXPLAINS HOW TO PRINT OUT A document. It begins by explaining the various print-setup choices you can make. You'll learn how to modify the printout so you can print selected areas, suppress widow and orphan lines, number the pages, and more. Finally, this chapter lists some of the special embedded printer codes available for the word processor. These codes offer special controls and features for your documents.

USING THE PRINT FORMS

The first time you print each document, you will probably want to select various print-setup options. Each document has its own set of these options that can be saved with it. Unless you change the options, Enable supplies default settings for each document.

There are four screens full of options available for printing. These four screens can be viewed from within the word processor document by pressing F10 to show the Top Line menu, then selecting the *Print* option. The first of the four screens appears. You can "flip" through the screens by pressing PgUp or PgDn.

Each screen has a series of prompts, or questions. Each prompt offers at least two different options from which to choose. By choosing the desired options for each prompt on each screen, you can control the appearance of the printout.

Besides the PgUp and PgDn keys, Enable offers other commands for manipulating these screens and selecting options. Some of these are shown at the bottom of the setup screen. Table 3.1 summarizes these commands.

Table 3.1: Summary of Enable Print-Screen Keys

KEY	EFFECT
PgUp	Moves one screen back
PgDn	Moves one screen forward
↵	Moves to the next prompt and selects the option that is currently highlighted
↓	Moves to the next prompt, selecting the option that is currently highlighted
↑	Moves to the previous prompt
Tab	Moves to next option within current prompt (Also provides a brief explanation of the option toward the bottom of the screen)
← or →	Moves to next choice within current option (also provides explanation) or the next option if no choices exist
Alt-F2	Begins printing using the options currently set
Alt-F10	Accepts the options as they are currently set, and saves them with the final document
Esc	Exits the options screens without accepting your changes (This is useful when you change your mind about the options or for printing a document with temporary changes to the options.)

If you find yourself changing the same options over and over for each document you print, you might find a custom profile helpful. See Chapter 22.

When you use ← or ↓ to move to the various prompts, Enable highlights the currently selected option for that prompt. You can see what options are currently set by pressing ↓ to flip through the prompts. Of course, when you change the options and save the changes, the new options will be highlighted the next time you view the screens. But what determines the options that are highlighted on new documents (that is, the first time you use the screens)? A profile, of course. In this book, we are using the *default* profile that comes with the program. This profile provides a standard selection of options on these screens. You'll probably find these options adequate for most of your printouts. Of course, you can create a custom profile (or several) to change these defaults. If you create a custom profile, you can still change the options using the commands described above.

The next few pages describe the most important options on the print setup forms and provide a step-by-step example using the DEMOMEMO document. Then, each option on these setup screens is described for future reference.

CHOOSING YOUR PRINTER

Profile Option: You can use a profile to set the default printer to your active printer. This way, you do not have to select the correct printer at this point—it will already be selected.

Probably the most important thing to do in the printer setup screens is to choose your printer from the list provided. If you don't choose the appropriate printer, Enable will be unable to use special print features to enhance the printout. You select your printer on the second of the four setup screens.

1. With the DEMOMEMO document on the screen, press F10 to display the Top Line menu. Then press **P** for the *Print* option.

2. Press PgDn to move to the second screen (Figure 3.1). The cursor should be in the space available for your printer name.

3. Press F7 to view the list of available printers at the bottom of the screen. These are the printers you selected when installing Enable for your system. If no printers are shown, refer to the installation process described in the Appendix.

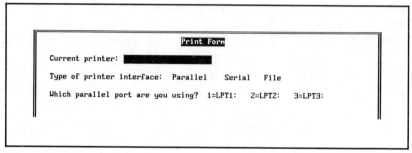

Figure 3.1: The print form for selecting your printer

4. Highlight the desired printer, then press ◄──. Enable inserts the name into the "Current printer" prompt. Press ◄── again to move on.

5. Select either *Parallel* or *Serial*, depending on the type of printer interface you have. Then press ◄──.

6. If you have a parallel interface, highlight the appropriate printer port (LPT1, LPT2, or LPT3) then press ◄──. If you have a serial port, select COMM1 or COMM2 for the printer port and press ◄──.

7. Select the baud rate and other serial transmission options if your printer is a serial type. Consult your printer and interface manuals for these settings. (Most printers use a 9600 baud rate and parity option *None*. Choose these options if you are unsure.) Press ◄── to move to the next screen.

SETTING TOP AND BOTTOM MARGINS

Another set of options you might use frequently are the *Top margin* and *Bottom margin* options. These are set on the third setup screen, unlike the left and right margins, which are set on the document rulers. Follow these steps to set the top and bottom margins. The cursor should already be at the top of screen three (Figure 3.2). If not, press PgDn until screen three is in view.

```
                        ┌─────────────────────────────────┐
                        │         Page Form               │
                        │                                 │
                        │  11.00 ... Length               │
                        │  8.00  ... Width                │
                        │  6     ... Lines per inch        │
                        │                                 │
                        │  6     ... Top margin (number of lines)     │
                        │  6     ... Bottom margin (number of lines)  │
                        │                                 │
                        └─────────────────────────────────┘
```

Figure 3.2: The page form for setting top and bottom margins

1. Press ↓ three times to move to the *Top margin* prompt. The default top and bottom margins are six lines (one inch). Change the *Top margin* setting to three lines by typing a **3** over the 6, then pressing ←.

2. Change the *Bottom margin* setting to nine lines by typing a **9** over the 6, making it 1.5 inches. Press ← to accept the change.

NUMBERING PAGES

You can number the pages of your document using an option on screen four. This option provides a simple page numbering system for your document that automatically prints the numbers on each page.

1. Press PgDn to move to screen four, a page form (Figure 3.3). The prompt ''Should pages be numbered'' should be highlighted.

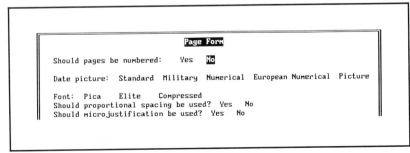

Figure 3.3: The print options screen for page numbering

2. Press → to highlight Yes, then press ←⏎. You'll see some options for the location of the number.

3. Press → to highlight *Bottom of Page*, then press ←⏎. This places the numbers at the bottom of each page of the printout.

4. Press ←⏎ to select the *Center* option.

5. Enter **1** as the beginning page number, then press ←⏎.

You have now activated page numbering for the document. The page numbering option is normally turned off for all new documents because Enable assumes that you'll want to use a different, more powerful method of numbering the pages. You should not use both methods together or you will end up with two sets of numbers. The alternative method of page numbering is described in Chapter 5.

CHOOSING A TYPE SIZE

If you want to change from Pica to either Compressed or Elite type for the entire document, Enable offers a print-setup option for this purpose. This option also appears on screen four and is labelled *Font*. Whichever type style you choose in this option, Enable will print the entire document in that style.

The attribute commands described in Chapter 4 provide more control than the *Font* option because they let you turn the type styles on and off at specific locations in the document. If an attribute conflicts with a print-setup option, the attribute takes over.

ACCEPTING AND SAVING THE PRINT OPTIONS

Now that you have set some of the more important print options, you need to accept the options if you want to reprint the document without having to reset these options again. If you then save the document, the options are saved with it. This means you won't have to make the same changes ever again (to this document). Remember, each document has its own print-setup options saved. From the Setup screens, press Alt-F10 to accept your changes and return to the document. Press the Esc key to exit the options screens and reject the changes you made, returning the options to their default status. If you print the document before pressing the Esc key to reject the changes (that is, print with the options screens still in view), the changes will affect the printout. This can be useful for making temporary setup changes for special printouts.

Accept the Setup options you've made and save the options with DEMOMEMO.

1. Press Alt-F10 to accept the setup changes.

2. Press F9 S E to save the document.

PREVIEWING AND PRINTING THE DOCUMENT

Previewing the document before printing is a handy way to spot errors in the print setup. Using Enable's Preview feature, you can see just what the final printout will look like—right on the screen. Not all page setup changes appear on the screen preview, but the changes we made so far do. Previewing the document is simple.

1. Switch to Final mode using the command F9 O D. The document should look like Figure 3.4.

Notice the page numbers at the bottom of each page and the amount of space allotted for the top and bottom margins.

The final step is printing. Since you have seen the preview already, you have a pretty good idea of what the document will look like on paper. Here's the command for printing:

2. Press Alt-F2 to print.

If the printout was unsuccessful, you will get the following message at the bottom of the screen:

Printer fault R to RETRY, C to CLOSE PRINT WINDOW, A to ABORT ENABLE

If your screen does not look exactly like the one shown in Figure 3.4, don't worry. You probably have some screen elements in view that were hidden in the example. See Chapter 5 for a summary of the commands for hiding screen elements.

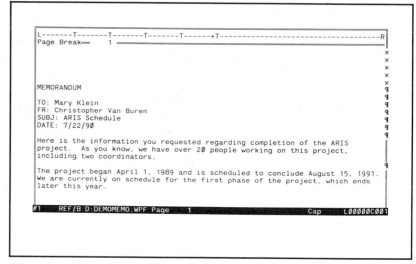

```
L-------T-------T-------T-------T------+T---------------------------------R
Page Break═      1 ════════════════════════════════════════════════════
                                                                          x
                                                                          x
                                                                          x
                                                                          x
MEMORANDUM                                                                q

TO: Mary Klein                                                            q
FR: Christopher Van Buren                                                 q
SUBJ: ARIS Schedule                                                       q
DATE: 7/22/90                                                             q

Here is the information you requested regarding completion of the ARIS    q
project.  As you know, we have over 20 people working on this project,
including two coordinators.

The project began April 1, 1989 and is scheduled to conclude August 15, 1991.  q
We are currently on schedule for the first phase of the project, which ends
later this year.

#1      REF/B  D:DEMOMEMO.WPF Page       1                         Cap     L0000C001
```

Figure 3.4: The document in Final mode

Check that the printer is connected properly and is selected. Then press **R** for *Retry*. If that doesn't help, select **C** to return to the document, then try changing the printer and interface setup options in steps 1 through 6 in the section "Choosing Your Printer." Consult your system configuration for the correct choices, or just try all combinations until you strike gold. Enable technical support may be able to help if you still can't get the document to print.

A CLOSER LOOK AT THE PRINT OPTIONS

Remember that you can get to these screens by pressing F10, then selecting the *Print* option. You can flip through these screens by pressing PgUp or PgDn.

The next few pages describe each of the print options on the four print-setup screens. Go ahead and experiment with these options on the sample document.

SCREEN ONE: SELECTING WHAT TO PRINT

The first setup screen contains some basic options for printing (see Figure 3.5). In this screen you can choose the portion of the document to print, the orientation, the paper type, and more.

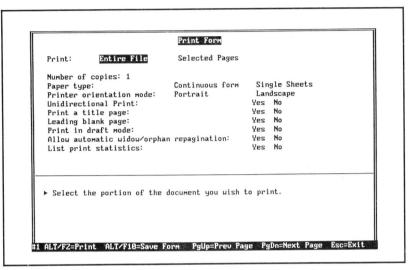

Figure 3.5: The first print-setup screen with basic print options

The *Print* option lets you print the entire file or specific pages of the document. Normally, the *Entire File* option is highlighted. If you select *Selected Pages*, Enable presents two more options. *Pages Selected* asks for the specific pages you want printed. If the pages are not consecutive, enter the page numbers separated by commas. For example, to specify pages 1, 3, 5, and 9, enter **1,3,5,9**. To specify a range of pages, enter the first and last page number, separated by a hyphen. For example, to print pages 3 through 8, enter **3-8**. You can combine ranges and individual pages if desired. For example, entering **1-5,9** prints pages 1 through 5 and page 9.

The *Page range selection should be* option determines whether Enable prints the *absolute* pages whose numbers are specified in the previous option (*Pages Selected*) or the *relative* pages, counting from the top of the document with "page 1." The only way this would make a difference is if you have used a page numbering feature to change the normal flow of numbers from the top of the document. That is, page 10 may not be the tenth page from the top if you have used special numbering in the document. The *Absolute* option will print page 10 and the *Relative* option will print the tenth page from the top.

Number of copies determines the number of copies that will print. This is normally set to 1 copy.

Paper type lets you use continuous paper or single sheets. Selecting *Single Sheets* pauses the printout at the end of each page so you can insert a new page.

The *Printer orientation mode* option prints the document upright on the page (Portrait) or sideways on the page (Landscape). When using Landscape mode, you should adjust the margins of the document to allow access to the entire width of the page. (Do not use the Landscape setting in the print options if you plan to use the embedded commands instead. See "Changing Print Orientation: %LAND-SCAPE and %PORTRAIT" in this chapter for more information.)

Unidirectional Print activates one-way printing for dot-matrix printers. This is useful when you have graphics in your document, such as boxes or borders drawn with the special box-drawing characters. One-way printing helps align text vertically.

The *Print a title page* option prints or does not print the document title that appears in the document. Of course, if you have removed the title, this option is unnecessary.

Leading blank page leaves a blank page at the beginning of the document and between multiple copies of the document.

Print in draft mode prints the document as it appears in the Draft mode on the screen, including any visible rulers, footer entries, comments, paper clips, and so on. This is useful for editing documents.

The *Allow automatic widow/orphan repagination* option determines whether or not Enable will suppress widow and orphan lines. A widow is the first line of a paragraph printed at the bottom of a page. An orphan is the last line of a paragraph printed at the top of a page. Select *Yes* to suppress these unwanted lines or *No* to allow them. (See "Keeping Text Together: %PAGES and %PAGEE" in this chapter for more information.)

The *List print statistics* option prints a page with the various print statistics at the end of the document when set to Yes. Choose No to avoid this extra page. Figure 3.6 shows a sample statistics page.

SCREEN TWO: OPTIONS FOR PRINTER SELECTION AND INTERFACE

Figure 3.7 shows the options on the second print-setup screen. This screen controls the printer and interface selection for the printout. The list of available printers that appears in this screen is based

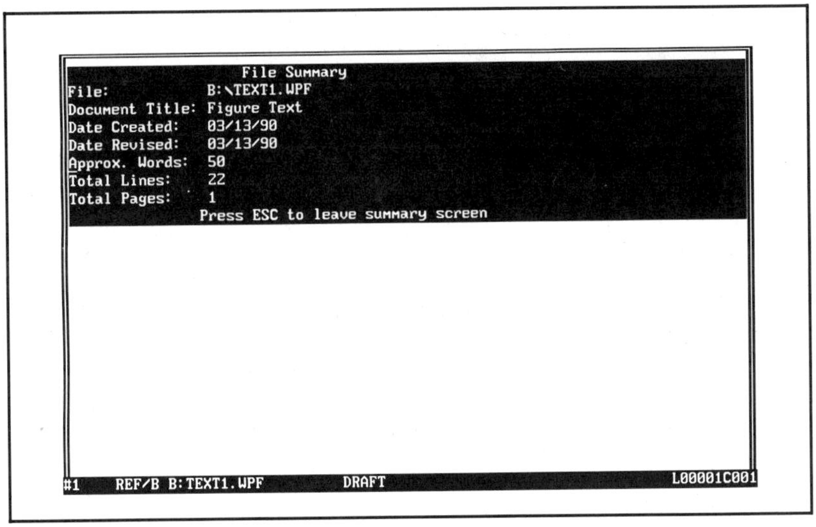

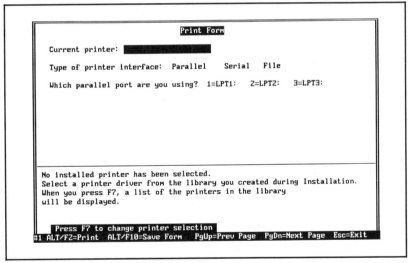

Figure 3.6: Sample statistics page

Figure 3.7: The second print-setup screen, showing printer and interface
selections

on the printer you installed. Interface options relate to your hardware
configuration.

Current printer selects the printer. If no printer is currently entered
for this prompt, press F7 to display a list of available printers. This

list comes from the printers you chose during installation. Highlight one of the printers in the list and press ←┘. You also can type in a printer name, but if that printer does not appear on your list, Enable will not accept the entry.

Type of printer interface prints to the parallel port, the serial port, or to a file. If you are printing to a printer, choose either *Parallel* or *Serial*, depending on the printer. Consult your printer manual if you are unsure which type it is. Choose *File* to print the document to a DOS print file on disk. Enable will automatically name the file with the document name plus the extension .PPD.

Which parallel port are you using is an option that appears when you select *Parallel* for the previous option. Enter the number associated with the LPT port to which your printer is connected. (If you are unsure, try each one and see if anything prints.)

Which serial port are you using appears when you select *Serial* for the previous option. Enter the number associated with the COM port to which your printer is connected. If you select *Serial*, the following options appear.

Baud rate is an option that allows you to select the baud rate of your printer interface. Consult your printer manual for details. The default option is 110 to allow access to all printers. However, this is a very slow rate. You should change the default if possible. Most newer serial printers offer a 9600 baud rate.

Choosing *Select one of the options described below* displays four sets of options at the bottom of the screen. These options display various communication protocols involving parity, stop bits, and word size. Choose the option that corresponds to your setup.

SCREEN THREE: OPTIONS FOR PAGE LAYOUT

The third print-setup screen (Figure 3.8) presents page layout options. These options control the margin and page dimensions of the printout. Here you can choose how much information is printed on each page.

Length sets the page length of the document. Standard letter-size paper is 11 inches long. If you are printing in Landscape mode, switch the length and width measurements.

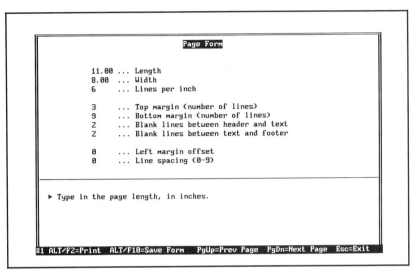

```
                           Page Form

        11.00 ... Length
        8.00  ... Width
        6     ... Lines per inch

        3        ... Top margin (number of lines)
        9        ... Bottom margin (number of lines)
        2        ... Blank lines between header and text
        2        ... Blank lines between text and footer

        0        ... Left margin offset
        0        ... Line spacing (0-9)


    ▶ Type in the page length, in inches.




#1 ALT/F2=Print  ALT/F10=Save Form   PgUp=Prev Page  PgDn=Next Page  Esc=Exit
```

Figure 3.8: Screen three: options for page layout

Width sets the page width. This should correspond to the margin settings set throughout the document. Standard printers allow an 8-inch width. Wide printers allow a 15-inch width.

Lines per inch determines the number of lines that will print vertically on 1 inch of the paper. This has no effect on line spacing; line spacing is controlled separately. Six lines per inch is standard on most printers. Check your printer for other available lines-per-inch settings.

Top margin determines the number of lines between the top edge of the paper and the first line of text (or the header). Enter the number of lines desired. Measurements can be calculated based on the lines-per-inch setting.

Bottom margin determines the number of lines between the bottom edge of the paper and the last line of text (or the footer). Enter the number of lines desired. Measurements can be calculated based on the lines-per-inch setting.

Blank lines between header and text determines the number of lines printed after the header and before the first line of the text. If you have not defined a header for the document, this space will appear in the top margin. You can also add the blank lines in the header entry area for the same effect. Headers are described in Chapter 5.

Blank lines between text and footer determines the number of lines printed before the footer—after the last line of the text on each page. If you have not defined a footer for the document this space appears in the bottom margin. You can also add the blank lines in the footer entry area for the same effect. Footers are described in Chapter 5.

Left margin offset adds extra space to the left margin. For example, if the left margin is set at column 5, you can print it at column 15 by setting this option to 10. This is a *global* offset for all left margin settings on all rulers throughout the document. Be sure that the line length, including this offset, does not exceed the page width.

Line spacing sets spacing between the lines for the entire document. If you have set line spacing using the *Layout* menu option or the equivalent expert command, those settings will override the one on this screen.

The command version for line spacing offers more flexibility than the print-setup option because you can place it at specific locations in the document.

SCREEN FOUR: OPTIONS FOR PAGE NUMBERING AND TEXT APPEARANCE

The options in screen four control page numbering and text formatting (see Figure 3.9). Formatting includes options for changing the type size, applying justification, and printing graphs. These are all options that rely on your hardware for support.

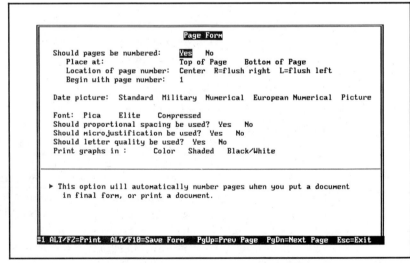

Figure 3.9: Options for page numbering and text appearance

Should pages be numbered turns page numbering on or off for the entire document. If you select Yes, three more options appear for the placement of the number. (For more control over page numbers, use the automatic page numbering feature described in Chapter 5.) This option should not be used if the automatic page numbering feature is being used, or you'll end up with two sets of page numbers.

Place at determines where the page numbers will appear on the page. You can position the numbers at the top or bottom of the page.

Location of page numbers determines where the page numbers will appear on the line. You can place them at the center, flush right, or flush left on the line.

Begin with page number starts printing the numbers at the specified page number. This is useful when your document begins at a page other than 1. Enter the desired starting page number.

Date picture displays the date in the format chosen. The date formats include the following:

FORMAT	*DISPLAY*
Standard	October 25, 1990
Military	25 October 1990
Numerical	10/25/1990
European Numerical	25/10/90
Picture	(See below)

If you choose the *Picture* option, you can create whatever format you like. This is done by combining the following elements in any order:

DD	Two-digit day (March *01* 1990)
MM	Two-digit month (*03*/01/1990)
YY	Two-digit year (03/01/*90*)
MON	Three-character month (*Mar* 01 1990)
MONTH(MM)	Full month name (*March* 01 1990)
YYYY	Full four-digit year (March 01 *1990*)
/ - . , :	Separators

Some examples include

DD MON YY	25 Oct 90
MONTH(MM) YYYY	October 1990
MONTH(MM) DD	October 25

You can include the current date in a document using the embedded command %DATE described later in this chapter.

Font determines which of three type sizes will be used for the printout. The standard is Pica, which prints 10 characters per inch on each line. Elite uses 12 characters per inch. Compressed uses 15 characters per inch (some printers may vary). If you switch from Pica, you may want to change the document's right margin to account for more columns per line. Elite allows 96 columns on the standard 8-inch platen. Compressed allows 120 columns (some printers may vary). Also see the equivalent attribute commands in Chapter 4.

Should proportional spacing be used? prints the document in proportional spacing if your printer includes this feature. *Proportional spacing* uses an adjusted amount of space for each character printed. Narrow characters take less space than wide characters. For example, the character "M" gets more space than "i." The effect is a more professional-looking document. Since proportional spacing takes less room than mono spacing, each printed line will appear slightly shorter than normal (that is, in respect to the right margin). You can also activate proportional spacing using the attribute command Alt-P. Attribute commands offer more control than their equivalent print-setup options. (See Chapter 4 for details about Alt-P.)

Should microjustification be used? determines whether microjustification should be used. This feature enhances justified text. This option can be used only if your printer includes this feature and you justify the document using the justified right margin (J) on the ruler.

Should letter quality be used? prints the document in letter-quality mode if your printer includes such a feature. This enhances the quality of the type.

Print graphs in determines whether inserted graphs should be printed in color, black and white, or shaded. This option is discussed in more detail in Chapter 12.

USING EMBEDDED COMMANDS FOR MORE PRINTING CONTROL

Besides all the print-setup options, Enable provides several special commands that can be placed inside the document at specific locations. Called *embedded commands*, these commands affect various aspects of the printout.

Since embedded commands appear in the text of the document, they must have a format that distinguishes them from the rest of the text. Enable uses the percent symbol (%) in front of the command entered in uppercase letters for this purpose (as in %DATE). With the exception of %DATE, all embedded commands must begin in column 1 of a line. This section describes some of the most commonly used embedded commands. Then, you'll try out some of them on the DEMOMEMO document.

SENDING PRINTER CONTROL CODES: %CONTROL

Your printer may offer features that Enable does not directly support. Some printers, for example, offer color printing. You can access special printer features by issuing the *printer control codes* from the document.

Each manufacturer may use a different set of codes for a particular printer. The only way to know your printer's special codes is to look in the printer manual. The codes will usually be presented in three ways: ASCII, decimal, and hex. You need the decimal versions of the codes for Enable's embedded commands. If your manual does not provide the decimal versions of the codes, you may have to translate the ASCII versions to decimal using an ASCII chart.

Suppose your printer uses the command Esc K 3 to activate the color red for the printer. To turn on the color red, you first find the decimal equivalent to this ASCII command: 27,75,51. Then you enter this code after the embedded command %CONTROL in the document:

    %CONTROL 27,75,51

Be sure to use commas between the various parts of the code as shown above. Also, remember to start the code in column 1 of the line. The printer will begin printing in red where the code appears in the document. (You must have a color ribbon to print in color.)

ENTERING THE CURRENT DATE: %DATE

This is one of the most useful of the embedded commands; it inserts the current date (taken from the DOS startup date) into your document at the location of the %DATE command. Unlike the other embedded commands, this does not have to start at column 1, but can be placed anywhere in the text of a document. This is also useful in headers and footers, as described in Chapter 5. Simply type %**DATE** and Enable will replace the embedded command with the date when the document prints.

PRINTING DOCUMENTS WITHIN DOCUMENTS: %INCLUDE

You may have an occasion to link documents for printing, such as when you split a large document into several files. It would be nice if you didn't have to print each file individually, but could link them. The %INCLUDE command lets you do this. Simply place the command at the end of the first document and enter the name of the next document to print. Be sure to place the command in column 1. For example, to print the document CHAPTWO.WPF at the end of the document CHAPONE.WPF, enter this command at the end of the CHAPONE.WPF file:

```
%INCLUDE  chaptwo.wpf
```

Be sure to include a space between the command and the document name. Include the DOS pathname if the document is not in the current path, as in %INCLUDE \data\chaptwo.wpf.

You can print a document in the middle of another by placing this command in the middle of the text at the desired position of the inserted document. This is useful for including complex tables in long documents when the tables are stored in separate files.

CHANGING PRINT ORIENTATION: %LANDSCAPE AND %PORTRAIT

You saw earlier in this chapter how you can print a document in either Landscape (sideways) or Portrait (upright) mode using the print options. The limitation on that feature is that it affects the entire document at one time; you cannot print certain pages in Landscape and others in Portrait mode. This embedded command gives you that control. Simply enter %LANDSCAPE to begin printing sideways and %PORTRAIT to begin printing upright.

CHANGING LINES PER INCH: %LINES

Remember: Changing lines per inch is not the same as changing line spacing. Lines per inch is a function of the printer; line spacing is a function of Enable. You can combine lines-per-inch and line-spacing changes for various effects. For example, using a lines-per-inch setting of 8 with a line spacing setting of 2, gives you one-and-a-half line spacing.

This embedded command is equivalent to the print-setup option *Lines Per Inch* described earlier in this chapter. However, this command offers more control because you can use it at specific locations in the document, whereas the print-setup option is a global command. To change lines per inch, enter the command %LINES followed by the desired value. For example, to activate 8 lines per inch, enter %**LINES 8**. Remember to begin the command in column 1. The change takes effect for all text below this command, until another %LINES command is encountered.

KEEPING TEXT TOGETHER: %PAGES AND %PAGEE

These commands work together to keep lines of text from breaking between pages. If you place %PAGES (page start) at the beginning of a section of text and %PAGEE (page end) at the end, the text between these commands will not be split between pages, if a page break should happen to fall between them. This is useful for keeping section headings with the first few lines of the text, or for keeping all the lines of a table together.

Note that this command is different than the automatic widow and orphan suppression option on the first print-setup screen. Enable considers a stray line to be a widow or orphan only when it is normally part of a paragraph. (A paragraph has a carriage return marker only on the last line.) Therefore, headings and other lines of text that have carriage return markers in them are not considered widows. %PAGES and %PAGEE can be used to keep two or more entire paragraphs together.

PAUSING THE PRINTOUT: %PAUSE

This embedded command temporarily stops the printout at the location of the command. This command can be used for printing on individual sheets of paper. However, you can also use the print-setup option, *Paper Type*, for this purpose. The %PAUSE command is most useful when you want to pause the printing at a location other than the end of a page. Use ←┘ to resume printing.

USING EMBEDDED COMMANDS IN THE SAMPLE DOCUMENT

Just reading about the embedded commands may give you an idea of their uses, but there is no substitute for trying them out. If the DEMOMEMO document is not already on the screen, bring it up now. Then, try the following:

1. Start a new document: Press Alt-Home. Then, from the Main menu, select the commands *Use System*, *Word Processor*, *Create*. Enter the name **\DATA\TEMP** and press ←┘.

2. Enter a few lines into this new document, then save it with the command F9 S Home. This returns you to the DEMO-MEMO document. You have now created and saved a dummy document called TEMP.

3. Move the cursor to the ruler at the top of DEMOMEMO (on the ruler itself).

4. Press F3 to insert a line.

5. Press Ctrl-M to activate the margin release.

6. Move the cursor to column 1 by pressing ←, then type **%INCLUDE \DATA\TEMP.WPF**.

7. Move the cursor to the line containing "DATE: 7/22/90." Make sure the cursor is on the "7" in the date.

8. Press F4 to remove the date, then type %**DATE** in place of the date. Press ← once to move the cursor one line down.

9. Type %**PAUSE Just stopping to think** beginning at column 1. The document now should look like the one in Figure 3.10.

10. Now print the document by pressing Alt-F2.

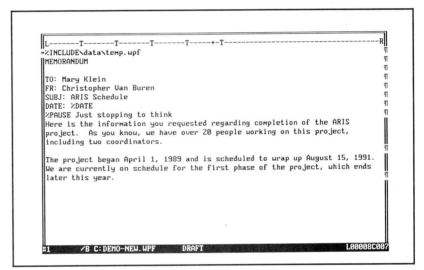

Figure 3.10: Using embedded commands on the sample document

The printout should include the TEMP file you created and the current date in the heading. The printing should pause just after this.

11. Press ← to continue printing the rest of the document.

If you have trouble with the printout, double-check the print-setup screens in the beginning of this chapter for the proper printer and interface designation.

The final step is to close the document and return to the Main menu without saving these recent changes. Here's how:

12. Press F10 Q Y (Q for Quit, Y for Yes).

CHAPTER

4

Formatting Your Document

THIS CHAPTER PROVIDES INFORMATION ABOUT formatting documents in the word processor, including how to create tables. Formatting includes changing the margins, using boldface, centering text, and so on. In this chapter, you'll learn how to control margins and tabs, how to align information on a line (including alignment within tables), how to apply character formats such as boldface, underlining, centering, and justification, and how to use hyphenation.

You will use the document prepared in Chapters 1–3. Be sure you have completed all the exercises in those chapters. If you have quit Enable since the previous session, follow the steps described in Chapter 2 for retrieving an existing document. Make sure that the Automatic Reformat feature is active by pressing F9 O A R.

CHANGING INITIAL RULER SETTINGS

When you first created the DEMOMEMO document, you saw the initial ruler at the top of the document. This ruler controls the margins and tab stops for the document. At that time you accepted the default ruler settings so you could begin working on the document right away. In the next exercise you'll discover how to change the ruler settings, insert new rulers, and reformat the document to your new settings.

The initial ruler is in view at the top of the DEMOMEMO document. Unless you move the cursor past the bottom of the first screen, the ruler stays in view at all times. You can move the cursor onto the ruler line to change the margins and tabs. Try this:

1. Press Ctrl-Home then ↑ to move to the ruler line.

2. Press → five times, then press Alt-L. This will move the left margin marker over five spaces. Notice that the text below the ruler adjusts to fit the new left margin.

3. Press ↑ again to move back to the ruler line.

4. Press Tab six times to move to the right margin, then press ← ten times to move ten spaces to the left.

5. Press Alt-R to move the right margin marker to the position of the cursor. The text below will reformat to the new right margin.

When you change the margins and tabs with the Automatic Reformat feature on, all text below the ruler automatically reformats to the new settings. You can change the settings at any time using the steps listed above. Table 4.1 lists the keys used to make changes to a ruler.

Table 4.1: Keys Used to Change a Ruler

KEY	EFFECT
For initial and new rulers:	
Tab	Moves to the next tab or margin
Shift-Tab	Moves to the previous tab or margin
→	Moves right one space
←	Moves left one space

Table 4.1: Keys Used to Change a Ruler (continued)

KEY	EFFECT
For initial ruler only:	
Alt-L	Sets the left margin at the cursor position
Alt-T	Sets a standard (left-alignment) tab at the cursor position
Ctrl-E	Removes the tab on which the cursor is located
Alt-R	Sets the right margin at the cursor position
Alt-J	Sets a justified right margin instead of the standard right margin. All text will be flush with the right and left margins.
Ctrl-A	Clears all tabs on the ruler
For new rulers only:	
Space or Hyphen	Removes a tab, margin, or other element
L	Sets the left margin at the cursor position
T	Sets a standard (left-alignment) tab at the cursor position
R	Sets the right margin at the cursor position
J	Sets a justified right margin instead of the standard right margin. All text will be flush with the left and right sides of the page.

For more information about text alignment, see "Controlling Text Alignment" later in this chapter.

Note that the Alt-J justified right margin is an alternative to the Alt-R standard right margin. The right edge of the page is either fully justified (Alt-J) or not (Alt-R). Also notice that Enable uses different commands for setting initial and new rulers. You will learn about new rulers in the next section.

INSERTING AND DELETING NEW RULERS

As you saw in the previous steps, when you change the margins of a ruler, all text below that ruler reformats to the new setting. But what if you want different paragraphs in the document to have different margin settings, as shown in Figure 4.1?

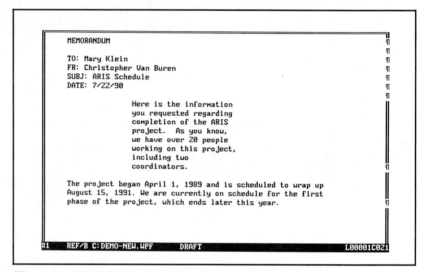

Figure 4.1: Multiple margin settings in a single document

To have several margin settings throughout the document requires several rulers. You can insert a ruler at any point in the document, set its left and right margins, and all text below the ruler will reformat to its settings. Text above the ruler is formatted by the settings of the previous ruler. The new ruler appears on the same line as the cursor when you enter the command Alt-F6. Once the ruler is in place, you can change the margins and tabs with the keys shown in Table 4.1. Complete the changes by pressing ◄┘.

When you insert a new ruler it will be set exactly like the one above it. If these are not the desired settings, you can opt to insert a ruler containing the default margin and tab settings instead of the previous ruler's settings. This is a variation on the Alt-F6 ruler insert command. Follow these steps:

- Press F10.
- Press **L** for the Layout menu.
- Press **2** to select the *Insert default ruler* option.
- Move the cursor to the desired line and press ⏎.

The result is a new ruler with the default margin and tab settings.

Now let's try some of the ruler commands on the sample document. First, you will insert a new ruler between the date and the first paragraph, and then you'll change its settings. Then, you'll delete that ruler and insert a default ruler instead:

Remember that you can hold down the Arrow keys for an auto-repeat effect.

1. Press Ctrl-Home to move the cursor to the top, then press ↓ six times to place the cursor between the date and the first paragraph.

2. Press Alt-F6 to insert a ruler at this position.

3. Press the space bar until the cursor is in column 17. (Use the line/column indicator as a guide.)

4. Press **L** to move the left margin.

5. Press → to move the cursor to column 56, then press **R** to move the right margin to that position.

6. Press ⏎ when finished. The screen should look like Figure 4.2.

7. Press ↑ once to move back to the ruler line.

8. Press Alt-F3 to delete the ruler. Notice that the text reformats to the settings of the previous ruler.

9. Press F10 L 2 ⏎ to insert a default ruler using the menu options.

10. Press ⏎ to accept the new ruler settings. The screen should look like Figure 4.3.

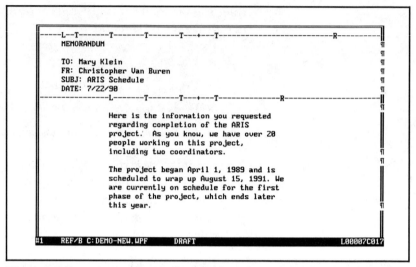

Figure 4.2: Inserting a ruler on the sample document

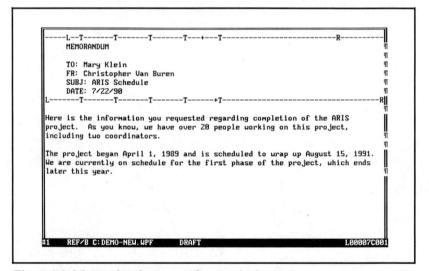

Figure 4.3: More ruler changes to the sample document

Removing a ruler is simple when you are already familiar with the delete commands. Just move the cursor onto the ruler line and press Alt-F3 to remove the entire line. Text below the ruler will reformat to the first ruler above it. You cannot delete the initial ruler at the top of the document. Instead, replace it with a new ruler by moving the cursor onto the ruler line and pressing Alt-F6. Or use the editing commands in Table 4.1 to change the ruler. Otherwise, you can use Ctrl-A to clear all the tabs on the ruler and start over.

USING THE MARGIN RELEASE

You've seen how you can control the margins for any part of a document by inserting rulers. But inserting new rulers can be a lot of work if you just want to extend the right margin on a single line—as you would on a typewriter with the margin release. It would be too much work to insert a new ruler for that one line, then insert another ruler to return to the correct margins. Instead, Enable offers a margin release command.

With the cursor on the desired line, press Ctrl-M. This extends the right margin for that line without changing the right margin setting for the rest of the paragraph. If the left margin is set to anything greater than column zero, using Ctrl-M also lets you move to the left of the current left margin (using the ← key).

Enable places a special double arrow symbol on the left border of the window to show where the margin releases occur (see Figure 4.4). When you see this indicator, you know that the right or left margin of the indicated line is wider (on each side) than the settings indicate.

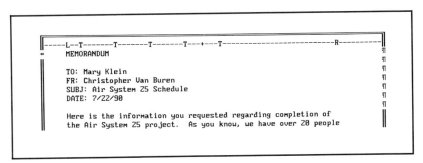

Figure 4.4: Margin release indicator

HIDING AND DISPLAYING RULERS

When you start accumulating rulers throughout the document, you may find them distracting to look at while you work. Thankfully, Enable lets you remove them from view without actually erasing them. They will remain invisible until you want to see them again. You can hide rulers with the simple command F9 O R O (O for On/Off, R for Ruler, O for Off). Try it now on the sample document.

To display rulers that have been hidden, use one of the following commands:

Enable offers menu versions of each of these expert commands. To access the menu versions, press F10, select *EditOpts*, select *Screen displays*, select *Rulers*, then select the desired option.

COMMAND	EFFECT
F9 O R T	Displays a single ruler at the top of the screen or removes the top ruler
F9 O R B	Displays a single ruler at the bottom of the screen or removes the bottom ruler
F9 O R W	Displays all rulers in their original locations within the text of the document

When you switch between ruler display locations, be sure to turn the rulers off first. Otherwise, Enable will keep the current rulers where they are and add the rulers you specify. In other words, you can display rulers at the top of the text, at the bottom of the text, *and* within the text, all at the same time, by using all three commands back to back without turning the rulers off between commands.

CONTROLLING TEXT ALIGNMENT

You can make any text in your document align with the left margin, the right margin, or both margins. Text aligned with the left margin is most common. This is called *left-justified* text, and it leaves the right margin ragged. Text aligned with the right margin, leaving the left side ragged, is called *right-justified*, and is relatively uncommon. Text aligned with both the right and left sides is called *fully-justified*, or simply *justified* text. The final alignment option is *centered* text.

Profile Option: You can make the default ruler use the J right margin instead of the R by customizing it with a profile option. Do this if you find yourself using full justification most of the time.

FULL JUSTIFICATION

Full justification is achieved by changing the right margin from an "R" to a "J" on the ruler line. To do this, move the cursor to the desired ruler, then use → to position the cursor in the desired column.

Now press Alt-J to make all text below this ruler (until the next ruler) fully justified with the right and left margins. That's it.

LEFT, RIGHT, AND CENTER

Aligning text with the left, right, and center of the margins requires a completely different approach than full justification. Luckily, the approach is the same for all three alignments. Using special commands, you can align a block of text or a single line at one time.

To align a single line of text, position the cursor on the desired line and use one of the commands in Table 4.2. If you want to align more than a line of text, use the block alignment options in Table 4.2. First, highlight the desired block using the F7 key at the beginning and end of the block (this is described in the previous chapter), then choose one of the block alignment commands.

Experiment with these commands on the example document, but return the lines to their original alignment when finished.

The block alignment options also have menu command equivalents. Select F10, choose *EditOpts*, then *Block Options*, then choose the desired alignment option.

Table 4.2: Text Alignment Commands

COMMAND	EFFECT
Alt-F4	Centers a line
F9 B +	Centers a block (the plus represents the plus sign on the ruler, which marks the center of the line)
Ctrl-]	Right-justifies a line
F9 B R	Right-justifies a block
Ctrl-[	Left-justifies a line
F9 B L	Left-justifies a block

WORKING WITH TABLES

Enable offers some useful features for manipulating tables. A table usually contains columns of numbers or text and often appears in the middle of a document. A table also may be imported from the Enable spreadsheet module. By aligning tab stops on the ruler, you can set the left side of each column then use the Tab key to move from column to column in a table. As you enter line after line, the information will align with the tab stops for each column, as shown in Figure 4.5.

This section discusses the various types of columns available for your tables and how to use them.

TYPES OF COLUMNS FOR TABLES

Figure 4.5 shows how tab stops on the ruler form the basis of columns. But this is only the beginning. Enable offers several types of columns for creating tables and some special features to go along with them. Each type of column is marked with a special character. Table 4.3 shows the column characters, the types of columns they create, and the characters that can be typed into each type of column.

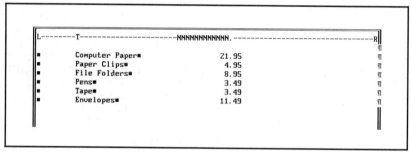

Figure 4.5: A typical two-column table

Table 4.3: Column Characters, Type of Column, and Acceptable Characters

COLUMN CHARACTER	TYPE OF COLUMN	ACCEPTABLE CHARACTERS
T	Standard left-aligned	All characters
X	Right-aligned	Numbers and letters; no punctuation or spaces
N	Decimal-aligned (for numbers)	Numbers and numeric characters − { [(+ $ # ' and ''. Use period or alphabetic character for decimal point.
^	Centered	All characters

Figure 4.6 shows an example of each type of column. With the exception of the T character, the number of these column characters that are displayed on the ruler line corresponds to the width of the column. Text that exceeds this width will not align with the rest of the column. For example, in Figure 4.6, the five X's create a five-character column that aligns on the rightmost edge (right-aligned).

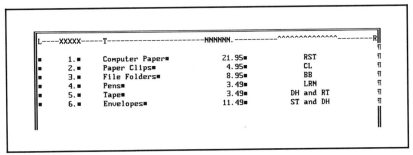

Figure 4.6: Various column types using characters on the ruler

CREATING A TABLE

When creating table columns, anticipate enough room for the widest line. To place these characters on a ruler, first insert a new ruler at the desired location. Next, move to the desired location on the ruler and type the characters of choice. Press ◄─┘ when finished. *You cannot type these column characters on an existing ruler—only on a new one.*

Once you've established the columns, you're ready to enter information into them. To use columns, position the cursor at the beginning of the first line, then press the Tab key to move to the first tab stop. If this is a numeric or right-aligned column, the cursor will align itself with the last N or X for that column (that is, the rightmost edge). If this is a centered column, the cursor will align itself in the center.

As you begin typing, the information will align itself in the column. Do not use the Backspace key to erase characters to the left. If you make a mistake while typing, use ← to move over to the mistake, then press Del to erase it. This will keep the alignment intact (more on editing columns later). Finally, make sure that the text in the column does not exceed the allotted space for that column, or text

If you must replace a ruler, just insert a new ruler under the one you want to replace, then remove the unwanted ruler. This will save time resetting the new ruler.

will not align properly. Unfortunately, if you underestimate the required column width when you set up the ruler, you cannot change it; instead, you have to remove the ruler and start over.

When you are finished typing in a column, press Tab to move to the next. When finished with the last column on the line, press Tab to move to the right margin, then press Tab again to move to the next line. Keep using Tab to move from column to column and line to line.

Try adding a table to the sample document using the steps below. You'll enter a table containing the phases of the ARIS project, their completion dates, and costs. First, prepare the document with these steps:

1. Press Ctrl-S as many times as needed to reach the end of the document (after the word "year" in the last sentence).

2. Press F9 Del ⟵ to remove the carriage return at this line.

3. Enter the following sentence:

   Following is a list of the four phases of the operation, their completion dates and costs: ⟵

The cursor should be on the line below the last line of the memo. Now insert a new ruler and apply the column markers using these commands:

4. Press Alt-F6.

5. Referring to the row/column indicator at the bottom of the screen, place the left margin at column 6 by pressing **L**. Press the space bar until you reach column 10, then place N's in columns 10 through 12 for a narrow number column. Then, space to column 15 and place a **T** in that column. Space to column 41, then place X's in columns 41 through 48, and N's in columns 54 through 62. Finally, the right margin should be on column 68. The ruler should look like the one in Figure 4.7.

6. Press ⟵ twice when finished.

Now you're ready to add data to the columns. The first column is set up to align the numbers on the periods. Since there are only three

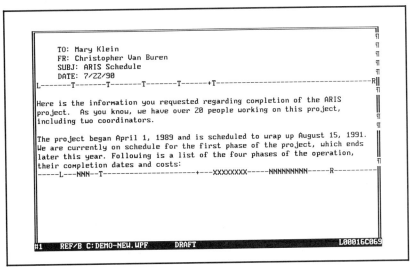

```
TO: Mary Klein                                                          ¶
FR: Christopher Van Buren                                               ¶
SUBJ: ARIS Schedule                                                     ¶
DATE: 7/22/90                                                           ¶
L-------T-------T-------T-------T------+T------------------------------R¶
                                                                        ¶
Here is the information you requested regarding completion of the ARIS
project.  As you know, we have over 20 people working on this project,
including two coordinators.                                             ¶
                                                                        ¶
The project began April 1, 1989 and is scheduled to wrap up August 15, 1991.
We are currently on schedule for the first phase of the project, which ends
later this year. Following is a list of the four phases of the operation,
their completion dates and costs:                                      ¶
-----L---NNN--T--------------------+---XXXXXXXX-----NNNNNNNNN-----R---------
```

```
#1    REF/B  C:DEMO-NEW.WPF       DRAFT                       L00016C069
```

Figure 4.7: Setting up several columns on a new ruler

N's in this column (that is, the column is only three characters wide), you can fit only two-digit numbers in it. The third column is set up for dates. Unfortunately, you cannot enter a slash character (/) in these columns because it destroys the alignment of the text. Instead, you'll use the hyphen character (-) to split the dates. (Actually, since the dates are all the same number of characters, it is not important to use a right-aligned column in this case—a standard left-aligned column would work just as well.)

7. Make sure that Num Lock mode is active by pressing the Num Lock key. An indicator will appear on the bottom line of the screen. Press Tab once, then type **1.** (include the period).

Notice that each time you press the Tab key, Enable inserts a square in the document. These will not appear on the printout—they are merely to show you where the tabs occur. As you will see later, knowing where the tabs occur can be useful.

8. Press Tab again, then type **Setup and Modeling**.

9. Press Tab again, then type **12-01-89**.

10. Press Tab again, then type **12,110.85**.

11. Press Tab three more times to position the cursor at the second line of the first column.

12. Using only the Tab key to move between columns, enter the rest of the table, as shown in Figure 4.8.

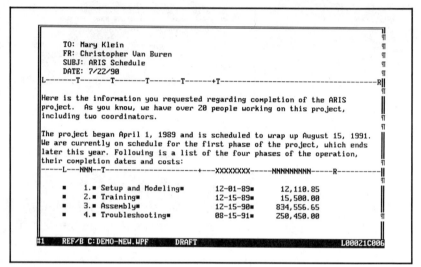

Figure 4.8: Finished table for the sample document

EDITING INFORMATION IN TABLES

Editing information in a table is not the same as editing regular paragraphs of text. Extra care is needed to keep the table's columns aligned. It's easy to accidentally remove tabular information and mess up the alignment—especially when using right-aligned and numeric columns. Here are some basic instructions.

First, make sure you're using the overstrike cursor (blinking underline). Use Tab or Shift-Tab to move to the desired column and row. Then use ← to position the cursor at the beginning of the text in that column. Now type over the text in the usual way. If you need to add characters to the end of the column (that is, if the new text is longer than the old), just keep typing in Overstrike mode as long as you remain within the bounds of the column. If you need to delete characters, use the Del key to remove characters at the cursor position; don't use the Backspace key. When using the Del key, be careful not to erase any tab markers (square markers in each column) or text will fall out of alignment. If you accidentally remove a tab marker, you can replace it by switching to Insert mode (blinking block) and pressing the Tab key in the desired position. Be sure to switch back to Overstrike before continuing with the edits.

USING CHARACTER ATTRIBUTES

Character attributes include boldface type, underlining, and other character enhancements. Enable lets you apply these character attributes at any time in your documents. You can use attributes on a single character, a word, a sentence, or the entire document. And Enable shows you what text you have formatted with what attribute—often by displaying the attribute right on the screen.

When you choose your printer(s) in the installation process, you assure that Enable knows how to communicate to your printer for such purposes as applying attributes. If your printer does not support a character attribute offered by Enable, the printout will not include that attribute change and the text will appear normal. Some printers can print attributes beyond those offered by Enable, such as printing in color. Enable does not limit your printer to the attributes described here—you can access any feature of your printer at any time.

Applying character attributes is just like marking text (described in Chapter 2). The procedure is simple: First, move to the beginning of the text you want to set. Next, press the attribute command (over a dozen exist). Then use one of seven special cursor movement commands to move the cursor to the end of the text, applying the attribute along the way. Finally, press the attribute command again to turn it off. Table 4.4 lists the character attribute commands, followed by a list of the cursor-movement commands that apply the attribute to the text.

Character attributes are actually "printer attributes," so they rely on the capability of your printer to print the attribute. Most printers can print the attributes offered by Enable.

Enable will display the character attributes and their commands for quick reference at the top of the screen: press F10 EditOpts Attribute Help on (F10 E E). Press the command sequence again to remove it.

Table 4.4: Character Attribute Commands and Applicable Cursor Movement Commands

ATTRIBUTE COMMAND	EFFECT
Alt-B	Boldface
Alt-C	Compressed

Table 4.4: Character Attribute Commands and Applicable Cursor Movement Commands (continued)

ATTRIBUTE COMMAND	EFFECT
Alt-D	Double-strike
Alt-E	Elite type (12 characters per inch)
Alt-I	Italic
Alt-F	Lower- to uppercase
Alt-K	Upper- to lowercase
Alt-M	Marked text
Alt-N	Normal (removes attributes)
Alt-O	Overstrike
Alt-P	Proportional text
Alt-Q	Quality print
Alt-V	Subscript
Alt-A	Superscript
Alt-U	Underline
Alt-W	Wide print
CURSOR MOVEMENT COMMAND	**EFFECT**
Ctrl-W	Formats the next word
Ctrl-C	Formats the next character
Ctrl-L	Formats from the cursor to the end of the line
Ctrl-G	Formats from the cursor to the end of the page
Ctrl-P	Formats from the cursor to the end of the paragraph
Ctrl-S	Formats from the cursor to the end of the sentence
Ctrl-B	Formats the current block (see explanation below)

THE ENABLE CHARACTER ATTRIBUTES

This section describes the various character attributes available in Enable. Remember that some of the attributes appear only on the printer, and others are simulated on the screen. Check your printer manual for more information about each of these attributes.

BOLDFACE AND DOUBLE-STRIKE Boldface and double-strike make type look heavier, or bolder. Unless you are using a dot-matrix printer, you may not notice any difference between them. However, dot-matrix printers handle these two attributes differently: bold-face places the second set of dots next to the first, whereas double-strike places the second set below the first.

ELITE, WIDE, PROPORTIONAL, AND COMPRESSED These attributes affect the width of characters or lines containing them. By default, text prints at 10 characters per inch. This is called *pica* width. Setting *elite* width changes the characters to 12 per inch. Some printers actually use smaller characters for elite type; others use less space between the characters. The result is the ability to fit more characters on each line of the page. If you are using a standard platen width (standard on letter-size printers), you can fit up to 80 pica characters or 96 elite characters on each line (assuming you have zero left and right margins).

When you switch from pica to elite, Enable does not automatically place more characters on each line to reflect the smaller character size. Instead, elite width will appear as short lines containing the same number of characters as pica width. You have to change the margins if you want more characters on each line. Set the right margin to column 96 for starters. That's the maximum for elite on standard printers. (If you have a wide-carriage printer, the maximum could be as much as 180 for elite and 150 for pica.) Move the margin in from there if you want more space. Make sure Automatic Reformat is on so the text adheres to the new margin settings.

Wide printing is less common and varies from printer to printer. Many printers use 8 characters per inch for wide printing. Since this is often used for headings, which usually do not extend across the entire width of the page, you may not need to change margins when using wide print.

Compressed print is smaller than Elite. Many printers use 15 characters per inch for this attribute (18 characters per inch is also common). This makes the maximum right margin 120 for standard printers and 225 for wide-carriage printers.

Proportional print does not change the size of the characters, but the space used by each character. This means that narrow characters, like "i", "l", and "!" use less space than wide characters like "m" and "w." Proportional type can make your document look more professional. However, it's impossible to know how many proportional characters will fit on each line, since each character is a different width. An inch of l's contains more characters than an inch of M's. Experiment with your right margin for best results.

When you apply these character width attributes, Enable uses special diamond-shaped markers in the document to indicate where the attribute begins and ends. Figure 4.9 shows the various markers for elite (E), compressed (C), proportional (P), and wide (W) type.

> Enable offers a way to activate elite or compressed type for the entire document with one command. By using a special *global* setting, you can avoid using the attribute commands for elite and compressed. This global setting is discussed in Chapter 3 along with the print-setup options. See "Choosing a Type Size" in Chapter 3.

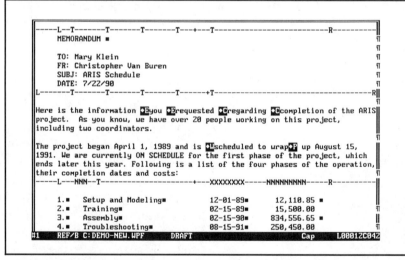

Figure 4.9: Document markers for elite, compressed, proportional, and wide attributes

ITALIC, LOWERCASE AND UPPERCASE, MARKED, AND QUALITY   Some printers do not offer italic print because it requires at least two complete character sets in the printer. If your printer offers

italic print, the switch between character sets will be automatic and invisible.

Lowercase and uppercase are two attributes that are not controlled by the printer. These are, in fact, screen attributes, since upper- and lowercase letters are determined for the printer by what is shown on the screen. You can think of these attributes as simple conversion tools from upper- to lowercase.

Marked text serves no purpose by itself. It is used with other commands and options that manipulate text, such as the Copy command.

Quality print is usually associated with high-quality dot-matrix printers, such as those using 24-pins, although many 9-pin printers offer quality print. In any case, it is a feature that enhances the quality of the type—sometimes at the cost of speed.

SUPERSCRIPT AND SUBSCRIPT   Superscript and subscript type is often required in numeric expressions. Superscript places text above the normal baseline as in

$$10^4$$

and subscript places text below it:

$$H_2O$$

UNDERLINE AND OVERSTRIKE   Underlining is a simple attribute for adding an underline to text. All printers are capable of accomplishing this attribute in one way or another.

The overstrike attribute lets you type one character on top of another, or several others. This can be used to produce special symbols, such as the "does not equal" sign ($\neq$), which is the / character typed over the = character. To activate overstrike, press Alt-O, then enter the character that is to strike over the other (such as the / in the $\neq$ symbol). Next, enter the second character. Finally, press Alt-O to turn overstrike off. The result will be two characters surrounded by the overstrike markers.

At times, you may need one character to overstrike others, as in "lining out" a section of text:

~~This is lining out text by overstriking the Dash character with text.~~

This is accomplished the same way as with two characters, except that the entire block is surrounded by the overstrike markers. Press Alt-O at the beginning of the text, then make sure the first character after the marker is the overstrike character. Finally, press Alt-O at the end of the text.

APPLYING ATTRIBUTES TO SELECTED TEXT

Since you've used the Alt-M and Alt-N commands earlier in this book to mark and unmark text, you should be somewhat familiar with the procedure for using character attributes on selected text. In this exercise you'll use some other attributes. Try this on your example document:

1. Move the cursor to the second paragraph on the "A" in the word "April."

2. Press Alt-B for boldface. Notice that a lowercase "b" appears at the bottom of the screen next to the mode indicator. This is the attribute indicator, telling you that the boldface attribute is active.

3. Press Ctrl-W three times to format the date in boldface type.

4. Press Ctrl-→ five times to move to the beginning of the next date (the "A" in "August").

5. Press Ctrl-W three more times to format that date in boldface type.

6. Press Alt-B to turn boldface off. The printed document would look like Figure 4.10.

Notice that the boldface attribute was on during the entire process, even though you moved the cursor without applying boldface. This is because only the special cursor movement commands listed above will apply the current format to the text. Other cursor movement commands work as usual without applying the attributes. Now try this:

7. Move the cursor to the "W" in "We are currently...." if it's not already there.

8. Press Alt-U to activate underline print.

```
·MEMORANDUM

        TO: Mary Klein
        FR: Christopher Van Buren
        SUBJ: ARIS Schedule
        DATE: 7/22/90

Here is the information you requested regarding completion of the
ARIS project.  As you know, we have over 20 people working on
this project, including two coordinators.

The project began April 1, 1989 and is scheduled to wrap up
August 15, 1991. We are currently on schedule for the first phase
of the project, which ends later this year. Following is a list
of the four phases of the operation, their completion dates and
costs:

        1.    Setup and Modeling      12-01-89      12,110.85
        2.    Training                02-15-89      15,500.00
        3.    Assembly                02-15-90     834,556.65
        4.    Troubleshooting         08-15-91     250,450.00
```

Figure 4.10: The example document with character attributes

9. Press Ctrl-W three times to highlight the first three words of the sentence.

10. Press Alt-F to turn the lowercase to uppercase attribute on. Notice that the bottom of the screen displays "uf" to show that two attributes are active.

11. Press Ctrl-W two more times to highlight the next two words. Notice that both active attributes are applied to the words.

12. Press Alt-N to turn the normal attribute on. This is also a way to turn active attributes off, since you cannot mix normal with anything else. The printed document would look like Figure 4.11.

APPLYING ATTRIBUTES TO BLOCKS

When you want to format a large area of the document, you can use the Block-Formatting command to accomplish this quickly. Here are the steps for applying attributes to a block of text at one time:

If you have a color monitor, use the command F10, MCM, Screen to select the "Co80" screen setting. This will display character attributes as high-intensity text. If your system supports graphics, use the same command to select the *Graphics* screen setting. This displays character attributes as they will appear on the printer.

- Highlight the desired text using the F7 key at the beginning and end of the block. This is the standard Block-Highlighting command described earlier in this book.

```
MEMORANDUM

     TO: Mary Klein
     FR: Christopher Van Buren
     SUBJ: ARIS Schedule
     DATE: 7/22/90

Here is the information you requested regarding completion of the
ARIS project.  As you know, we have over 20 people working on
this project, including two coordinators.

The project began April 1, 1989 and is scheduled to wrap up
August 15, 1991. We are currently ON SCHEDULE for the first phase
of the project, which ends later this year. Following is a list
of the four phases of the operation, their completion dates and
costs:

     1.    Setup and Modeling        12-01-89        12,110.85
     2.    Training                  02-15-89        15,500.00
     3.    Assembly                  02-15-90       834,556.65
     4.    Troubleshooting           08-15-91       250,450.00
```

Figure 4.11: More character formatting on the example document

The command
F2 ↑ B is one of the
advanced cursor move-
ment commands dis-
cussed in Chapter 5.

- Move the cursor back to the beginning of the block using the command F2 ↑ B.

- Turn on the desired character attribute(s) using the appropriate Alt key command(s).

- Press Ctrl-B to apply the active attribute(s) to the current block.

- Press Alt-F7 to clear the block highlight so you can see the character attributes.

Note that this procedure applies only to the attributes bold, italic, lower to upper, upper to lower, marked, normal, superscript, subscript, and underline. All other attributes use special start and end markers to designate text being affected by an attribute.

DISPLAYING CHARACTER ATTRIBUTES

Enable displays some character attributes on the screen. Others, however, cannot be shown and are displayed as bold type. So, if you use several of these attributes together in the same document, how can you tell them apart? The answer is to turn on the attribute indicator. The indicator shows you what attribute applies to the text in your document. You saw how the indicator uses lowercase letters to show an active attribute when you are typing. The same indicator uses uppercase letters to show which attributes apply to existing text. Simply move the cursor to the desired text and look at the bottom of the screen for the indication. Try this:

1. Press Alt-S to turn the indicator on.

2. Move the cursor to the formatted text and watch the bottom of the screen. The indicator displays the name of the format active at the cursor position (see Figure 4.12). As the cursor moves over formatted text, the indicator changes.

3. Press Alt-S again to turn the indicator off.

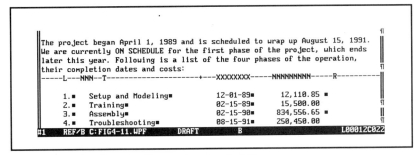

Figure 4.12: Attribute indicator showing boldface text

You may want to leave the attribute indicator on at all times. It does no harm to leave it on, and it serves a useful purpose.

INSERTING TEXT WITH CHARACTER ATTRIBUTES ACTIVE

So far, you've seen how to apply character attributes to existing text. But often, you'll want to apply them as you create a document so you don't have to go back and apply them later. This is very simple. As you type, simply turn the desired attributes on with the appropriate Alt-key command. Then just continue typing. Everything you type with the attribute active appears in that attribute. Turn the attribute off when finished.

ATTRIBUTES AND TABS—A POTENTIAL PROBLEM

Many of the attributes change the widths of the characters. Compressed, elite, and proportional attributes have significant effects on character width. But quality and double-strike also change character widths. When you change the widths of such characters, they *may not* align properly with tab stops. This can be a significant problem when you use these attributes along with tables.

HYPHENATING WORDS

Enable offers some special tools for hyphenating words at the ends of lines. There are two reasons for using hyphenation: when using hyphenated words, such as "half-hearted" and "self-inflicted," and when breaking a word at the end of a line.

Often, you'll want a hyphen to appear permanently with a word or compound modifier—whether at the end of a line or not. In this case, you need a regular hyphen, called a *hard hyphen*. To insert a hard hyphen, simply press the hyphen key where needed and continue typing normally. This you may have already assumed. If the hyphenated word appears at the end of a line, Enable may wrap the word (including the hyphen) to the next line.

When a word is hyphenated at the end of a line and would not normally be hyphenated in the middle of a line, you need what's called a *soft hyphen*. A soft hyphen appears only as long as the hyphenated word is at the end of a line. If you change the margins or insert or delete text—causing the hyphenated word to move to the middle of a line—the soft hyphen will disappear and the word will be joined normally. This is ideal for breaking long words between lines, making

You may want to insert a *hard space* at the end of a line to prevent the words on either side from breaking between lines. This can be handy for proper names and elipses (. . .). Press Alt- = where the normal space would occur. This will produce a diamond and will cause the words on either side to be treated as one word. When your document is printed, the diamond will disappear and look like a space.

the right edge of the text more uniform. Use these steps to insert a soft hyphen as you approach the end of a line:

- Begin typing the word at the end of the line. Insert the hyphen at the desired break point using the hyphen key.

- Press the → key until the cursor moves to the beginning of the next line.

- Finish typing the word at the beginning of the next line.

Enable knows to remove this hyphen if it appears anywhere but at the end of the line (that is, if it moves).

So what if you need a hard hyphen at the end of a line, but want to break the word between lines, for example, if a word like "self-inflicted" appears at the end of a line? First, the hyphen is permanent and should be preserved wherever the word appears. But you decide you also want to break the word between lines, so that "self-" appears at the end of one line and "inflicted" appears at the beginning of the next. You can break the word between lines by using a soft hyphen, but if the margins change, the hyphen will disappear. Instead, insert an *end-of-line* hard hyphen using the following steps:

- Begin typing the word at the end of the line. Insert the hyphen at the desired break point by pressing Alt-Hyphen (Alt with the hyphen key).

- Press the → key until the cursor moves to the beginning of the next line and finish typing the word.

As you see, this is similar to the soft hyphen, but the Alt key is used with the hyphen key to make a hard hyphen appear at the end of the line.

If you commonly use two hyphen characters (--) to represent an em dash (—), you might need to insert these characters at the end of a line, breaking the line after the dash so the word immediately following the dash wraps to the next line. Try making the second dash a hard hyphen as described above. This will ensure that the information reformats correctly if the margins should change.

INSERTING HYPHENS AS YOU TYPE

Let's try the hyphenation features on the example document. First, prepare the document by inserting a default ruler at the bottom of the memo (under the table). Remember how? Here are the steps:

1. Use ↓ (or other cursor movement commands) to place the cursor at the bottom of the document, one line below the table.

2. Press F10 L 2 ⏎ to insert a default ruler at the cursor position.

3. Press ⏎ twice to move to the starting position.

Now you're ready to insert the text with hyphenation:

4. Type the following:

    I hope this information is satisfactory and that the schedule meets your ap-

5. After typing the hyphen, press → two times to move to the beginning of the next line. Then type the following:

    proval. We should not have any problems meeting our goals, which are self

6. After you type "self" press Alt- (Alt with the hyphen key).

7. Press → three times to move to the next line.

8. Finish with the word **inflicted.**

9. Now change the right margin by pressing ↑ four times to position the cursor on the ruler line.

10. Press → until the cursor is in column 68, then press Alt-R. The screen should look like Figure 4.13.

Notice that the word "approval" is no longer hyphenated since it moved to the middle of a line. But the word "self-inflicted" remained hyphenated.

INSERTING A HYPHEN IN EXISTING TEXT

Now that you have seen the effect of hyphenation with changes in the margins, what happens when you return the margin to its original

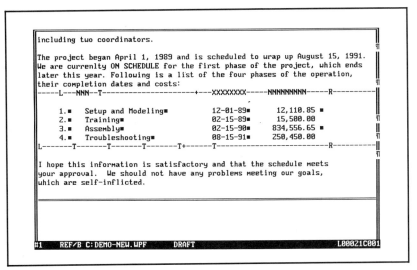

```
including two coordinators.                                              ¶
The project began April 1, 1989 and is scheduled to wrap up August 15, 1991.
We are currenlty ON SCHEDULE for the first phase of the project, which ends
later this year. Following is a list of the four phases of the operation,
their completion dates and costs:                                       ¶
-----L---NNN--T---------------------+---XXXXXXX-----NNNNNNNN-----R---------
              1.■   Setup and Modeling■       12-01-89■     12,110.85 ■
              2.■   Training■                 02-15-89■     15,500.00       ¶
              3.■   Assembly■                 02-15-90■    834,556.65 ■
              4.■   Troubleshooting■          08-15-91■    250,450.00       ¶
L-------T-------T-------T-------T+------T------------------------R---------
                                                                        ¶
I hope this information is satisfactory and that the schedule meets
your approval.  We should not have any problems meeting our goals,
which are self-inflicted.




#1    REF/B C:DEMO-NEW.WPF        DRAFT                        L00021C001
```

Figure 4.13: Using hyphenation on the example document

position? Do the words rehyphenate themselves as before? Try it:

1. Return the cursor to the ruler, then press → until you reach column 78.

2. Press Alt-R to move the right margin.

The old hyphenation is no longer in place. Here's how to put it back (make sure you are in Insert, not Overstrike mode):

3. Move the cursor to the second "p" in "approval."

4. Press the hyphen key to insert a hyphen, then press the space bar.

5. Press ← five times to position the cursor at the end of the previous line.

6. Press the Del key once.

7. Move the cursor to the first "i" in "self-inflicted." Then press the space bar to insert a space after the hyphen.

8. Press ← seven times to position the cursor at the end of the previous line.

9. Press the Del key once.

Since "self-inflicted" already contains a hard hyphen, it will remain in place the next time the margins change. Otherwise, you would need to replace the existing hyphen with a hard hyphen (Alt with the hyphen key) when hyphenating existing text like this.

10. Press F9 S Home to save the document and return to the Main menu.

AUTOMATIC HYPHENATION

Now that you are familiar with hyphenation and the use of soft and hard hyphens, take a look at Enable's Automatic Hyphenation feature. This feature does most of the hyphenation work for you.

Rather than insert a hyphen in every word that needs one, you can tell Enable to hyphenate as needed at the ends of lines. This is done by specifying a hyphenation zone. All words that exceed the width of this zone are automatically hyphenated by Enable. You decide the width of the zone by placing a Z on a ruler prior to the right margin (see Figure 4.14). The distance between the Z and the right margin (R) is the zone. Usually, the zone is from 4 to 8 spaces wide.

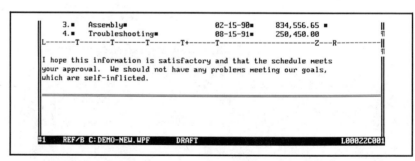

Figure 4.14: A hyphenation zone

Since you cannot type the Z on an existing ruler, you must insert a new ruler to apply Automatic Hyphenation. If text already exists below this ruler, it will reformat (hyphenate) according to the zone. If Enable is unsure how to hyphenate a word, it will prompt you for the correct hyphenation.

LINE SPACING

The line-spacing option controls the distance between the lines of text. You can set line spacing to double-space or triple-space your documents, but there are actually many more spacing options available. Here's how to set line spacing:

- Move the cursor to the line where you want the line spacing change to take effect.

- Press F9.

- Press Ins.

- Enter the amount of spacing you want. The spacing can be any whole number from 1 to 231.

- Press **S**.

Line spacing will not appear on screen in Draft mode. To see the line spacing change, switch from Draft mode to Final mode (F9 O D). Experiment with line spacing changes on the sample document if desired. When finished, remove the line spacing markers by returning to Draft mode, then moving to the line containing the marker and pressing Alt-F3 to remove the line. Note that line spacing affects all text below the marker—until another line spacing marker is encountered.

CHAPTER 5

Working with Large Documents

THIS CHAPTER CONTAINS HELPFUL INFORMATION about some Enable features that you will use frequently when creating and editing longer documents. If you use the word processor for reports, books, manuals, or any documents more than three or four pages long, you'll probably need to use headers, footers, and page numbers, insert page breaks, search for specific text, mark a place in the text for future reference, and move the cursor quickly through the document. You'll use the memo you've been working on in earlier chapters to learn about these features.

FINDING INFORMATION IN A DOCUMENT

There are three ways to find and handle information in an Enable document: finding, finding and marking, and finding and replacing. You can use either the Top Line menu or the expert commands to accomplish any of these three tasks. Using either method, you can

CH. 5

change a series of options that affect the way Enable searches—or you can accept these options the way they are. The options are currently set for the most common use.

FINDING

The longer the document, the more difficult it can be to find occurrences of a word or phrase. Enable's Find commands provide the necessary tools.

Here's how to find text using the Top Line menu. If you'd like, try out this feature on the DEMOMEMO document.

- Press Ctrl-Home to move the cursor to the top of the document. Unless you request otherwise, Enable searches from the current location of the cursor.

- Press F10 to invoke the Top Line menu.

- Press **F** for the Find menu.

- Press ◄─┘ to select the *Find only* option.

- Enter the word or phrase you want to find and press ◄─┘. Unless you specify otherwise (using the *Change Options* options listed below), Enable will find matching words in either upper- or lowercase.

Finding a particular heading is an easy way to jump to a specific location in the text.

- Press ◄─┘ to select the *Accept Options* option. (At this point you could change the find options by choosing *Change Options*— see the discussion below.) Enable moves the cursor to the first character of the first occurrence of the specified text.

- Press F5 to find the next occurrence of the specified text. (You also can use the expert command F9 F A to find the next occurrence.) When Enable cannot find another occurrence, it responds with a beep. (Use F6 to move to a previous occurrence.)

Profile Option: If you find that you always select the *Change Options* option, you might want to permanently change the find option defaults using a profile.

Enable lets you change the basic find options for your search. When you use the *Change Options* option, you'll see the following five prompts:

- *Case*—Choose *Ignore* to find all matching words, regardless of upper- and lowercase letters. This is the default option.

Change the option to *As Entered* to have Enable find only those words that match the case of the word you entered.

- *Find From*—Choose *Top* to search from the top of the document downward (forward), regardless of the cursor position. Choose *Current* to search from the current position of the cursor downward (this is the default option). Choose *Bottom* to search from the bottom of the document upward (backward).

- *To*—The *Find From* option determines the starting position for the search, and *To* determines the stopping position. Choose any option other than the one you used in the previous prompt. If you choose the same option, Enable will ask you to reselect.

- *Find From Column*—This is used in multiple-column documents to find words that occur only in a specific column. You can ignore this option by pressing ←┘.

- *To Column*—This is used with the previous option. Ignore this by pressing ←┘.

Here's how to find text using the expert commands:

- Press Ctrl-Home to position the cursor at the top of the document. Enable will search from the current position of the cursor to the bottom of the document—unless you request otherwise by using the find options.

- Press F9 F T (F for Find, T for Text).

- Enter the text you want to find and press ←┘. Unless you specify otherwise, Enable ignores the case of the letters you enter.

- Here you can change the various find options (listed above) or press ←┘ to accept the default options.

- Find the next occurrence of the text by pressing F5 or by using the expert command F9 F A.

FINDING AND MARKING

Finding and marking is identical to finding except that matching text is marked (highlighted). Marked text can then be formatted, moved, or copied. This can save some time when a frequently used word or phrase is also formatted in a consistent way throughout a document.

Here are the basic steps for finding and marking using the menu. Again, try out this feature on DEMOMEMO if you want.

- Press Ctrl-Home to position the cursor at the top of the document. Otherwise, position the cursor where you want to begin searching.

- Press F10 to invoke the menu.

- Press **F** for the Find menu.

- Press ↑ once to highlight the option *Find and Mark*, then press ←.

- Enter the word or phrase you want to find and press ←. Unless you specify otherwise (using the *Change Options* options listed in the previous section), Enable will find matching words in either upper- or lowercase.

- Press ← to select the *Accept Options* option. (At this point you could change the find options by choosing *Change Options*— see the description in the previous section.) Enable will move the cursor to the first character of the first occurrence of the specified text.

- Press F5 to find the next occurrence of the specified text. (You also can use the expert command F9 F A to find the next occurrence.) When Enable cannot find another occurrence, it responds with a beep. (Use F6 to move to a previous occurrence.)

You can also use the expert commands to find and mark text:

- Press Ctrl-Home to position the cursor at the top of the document. Otherwise, position the cursor where you want to begin searching.

- Press F9 F M (F for Find, M for Mark).

- Enter the text you want to find and press ←. Unless you specify otherwise, Enable ignores the case of the letters you enter.

- Here you can change the various find options or press ◄━┛ to accept the default options.

- Find the next occurrence of the text by pressing the F5 key or by using the expert command F9 F A. As you find other occurrences of the text, Enable will highlight (mark) them all.

FINDING AND REPLACING

Sometimes you may need to replace certain words throughout the document. Suppose you have written a long report about the ARIS project and, after the report is completed, the project is renamed "Air System 25." Throughout the document, references to ARIS have to be changed. The automatic find and replace options handle this for you. The options are similar to those for finding or finding and marking.

Retrieve DEMOMEMO for the next exercise. You'll use the Top Line menu to find the word "ARIS" and replace it with "Air System 25."

1. Press Ctrl-Home to position the cursor at the top of the document.

2. Press F10 to invoke the Top Line menu.

3. Press **F** for the Find command.

4. Press ↓ once to highlight the *Find and Replace* option, then press ◄━┛.

You should see the "Enter string to find" prompt. Unless you specify otherwise, Enable will ignore the case of the letters you type.

5. Enter the word **ARIS**, then press ◄━┛.

Now you see the "Enter replace string" prompt. When finding and replacing, Enable considers upper- and lowercase letters.

6. Enter **Air System 25** and press ◄━┛.

7. Press ◄━┛ to select the *Accept Options* option. Enable replaces the first occurrence (following the cursor) with the

replacement text you entered—respecting the upper- and lowercase letters.

Move to the next occurrence, previewing it before replacing it.

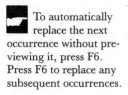
To automatically replace the next occurrence without previewing it, press F6. Press F6 to replace any subsequent occurrences.

8. Press F5. This will find the next occurrence and wait for your command to replace it or skip it. Press F5 to skip this occurrence and move to the next without replacing; press F6 to replace this occurrence.

9. Repeat step 8 to replace or skip the remaining occurrences. Be sure to replace all occurrences in the sample document before continuing to the next chapter.

Here's how to find and replace using the expert commands:

- Press Ctrl-Home to move to the top of the document. Otherwise, position the cursor at the desired location.

- Press F9 F R (F for Find, R for Replace).

- Enter the text to find and press ◄┘.

- Enter the text to replace and press ◄┘.

- Press ◄┘ to accept the default options or change them by highlighting the *Change Options* option and pressing ◄┘. These options are described under "Finding" earlier in this chapter.

- Press F5. This will find the next occurrence and wait for your command to replace it or skip it. Press F5 to skip this occurrence and move to the next without replacing; press F6 to replace this occurrence.

FINDING PARTIAL WORDS USING A WILDCARD

When using the find commands, you'll notice that Enable finds only complete words or phrases that match the text you specify. In other words, Enable will not find your word when it appears as part of another word. For example, when you specify "the" as the word to find, Enable will not find "therefore," "them," "either," and so on (all containing "the"). While this is usually desirable, there may be times when you want to find partial occurrences of the specified word. For example, you might want to find "string," "strings," and "stringlike" without searching three separate times. You can accomplish this with special characters called *wildcards*.

By using wildcards as part of the search text, you can change the number of possible matches to your text. The most common wildcard is the dollar sign ($). This character, when entered with the search text, represents any character(s). For example, entering "the$" will locate "the," "therefore," "their," and all other words beginning with "the." It will not locate "either" because it does not begin with "the." To find "the" when it appears anywhere in a word, you would enter "the" as the search text.

The second wildcard is the question mark (?). This represents any single character in the exact position it appears in the search text. For example, if you enter "the?" as the text to find, Enable will find "them" and "they," but will not find "the" or "their." Only words with exactly one character following "the" are considered matches.

INSERTING PAGE BREAKS

When you view your document in Final mode using the command F9 O D, Enable displays the document on the screen just as it would print on paper (except for some attributes and embedded commands). This reveals where the page breaks occur. Try switching to Final; the screen should look like Figure 5.1. Presently, the sample document has only one page, as indicated at the top of the screen in Final mode.

If the document had more pages, each would be clearly marked at the top with the page marker shown in Figure 5.1. Now return to Draft mode by selecting the command F9 O D. Notice that the page marker remains in the document. Enable leaves these markers in the document when you return to Draft mode, even though the markers could change positions when you make edits and would no longer reflect the page break locations accurately. Unfortunately, the only way to get rid of these markers in Draft mode is to move the cursor to each one and press the familiar Alt-F3 key to delete the entire line. However, when you view the document in Final mode again, the markers will come back to haunt you. Best get used to them.

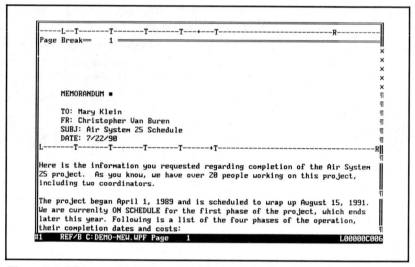

Figure 5.1: The sample document in Final mode, showing a page number

Knowing where Enable naturally breaks the pages is useful for certain formatting needs. For one thing, you can determine if a natural page break occurs in an unwanted location. For example, when you work with a large document, you may want to start a section of text on a new page, such as when you begin a new chapter. How can you be sure that the section begins on a new page? The answer is to insert a *page break,* which will begin a new page at that point. The page marker indicates the top of the new page.

If the break occurs prior to a natural break (and it most likely will), the end of the previous page will simply be left blank. Try this on the sample document:

1. Move the cursor to line 15 of the document, above the ruler that controls the table of completion dates.

2. Press F9 Ins M P to create a page break at this line. The page break appears at the position of the cursor, as shown in Figure 5.2.

Notice that the page break marker indicates a "user defined" page break. This distinguishes it from natural breaks.

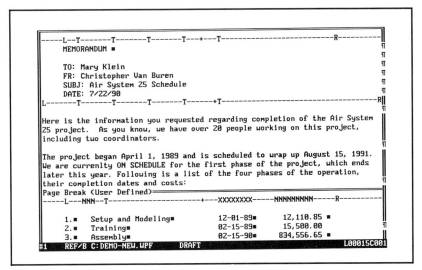

Figure 5.2: A page break inserted with the F9 Ins M P command

3. View the document in Final mode again; the user-defined page break marks the beginning of page 2, as shown in Figure 5.3.

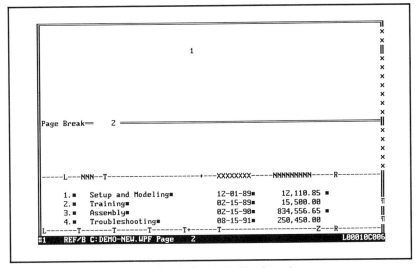

Figure 5.3: The user-defined page break in Final mode

You will notice a number of empty lines before and after this marker. The lines before the marker are the lines left blank at the end of the previous page. The eight blank lines immediately following the page break indicate the top margin of the page. The right edge of the document window displays an "x" at each of these blank lines.

CREATING HEADERS AND FOOTERS

Headers and footers are common in large documents. A *header* is a line of text at the top of the page that repeats throughout the document—or, at least, throughout a section of the document. A *footer* is a line of text at the bottom of the page. Usually, the header or footer will contain the page number, name of the section or chapter, or other descriptive text. Headers and footers in Enable can be more than one line; they can contain as many lines as are allowed on each page. But this reduces the number of lines available on each page for your document. Headers appear just below the top margin of each page and footers appear just above the bottom margin.

To insert a header, first position the cursor at the top of the first page on which the header should appear. It's very important to move to the top of a page because inserting a header also inserts a page break. Next, use the menu command F10, Layout, Insert a Header.

Footers can be inserted anywhere in the page (preferably below the header), and use the command F10, Layout, Insert a Footer.

The equivalent expert commands are shown here:

COMMAND	RESULT
F9 Ins H	Inserts a header
F9 Ins F	Inserts a footer

You then type the text for the header or footer into the entry space. Whatever you type into the entry space is printed on each page. The alignment and attributes of this text also apply to each page. If the header is centered in the entry space, it will be centered on each page. If it's boldface in the entry space, it will be boldface on each page.

Let's create a header for the sample document:

1. Press Ctrl-Home to move the cursor to the top of the document. Then press ↑ to move the cursor to the initial ruler line. (Make sure you're in Draft mode.)

2. Press F9 Ins H to insert a header. The header adheres to the margins of the initial ruler.

3. Now type the following in the header entry space (see Figure 5.4):

    Special Memo

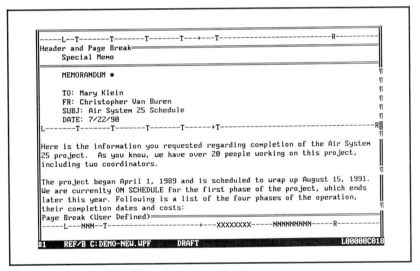

Figure 5.4: Typing the header text into the entry space

4. Press F9 O D to view the document in Final mode. Use the Arrow keys to view the entire document. The header appears below the page break markers for each page.

You can always return to the header or footer entry area and edit the text in it. Of course, this must be done in Draft mode. To remove a header or footer, move the cursor to the top line of the header or footer entry space, then press Alt-F3. You can also hide header and footer entry areas from view. This cleans up the screen while you're working, but leaves the headers and footers intact. To hide headers use F9 O H; to hide footers use F9 O F. Repeat the command to display the header or footer again.

NUMBERING PAGES AND DATING DOCUMENTS

Page numbers are related to headers and footers in that they appear in the header or footer area. Enable has a page numbering feature that works with headers and footers to automatically number the pages in your documents. This numbering feature is different than the one described in Chapter 3. It's very simple—just insert the character # anywhere in a header or footer. When you print the document or view it in Final mode, this symbol will become a page number. Try it out on DEMOMEMO:

1. In Draft mode, place the cursor in the header entry area and move out to column 58.

2. Type **Page** # (if you wanted only the number to appear, you would just type #).

3. Press F9 O D to view the results in Final mode. The page number appears in the header for each page on which the header is printed.

You may want to begin numbering pages at something other than 1. For example, you might have the chapters of a book in separate files. Thus, if Chapter 1 contains 124 pages, Chapter 2—even though it is a separate document—should begin at page 125. To specify a starting page number, type the page number symbol (#) followed by an equal sign (=) and the starting page number. For example,

    # = 125

would start numbering with 125. Do not type any spaces in this formula.

For more informa-
tion about using
dates in documents,
including changing the
date format, see the
%DATE embedded
command in Chapter 3.

Enable also offers a special date command that automatically places the current date on your document inside the header area. This date comes from the Enable startup screen. Just insert the command %DATE anywhere in a header or footer. When the document is printed or viewed in Final mode, the date will appear in place of this command. Try it on the sample file:

1. In Draft mode, place the cursor in the header entry area and move out to 27.

2. Type %**DATE**.

3. Press F9 O D to view the results in Final mode. The correct date appears in the header for each page on which the header is printed. Your document should now look like Figure 5.5.

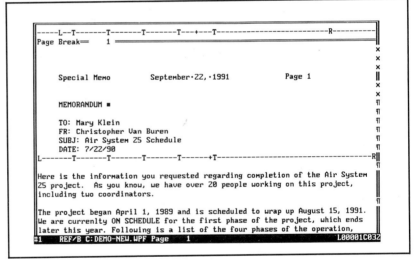

Figure 5.5: Sample document with page number and date in header

You might notice a second page number at the bottom of each page. You created this in Chapter 3 when you experimented with the print-setup screens. You can remove this second page number by returning to the print-setup screens and turning the numbering feature off. See "Numbering Pages" in Chapter 3 for details.

CREATING A TITLE PAGE

Enable has a special feature for creating document title pages. In Enable, a document title page is not considered part of the document text. Page numbers do not appear on the title page, nor do headers and footers. Enable takes the information you specify for the title and prints it in the center of this special page.

Create a title page for the sample document with the following steps.

1. Press Ctrl-Home then ↑ to move the cursor to the initial ruler line.

You may remember from Chapter 1 that we deleted the document title area from the DEMOMEMO document. To get the title area back again, we have to insert a new one.

2. Press F9 Ins N T to insert a new title. The document title area appears at the location of the cursor, as shown in Figure 5.6.

You'll enter a two-line title inside this area. The information will be centered vertically on a separate page in front of all other pages.

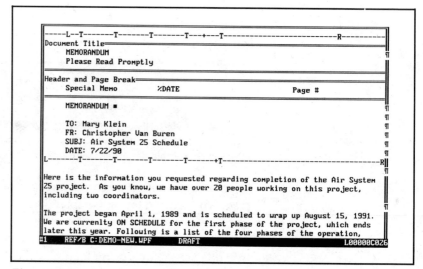

Figure 5.6: Inserting a document title area

3. Type **MEMORANDUM**, then press ◄─┘. Notice that pressing ◄─┘ expands the title area. This is so you can create titles of any length.

4. Type **Please Read Promptly** (do not press ◄─┘).

5. Press ↓ until the cursor is outside the title area.

You can view the effects of this title by switching to Final mode.

You can remove the document title by moving the cursor to the top line of the title area and pressing Alt-F3. You can also hide the title area from view. This keeps it active for the document but removes it from view while you're working. Do this with the command F9 O N T. You can redisplay a hidden title by entering the same command again.

Profile Option: You can have all new documents start out with the title area hidden rather than being in view. You could then display the title area when desired.

USING THE PAPER CLIPS AND COMMENTS FEATURES

Paper clips and comments are used to mark certain parts of a document. When you work with large documents, it can be useful to insert special comments throughout the document—comments that will not print with the rest of the document but will appear on screen. Clips are handy devices for marking a section so you can return to it later.

INSERTING PAPER CLIPS

When you work with large documents, you may want to mark certain sections in order to quickly locate sections you frequently refer to. Although the Find command can be used for this purpose, it may not be the fastest way to locate the section you want. Therefore, Enable lets you place special markers within the text of your documents. You can quickly jump to these markers, called *paper clips*, at any time.

You can add as many paper clips to a document as you like. Each has a number. To add a paper clip, do the following:

- Press F10.

- Press **E** for EditOpts.

- Select *Insert a paper clip* and press ◄─┘.

- Position the cursor where you want to insert the clip, then press ◄─┘.

- Enter a number for the paper clip you are inserting. Although you can use the same number more than once, you will usually use a different number for each clip.

The equivalent expert command to insert a clip is F9 Ins [*n*] M C, where *n* is the number of the clip you are inserting. For example, typing F9 Ins 5 M C inserts a paper clip with the number 5. When using the expert command, be sure to position the cursor before entering the command.

To jump to a paper clip, press F2, enter the number of the clip you want to locate, and type **M C**.

You can remove a paper clip by moving the cursor to the line containing the clip and pressing Alt-F3. You can also hide paper clips from view and return them to the screen by pressing F9 O M C.

ADDING COMMENTS

Paper clips are for marking locations in a document, whereas comments are for notating the text.

A comment is like a paper clip, but you can enter text into it. The text you enter in the comment area will not print with the document. You can think of a comment as a sort of Post-It™ note in the document. Like paper clips, comments can be placed anywhere, and you can use as many as you like. Unlike paper clips, however, comments are not numbered, so you cannot jump to a comment as easily as you can a paper clip. Here's how to insert a comment:

- Press F10.

- Press **E** for EditOpts.

- Select *Insert a comment* and press ◄─┘.

- Position the cursor where you want to insert the comment, then press ⏎.
- Type the comment inside the entry area. Use ↓, not ⏎, to leave the entry area when finished.

There are a number of expert commands that apply to comments:

COMMAND	RESULT
F9 Ins N C	Inserts a comment at the cursor location
F2 N C	Jumps to the next comment (relative to the cursor position) and displays comments if they are hidden
F2 ↑ N C	Jumps to the previous comment (relative to the cursor position) and displays comments if they are hidden
Alt-F3	Deletes the comment at the cursor position
F9 O N C	Hides or displays comments

Insert a comment in the sample document using these steps:

1. Move the cursor to line 15 in the document. This should be directly above the ruler that formats the table.

2. Press F9 Ins N C. The margins of the comment entry space are set to the left and right edge of the screen, but the tabs are controlled by the ruler above it. You can enter as much text as you like into this entry space.

3. Type **Get new figures from Janice for this table.** as the comment. Do not press ⏎ when finished. Press ↓ to leave the entry space.

4. Press F9 O N C to hide the comment.

HIDING SCREEN ELEMENTS

By now you've accumulated a lot of screen elements that mark places in the document. These include headers, page breaks, comments, paper clips, and so on. If they were all showing at one time, the screen might look something like Figure 5.7.

These elements can be distracting, but Enable's On/Off commands let you hide or show these elements (that is, turn them on or off). Type the commands once to turn the elements off and again to turn them back on. Table 5.1 summarizes these commands.

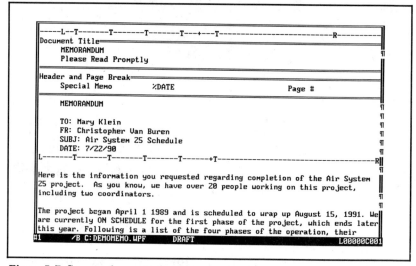

Figure 5.7: Screen elements showing

Table 5.1: On/Off Commands for Hiding and Displaying Screen Elements

COMMAND	AFFECTS
F9 O N C	Comment entries
F9 O N T	Document title entry
F9 O F	Footers
F9 O H	Headers
F9 O S	Line spacing marker
F9 O M P	Page break marker
F9 O M C	Paper clips
F9 O R O	Ruler

AUTOMATIC SCROLLING

The automatic scrolling commands move the cursor through the document as you observe. These commands let you view your document a character at a time, a line at a time, or a half-screen at a time. The best way to understand this feature is to try it. Use these steps with the DEMOMEMO document:

1. Move to the top of the document by pressing Ctrl-Home.

2. Press Alt-F9, then press →. This will start the cursor moving through the document one character at a time. It will stop when it reaches the end of the document or when you press Ctrl-Break.

3. Press Pause to stop the scrolling (or Ctrl-Num Lock).

4. Press → to continue the scrolling again.

5. If the cursor has not reached the bottom of the document yet, press Ctrl-Break to stop it.

Table 5.2 summarizes the automatic scrolling commands.

Table 5.2: Automatic Scrolling Commands

COMMAND	SCROLLS
Alt-F9 ↓	Down one line at a time
Alt-F9 ↑	Up one line at a time
Alt-F9 →	Right one character at a time
Alt-F9 ←	Left one character at a time
Alt-F9 PgDn	Down one-half screen at a time
Alt-F9 PgUp	Up one-half screen at a time
Pause (Ctrl-Num Lock)	Temporarily pauses the scrolling (Press any key to start again.)
Ctrl-Break	Stops the scrolling

As you can see, these commands can come in handy on large documents when you want to examine the entire document. Experiment with these commands on the sample document.

SPECIAL DELETE OPTIONS

You learned the basic delete commands in Chapter 2. However, Enable has some additional delete commands that are especially useful when you're working on large documents. When you have a large document, it is more likely that you'll have large areas of text to delete now and then; that's what the delete commands in Table 5.3 handle.

Table 5.3: Advanced Delete Commands

COMMAND	DELETES
F9 Del Ctrl-Home	From cursor to the beginning of the document
F9 Del Ctrl-End	From cursor to the end of the document
F9 Del PgDn	From cursor to the next page break (user defined or system defined)
F9 Del PgUp	From cursor to the previous page break
F9 Del M P	All system-supplied page breaks displayed in Final mode
F9 Del M C	All paper clips
F9 Del End	From cursor to bottom of screen
F9 Del Home	From cursor to top of screen

SUMMARY OF ADVANCED CURSOR MOVEMENT COMMANDS

In Chapter 1 you learned the basic cursor movement commands for the word processor. But sometimes there are faster ways to move the cursor. Throughout this chapter, you've been discovering some other more specialized cursor movement commands, such as a command to move to the next comment. Table 5.4 presents a summary of these advanced commands. These are expert commands that begin with the F2 key. The last two commands are covered in Chapter 6.

Table 5.4: Advanced Cursor Movement Commands

COMMAND	MOVES CURSOR TO
F2 Tab	Beginning (if the cursor is not at the beginning of the line) or end of the current line
F2 PgUp	Beginning of the page on which the cursor is located; that is, the previous page break visible when you view the document in Final mode. If you add a number prior to pressing PgUp, this moves the cursor up by the specified number of pages.
F2 PgDn	End of the page on which the cursor is located; that is, the next page break. (See above command for details.)
F2 M C	Next paper clip relative to the cursor position. If you insert a number after pressing F2, cursor will move to the paper clip of that number.
F2 ↑ M C	Previous paper clip relative to the cursor position
F2 P	Bottom of the current paragraph
F2 ↑ P	Top of the current paragraph
F2 R	Next ruler
F2 ↑ R	Previous ruler
F2 A	Next attribute
F2 ↑ A	Previous attribute
F2 N C	Next comment
F2 ↑ N C	Previous comment
F2 F	Next footer
F2 ↑ F	Previous footer

Table 5.4: Advanced Cursor Movement Commands (continued)

COMMAND	MOVES CURSOR TO
F2 H	Next header
F2 ↑ H	Previous header
F2 N F	Next footnote
F2 ↑ N F	Previous footnote
F2 I	Next index entry
F2 ↑ I	Previous index entry

Since there are so many cursor movement commands, determine which ones you use most often and commit those to memory. Cursor movement is supposed to save time and effort, so don't get bogged down with learning too many commands if you don't use them frequently.

Special Word Processing Features

ENABLE PROVIDES MANY POWERFUL FEATURES FOR serious word processing jobs. In this chapter, you'll discover how to use many of Enable's organizational tools, as well as other special features. First, you will learn how to use Enable's built-in spelling checker and thesaurus. You will then discover how to generate a table of contents and indexes for your documents.

CHECKING YOUR SPELLING

Checking the spelling of a document is an important step to accomplish before printing. Computerized spelling checkers often find errors that are missed by the human eye. The computer compares every word in the document to its list of words (dictionary). If any do not match, the spelling checker highlights them as possible errors. The spelling checker also gives you a chance to correct words and offers suggestions on how to spell words.

Spelling checkers make two common mistakes. Often, words that do not match its dictionary are "flagged" as misspelled even though they are correctly spelled words. They are just not in the dictionary. For this reason, you can add words to the dictionary. Another mistake is that spelling checkers cannot locate improperly used words that are spelled correctly (such as "there" instead of "their") or typographical errors that happen to result in a correct word (such as a missing "d" in the word "and"). For this reason, spelling checkers should not totally replace human proofreading. In the following sections, you'll discover how to invoke and use the Enable spelling checker on the sample document, and you'll learn about these features:

- Checking words against its 80,000-word dictionary
- Finding unmatched words
- Adding words to a custom dictionary
- Using the custom dictionary along with the standard dictionary for checking
- Finding double words

Before continuing with this chapter, add a few spelling errors to your DEMOMEMO document. These will help make the explanations more meaningful. Use the editing commands covered earlier to make the three changes shown in Figure 6.1. If you haven't already removed the rulers from your document, you may want to do so now (F9 O RO).

INVOKING THE SPELLING CHECKER

Now that you've prepared the document, you're ready to begin using the spelling checker. Use the following steps to start the spelling checker:

1. Move the cursor to the beginning of the first paragraph in the document. The cursor should be on the "H" in "Here."

2. Press F10.

3. Highlight option 2 (*Dictionary*) and press ←.

4. Select *Spell Check* by pressing ←. The screen should look like Figure 6.2.

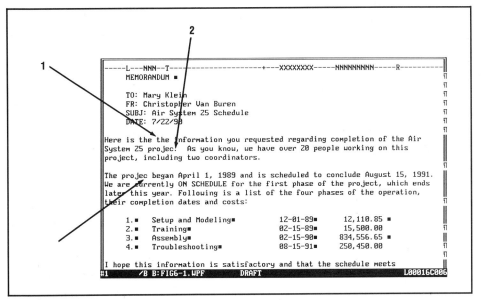

Figure 6.1: Add these spelling errors to the document.

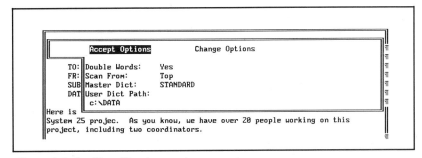

Figure 6.2: Spelling Checker options

CHOOSING SPELLING CHECKER OPTIONS

You have now invoked the spelling checker and are ready to use the various checking options. Like many other commands in Enable, you can use standard, or default, options with the spelling checker, or you can change the options individually. Here are the options available if you select *Change Options*:

- *Check Double Words*—Enable asks if you want it to look for words that appear twice in a row. This is a common error that is difficult to catch manually. The spelling checker can search for these double words for you. Select Yes to locate double words or No to ignore them.

- *Scan From*—You can begin checking from the top of the document or from the position of the cursor. Often, you'll want to skip sections of the document and start from the cursor position; using the *Current* option lets you do this.

- *Select Master Dictionary*—You can purchase a medical and legal dictionary for use with the Enable spelling checker. If you purchased either of these dictionaries and they appear as options, select *Standard* as the dictionary.

- *User Dict Path*—This is the directory location of the custom user dictionary. This dictionary contains words that you add when checking the spelling of documents. Because many valid words are not included in the standard dictionary, accumulating a good custom dictionary is helpful. Enter the directory path where you would like to keep this dictionary. If Enable finds an existing custom dictionary in the specified location, it uses that one; otherwise, it creates a new dictionary. It assigns the name USERDICT.TSG unless you specify the file name along with the path.

Now continue with the spelling checker options.

1. Select *Change Options*.

2. Press ◄—┘ to check double words.

3. Press **C** to select the *Current* option so Enable checks from the location of the cursor.

4. Press ◄—┘ to select the Standard dictionary.

5. Enter the user dictionary path as follows—**C:\DATA**—then press ◄—┘.

Enable begins checking the document for errors, stopping at the first error it finds—the double "the." The screen should look like Figure 6.3.

> Profile Option: You can specify a user dictionary path in a profile option. This causes Enable to check for the dictionary in the same path each time.

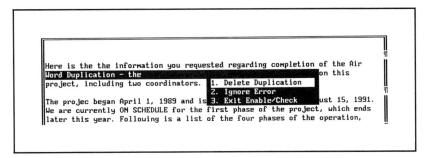

Figure 6.3: The spelling checker finds the first error

CHECKING THE DOCUMENT

The spelling checker now is waiting for your response. You can choose to delete the duplication, leaving only one occurrence of the word; you can ignore the duplication, leaving both words in place; or you can quit the spelling checker.

1. Press ⏎ to select option 1, deleting the duplication.

Enable moves to the next spelling error and stops on the word "projec" as shown in Figure 6.4. Notice that the word in question

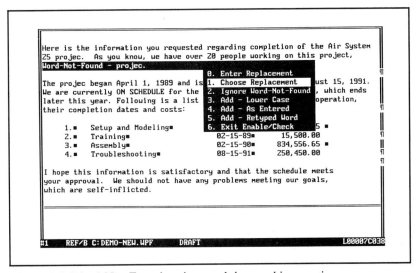

Figure 6.4: Word-Not-Found options and the word in question

appears in the menu bar. Also, Enable lets you see the word as it's used in context in the line above the menu bar. Since this word does not match any in the Enable dictionary, the standard "Word-Not-Found" menu appears with various options for correcting the error. In this case, we're going to replace the word. But first let's take a look at the other options.

Enter Replacement lets you type a new word to replace the one shown on the menu bar. Just type the new word and press ⏎ to replace the current word.

Choose Replacement presents a list of choices for the word in question. You can choose one of the alternatives provided by Enable, or enter the replacement word yourself. If Enable is unable to suggest alternatives, you'll have to enter the word yourself.

Ignore Word-Not-Found ignores the word in question and moves to the next error. This is useful when Enable catches names as misspelled words. You can also use the Esc key to ignore words. If you ignore a word once, Enable will skip the same word if it appears later in the document.

Add—Lower Case adds the word to the custom dictionary in all lowercase letters. Once the word is added, it will not be considered misspelled in any other document again—as long as the word appears in lowercase letters or with an initial capital letter.

Add—As Entered adds the word to the custom dictionary as it is shown on the screen. If Enable finds the word (exactly as typed) again, it will consider it correct. Use this option when uppercase letters are important to the word. For example, the word "Florida" should always begin with a capital letter. Therefore, when you add the word to the dictionary, it should begin with a capital "F." Lowercase spellings of this word will then be considered incorrect.

Add—Retyped Word lets you retype the word and then adds it to the document and dictionary. This can be useful for making minor changes to a word before adding it. However, you should be sure that the word is not already in the dictionary.

Exit Enable/Check quits the spelling checker.

All these options, except *Exit*, continue to the next misspelled word. Now let's try it with the sample document. In this case, the word "projec" is in question. You could simply enter a replacement, but instead try another option.

2. Select *Choose Replacement*. Enable displays a list of possible corrections, as shown in Figure 6.5.

3. Select the correct word and press ◄─┘ to make the correction.

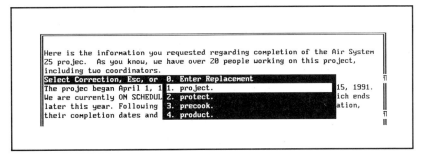

Figure 6.5: Enable's list of suggested words

Notice that Enable flags the same misspelled word again. This is because Enable does not automatically replace all occurrences of a misspelled word with the corrected word. If the error occurs throughout the document, consider exiting the spelling checker and using the Find and Replace feature to correct the word.

4. Repeat steps 2 and 3 for the word "projec."

5. Continue to check the remainder of the document. When Enable cannot locate any more misspellings, you'll see the Enable/Check Summary screen, as shown in Figure 6.6. This screen shows the number of words in the document, the number that were misspelled, how many were corrected, and so on.

Enable will consider some hyphenated words incorrect. The spelling checker can not tell if a word appears at the end of a line, so many end-of-line hyphenations will be considered incorrect. Use the *Ignore Word-Not-Found* option on these hyphenated words.

MAINTAINING THE USER DICTIONARY

When you add your first word to the custom dictionary, Enable creates the dictionary at the location you specified. When checking

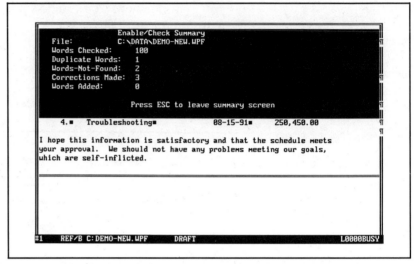

Figure 6.6: Enable/Check Summary screen

future documents, Enable will automatically check the user dictionary if a word is not found in the standard dictionary. You can start a new user dictionary by deleting or renaming the current one. Enable will start a new dictionary whenever it cannot find an existing one.

The user dictionary appears with the name USERDI__.TSG in the specified directory. The standard dictionary appears with the name SPLLDICT.TSG in the EN300 directory.

You can view the contents of the user dictionary at any time—you can even add or remove a word from it. Here's how:

- Start at the Main menu.

- Select *Use System*.

- Select *Word Processing*.

- Select *Dictionary*.

- Enter the name of the dictionary, including the directory path. If you followed the exercises in this chapter, you would type **C:\DATA** and press ←. Notice that you don't need to type the name of the dictionary itself. Enable knows to look for the file name USERDI__.TSG.

Get to the Main menu by quitting the word processor with F10 Quit Yes, or use the command F9 S Home to save the current document and return to the Main menu.

- With the dictionary on the screen, use standard word processing commands to edit the words shown. Be sure to keep all words on separate lines.

- Save the dictionary using the standard word processor save commands.

USING THE THESAURUS

Enable's online thesuarus provides synonyms for words used in your document. Whereas the spelling checker can be used on an entire document at one time, the thesaurus is meant to be used as you type—one word at a time. When you come across a word for which you want to examine synonyms, just call up the thesaurus and choose the word on the spot. Let's try it out.

1. Move the cursor to the first "c" in the word "conclude" located in the second paragraph.

2. Press F10.

3. Press **2** to select the *Dictionary* option.

4. Press **2** to select the *Thesaurus* option.

At this point, Enable reads the word "conclude" and brings up a list of possible meanings. These are standard dictionary meanings for the word. The screen should look like Figure 6.7.

Enable shows three possible meanings for the word, all verbs. You can choose to find synonyms for one of these three meanings, based on the usage in the document.

5. Press **2** to select the second meaning from the list.

If you have trouble finding applicable synonyms for a word, try looking up a contrasting word. Just type the contrasting word in the document and invoke the thesaurus on that word. Both synonyms and antonyms will be displayed.

Enable now shows you the synonyms (and some antonyms) for the chosen word, as shown in Figure 6.8. At the top of the box, Enable repeats the definition for your convenience. The bottom of the box describes the keys you can use at this point. You can also look up the definitions of any of these words by highlighting the word, then pressing ◄─┘. This lets you "branch" to a different set of synonyms.

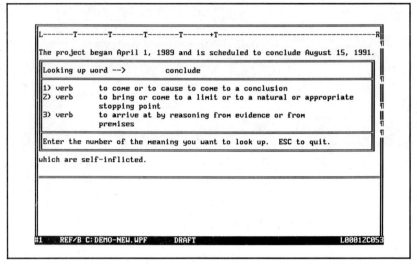

Figure 6.7: Thesaurus meanings for the word "conclude"

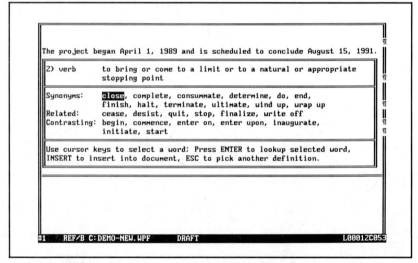

Figure 6.8: Enable lists the synonyms for the chosen word

    6. Press → until "wrap up" is highlighted.

    7. Press Ins.

Be sure to save the changes you make using the spelling checker and thesaurus. The spelling checker and thesaurus change the document that's currently in memory. If you don't store this on disk, the changes will not be permanent. Save the sample document with this command: F9 S E. This will, of course, replace the existing copy on the disk with the changed version.

CREATING AND EDITING A TABLE OF CONTENTS

Enable provides a time-saving feature that automatically creates a table of contents for your document. When you type the contents entries, Enable will compile the table of contents, showing the appropriate page numbers. If the page numbers change due to inserted or deleted text, Enable can generate a new table of contents containing the updated page numbers.

Enable also gives you some control over the display of the contents. You can use up to four indented levels for the entries, and you can print the entries with reference numbers and page numbers:

```
    1. First Unit Entry ................................................... 1
        1.1 Chapter Entry 1 ........................................... 2
        1.2 Chapter Entry 2 ........................................... 4
            1.2.1 Section Entry 1 ................................... 4
            1.2.2 Section Entry 2 ................................... 5
                1.1.1.1 Minor Section Entry 1 ..................... 7
                1.1.1.2 Minor Section Entry 2 ..................... 7
    2. Second Unit Entry ............................................. 9
```

or without reference numbers or page numbers:

```
    First Unit Entry
        Chapter Entry 1
        Chapter Entry 2
            Section Entry 1
            Section Entry 2
                Minor Section Entry 1
                Minor Section Entry 2
    Second Unit Entry
```

Simple commands adjust the formatting of the table of contents. Once you've created the entries, Enable will compile the table at your command and store it in a separate word processor document. This can be printed with the original document or separately.

CREATING THE CONTENTS ENTRIES

The first step to creating a table of contents is to type the entries. Since contents entries are almost always titles or phrases that occupy only one line, Enable allows only one line per entry. If you use more than one line, the second and subsequent lines will be considered other entries. Most likely, your entries will duplicate section headings in the document. Here are the steps:

- Press F10.
- Press **L** to select the *Layout* option.
- Select *Table of contents options*.
- Select option 1, *Create an entry*.
- Position the cursor on the line that is being referenced by the contents entry. If this is a section heading, place the cursor on the line containing the heading. Press ◄─┘.
- Type the contents entry in the entry area provided. Use ↓ to move the cursor out of the entry.

You can designate the "level" of an entry by typing one of the following characters in the first column of the entry:

CHARACTER	LEVEL OF ENTRY
U	Unit Entry
C	Chapter Entry
S	Section Entry
M	Minor Section Entry

These are listed in order of their level. Each new level will be indented from the preceding level, creating subheadings. Be sure to include a space after the level indicator. Use this procedure for all entries, so that each has a separate entry area.

FORMATTING THE ENTRY

Unless you specify otherwise, Enable will include entry numbers and page numbers for your table of contents (as shown earlier). You can omit the entry numbers and page numbers for each entry individually by including special commands in the contents entry area.

To omit the entry number for a particular contents entry, type the following in the first line of the entry area: **N#** (for "no number"). To remove the page number, enter **NP** as the first line of the entry. To remove both elements, Type **N#** on the first line and **NP** on the second line.

Let's create and format a table of contents for the sample file. Even though this file is only a few pages long, we can effectively use the contents feature. Here are the steps:

1. Move the cursor to line 1 of the document. This should be the line containing the word "MEMORANDUM."

2. Press F9 Ins T.

3. Type **N#** and **NP** and press ⏎.

4. Type **U Memorandum**. The entry should look like Figure 6.9.

5. Move the cursor to the line containing "TO: Mary Klein." This should be line 3 of the document.

6. Press F9 Ins T.

7. Type **To** then press ↓ two times to move to the next line of the document.

8. Press F9 Ins T.

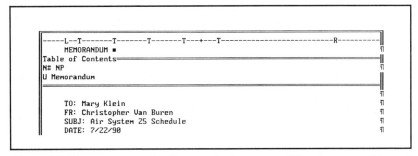

Figure 6.9: Contents entry for the sample document. (The document title and header have been hidden.)

9. Type **From**.

10. Move the cursor to the first line of the table in the document.

11. Press F9 Ins T.

12. Type **U Schedule and Costs**. (The controlling ruler may cause distortions in this entry—don't worry about this for now.)

That's it for the entries. Keep this file on your screen—in a moment you'll compile the table.

To remove a contents entry, move the cursor to the first line of the entry area and press Alt-F3. Also, you can hide the contents entries by pressing F9 O T (O for On/Off, T for Table of Contents).

COMPILING THE TABLE OF CONTENTS

Once you have completed the entries, you're ready to compile the table of contents. Remember that Enable stores the table in a separate file from the document. This file is automatically saved onto the disk in the same directory as the document from which you are creating the contents. Here are the steps for compiling the table:

- Press F10.

- Press **L** for *Layout*.

- Press **9** for the *Table of contents options*.

- Press **2** for the *Compile the table* option.

- Enable will ask if you want periods between the entries and the page numbers. Assuming you have not supressed the page numbers as described above, choose Yes or No as desired.

- Change the margins and table on the ruler, or just press ↵ to accept the ruler as is. Enable creates the table of contents on disk and returns to the original document.

When you use these commands, Enable displays a ruler that controls the tabs and margins for the table. You can use this default ruler or you can change the settings using the commands listed in Chapter 2.

The name given to this new contents file is the same as the document name from which it was created—but with the .WPT extension instead of the standard .WPF extension.

Follow these steps to compile the table of contents for the DEMO-MEMO file.

1. Press F10.

2. Press **L** for Layout.

3. Press **9** for *Table of contents options.*

4. Press **2** for *Compile the table.*

5. Enable asks if you want periods between the entry and the page number. Press Y.

6. Enable now displays a ruler at the top of the screen. Press ◄─┘ to accept this ruler as is. Enable now writes the table of contents to the disk.

You can't see the table at this point—to do that you have to select the saved file, which is explained in the next section.

VIEWING AND EDITING THE TABLE OF CONTENTS

To hide or show table of contents entries on the screen, use the On/Off command F9 O T.

When you create the table of contents, you are not shown the results immediately. Instead, you have to access the file that was saved on the disk. These are the steps:

- Return to the Main menu with the command Alt-Home. (This command gets you to the Main menu when you are currently in a document.)

- Select the options Use System, Word Processing, Revise.

- Enter the name of the table of contents file (remember, this is the name of the original file plus the .WPT extension) and press ◄─┘. The contents file will be in view on the screen.

You can move from the contents file to the original document by pressing Alt-↑.

If you followed the steps listed above, your original file will still be open. Follow these steps to view the table you just compiled.

1. Press Alt-Home to move to the Main menu.

2. Select the options *Use System*, *Word Processing*, and *Revise*.

3. Type the name for the table of contents: **\DATA\DEMO-MEMO.WPT** (be sure to include the extension).

4. Press ⏎ when finished entering the name. The screen should look like Figure 6.10.

```
L----T----T----T----T---------------------------------------------R
L----T----T----T----T---------------------------------------------R
■     Memorandum                                                   ¶
2.■   TO.........................................................1¶
3.■   From.......................................................1¶
4.■   Schedule   and Costs.......................................2¶
```

Figure 6.10: Sample table of contents

Notice that the first entry is not numbered with the rest. However, it's still considered entry 1. If you make changes to the document or the contents entries, simply recreate the table. For now, let's remove the table of contents from the screen:

5. Press F10 Q Y.

6. If you haven't already done so, save your sample document now. Use the command F9 S E if you plan to continue, or F9 S End if you want to quit.

You can make changes to the table of contents while it's in view—adjust the ruler, add new entries, use character attributes, and so on. When you're finished making these changes, save the table again with one of the standard document save commands.

PRINTING THE TABLE OF CONTENTS

There are two ways to print the table of contents: with the original document and separately. If you print the table of contents separately, you can either open the contents document or print it directly from the original document. If the contents document is open, just use the standard Alt-F2 print command to print it. However, you can print the contents document from its original document (that is, the document that created it) by using the following steps:

- Press F10.
- Press **L** for Layout.
- Press **9** for *Table of contents options*.
- Press **3** for *Print table of contents*.

To print the table of contents along with the original document, use the embedded command %INCLUDE. This command is described in Chapter 4, but a brief review is included here:

- Get the original document in view on the screen.
- Move the cursor to the top (or wherever you want the table of contents to appear). You may have to move below special document markers, such as headers, the document title, and others.
- If you do not have a blank line on which to type, insert one with the F3 key.
- Move the cursor into column 1 of this blank line. If the left margin does not allow this, press Ctrl-M (the Margin Release command), then move out to column 1.
- Type %**INCLUDE**, followed by a space and the name of the table of contents document (including the extension). For the sample document, you would type

  ```
  %INCLUDE \data\demomemo.wpt
  ```

  Be sure to type the word INCLUDE in uppercase letters. See the %INCLUDE embedded command in Chapter 4 for more details.

USING AN ALPHANUMERIC SYSTEM FOR A TABLE OF CONTENTS

With Enable you can change the entry numbering system. You have a choice of using the numeric system, which is the type you used for the DEMOMEMO table, or you can use an alphanumeric system. In the alphanumeric system, unit entries use Roman numerals, chapter entries use uppercase letters, section entries use Arabic numerals, and minor section entries use lowercase letters, as shown here:

Here's how to make the change. Try it on your sample document:

1. Press F10 L 9 to get to *Table of contents options*.

2. Press **4** to select *Modify table of contents options*. The screen should look like Figure 6.11.

3. Press ◄┘ to answer No to the first prompt. This is a specialized feature that can be very tricky to use.

4. Press Tab three times to move to the option *4 = I*, which specifies the uppercase Roman numerals for the unit numbers. Then press ◄┘.

5. Press Tab once to move to *2 = A*. Then press ◄┘. This selects uppercase letters for the chapter numbers.

6. Press ◄┘ to select Arabic numerals for the section numbers.

7. Press Tab four times, then press ◄┘ to select lowercase Roman numerals for the minor section numbers.

8. Press Y to select Yes for the *Optional outline style*. This goes with the alphanumeric style you've set up.

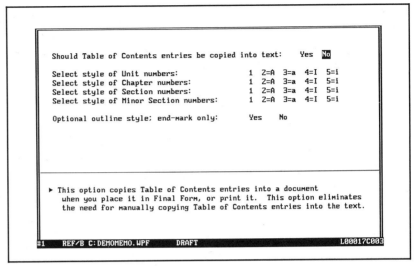

Figure 6.11: Modifying the table of contents options

9. Recompile the table of contents by entering the command F10 L 9 2.

10. Press Y to include the periods in the table.

11. Press ◄─┘ to accept the ruler. The new table is saved in place of the old one. To view the new table, see the "Viewing and Editing the Table of Contents" section earlier. The screen should look like Figure 6.12 when finished.

12. Be sure to save the document for this change to take effect.

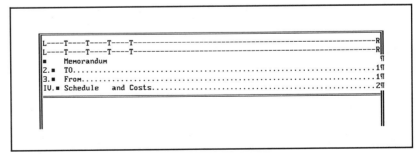

Figure 6.12: Sample document table of contents with alphanumeric numbering system

Note that if you save your document after making these contents option changes, the changes will be saved with the document. In other words, the next time you prepare a table of contents with this document, the new numbering system will be used. Of course, you can change the system back again if desired.

CREATING INDEXES

Creating an index is very much like compiling a table of contents. Enable tracks a series of entries you make throughout the document and creates an index using the appropriate page references for occurrences of that entry. You must mark each index item and each occurrence you want listed. When you compile the index, Enable creates a new document containing the entries and their respective page numbers. Enable uses only one heading for each different entry—multiple occurrences of the same item appear as multiple page references under the same heading.

When the document can be saved on disk, Enable gives it the .WPI extension. Like contents documents, index documents can be edited and printed as independent files. In addition, you can print the index along with the original document using the %INCLUDE embedded command.

MARKING INDEX ENTRIES IN TEXT

There are two ways to create an index entry—by marking text that already appears in the document, and by typing in the entries manually. Marking text is the easiest. You simply move the cursor to the desired word or phrase and highlight the word using the Alt-X command. Here are the steps:

- Position the pointer at the beginning of the desired word or phrase.
- Press Alt-X to activate the index attribute.

- Use one of the following cursor movement commands to highlight the desired information:

Ctrl-C	Highlights a character
Ctrl-W	Highlights a word
Ctrl-S	Highlights a sentence (to the next period)
Ctrl-L	Highlights from the position of the cursor to the end of the line

- Press Alt-X again to turn off the index attribute.

You cannot highlight text that appears in headers, footers, footnotes, or comments, and you cannot highlight text that contains the attributes bold, italic, underline, superscript, or subscript.

There are a few disadvantages to this method of making an entry. One is that the text in the document must be exactly the way you want it to appear in the index (except for upper- and lowercase letters, which Enable ignores). Often, a section of a document will refer to a subject that you want in the index—but not refer to the subject in the way you would list it in the index. Also, there are restrictions to the information you can highlight this way. You cannot highlight text that contains a boldface attribute, for example. Finally, this highlighting method makes all entries the same "level." Often, some entries are subordinate to others. To create subordinate entries, and to overcome the other liminations mentioned, you must use the manual index entry, as explained below.

TYPING MANUAL INDEX ENTRIES

Creating a manual index entry is like creating a contents entry. You can type the exact information you want in the index and enter it in a precise location of the document. Here are the steps:

- Position the pointer on the line containing the desired index item. This will be the line tracked by Enable.

- Press F9 Ins I to create an index entry space at this location. Alternatively, you can use the commands F10, Layout, Index Options, Create an Entry.

- Enter the desired index entry in the space provided.

Unless you specify otherwise, your entry will be a main heading in the index. To create a subheading, enter the main heading along with the current entry in the following manner:

Main heading;Subheading

You can specify up to five levels of subheading this way. Here's an example of a four-level subheading:

Aircraft;helicopters;piloting;radio controls

The index entry this creates would look like this:

Aircraft
　helicopters
　　piloting
　　　radio controls

Be sure that you enter the main heading the same way each time it appears.

COMPILING THE INDEX

After marking or entering the desired index entries, you are ready to compile the index. Use the commands F10, Layout, Index Options, Compile the Index to compile the index. Enable now presents the message, "Do you want periods between the entry and the page number?" Choose Yes or No and press ←. Next, Enable displays the default ruler for the index document. You can make changes to this ruler to alter the way Enable displays the index. Otherwise, just press ← to accept the ruler.

Once you accept the ruler, Enable compiles and saves the index, then returns to the document. You can view the index by returning to the Main menu and entering the following commands:

- Use System
- Word Processing
- Revise
- <*name of original document*>.WPI

To hide or show index entries on the screen, use the On/Off command F9 O I.

This brings the index into view in Enable. You can now make changes to the document and save it again if desired. Remember, also, that you can print the index along with the document by using the %INCLUDE command as described earlier in this book.

If you make changes to the document, you should recompile the index as described above. Remember that this will save a new index over the old one. If you have made changes to the old index, those changes will be gone.

SORTING LINES OF TEXT

You may often type information into a document that you would like to arrange in alphabetical order, such as a list of names. Enable offers a special word processor sorting command that arranges a section of word processor text in alphabetical order. The sorting command, when used with the *Lines* option, rearranges the section of text, line by line. Of course, this would serve little purpose in a normal paragraph of text. Therefore, Enable also lets you sort paragraphs of data so that each paragraph remains intact. This is done with the *Paragraphs* option. Sorting is primarily used for lists and tables of data. Enable will sort lines between the cursor position and the first blank line or ruler. All you have to do is position the cursor at the top of the area you'd like to sort, then invoke the sorting command. Let's try it on the sample document:

1. Position the cursor on the first line of the table in the sample document. This should be line 19. (Place the cursor anywhere on the line that begins with the number 1.)

2. Press F10.

3. Press **L** for Layout.

4. Press **B** to select Sort.

5. Press **C** for Change Options.

6. Enable asks if you want to sort by line or by paragraph. Press **L** for Line.

The paragraph sort will not allow paragraph markers in the middle of the sorted text (that is, it keeps the paragraph intact). This option is used rarely.

7. Enable asks if you want the lines in ascending or descending order. Press ◄┘ to choose ascending.

Enable now asks for a field number. This is another way of asking, "By which column would you like to sort?" As you know, columns are designated by tab stops on the ruler line. Rather than sorting the lines by the first characters in each line, Enable will start with any column position on the line. If the information you're sorting has no columns, you would enter 1. However, if you're sorting a table like the one in the example, you can choose any of the left-aligned columns. In the example, for instance, there are four columns that are available for sorting: the numbers, the phases of operation, the dates, and the costs.

Notice that only left-aligned columns marked with the standard tab stop (T) are used in sorting. This is a limitation in the sorting feature. Right-aligned or numeric tabs are not considered fields for sorting. The left margin is considered the first field. The next T tab stop is the second, and so on.

In the example, let's sort by the description of the phases of operation in the table. This would be tab position 2, or field 2.

8. Enter **2** as the field number, then press ◄┘.

The length of the keyword is the next prompt. This determines the number of characters, starting with the tab position, that will be used for sorting. Normally, five characters is enough for a sort. But if your list includes, for example, the words *convoluted* and *convoy*, then these two words may not appear in proper order because Enable will quit sorting after the first five characters (which are identical in these words).

9. Enter **5** and press ◄┘.

10. Enable now asks if you want to sort from the top of the document or from the current cursor position. Press **C** for Current.

Enable now highlights the specified length of the specified field and asks if the keyword field is identified correctly (see Figure 6.13). Before sorting, Enable want you to verify that the field you entered and the length you specified are correct. Enable also uses the highlight to show you how much text will be sorted.

11. Press Y to continue with the sort. The screen should look like Figure 6.14.

12. Try sorting these lines back to their original order by using field 1 and a length of 6. Remember to place the cursor in the top line before starting.

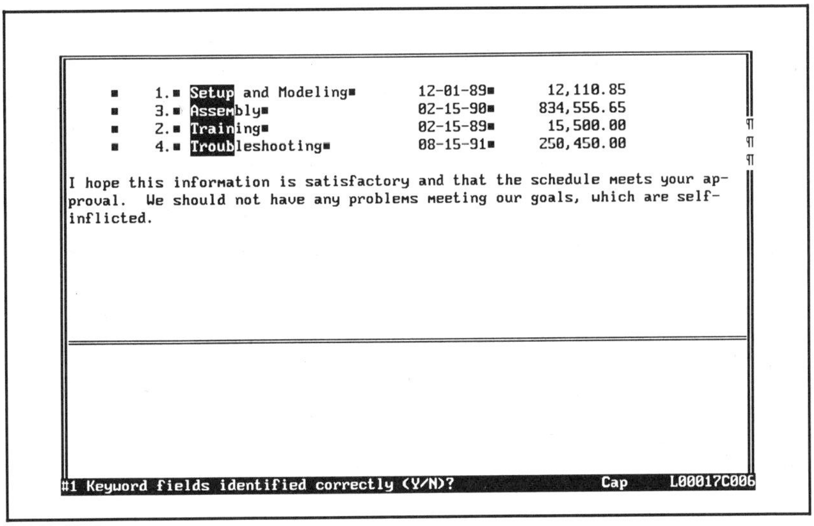

```
          ■      1.■ Setup and Modeling■         12-01-89■       12,110.85
          ■      3.■ Assembly■                   02-15-90■      834,556.65
          ■      2.■ Training■                   02-15-89■       15,500.00       ¶
          ■      4.■ Troubleshooting■            08-15-91■      250,450.00       ¶
                                                                                 ¶
    I hope this information is satisfactory and that the schedule meets your ap-
    proval.  We should not have any problems meeting our goals, which are self-
    inflicted.




    #1 Keyword fields identified correctly (Y/N)?                 Cap    L00017C006
```

Figure 6.13: Verifying that everything is ready for sorting

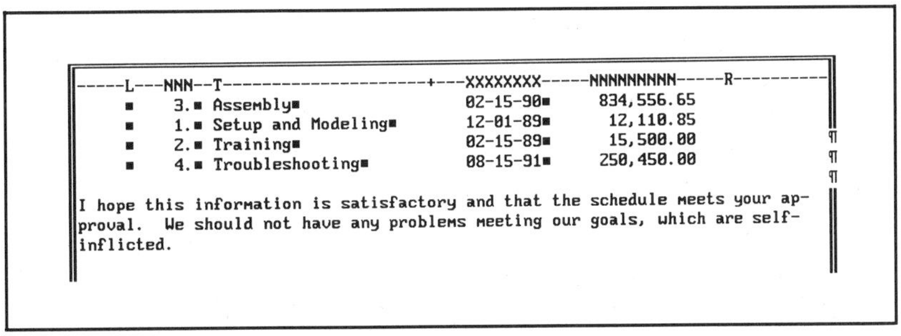

```
    -----L---NNN--T--------------------+---XXXXXXX-----NNNNNNNNN-----R---------
          ■      3.■ Assembly■                   02-15-90■      834,556.65
          ■      1.■ Setup and Modeling■         12-01-89■       12,110.85
          ■      2.■ Training■                   02-15-89■       15,500.00       ¶
          ■      4.■ Troubleshooting■            08-15-91■      250,450.00       ¶
                                                                                 ¶
    I hope this information is satisfactory and that the schedule meets your ap-
    proval.  We should not have any problems meeting our goals, which are self-
    inflicted.
```

Figure 6.14: Sorting complete

DRAWING BOXES, LINES, AND BORDERS

Enable provides a set of graphic characters for drawing boxes, lines, and borders within your word processor documents. Containing 22 characters, this special set provides graphic characters that correspond to standard keyboard characters. When the character set is active, typing the standard character will produce the corresponding graphic character. Figure 6.15 shows the available graphic characters and their corresponding standard characters.

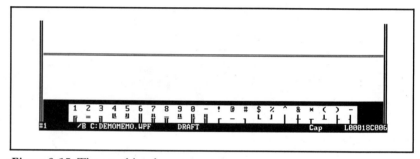

Figure 6.15: The graphics character set

To use these characters, follow these steps:

- Press F10.

- Select the *Layout* option.

- Select the *Use Special Characters* option.

- Select the *Box Drawing Set* option. This produces the menu of characters at the bottom of the screen, shown in Figure 6.15.

- Type the keyboard character shown on the top line of the menu corresponding to the desired box character to create the desired graphic effect.

These characters include the corners and intersection points needed to draw a variety of lines and boxes. Figure 6.16 shows some drawings that were created using the various graphic characters.

You also can type standard text along with the graphics characters; only the corresponding numbers and symbols are unavailable. You can combine graphics characters with left and right tabs to align them and to create vertical borders within text. Figure 6.17 shows an example.

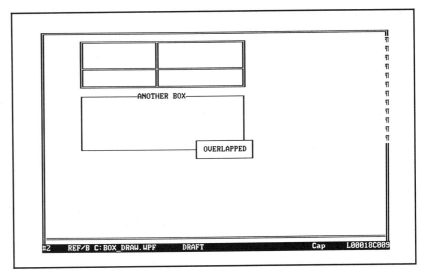

Figure 6.16: Graphics drawn with the box drawing characters

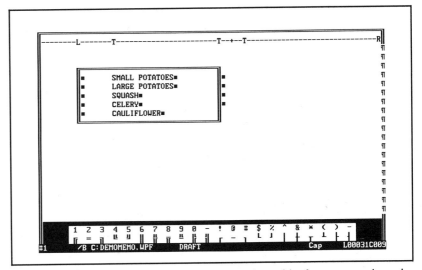

Figure 6.17: A graphic with text characters and graphic characters, using tabs to align vertical borders

PART

2

Spreadsheets and Graphs

Creating a Spreadsheet

THIS CHAPTER INTRODUCES THE ENABLE SPREAD-sheet module. The basic purpose of the spreadsheet and some of the things you can accomplish with it are covered in the Introduction to this book. This chapter shows you how to begin a spreadsheet file and enter data into it, how to save your work on disk, and other basic spreadsheet tasks. By the end of the chapter, you will be able to create simple spreadsheets that contain data and formulas for calculation.

STARTING A SPREADSHEET FILE

Starting a spreadsheet file is not much different than starting a word processor file. Begin at the Main menu and use the sequence of commands shown below. If you already have a document open—say, a word processor document—you can either remove it from memory before starting (that is, close the document window) using the command F10 Q Y or you can leave it in memory (leave the window open) using the command Alt-Home.

1. Press ⏎ to select *Use System*.

2. Press **S** to select *Spreadsheet/Graphics*.

3. Press **C** to select *Create*.

4. Enter a name for the file. This name can include a DOS directory path if desired. Otherwise, Enable uses the current path. You can change this name at any time whether you've saved the file or not. For this example, use **\data\expenses**, then press ⏎.

The screen should look like Figure 7.1. This is a blank spreadsheet file, ready for your information. The labels on this figure point out the various elements of the spreadsheet screen, which you'll learn about in a moment.

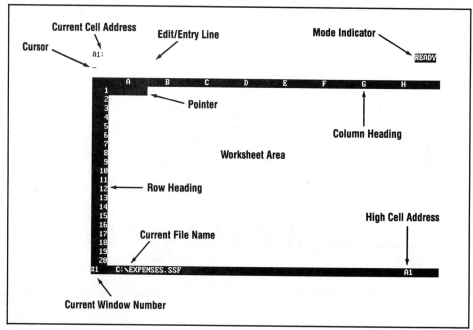

Figure 7.1: New spreadsheet file

As you know from the Introduction, spreadsheets are made up of a series of rows and columns. Columns contain letter names and rows are numbered. The intersection of a row and a column is called a *cell*. Cells are the basic element of the spreadsheet; all information is entered into the cells. Since the rows and columns are labeled with numbers and letters, the identification of a cell is the column letter and row number. For example, cell C5 is the intersection of column C and row 5. The cell name (C5) is called the *address* of the cell.

The spreadsheet offers 9999 rows and 1024 columns, for a total of 10,238,976 cells. The screen shows only 160 cells at one time (unless you change the size of the cells). To see more of the spreadsheet, you must move the screen to the desired location. This is done through pointer movement commands, which are discussed later in this chapter. For now, just remember that there is more to the spreadsheet than is showing in one screen.

EXAMINING THE SPREADSHEET SCREEN

Let's take a moment to examine the screen. There are many elements of a spreadsheet and it helps to be familiar with them. Refer to the labels in Figure 7.1 as you read the following descriptions of the basic elements.

The *pointer* is the highlight block that can be moved from cell to cell. Whichever cell the pointer is currently highlighting is called the current cell. This simply means that you have moved the pointer to that cell. Later, you'll learn many ways to move the pointer.

The *current cell address* is displayed in the top-left corner. That is the cell on which the pointer is currently located. As you move the pointer, the current cell address in this corner of the screen changes to reflect the current cell. After the current cell address, Enable places a colon, then displays the contents of the current cell. Of course, you can also see the cell contents in the cell itself, but in a moment you'll see how this contents line can be useful.

The line below the current cell address is the *edit/entry line*. When you enter information into the spreadsheet, this is where it appears as you type it. Then, if you like what you have typed, you can place the information into the work area. Also, when you edit the contents

You should not invoke the Top Line menu when you are in the middle of entering or cditing text on the edit/entry line.

of the current cell, this is where the work is done. When you press the
F10 key, the Top Line menu appears on this line. Press Esc to remove
it from view.

The *cursor* is the insert point of your typing. When you begin typing, this is where the text will appear. The cursor remains in the edit
line at all times.

The *mode indicator* at the top-right shows you which of several
modes is active. Certain actions can be performed in certain modes
and not in others. Usually, you'll know which mode is active, but
glancing at the indicator now and then can be helpful. Modes are
explained as they are encountered throughout this chapter.

The *worksheet area* consists of the cells collectively. This is where all
information appears and calculations are made.

As in the word processor and database, the status line at the bottom of the screen shows you the *current window number* (that is, the current file). If you use multiple documents at one time, this can be
useful. (See Chapter 23 for more information about using multiple
files.) Enable also displays the *current file name* in the status line. This is
the name entered when you started the document. This is also the
name that will be used if you save the document. This name can
include a DOS directory path if desired, and you can change the
name at any time. In the lower-right corner of the screen is the *high cell
address*. The high cell is the the intersection of the rightmost column
and lowest row that contains information. The high cell does not
have to contain information, it represents the highest row and
column that contain information. Uses for the high cell are discussed
throughout the chapter.

The status line will often present other information, such as the
status of the Caps Lock and Scroll Lock keys and special messages.
Also, the F9 expert command summary appears on this line when
you press F9.

ENTERING DATA

Three types of data can be entered into a spreadsheet: labels, numbers, and formulas. Labels include headings, descriptions, and other
text information. Numbers are simply values. Formulas are entries
that calculate values based on information in other areas of the

spreadsheet. In this section we'll work with labels and numbers. Formulas are discussed later in the chapter.

All information goes into the cells in the spreadsheet. To indicate the cell in which to place your information, move the pointer to the desired cell before typing. You can move the pointer using the Arrow keys. As you type the information, it will not appear in the cell right away. Instead, it appears on the edit line. This is so you can make changes as you type. To place the entry into the cell, press ← or one of the Arrow keys. Following are the steps for entering data into the spreadsheet:

- Use the Arrow keys to position the pointer on the desired cell. This is the cell that will contain the information you type.

- Begin typing your entry. Use any special characters for alignment if desired (these are discussed in a moment). Enable will determine if your entry is a label, number, or formula.

- Use the Backspace key to make corrections as you type, or press Esc to completely start over.

- Press ← to accept the entry. This leaves the pointer in the current cell. You can also press one of the Arrow keys to accept the entry. This moves the pointer one cell in the direction of the arrow.

ENTERING AND ALIGNING LABELS

A label is any information that begins with an alphabetic character. Actually, "nonnumeric character" is more accurate; labels can include any character from the keyboard as long as the first one is nonnumeric. You can begin with a nonnumeric character and then type numbers if you like. These entries are still considered labels. For example, the entry "AB200" is accepted as a label.

If you must enter a label that begins with a number (as in 24EG), you can begin by typing a space. The space character is considered nonnumeric. You can remove the space later. Another way is to start with one of the alignment characters discussed below.

You can align labels with the left side, right side, or center of the cell—provided they don't exceed the limits of the cell (see Figure 7.2).

If you move the pointer to a cell that already contains information, then type your entry, Enable replaces the previous entry with the new one. Normally, you'll want to move the pointer to an empty cell before typing. However, you can use this method to replace unwanted data.

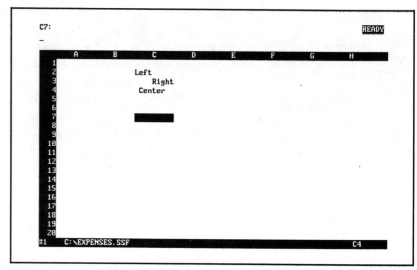

Figure 7.2: Label alignment

To align your entry, you must enter one of the following alignment characters, then type your entry:

ALIGNMENT CHARACTER	TYPE OF ALIGNMENT
^	Center
>	Right
<	Left

All alignment characters are considered nonnumeric characters and define your entry as a label.

If you don't enter an alignment character, Enable centers the entry according to the default global alignment. You can change this with the F10, Worksheet, Global, Alignment, Labels command.

Let's try entering some labels into the Expenses spreadsheet. If you make a mistake while typing, use the Backspace key to back up and erase.

1. Press ↓ three times to get to cell A4. (Check the current cell address in the top-left corner of the screen to be sure.)

2. Type **Rent** then press ⏎. The entry appears in the cell and the pointer remains on the cell.

Notice that the mode indicator changes from Ready to Label, indicating that you are entering a label, and that the entry is centered. Let's retype this entry so it is left-aligned.

3. The pointer should still be on cell A4. Type <**Rent** and press ↓ to accept the entry and move to the next cell (A5). Notice that the new entry has completely replaced the old.

4. Type <**Supplies** and press ↓ when finished.

5. The pointer should be on cell A6. Type <**Phone** and press ↓.

6. Continue entering the labels shown below. Press ↓ to move to the next cell after each entry:

   ```
   <Utilities
   <Entertainment
   <Advertising
   <Professional Svcs
   <Personnel
   <Insurance
   ```

When you're finished with these entries, the screen should look like Figure 7.3. Notice that some entries exceed the boundaries of their cells. This is no problem. As long as the adjacent cell is empty, labels that are too large for a cell are partially displayed in the next. However, if the adjacent cell contains information, then your entry will be displayed only as far as the limits of its own cell; the data in the next cell will cover up the rest. You'll see how this works later.

Now you'll enter the labels across the top of the spreadsheet. These include the main title for the expense report. Add these labels using the following steps:

7. Move the pointer to cell C1.

8. Type **Expenses** and press ⏎.

9. Move the pointer to cell B2.

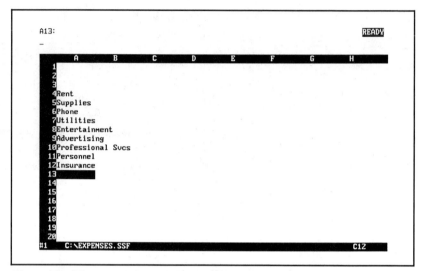

```
A13:                                                    READY
 ─
        A       B       C       D       E       F       G       H
  1
  2
  3
  4Rent
  5Supplies
  6Phone
  7Utilities
  8Entertainment
  9Advertising
 10Professional Svcs
 11Personnel
 12Insurance
 13
 14
 15
 16
 17
 18
 19
 20
#1     C:\EXPENSES.SSF                                   C12
```

Figure 7.3: The sample spreadsheet so far

   10. Type **First Quarter 1991** and press ←.

   11. Enter the labels **Jan Feb Mar** across cells B3, C3, and D3.

Notice that these labels are centered in their cells because they lack alignment characters. This will work out fine for the column headings. The "First Quarter 1991" subtitle in row 2, however, is off center. Try entering it again with some extra spaces this time.

   12. Move the pointer to cell B2. Notice that the current cell address line displays the contents of the cell in addition to the address. Now retype the entry leaving six spaces before the word "First." Press ← when finished. The screen should look like Figure 7.4.

ENTERING VALUES

Do not use commas in your numbers, or symbols such as $ or %. You can add these things later using special formatting commands. This is discussed in the next chapter.

Now that the sample spreadsheet has all its labels in place, you're ready to enter the numbers. Numbers, also called *values*, must begin with a numeric character. Numeric characters include all numerals and the symbols − (. and + . At this point, you'll be using only the numerals, the minus sign (to designate a negative number), and the period (decimal point). As soon as you begin your entry with one

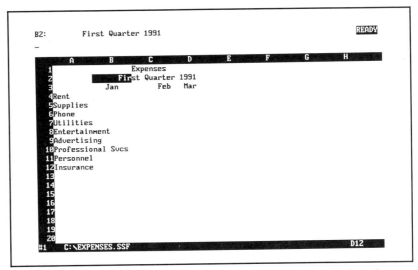

Figure 7.4: The sample spreadsheet with all labels entered and aligned

of these characters, Enable assumes you are typing a number and does not allow any nonnumeric characters in the entry.

The significance of numeric entries is that they can be calculated with other numeric entries. Later, you'll see how calculations work in the spreadsheet. For now, let's enter some numbers into the Expenses spreadsheet:

1. Move the pointer to cell B4, type **1500**, then press →.

2. Now enter the following numbers as shown (use the Arrow keys to move to the appropriate cells):

Rent	1500	1500	1500
Supplies	125	125	130
Phone	400	300	300
Utilities	120	100	100
Entertainment	600	250	250
Advertising	3000	1200	2000
Professional Svcs	2200	1200	1200
Personnel	8500	8500	9000
Insurance	1000	1000	1100

Notice that the labels in column A no longer extend into column B as before. This is because column B is no longer empty. Another thing to notice is that numeric entries are aligned with the right edge of the cell. This is automatic and cannot be changed. The spreadsheet should now look like Figure 7.5.

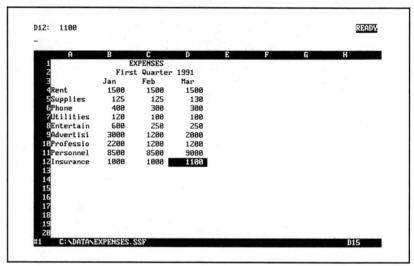

Figure 7.5: The sample spreadsheet after entering values

CHANGING COLUMN WIDTHS

Another important spreadsheet feature is the ability to adjust the widths of the columns. The Expenses file has already illustrated this need with its long labels in column A. No doubt, changing column widths is one of the first things you'll do to any spreadsheet—to make it more readable. Here are the steps for changing a column's width:

You can invoke the Top Line menu by pressing the slash key instead of F10.

- Move the pointer into the column you want to change. Any row of the column is acceptable.
- Press F10 to display the Top Line menu.
- Press **W** to select the *Worksheet* option.
- Press **W** to select the *Width* option.
- Press **S** to select the *Set* option.

- Type the number indicating the desired width. Replace the default number with your new number—maximum is 72 characters wide; minimum is 0 (invisible). When you press ↵, the change is made.

The goal in column-width settings is to make the column slightly wider than the widest entry in it. This leaves a bit of space before the next column. Of course, you can change the column width at any time. Let's change column A in the Expenses worksheet:

1. Move the cursor to column A.

2. Press F10 W W S.

3. Enter **16** for the new width and press ↵. Keep the worksheet on your screen—in a moment you'll save it.

Enable also lets you change the widths of all the columns at once. This is called setting (or changing) the *global column width*. This is handy when most of the columns in a spreadsheet are the same width—but wider or narrower than the default. In fact, by setting the global column width, you are setting a new default. The procedure is similar to changing a single column:

- Press F10 to display the Top Line menu.

- Press **W** to select the *Worksheet* option.

- Press **G** to select the *Global* option.

- Press **W** to select the *Width* option.

- Type the number indicating the desired width. Replace the default number with the new default. Press ↵.

The change is made to all columns that have not already been changed. In other words, if you change the width of an individual column, it is not affected by global width changes.

To return a column to its original (default) width, use the *Current* option (C) instead of the *Set* option. The entire command is: F10 W W C (W for Worksheet, W for Width, C for Current).

WORKING WITH HIDDEN COLUMNS

If you make a column's width 0 characters wide, the column is no longer visible on the screen, but the data in the column is still part of the spreadsheet. The column heading (that is, the column's letter) will also be missing. This can be an effective way to hide information. Hidden columns will not show up on printouts or when you highlight information in the spreadsheet.

Since you cannot move the cursor into a hidden column, you cannot use the column-width procedure to redisplay the column (that is, to enlarge it) because this procedure requires that the pointer be in the column you're changing. So to redisplay a hidden column, use the *Hidden* option in place of the *Set* option. The entire command is F10 W W H. Enable will prompt

Enter range that includes columns or levels to be reset: ALL

With this command, you can redisplay all hidden columns by accepting the "ALL" entry. Or you can specify the range of columns that has hidden columns in it. For example, if column C is hidden, you can specify columns A through D. Just move the pointer to the starting column, then press the period key. Then move to the ending column and press ◄┘.

SAVING SPREADSHEETS

Enable offers many options for saving your spreadsheet. If you are familiar with the word processor or database, the save procedures in the spreadsheet will be familiar. Follow these steps to save the Expenses file:

1. Press F10 to display the Top Line menu.

2. Press **S** to select the *Save* option.

3. Press ◄┘ to select the *Accept Options* option.

Enable will save the file under the current name (including the directory path). In this case, the name is C:\DATA\EXPENSES. The file will appear on disk with the .SSF extension and a backup copy is stored with the .SS@ extension.

ENABLE SAVE OPTIONS

If you want to change the name of the file, the directory path, or the format of a saved file, you can use the *Change Options* option instead of accepting the options. This option also lets you save a portion of the spreadsheet rather than the entire file. Following is an explanation of the options.

FORMAT TO SAVE   You can save the document in Enable OA format, Enable 2.0 format, or any of the formats listed in Table 7.1. If you select the Enable OA format, you then have the choice of saving the file with or without the formulas. *All* saves the entire file, and *Values* saves the file without formulas—that is, just the values in the cells.

Table 7.1: Formats for Saving Enable Documents

FORMAT	DESCRIPTION
123/1A	Saves the file with the .WKS extension, which is compatible with version 1A of Lotus.
123/2	Saves the file with the .WK1 extension, which is compatible with Lotus 1-2-3 version 2.0 and later.
DIF	Data Interchange Format. DIF is a standard format for spreadsheets. Its primary use is when converting data between programs or computers. DIF keeps the spreadsheet information in row and column order but strips out all formulas and other formatting from the data.

Table 7.1: Formats for Saving Enable Documents (continued)

FORMAT	DESCRIPTION
ASCII	Saves spreadsheet data without formatting of any kind. The formulas are not saved—only the values in cells. The row and column arrangement of the data is also lost. This option should be used only when one of the others cannot.
SuperCalc	Saves the spreadsheet in a format readable by SuperCalc.
Enable 2.0/LAN	Saves the spreadsheet in Enable local area network version 2.0.

ENTER RANGE TO SAVE   You can save the entire spreadsheet or a portion of it. To select a portion of the spreadsheet, move the pointer to the first cell in the portion you want to save (that is, the upper-left corner). Then press the period key. Next, move the pointer to the last cell (lower-right corner) of the desired portion; the entire block will be highlighted. When the desired portion of the file is highlighted, press ⬅.

ENTER FILE NAME   Enter the name you would like for the file. Be sure to include the drive and directory location if it's different than the one shown. If you don't specify a DOS directory path, Enable will use the default path. Press ⬅ when finished. Enable saves the document with the specified name in the specified directory. If a file with that name already exists, Enable will ask if you want to *Cancel* the save procedure or *Replace* the existing file with the current spreadsheet.

USING QUICK SAVE

Like the other modules, the spreadsheet offers some Quick Save options so you can avoid using the Top Line menu. These include the expert commands under the F9 key. Table 7.2 shows a list of the various Quick Save options.

Table 7.2: Enable Quick Save Options

COMMAND	EFFECT
F9 S E	Saves the file and leaves it on the screen for further changes.
F9 S End	Saves the file and returns to DOS (provided other windows are not open).
F9 S N	Prompts you for a new file name before saving the spreadsheet. After saving, Enable returns to the current file.
F9 S Home	Saves the file and returns to the Main menu or to the previously opened window. The file's window will be closed.
F9 S R	Saves the file, closes its window, and prompts for the name of a different file to revise. This bypasses the Main menu when you want to revise another file.
F9 S C	Saves the file, closes its window, and prompts for the name of a new file to create. This bypasses the Main menu when you want to create a new file.
F9 S B	Prompts for a range (portion) of the current file before saving. Enable will save only the portion you specify. (See the *Enter range to save* option in the "Enable Save Options" section of this chapter.)

QUITTING
THE SPREADSHEET MODULE

You can also opt to quit the spreadsheet module or return to the Main menu without saving anything. This is done in one of two ways. First, you can quit the spreadsheet module without saving the current file. Just enter the command F10 Q Y (Q for Quit, Y for Yes). You will be returned to the Main menu where you can choose any Main menu option.

You can also return to the Main menu and leave the current spread-sheet open. This is useful for starting new files or editing other files. You can return to the open spreadsheet window using the various window manipulation commands discussed in Chapter 23. To return to the Main menu with the current window open, press Alt-Home.

MAKING CALCULATIONS WITH FORMULAS

The third type of information you can enter into a spreadsheet is a formula. A formula calculates its value based on the information in other cells. Most often, this means calculating numeric values; but you'll see how Enable can even calculate label or text values. A formula is the essential element in a spreadsheet that lets you create "what if" scenarios and save the time and trouble of calculating by hand.

Formulas can be simple or complex. But some of the most useful spreadsheets contain only simple formulas. This section introduces simple formulas and the basics of creating them.

ENTERING A SIMPLE NUMERIC FORMULA

Because formulas calculate results based on other cell values, they must be entered in a special way, using references to the cells they calculate. The simplest formula is just a reference to the value of another cell: + B4. This formula says, "Get the value currently in cell B4." It can be entered into any cell other than B4; the result will be the same value as contained in cell B4.

Notice that the formula starts with a plus sign. This is to let Enable know that you're typing a formula and not a label. If you typed "B4" without the plus sign, Enable would think you're entering a label. Any numeric character can be used to start a formula. Since cell addresses start with nonnumeric characters, you must insert the plus sign first (this sort of fools Enable into thinking you're entering a number). Try this on the Expenses example:

1. Move the pointer to cell B14.

2. Type **+ B4** and press ◄─┘.

This formula produces the amount 1500—the value in cell B4—in cell B14. Now, to see the real usefulness of a formula, try changing the value in cell B4. Since cell B14 depends on the value of B4, it too will change when B4 changes:

3. Move the pointer to cell B4.

4. Type **1000** and press ←┘.

As soon as you enter the new number in cell B4, the formula in cell B14 recalculates its value. This is the dynamic nature of spreadsheet formulas. Your spreadsheet should look like Figure 7.6.

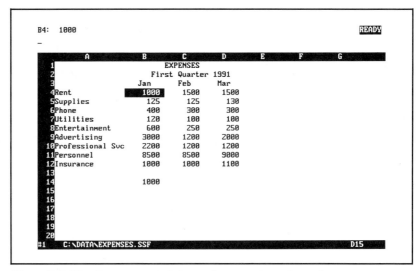

Figure 7.6: The Expenses worksheet after entering a formula

Another formula might add the values in two or more cells. You can add, subtract, multiply, and divide. All you need is the appropriate *operator* along with the cell addresses. For example, to add cell B4 to cell B5 you would enter

+ B4 + B5

The first plus sign is to let Enable know that this is a formula; the second is to add the two values together. Try replacing the formula in

B14 with this formula:

5. Type **+B4+B5**. The resulting value in B14 is 1125. Keep the spreadsheet on your screen. You'll enter some more formulas into it using a different method.

Following are the basic mathematical operators you can use in formulas such as this:

OPERATOR	OPERATION
+	Addition
−	Subtraction
/	Division
*	Multiplication
**	Exponentiation
&	Concatenation (for text only)

COMBINING TEXT STRINGS WITH CONCATENATION

Concatentation is the combining of information into a text string. For example, the formula

+"Mastering   "&"Enable"

produces the result *Mastering Enable*. Of course, the formula can refer to cells that contain values: +"Mastering   "&C5. Where cell C5 contains "Enable" this produces *Mastering Enable*. Notice the space after the word "Mastering." This ensures that the space will be present between the words. If the formula contains only cell references, as in +A5&C5, you can create the space by placing it in quotation marks: +A5&"   "&C5.

Concatenation applies only to text strings. In the above example, if cell C5 contains a numeric value, the formula would produce an error. To concatenate a numeric value with other information, you must convert the value to text using the function @STRING. See Chapter 10 for details.

CALCULATING CONSTANT VALUES

Besides calculating the values of other cells, which can be variable (since you can change their values), formulas can also calculate *constant values*. A constant value is simply a number entered as part of the formula. For example, you can add 100 to the contents of cell B4 using this formula: 100 + B4.

Notice that the formula does not begin with a plus sign. This is because the first character is a numeric character, which makes the plus sign unnecessary. Try this formula in cell B14 of the Expenses spreadsheet. The result should be 1100.

You can also just add constant values, as in the formula 100 + 45. This makes the spreadsheet act like an expensive calculator, letting you make simple calculations while you work. The power of a spreadsheet is in the variables (or cell references).

ORDER OF OPERATIONS

When you combine cell references (variables) with the various operators, you might get some lengthy formulas. There is practically no limit to the size of the formula you can enter. However, lengthy formulas can involve *operation order*. This is simply a system of ordering calculations for desired results. By surrounding a calculation with parentheses, it is treated with priority in calculation order. For example, these two formulas contain the same numbers and operators, but produce different values:

$$5 + (2*2) = 9$$
$$(5 + 2)*2 = 14$$

The only difference is the order of operation. If you do not include parentheses to order the calculations, Enable will use the following order:

1. Exponentiation

2. Positives and negatives

3. Multiplication and division (left to right)

4. Addition and subtraction (left to right)

Note that Enable considers the sign of a number (positive or negative) separately from addition and subtraction. If you are ever unsure about the calculation order of a formula, use parentheses to "force" the calculation order you want.

ENTERING FORMULAS WITH THE POINTING METHOD

When formulas use cell references, you must be careful to enter the correct reference. When the referenced cell is in view on the screen, it's easy to get it right. But when the referenced cell is in an undisplayed part of the spreadsheet and you don't know its address, you may have to view the cell before you can complete the formula.

Instead, try using the *pointing* method of entering formulas. This method lets you enter a cell address in a formula by moving the pointer to the cell. Try adding all the cells in column B of the Expenses spreadsheet using this method:

Notice that as you begin pointing, Enable displays the word POINT as the mode indicator.

1. Move the pointer to cell B14. The formula will make this cell display the total of all cells in the range B4 to B12.

2. Type + (plus sign). This is the beginning of the formula. You can now begin pointing to the cells you want.

3. Press ↑ until you reach cell B4. Notice that the entry/edit line shows the formula as you are pointing.

4. Press + again. The pointer jumps back to the current cell, ready for the next part of the formula.

5. Move the pointer to cell B5 and type +.

6. Move the pointer to cell B6 and type +.

7. Continue this process until you type the plus sign after cell B11. The formula should look like this:

    +B4+B5+B6+B7+B8+B9+B10+B11+

8. Move the pointer to cell B12 and press ↵. Pressing ↵ instead of another plus sign tells Enable that the formula is finished. The value in cell B14 is 16945.

You have now calculated the total of column B, using the pointing method of entering a formula. Be sure to begin the formula with a numeric character, then begin pointing. You can use the Arrow keys to point, starting anywhere in the formula. For example, to enter the formula $+125*B6-(A6+A7)$ you would type

+ 125 * B6 – (

then point to cell A6, enter a plus sign, and point to cell A7. Whenever you can type a cell address, you can point instead.

USING FUNCTIONS IN FORMULAS

You've seen how cell references can be combined with operators to create formulas. And you used the pointing technique to add the cells in a column using a series of additions (plus signs). You may already have begun to think that some formulas will be too much work for practical purposes. Formulas that add rows and columns, for example, can be tedious to enter.

But Enable provides some shortcuts to formula-making. These shortcuts are called *functions*. Functions can be entered in place of (or along with) your formulas for various effects. And functions are always easier to use. Functions consist of three parts: the @ sign, the function name, and the argument. For example, in this function—@SUM(A1..A6)—the function name is SUM and the argument is (A1..A6).

The key to using functions is to enter the argument properly. The *argument* specifies the cells used in the function and any other values applicable to the calculation. A complete discussion of arguments and functions appears in Chapter 10. The function listing contains only brief explanations of each function, however, so some of the more useful functions are explained in detail on the next few pages.

ADDING ROWS AND COLUMNS WITH @SUM

Like all functions, @SUM begins with the @ sign. This lets Enable know that SUM is a function and not a label. The purpose of the @SUM function is to add a set of values, such as the values in a column. Try replacing the lengthy formula in cell B14 of the Expenses spreadsheet using the @SUM function as follows:

1. Move the pointer to cell B14.

2. Type **@SUM(**. Do not press ◄—┘.

3. Press ↑ until you reach cell B4, then press the period key.

4. Press ↓ until you reach B12, then press) (the right parenthesis).

5. Press ◄—┘ to accept the formula. The formula should read

    @SUM(B4..B12)

and the result is the same as the previous formula.

A range can also include a "block" of cells, as in the range B4..D12.

The @SUM function used in these steps uses a *range* of cells as its argument. A range specifies the first and last cells in a column or row and implies all the cells from the first to the last. The above example specifies the range B4..B12, meaning all the cells from B4 through B12 should be added in the function.

These steps show how to enter a range using the pointing method of referencing cells. Of course, you could simply type the beginning and ending cell addresses, separated by two periods (yes, type the periods too).

The function @SUM also adds a noncontiguous range, or list of cells. For example, you can enter

@SUM(B4,B5,B8,B12)

and the function adds only those cells in the list. Notice that listed cells are separated by commas.

GETTING AVERAGES WITH @AVG

As its name implies, this function calculates the average of a group of values. Like the @SUM function, you can enter a *range* or a *list* as the argument. Try using this function in the Expenses spreadsheet using these steps:

1. Enter the label <**Total** in cell A14.

2. Enter the label <**Average** in cell A15.

3. Move the pointer to cell B15.

4. Type **@AVG(B4..B12)** and press ←. The average of the values in column B will appear in cell B15. Figure 7.7 shows the spreadsheet so far.

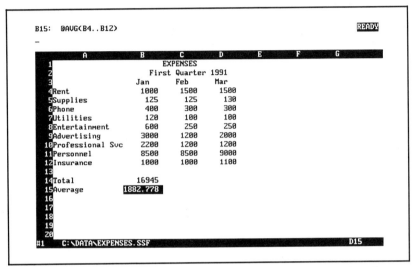

Figure 7.7: The Expenses spreadsheet with @SUM and @AVG functions

This time, instead of pointing to the cells in a range, you entered them directly. Remember that you can also list values for the @AVG function, as in @AVG(B4,B6,B9,C25,M4).

USING @IF TO MAKE DECISIONS

The *syntax* of a command or function is the required structure in which you must enter it. The syntax includes all the parts of the command or function that should be included when you use it—in the correct order.

Perhaps the most important of all spreadsheet functions is @IF. This function empowers the spreadsheet with decision-making qualities. The spreadsheet can perform different calculations based on different values throughout the sheet. The function uses the following syntax:

@IF(*test, result if true, result if false*)

The first part of the argument is a test (also called an *IF test*). A *test* asks if a condition is true, such as whether the value of cell B4 is greater than the value of C4. If the test is true then the first result is used. If the test is false then the second result is used. All tests are either true or false. All three elements in the argument must be separated by commas.

To perform a test requires the use of a *logical operator*. Following are the logical operators you can use in an IF test:

OPERATOR	MEANING
=	Equal to
< >	Not equal to
>	Greater than
<	Less than
> =	Greater than or equal to
< =	Less than or equal to

One of these operators must be used in the IF test. Here are a few examples:

@IF(G5 = 100,F3,F4)

This says, "If the value of cell G5 equals 100, then get the value of cell F3, otherwise, get F4." It does not matter if you use cell references or constant values in the function. The only requirement is that the IF test can be evaluated to either *true* or *false* and that the three elements are separated by commas.

@IF(G5 < 100,G5,F3*G3)

This says, "If the value of cell G5 is less than 100, then get the value of G5, otherwise, multiply the value of F3 by G3." This shows that any portion of the function can include calculations (or formulas).

@IF(G5>G6 + 100,G5,G6 + 100)   This says, "If the value of cell G5 is greater than the sum of G6 and 100, then return G5, otherwise return the sum of G6 and 100." This shows that you can use a calculation as part of the IF test expression. Notice that the comma appears after the entire IF test.

Try entering the following IF test in the Expenses spreadsheet:

1. Move the pointer to cell B16.

2. Type

    @IF(B14<20000,B14,20000)

   then press ←┘.

This formula makes sure that the total in cell B14 does not exceed 20,000. It says, "If B14 is less than 20,000 then use it, otherwise, use 20,000." Now try changing one of the values in the column so that the total in B14 is greater than 20,000. For example, change cell B12 to 10000. Since the total is greater than 20,000, the IF statement returns 20000 to cell B16.

USING @IF WITH LABELS   One of the most useful things about the @IF function is that you can use it with labels or text strings. This provides dozens of different uses for the function. For example, you can test whether a particular label has been entered, then perform different calculations based on the label:

@IF(A1 = "Yes",C25,B5 + 5)

This says, "If the label *Yes* has been entered into cell A1, then get the value of cell C25, otherwise, return the sum of B5 and 5." The text string must be enclosed in quotation marks as shown above. Other than that, the syntax is the same as a numeric test.

You can also use text strings in the results of the test. This can be useful for printing messages and other comments based on values in the spreadsheet. Try this in the Expenses spreadsheet:

1. Move the pointer to cell B16.

2. Type

@IF(B14>20000,"SEE BUDGET","")

Press ↵ when finished. The result is shown in Figure 7.8.

This function prints the message "SEE BUDGET" when the total of the month's expenses is greater than 20,000. If the total is less than

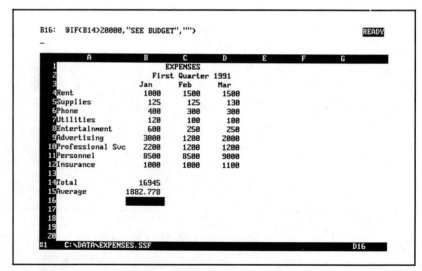

Figure 7.8: Adding an IF function to print messages

20,000, the function returns the value "". This means "return nothing," or null. Change the values in column B to see the various effects.

Note that when using text strings in an IF test, upper- and lowercase letters do not matter. However, except for upper- and lowercase, the two strings must match *exactly* or Enable will not consider them the same.

MAKING TWO OR MORE TESTS   So far, the IF tests discussed have evaluated one condition as either true or false. Based on the result of that test, one of two values is returned. Occasionally, you will find the need to return a value based on the result of two tests. Then, if *both conditions* are true, the test is true. An example might be, "If the value of A1 equals 25 *and* the value of A2 equals 40, then return X, otherwise, return Y."

Performing multiple tests in one IF function requires one of the *conditional operators* shown here:

AND   Both tests must be true for the statement to be true.

OR   Either or both tests can be true for the statement to be true.

Note that when using the OR operator, *either or both* of the tests can be true for the entire statement to be true. Both tests must be false for the statement to be false. The example:

@IF(A1 = 1 AND B1 = 2,G5,G6)

says, "If the value of cell A1 equals 1 and the value of B1 equals 2, then return G5, otherwise, return G6." Both tests must be true for the function to return G5.

The example

@IF(A1 = 1 OR B1 = 2,G5,G6)

says, "If the value of cell A1 equals 1 and/or the value of B1 equals 2, then return G5, otherwise, return G6." Either or both tests can be true for the function to return G5. Both tests must be false for the function to return G6.

You can combine AND and OR operators in a formula to extend the test. Simply insert the conditional operator between each IF test. Although it's uncommon for a function to require more than a few tests, if several tests are needed, consider using parentheses to order the logical flow of the formula. For example, these two functions test differently:

@IF(A1 = 1 AND B1 = 1 OR (A2 = 2 AND B2 = 2 OR C2 = 5),1,0)
@IF(A1 = 1 AND (B1 = 1 OR A2 = 2) AND B2 = 2 OR C2 = 5,1,0)

The tests grouped into parentheses are treated as one condition in the logical process of the formulas, and the outcome, in this case, could vary.

TESTING IF A CONDITION IS NOT TRUE   Another important addition to the @IF function is the use of the modifier NOT. The NOT modifier flips the logic of an IF test so that it becomes *true* when the test does *not* work. For example, a typical IF test says, "If A1 is greater than 1, then X, otherwise Y" and looks like this: @IF(A1>1,X,Y). The NOT version says, "If A1 is not greater than 1, then X, otherwise Y" and looks like this: @IF(NOT(A1 = 1),X,Y). The test must be placed in parentheses and preceded by the NOT modifier.

Here is another example. The formula

@IF(NOT(A5 = 25),S5,S6)

says, "If A5 does not equal 25, then return S5, otherwise return S6." This flips the statement into the negative: the statement is *true* if the condition is *not* true.

You can use NOT with multiple IF tests by enclosing each test in a separate set of parentheses preceded by NOT.

ENTERING DATES IN A SPREADSHEET

Enable lets you enter dates for various purposes in the spreadsheet. Besides being able to enter a date, Enable offers calculations that you can perform on dates, such as adding a certain number of days to a date or subtracting one date from another to determine the elapsed days.

Enable views a date as the number of days elapsed since December 31, 1899. This means the date January 1, 1900 has the value 1. This value is called the date *serial number* and is used by Enable for all dates.

Since the date serial number is really just a number like any other number, Enable does not distinguish between dates and numbers. Dates are simply numbers formatted to look like dates. In other words, you can take the value 100 (not a date) and format it using one of the date formats in the command F10 W R F D and it will appear as the date April 10, 1900.

Enable will not recognize a common date entry as a date. For example, if you enter 10/5/91, Enable considers this the formula 10 divided by 5 divided by 91 and enters .021978 into the cell. This is hardly the date you were expecting. Does this mean you have to enter dates as date serial numbers? Well, yes. And this is quite an inconvenience. But there are ways around the problem. One way is to enter all dates with the function @DATE. This is how you would enter the date October 5, 1991:

Dates do not have to be entered as serial values if you don't plan to use them in calculations. Just enter them as text labels.

@DATE(91,10,5)

This results in the date serial number 33515, which can then be formatted using the F10 W R F D command. For more information about the @DATE command, see Chapter 10. For more information about date formats, see Chapter 9.

Editing
Spreadsheets

BY NOW YOU KNOW THE ESSENTIALS OF BUILDING A simple spreadsheet—entering data, making calculations with formulas, and using special functions. This chapter uses the Expenses worksheet to show you how to edit the information in a spreadsheet. Editing involves changing the data in the cells, copying information, formatting data for specific visual needs, and much more. Before you start, bring up the Expenses spreadsheet as you last saved it in Chapter 7.

MOVING AROUND THE SPREADSHEET

As your spreadsheets grow, so will the need to move around the sheet quickly. Using the Arrow keys is not always the easiest way to get around. Thankfully, Enable provides numerous pointer movement commands that become useful as your spreadsheets become larger. Table 8.1 presents a list of these movement commands.

Table 8.1: Enable Pointer Movement Commands

COMMAND	MOVES POINTER
PgDn	One screen down
PgUp	One screen up
Tab	One screen right
Shift-Tab	One screen left
Home	To cell A1
End Home	To high cell, shown in the lower-right corner of the screen (intersection of the highest row and column in use)
F2 [*n*] ⏎	To specified cell (where [*n*] indicates any cell address)
F2 [*name*] ⏎	To first cell in the specified range (where [*name*] indicates any range name)
F2 →	To last used cell in the current row
F2 ←	To the first used cell in the current row
End [*arrow*]	To the next used cell in the direction of the arrow (where [*arrow*] indicates any arrow)

Experiment with these movement commands on the Expenses spreadsheet. Try jumping to cell AA52 by using the command F2 AA52 ⏎. Then move back to cell A1 by pressing Home. The command End Home should take you to cell D16. To see the value of the End-Arrow commands, try the following:

1. Enter data (anything) into cells G5 and G12.

2. Move the pointer to cell A5.

3. Press End-→. The pointer should move to cell D5. This is because D5 is the rightmost cell in the block. In other words, there are no blank cells between A5 and D5, so D5 is the end of the block.

4. Press End-→ again. The pointer should move to cell G5. This is because G5 is the first cell of the next block. The command skips all blank cells between these blocks and move from the first to the last cell of each block.

The End-Arrow commands are useful for jumping to the various sections of your large spreadsheet. By skipping all blank cells between the blocks, or sections, you can move quickly from block to block.

EDITING CELL CONTENTS

You've seen how you can change the information in a cell by typing a new entry. Entering new data into a cell replaces any old data in the cell. But this can be a lot of work when you just want to make a small change to the original entry—especially if the entry is large. So Enable lets you use many of the word processor editing and cursor movement commands to change the information in a cell without retyping it.

See Tables 1.1 and 2.1 for the Enable editing commands.

If you're familiar with the word processor, these editing commands will come naturally. First move the pointer to the cell you want to change, then press F4. This function key puts you into Edit mode and places the cell contents on the edit/entry line. You can now use some familiar editing commands to change the data.

Try the following example on the Expenses spreadsheet:

1. Move the pointer to cell B2.

2. Press F4.

3. Use the → key to move to the "F" in "First."

4. Type **Secon** then press the Ins key.

5. Type **d** to finish the word "Second," then press ←.

Now change the label back to "First."

6. Press F4 again.

7. Use the → key to move to the "S" in "Second."

8. Press the Del key six times to remove the word.

9. Press Ins to switch to Insert mode (flashing block).

10. Type **First** and press ⏎.

You can use this process to change formulas, numbers, or labels throughout the spreadsheet.

ERASING INFORMATION

Erasing information is a common need in spreadsheets. Using the F10 W R E command, you can erase any cell or block of cells at one time. This removes the information contained in the cell—not the cell itself. Here is the basic process:

- Press F10 to activate the Top Line menu.

- Press **W** to select *Worksheet*.

- Press **R** to select *Range*.

- Press **E** to select *Erase*.

- Move to the cell that has the information you want to erase. If you want to erase data in a block of cells, move to the first cell in the block (that is, the upper-left cell), then press the period key.

- If you are erasing data in a single cell, press ⏎ and the information is removed. If you are erasing data in a block, move to the last cell in the block (that is, the lower-right cell), then press ⏎.

Enable offers an expert command version of this procedure. You may find it easier to use. The expert command works like this:

- Position the pointer on the cell that contains the information you want to erase. If you want to erase information in a block, position the pointer on the first cell in the block.

- Press F9 Del B.

- If you are erasing data in one cell, press ⏎. The cell will be erased. If you are erasing data in a block, press the period key, then move to the last cell in the block. Finally, press ⏎.

Earlier in this chapter you entered some temporary information into cells G5 and G12. Let's try erasing these entries now. Follow these steps:

1. Move the pointer to cell G5.

2. Press F10, then select the options *Worksheet*, *Range*, and *Erase*.

3. Press the period key.

4. Use the ↓ key to move down to cell G12. The screen should look like Figure 8.1. (Your screen will display the text you entered, of course.)

5. Press ⏎. The data is erased.

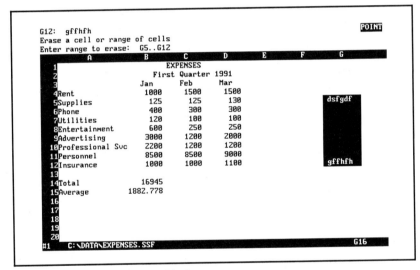

Figure 8.1: Highlighting the block you want to erase

INSERTING AND DELETING ROWS AND COLUMNS

When you start editing a spreadsheet, you may find the need to delete entire rows or columns. Likewise, you might want to insert new rows and columns between existing data. These are common operations that can be accomplished using keystroke commands or menu options.

INSERTING AND DELETING ROWS

Enable offers special function key commands for inserting and deleting rows. Simply position the pointer on the desired row, then press F3 to insert rows or Alt-F3 to delete rows. Try this example on the Expenses spreadsheet:

1. Move the pointer to row 5 (any column is okay).

2. Press F3. Enable prompts

   Enter number of rows to insert on this level:

3. Enter **3** then press ◄──┘. Immediately, three new rows are added at the pointer location. Your screen will look like Figure 8.2.

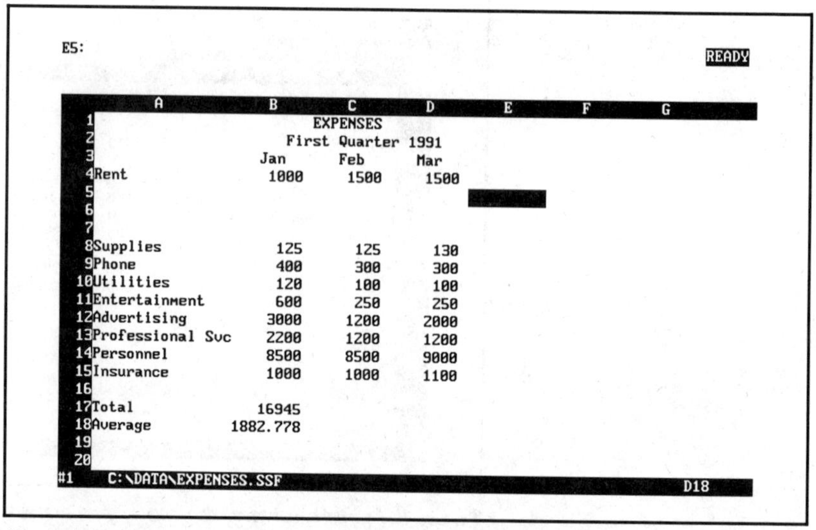

```
E5:                                                               READY

           A            B          C          D       E      F      G
  1                            EXPENSES
  2                       First Quarter 1991
  3                        Jan        Feb        Mar
  4 Rent                  1000       1500       1500
  5
  6
  7
  8 Supplies              125        125        130
  9 Phone                 400        300        300
 10 Utilities             120        100        100
 11 Entertainment         600        250        250
 12 Advertising          3000       1200       2000
 13 Professional Svc     2200       1200       1200
 14 Personnel            8500       8500       9000
 15 Insurance            1000       1000       1100
 16
 17 Total               16945
 18 Average           1882.778
 19
 20
#1     C:\DATA\EXPENSES.SSF                                       D18
```

Figure 8.2: Expenses spreadsheet with new rows added

When you insert rows like this, Enable automatically updates any cell addresses used in your formulas, so they reference the appropriate new cells. For example, cell B5 has become cell B8 since you inserted three rows in the Expenses spreadsheet. Any reference to cell B5 will automatically be changed to B8.

Formulas that use ranges, such as the one in cell B17, will also be updated. In this case, the range expands to include the new rows. Notice that the formula in cell B17 now reads @SUM(B4..B15). This means the range has expanded to include the inserted rows. If you enter data into cells B5, B6, or B7, it will be used in the formula in cell B17. However, if the cells remain blank, they will not affect the result. This is one of the intelligent features of the Enable spreadsheet.

Now let's delete these rows. Like inserting, deleting changes the addresses of all cells below those being removed. This is because they move up to fill the space left by the deleted rows. However, Enable takes care of updating cell and range references throughout the spreadsheet. Try it:

1. Move the pointer to cell F8.

2. Enter the formula **+B6**. This will display the value of cell B6 (which is now empty).

3. Move to cell B6, enter **25**, and press ←┘. Notice that the formula in cell F8 reflects the entry. Also, the total in cell B17 includes this new value.

Now delete the blank rows you added earlier.

4. Move the pointer to row 5 (pressing ↑ will do the trick).

5. Press Alt-F3.

6. Press the period key.

7. Press ↓ two times to highlight rows 5, 6, and 7. The screen should look like Figure 8.3.

8. Press ←┘ to remove the three rows.

Notice that the formula that was in cell F8 has moved up to cell F5 and now displays the message "ERR." This is because the cell it referenced no longer exists and Enable does not use the cell that has taken its place. Any formula that included a reference to the deleted cell would display "ERR."

Now take a look at the total in cell B14. The total no longer includes the deleted cells, but has been updated for the new range. Why doesn't

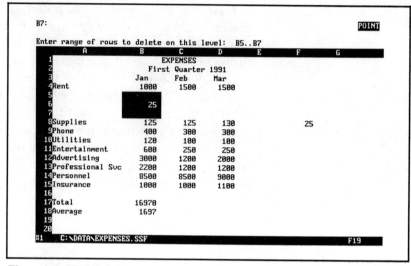

Figure 8.3: Highlighting rows to delete in a spreadsheet

this formula display "ERR" like the one in cell F5? Because the deleted rows were *within* the range used in this formula. If you were to delete the entire range, the total would then display "ERR."

In summary, be careful not to delete rows when specific cells in the rows are referenced in formulas; this will cause errors throughout the spreadsheet. However, if no formulas reference deleted cells, go ahead and delete; Enable will update references to cells that have new addresses due to the deletion (that is, cells *below* the deleted rows).

Although the method shown in the previous example is the fastest way to insert and delete rows, you might prefer to use the menu options. To insert rows using the menu, follow these steps:

- Position the pointer where you want to insert the rows. The new rows will appear at and below the pointer.
- Press F10.
- Press **W** to select *Worksheet*.
- Press **I** to select *Insert*.
- Press **R** to select *Row*.
- Enter the number of rows you want to insert, then press ◄─┘.

To delete rows using the menu, follow these steps:

- Position the pointer on the first row you want to delete.
- Press F10.
- Press **W** to select *Worksheet*.
- Press **D** to select *Delete*.
- Press **R** to select *Row*.
- Press the period key, then use the ↓ key to highlight the rows you want deleted.
- Press ◄─┘.

INSERTING AND DELETING COLUMNS

Inserting and deleting columns is almost identical to inserting and deleting rows with the menu options. Just select C (for columns) instead of R (for rows). Here are the steps:

- Position the pointer where you want to insert the columns. The new columns will appear at and to the right of the pointer.
- Press F10.
- Press **W** to select *Worksheet*.
- Press **I** to select *Insert*.
- Press **C** to select *Column*.
- Enter the number of columns you want to insert, then press ◄─┘.

To delete columns, follow these steps:

- Position the pointer on the first column you want to delete.
- Press F10.
- Press **W** to select *Worksheet*.
- Press **D** to select *Delete*.
- Press **C** to select *Column*.

- Press the period key, then use the → key to highlight the columns you want to delete.

- Press ←⏎.

ERASING
AN ENTIRE SPREADSHEET

Erasing a worksheet is similar to quitting without saving the file. However, when you quit, Enable takes you to the Main menu, where you have to start a new file by selecting the various menu options. On the other hand, if you erase the current spreadsheet, it's like quitting and starting a new file in one step.

This command is useful when you want to start a spreadsheet over, or if you have created a temporary spreadsheet and do not intend to save it. Here are the basic steps:

These steps remove the spreadsheet without saving it. If you want to keep a copy of the file, save it first using one of the many save commands described in Chapter 7.

- Press F10.

- Press **W** for *Worksheet*.

- Press **E** for *Erase*.

- Press **Y** to confirm your actions.

That's all there is to it. Enable erases the entire spreadsheet and presents an empty sheet. The name of the spreadsheet will remain the same. (Of course, you can change the name when you save it.)

MOVING INFORMATION

When you want to make room for new information in your spreadsheet, sometimes inserting rows or columns is the answer. And sometimes it's not. You'll undoubtedly find the need at times to control blocks of data—moving them around the spreadsheet.

Moving is accomplished with either the keystroke command Alt-F8 or with menu options. Here's the general procedure for the keystroke method:

You can save a step in this process by starting out with the pointer on the first cell of the destination before pressing Alt-F8. The pointer will automatically return to this cell when you finish specifying the range you want to move.

- Press Alt-F8.

- Move the pointer to the first cell in the block you want to move; this is the upper-left corner. (If you're moving one cell, just place the pointer on that cell.)

- Press the period key, then move to the last cell in the block; this is the lower-right corner. All cells between the first and last will become highlighted. Press ◄─┘ when finished.

- Move the pointer to the first cell in the block to which you want this data moved. Then press ◄─┘.

When you move the data, all information currently in the location to which it is moved will be replaced. In other words, if you move cell A1 to cell B5, any information in cell B5 will be replaced by the moved data. The data will, of course, no longer appear in cell A1.

Another thing to remember about the Move command is that formulas, when moved, remain *exactly as they were* in the original location. Any references to other cells will remain the same. Let's see how this works in the Expenses worksheet:

1. Start with the pointer on cell D14.

2. Now press Alt-F8.

3. Move the pointer to cell B14 and press the period key.

4. Move the pointer to cell B16 and press ◄─┘. The pointer jumps over to cell D14 (where we want to move this data).

5. Press ◄─┘ to move the data. The screen should now look like Figure 8.4.

Notice that the formulas remain the same—they calculate the same cells and display the same results. In this case, it would be confusing to leave this information where it is. It looks as if the cells should calculate the results of column D, but, indeed, they calculate

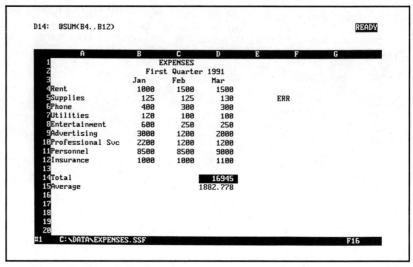

Figure 8.4: Moving a block of data to another location

information in column B. Try moving these three cells back again using the menu version of the Move command:

6. Move the pointer to cell B14.

7. Press F10.

8. Press **W** to select *Worksheet*.

9. Press **M** to select *Move*.

10. Move the pointer to cell D14 and press the period key.

11. Move the pointer to cell D16 and press ◄──┘. The cursor should return to cell B14.

12. Press ◄──┘ to complete the move.

At any point in the move process (using either the keystroke command or the menu command), you can change your mind by pressing the Esc key. If you have already selected the range to move, you may have to press Esc twice to return to the Ready mode.

COPYING INFORMATION

Copying is similar to moving—but it has some important differences. When you copy information from one location to another, the original stays intact and a duplicate copy is placed in the new location. Another difference is that when copying, the number of cells in the destination range can be larger than the number of cells you are copying. For example, you can copy cell A1 to cells C1..C3.

Most important, copying formulas is different than moving them. First, let's look at the basic Copy command using text and numbers, then we'll copy some formulas and discover the differences.

COPYING TEXT AND NUMBERS

Copying text and numbers is simple. Just use the F8 key, highlight the desired information, and specify the new location. Here is the exact process:

- Start with the pointer on the first cell of the destination.

- Press F8 to begin the Copy command.

- Move the pointer to the first cell in the source range (the range you want to copy). This is the upper-left corner.

- Press the period key, then move the pointer to the last cell in the range and press ←. If you are copying just one cell, simply press ←.

- If the number of cells in the destination is the same as the number of cells you are copying, just press ←. If the destination is larger than the source, then press the period key and move the pointer to the last cell in the destination range. Then press ←.

If information already exists in the destination range, it will be replaced by the new information. Be careful not to replace information needed in formulas. If you need more room in the destination, insert new rows or new columns as described earlier in this chapter.

Here is an example of copying one cell to many. Try this on the Expenses spreadsheet:

1. Move the pointer to cell F4.

2. Press F8.

3. Move the pointer to cell B3, then press the period key.

4. Move the pointer to cell D3, then press ←. You have now specified the source range, or the range that you will be copying.

5. Press the period key, then move the pointer to cell F12.

6. Press ←. This copies the three title cells to the range F4..H12. The screen should look like Figure 8.5.

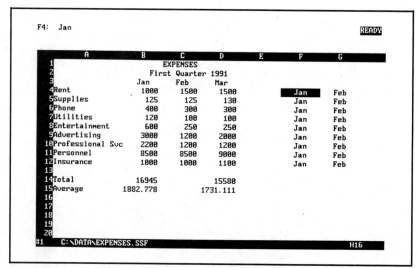

Figure 8.5: Copying cells to a larger destination range

You could have highlighted the entire block in the destination instead of just the first column; the result would have been the same. Since there were three cells in the row being copied, Enable assumes three cells across the destination (unless you specify more than three). So the rule is: When you specify more columns or rows than were in the source, Enable fills the cells you specify. If you do not specify more columns or rows (that is, if you highlight just one column or row), Enable uses the same number as were in the source. Here's another example to help make this clear:

1. Move the pointer to cell F4.

2. Press F8.

3. Move the pointer to cell C1.

4. Press ← to specify this one cell as the source.

5. Press the period key, then move the pointer to cell I13.

6. Press ← when finished.

The result of this example is that the information in the source cell is copied to the entire range specified.

7. Now erase the information in the range F4..I13 using the expert command F9 Del B command, as described earlier in this chapter.

COPYING FORMULAS

You'll find the Copy command a powerful feature of the spreadsheet when you need to duplicate formulas. When you copy a formula from one location to another, Enable adjusts the cell references in that formula to be *relative* to the new location. So rather than getting two identical formulas calculating the same result, you get two different formulas, each calculating the result of its relative cell references. Here's an example that will make this clear:

1. Move the pointer to cell D14.

2. Press F8.

3. Move the pointer to cell B14, then press the period key.

4. Move the pointer to cell B16, highlighting the range B14..B16. Press ← when finished.

5. Since the destination is supposed to be exactly the same size as the source (in this case, three cells), just press ← to let Enable copy the information. The result looks like Figure 8.6.

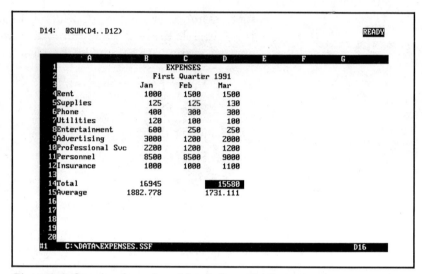

Figure 8.6: Copying formulas with relative cell references

Notice that the copies produce different results than the originals. In fact, the new formulas are relative to row D, just as the originals are relative to row B. Cell D14, for example, reads @SUM(D4..D12). The formulas are exactly as you would want them.

All the rules that apply to the number of cells in the source and destination range are the same as we saw in the previous example. For instance, you can copy one formula into a dozen cells by specifying the appropriate destination range during the Copy command. Try copying cells B14..B16 to the bottom of column C to complete the totals for the Expenses worksheet:

6. Move the pointer to cell C14.

7. Press F8.

8. Move to cell B14 and press the period key.

9. Highlight the range B14..B16, then press ↵.

10. Press ↵ to complete the copy. All three columns now calculate totals and averages.

There may be times when you don't want Enable to copy formulas relative to the new location. Perhaps you want a cell reference to remain exactly as the original. Since the Copy command automatically adjusts cell references, you have to specify cells that will remain the same. Cell references that do not change when copied are called *absolute references*.

Unless you specify otherwise, all cell references in formulas are relative; that is, they are adjusted when copied. The following formula uses relative cell references:

+A1 * A3

Suppose this formula appears in cell A4 of your Expenses spreadsheet. If you were to copy it to cell B4, the formula would read

+B1 * B3

To make a cell reference absolute requires that you insert dollar signs ($) between each part of the address. The above example in cell A4 would appear like this:

+$A$1 * A3

If this formula were copied to cell B4, the result would read

+$A$1 * B3

Notice that the cell containing the dollar signs (the absolute reference) does not change, but the other cell reference is adjusted. Any cell address in any formula or function can be made absolute by adding the dollar signs. Try this on the Expenses spreadsheet. First enter an example formula into the spreadsheet:

1. Move the pointer to cell F1 and enter the number **5**.

2. Move the pointer to cell B18.

3. Type the formula **+B14 +F1** and press ⏎. This adds 5 to the total shown in cell B14.

4. Now copy this formula to cell C18. First, move the pointer to cell C18, then press F8.

5. Move the pointer to cell B18 and press ←┘.

6. Press ←┘ again to finish the copy.

Notice that the formula in cell B18 adds 5 to the total in B14. The formula in cell C18, however, calculates the same result as the total in cell C14. The intent was to add 5 to this total also. If you look at the formula in cell C18, it reads

+C14+G1

Enable has made all references relative to the new location. Unfortunately, cell G1 contains nothing. Instead, the formula should have left the reference to F1 alone. Here's how to do it right:

1. Move the pointer to cell B18.

2. Press F4 to begin editing the formula.

3. Press the Ins key to switch to the Insert mode.

4. Insert $ in front of the F, and insert 1 in the cell reference F1. Then press ←┘. The formula should read

+B14 + $F$1

5. Now copy this formula to cell C18 again. First, move the pointer to cell C18, then press F8.

6. Move the pointer to cell B18 and press ←┘.

7. Press ←┘ again to finish the copy. The result should be correct and the formula in C18 should read

+C14 + $F$1

You can use absolute references in more advanced copy procedures. When spreadsheets get more complex, you might find the need to make only the row reference in a cell address absolute—or only the column. In this case, you would use only one dollar sign in a cell address.

SORTING YOUR DATA

Although Enable's spreadsheet hardly rivals the database for sorting capabilities, it does offer a useful sorting function for your spreadsheet information. In the spreadsheet, you can sort numbers in numerical order and text in alphabetical order. Also, dates can be sorted in chronological order. Enable automatically sorts the data in proper order; you just choose the data to sort and decide if you want the data in ascending or descending order. Spreadsheet sorting is perfect for arranging tables of data, such as the one in the Expenses spreadsheet. When sorting needs exceed the use of the spreadsheet, you should consider transferring the spreadsheet data to the database.

Sorting a range of cells in the spreadsheet requires several menu options performed in a specific order. These options are all found in the Worksheet, Range, Sort menu (F10 W R S) (Figure 8.7).

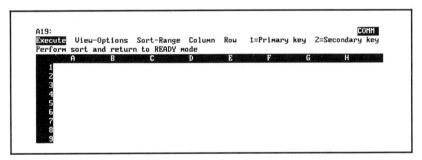

Figure 8.7: The options in the Worksheet, Range, Sort menu

Below is the procedure for using these options to sort a range of cells in the spreadsheet. Following this procedure is an explanation of each option. To sort a range of cells, follow these basic steps:

- Press F10 W R S to view the sort options.

- Select *Sort-Range* and specify the range of cells you want to sort.

- Select *Column* to sort the columns of the range (that is, sorting by rows while keeping the columns together) or *Row* to sort the rows of the range (that is, sorting by columns while keeping the rows together). The *Column* option is most common.

- Select the *1 = Primary key* option, then specify the cell containing the primary key. This is most likely the first cell in one of the columns you are sorting.

- Select the *Execute* option to sort the range according to your specifications.

THE SORT OPTIONS

With that brief description of the sorting procedure, let's take a look at each of the sort options. (These are listed in order of their recommended use for sorting.)

SORT-RANGE   This option specifies the range of cells you want to sort. Select this option, then specify the range by moving to the first cell (upper-left) and pressing the period key. Then, move to the last cell (lower-right) and press ◄┘. You can use the Arrow keys or other cursor movement commands to move to the last cell in the range.

COLUMN   This option sorts the chosen range column by column. In other words, the information will be in sorted order across the spreadsheet. Usually, the first row of information is used as the key sorting row. Figure 8.8 shows an example before and after columnar sorting.

ROW   This option sorts the range row by row. Information will be in order down the rows of the spreadsheet. Usually one column in the range is chosen as the key sorting column. Figure 8.9 shows an example before and after row sorting.

PRIMARY KEY   This is the row or column by which the information is sorted. In Figures 8.8 and 8.9, the first row and column in the range is used. The primary key applies to any row or column in the sort range specified.

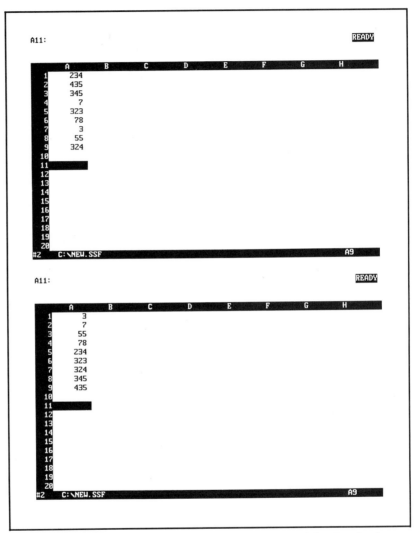

Figure 8.8: The lower screen shows columnar sorting of the data in the top menu; the upper screen shows the spreadsheet before sorting.

SECONDARY KEY The secondary key is used to "break a tie" when identical items appear in the primary key row or column. For example, if you are sorting by a column of last names, you might encounter two Smiths. In this case, you might opt to add a secondary

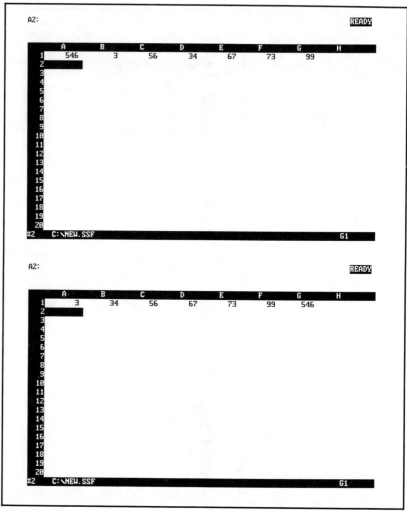

Figure 8.9: The upper screen shows the spreadsheet before sorting; the lower screen shows the spreadsheet after row sorting.

key using the column of first names. This way, John Smith will appear before Martha Smith.

VIEW OPTIONS This option displays the sorting options you have selected. This is useful for previewing your selections prior to executing the sort. The View Options screen looks like Figure 8.10.

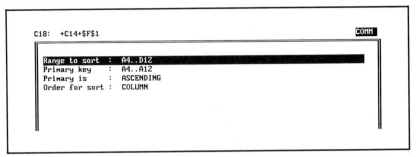

Figure 8.10: The View Options screen

EXECUTE This option sorts the specified range using the specified keys. This is, of course, the last action you should perform in the sorting process.

SORTING YOUR EXPENSES SPREADSHEET

Now try sorting the Expenses spreadsheet data. In this example, we'll sort the expenses and their quarterly values in alphabetical order by the name of the expense; then, we'll re-sort the range in order of ascending cost using the month of March as the key. Here are the steps:

1. Enter the command F10 W R S (Worksheet, Range, Sort).
2. Select *Sort-Range*.
3. Move the pointer to cell A4 and press the period key.
4. Move the pointer to cell D12 and press ←┘.
5. Select *Primary key*.
6. Select *Ascending* order for the sort.
7. Move the pointer to cell A4 and press ←┘.
8. Select the *Column* option.
9. Select the *Execute* option. The range will be sorted in ascending alphabetical order by the name of the expense. Figure 8.11 shows the result.

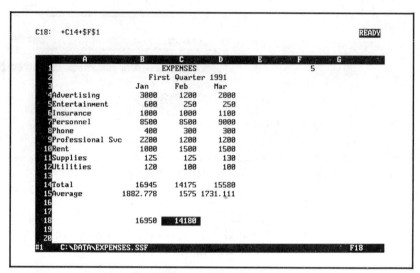

Figure 8.11: Result of sorting the Expenses spreadsheet

10. Choose the command F10 W R S, then select the *Primary key* option again.

11. Select *Ascending* order for the sort.

12. Move the pointer to cell D4 and press ←⎯.

13. Select *Execute* to re-sort the range.

Notice that you can re-sort a range by a different key without reselecting all the options. Enable remembers the current sort range until you select a new one. You can simply change the keys, or the order of the sort (Column or Row) and re-sort the range.

Another thing to notice is that the sorting process did not adjust the result of the formula in row 14. This is because the sorted range was within the range used for the formula calculation (for example, range B4..B12). However, sorting the spreadsheet can have adverse affects on formulas. Try entering this formula in cell B18:

@SUM(B5..B11)

Repeat the steps in the exercise above to re-sort the range and watch the result of the formula as you change the order of the cells. The formula calculates different values for each order.

To guard against accidental sorting problems, adjust your formula ranges to include a blank row above and below the actual values. As long as those rows do not contain values (preferably they will be blank), the result of the formula will not be affected. Then, when you sort the values, there is no chance of including the entire range used in the formula.

NAMING RANGES

Using range names makes your spreadsheets easier to understand and build. Many spreadsheet commands and functions require that you enter a range reference in the form A3..C9. Range references contain the address of the first and last cell of the range (that is, the two corners). But the Range Name command lets you apply an easy-to-remember name to any range reference. You can then use the name wherever Enable asks for a range reference. For instance, suppose you use the formula @SUM(A1..A5). You can apply the name SALES to the range A1..A5 and enter the formula like this:

@SUM(SALES)

There is no limit to the number of names you can use in a spreadsheet, but there are some restrictions on the names themselves. Always begin a range name with a letter. Do not use spaces or special characters in a range name. Avoid creating a name that looks like a cell reference, such as AA25. Range names can be a maximum of 15 characters. Following are some acceptable range names:

SALES

Budget

January

Sales91

To name a range, follow these simple steps:

- Enter the command F10 W R N (Worksheet, Range, Name).
- Select *Create*.

- Enter the desired name, following the rules outlined above, then press ←┘.

- Move the pointer to the first cell in the desired range, then press the period key. (Alternatively, just type the range reference where prompted.)

- Move the pointer to the last cell in the range, then press ←┘.

- When Enable asks for another name, press Esc. You could continue to name other ranges at this point or press Esc to exit.

Once you have named a range, Enable automatically updates the spreadsheet. Wherever the range reference was used, Enable converts it to the name you specified. For example, if you name the range A1..A5 to SALES, the formula @SUM(A1..A5) would change to @SUM(SALES). When you enter formulas that use this range, just enter the name instead of the range reference. The name should not be in quotation marks when it appears in a formula. If you create a name that has already been used for a range, Enable will apply the name to the last range named. In other words, the old range containing that name will no longer be named, and the new range will contain the name. This can cause problems in formulas that refer to the old range name. Enable will attempt to convert the range name to its standard range reference. Likewise, if you delete a range name that has been used in formulas, the formulas will convert back to the standard range reference.

Let's try using a range name in the Expenses spreadsheet. We'll name the range B4..B12 as "January." Here are the steps:

1. Enter the command F10 W R N.

2. Select the *Create* option.

3. Type **January** as the name.

4. Enter the range reference **B4..B12** and press ←┘.

5. Enable asks for another range name. This is so you can create several range names without reselecting all the menu options over and over. Just press Esc to exit this menu.

6. Move the pointer to cell B14 and examine the formula at the top of the screen. It should read

@SUM(JANUARY)

Notice that Enable converts your range name to uppercase letters. However, you can enter the name using upper- or lowercase letters. Remember, however, that Enable makes no distinction between the cases, so the names "January" and "JANUARY" are considered the same name.

ENTERING SEQUENTIAL NUMBERS WITH DATA FILL

The Data Fill command takes the work out of entering sequential numbers into your spreadsheet. Using your starting number and increment value, Enable will enter the series of numbers into your specified range or until a specific number is reached. Whenever you need to enter a series of numbers that increase in a standard increment, follow these steps:

- Enter the command F10 W R D (Worksheet, Range, Data Fill).
- Select *Initialize*.
- Specify the range that you would like to fill with values.
- Enter the starting value and press ←.
- Enter the step value and press ←. This is the increment between the numbers.
- Enter the ending number. This applies only if the specified range is large enough to accommodate the stop value. Otherwise, Enable will fill the range and then stop. To simply fill the range, press ←. Otherwise, enter the desired stop value and press ←.

Figure 8.12 shows an example of some filled ranges. The first range, A2..F2, uses a starting value of 1 and an increment of 1. The second range, A3..F3, uses a starting value of 100 and an increment

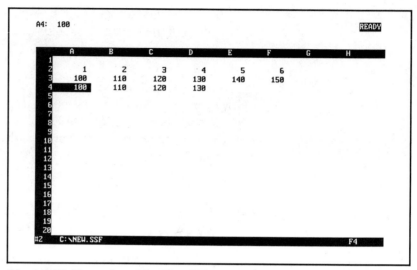

Figure 8.12: Examples of the Data Fill command

Figure 8.12 shows an example of some filled ranges. The first range, A2..F2, uses a starting value of 1 and an increment of 1. The second range, A3..F3, uses a starting value of 100 and an increment of 10. The third range, A4..F4, uses a starting value of 100, an increment of 10, and a stop value of 130.

USING CELL PROTECTION

If you create spreadsheets that are used by others, cell protection is almost a must. This feature "locks" spreadsheet cells and prevents them from being altered. Commonly, protection is applied to cells that contain formulas and not to those that require data entry. This way, the formulas cannot be altered or accidentally removed.

To protect the formulas in the Expenses spreadsheet, first specify the cells to be protected, then activate the cell protection feature. Follow these steps:

1. Enter the command F10 W R P (Worksheet, Range, Protection).

2. Enter the range reference **B14..D16** and press ←┘ (or highlight the range).

At this point, you have protected the cells containing formulas. However, cell protection is currently deactivated in Enable. To activate cell protection, use this command:

3. Enter the command F10 W G P (Worksheet, Global, Protection).

4. Select the *Disallow Changes* option to turn protection on.

Now you have activated cell protection throughout Enable. The cells you highlighted in steps 1 and 2 are now protected from changes. Test it by trying to type something into these cells.

The command F10 W G P is a sort of "master switch" for protection. Once you have protected cells and ranges individually, use this command to turn protection on or off. This master switch is useful when you want to make changes to protected cells. You can turn the master switch off without unprotecting each cell individually.

Formatting and Printing Spreadsheets

THE LAST TWO CHAPTERS HAVE EXPLAINED THE majority of spreadsheet features. You should be familiar with creating spreadsheets, entering data and formulas, changing the contents of a spreadsheet, and copying information. Using these fundamentals, you can build almost any basic spreadsheet in Enable.

Now you're ready for a few ideas on how to improve the appearance of your spreadsheets. This chapter will begin by explaining the various formatting tools you can use in your spreadsheets. These include alignment options, numeric formats, and the use of special characters.

When the spreadsheet looks just right, you'll be ready to print. This chapter will show you how. Spreadsheet printing can be very simple, or you can use special options that make it more complex, such as headers, page numbers, borders, and print-setup options.

ALIGNING SPREADSHEET TEXT

One of the most basic formatting options you can apply to your spreadsheet data is *alignment*. You saw in Chapter 7 that labels are normally centered in cells, and numbers are normally flush with the right side of the cell. If you simply type data with no regard for alignment, they will turn out like the example in Figure 9.1.

You can align information in a spreadsheet using one of two methods: you can add an alignment prefix or you can use the F10 W R A menu command.

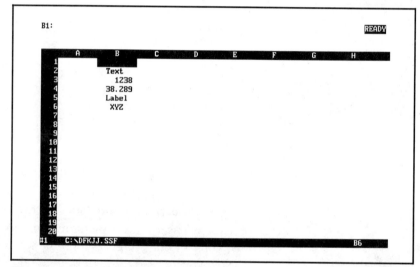

Figure 9.1: Default alignment

ALIGNMENT PREFIXES

When you enter text into a cell, you can begin the information with one of the three alignment prefixes. The prefix will dictate which type of alignment is used for the information. Remember that this alignment applies to each cell independently—the width of the cell can have an effect on the appearance of the information. For example, if your label just fits into the width of a cell, it does not much matter if the data is flush right, flush left, or centered, since there is no room for these alignments to appear. The three alignment prefixes are as follows:

PREFIX	*ALIGNMENT*
<	Flush left
>	Flush right
^	Centered

To align numeric entries using a prefix, just enter the prefix by itself and press ◀— to accept the entry. This will align the cell with no information in it. Then, type the numeric entry into the "prealigned" cell (type the number or formula without a prefix). Any information you enter will be aligned according to your prefix. Essentially, this is a way to prealign cells for data that you will enter later.

USING THE ALIGNMENT COMMAND

Another way to align information is to use the command F10, Worksheet, Range, Alignment. This command can act on a range of cells at one time—saving you much time and trouble when aligning large blocks of data. Try the following steps on the Expenses document.

1. Move the pointer to cell A4. This should be the first cell in the column of expense categories.

2. Press F10.

3. Press **W** for the *Worksheet* option.

4. Press **R** for the *Range* option.

5. Press **A** for the *Alignment* option.

6. Press **R** for the *Right* option.

7. Press the period key to anchor the top of the range. Then press ↓ until the range A4..A12 is highlighted. Finally, press ◀—. Figure 9.2 shows the result.

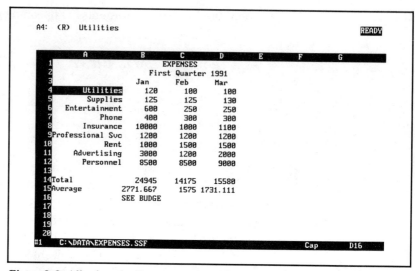

Figure 9.2: Aligning the Expenses spreadsheet with the Alignment command

You can align all the cells of the spreadsheet using the command F10, Worksheet, Global, Alignment. This command changes all cells globally—except those that have been aligned with a prefix or range alignment command.

Enable provides a keyboard version of the Alignment command. You might find the keyboard options easier to use. Just move to any cell and use one of the following commands:

COMMAND	ALIGNMENT
Ctrl-[	Flush left
Ctrl-]	Flush right
Alt-F4	Centered

You might find it convenient to use the Worksheet, Global, Alignment or Worksheet, Range, Alignment command to align most of the cells in your spreadsheet, then use one of the keyboard commands to adjust cells that do not adhere to the norm.

CHOOSING A FORMAT FOR DISPLAYING NUMBERS

Enable has 11 ways to display numbers. As you build spreadsheets, you may need to use several of the number formats. Following are the steps for choosing a numeric format:

- Press F10.

- Press **W** for *Worksheet.*

- Press **R** for *Range.*

- Press **F** for *Format.*

- Choose one of the formats described below.

- At this point, some formats first provide a second set of options and then a range; others will ask you to enter a range.

This section describes each number format and includes an example of each.

FIXED

The Fixed format displays numbers with a fixed quantity of decimal places. Numbers without decimal values will show zeros after the decimal point. After selecting this option, Enable asks you to specify the number of decimal places. The number of places must be from 0 to 14. After entering the number of places, you are asked for a range to format. Note that this format seems to round numbers so they will fit into the specified quantity of decimal places. These numbers are not really rounded, since calculations based on the numbers still use the full version. (See the @ROUND function in Chapter 10 for more details.) Below are some examples using fixed decimal places of 2:

YOU ENTER	ENABLE DISPLAYS
5	5.00
5.3878	5.39
− 5.4	− 5.40

CURRENCY ($)

Use this format to add dollar signs to a number. Like the Fixed format, this format also lets you specify a number of decimal places and a range to format, but this will usually be 2. In addition, it displays negative numbers with parentheses around them and includes commas between thousands. Following are some examples of the Currency format using fixed decimal places of 2:

YOU ENTER	ENABLE DISPLAYS
5	$5.00
−5.4	($5.40)
5778	$5,778.00

INTEGER

This format displays the number as an integer value. All decimal places are removed and the number is rounded to show the appropriate value. The number is not changed, however, since all calculations based on the number still use the original value. (See @TRUNC in Chapter 10 for additional information.) Below are some examples:

YOU ENTER	ENABLE DISPLAYS
5.3878	5
−5.4589	−5

COMMA

This format is identical to the Currency ($) format, but it does not include the dollar signs. This is useful for large blocks of values that represent dollar amounts. Too many dollar signs can be annoying.

PERCENT

This format displays values as percentages. It multiplies the value by 100 and adds the percent sign. Hence, to use this format accurately, you should multiply values by 0.01 (use decimal values) before entering them. After choosing this option, Enable asks you to specify a number of decimal places and a range to format. Following are examples with no decimal places:

YOU ENTER	ENABLE DISPLAYS
5	500%
.01	1%

DATE

This format should be used on valid dates only. Although a valid date is really just a numeric value that represents the number of days elapsed since 12/31/1899, formatting standard values will probably produce obscure dates. Instead, enter a date as described in Chapter 7, then use this command to specify a different date format. When you select this command, Enable provides a list of seven different date formats from which to choose.

TIME

This format, like the Date format, should be used on valid times only. Enter a time using the @TIME function described in Chapter 7, then use this format option to change the time format to one of the four formats offered.

SCIENTIFIC

This format uses scientific notation to display extremely large or small numbers. Enable asks for a number of decimal places and for the range to format. For example:

YOU ENTER	ENABLE DISPLAYS
− 30000030	− 3.00E + 07
378.002838	3.78E + 02

GENERAL

General is the format used by Enable when you do not specify another. This format is included so you can return formatted values back to the standard (General) format. This format displays numbers with the minimum requirednumber of decimal places—removing trailing zeros . Usually this is the same way you originally entered the number. Negative numbers are displayed with a minus sign, and no commas or other symbols are used. Extremely large numbers are displayed in scientific notation. For example:

YOU ENTER	ENABLE DISPLAYS
5	5
5.3878	5.3878
− 5.40	− 5.4

+ /−

This is a special format for creating charts and histograms without using graphics. Formatting a value with + / − converts it to a series of plus signs or minus signs. A full explanation is provided in the section ''Text-Based Graphs.''

RESET

Reset returns the chosen values to the format currently specified as the global format. You can specify the global format using the command F10 W G F.

TEXT-BASED GRAPHS

If you don't have graphics capabilities for your system, you may be under the impression that you cannot produce graphs of your Enable data. But Enable offers a special tool for creating bar graphs right on the worksheet with your data. As you update the numbers in the worksheet, the graph will automatically recalculate its values and rechart the information. These graphs don't look as nice as those

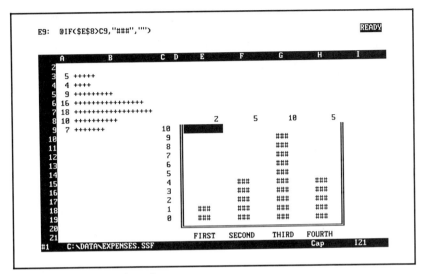

Figure 9.3: Two graphs using text

described in Chapter 11, but they suffice. Figure 9.3 shows examples of a horizontal bar graph and standard bar graph.

CREATING A HORIZONTAL BAR GRAPH

Creating a horizontal bar graph is easy. Enable provides a special format that does most of the work for you. This format turns any number into a series of plus signs (+) or minus signs (–). The number of plus signs equals the value of the number. Here are some examples.

ORIGINAL NUMBER	FORMATTED
6	+ + + + + +
13	+ + + + + + + + + + + + +
– 12	– – – – – – – – – – – –

Values of zero produce a single period (.), negative values produce minus signs, and positive values produce plus signs. Stacked on top of each other, these symbols can produce an effective graph. The only thing you have to do is expand the column containing these values and format the values with the correct symbols.

Here is a simple exercise to show the steps involved in producing a graph. Try it, starting with a blank worksheet.

1. Move the pointer to cell A3.

2. Enter the label **Oranges** then press ↓. Enter the label **Bananas** and press ↓. Enter the label **Pears** and press ↓. Enter the label **Grapes** and press ↓. Enter the label **Apples** and press ↓.

3. Move the pointer to cell B3, then enter the following values next to each of the labels. Press ↓ after each value:

    18
    15
    20
     9
    12

4. Enter the command F10 W W S (Worksheet, Width, Set).

5. Enter **20** to set the column width to 20 characters, then press ⏎.

6. Enter the command F10 W R F (Worksheet, Range, Format). Then choose the format + / − .

7. Enter the range B3..B7 to format the values in column B, then press ⏎.

8. Move the pointer to cell A2.

9. Enter the label **Fruit Sales** and press ⏎. The result is a simple horizontal bar graph.

You can enter any values into cells B3..B7 and the bars will change to reflect the new value. These values can also be the results of formulas that refer to other cells. When the formulas calculate new values, the bars will change.

You might find that your numbers are too large to create horizontal bar graphs effectively; if the numbers are in the hundreds or thousands, you would not want to expand the columns that much. Instead, use formulas to reduce the values to a more ''graphable'' size. Try multiplying the values by .01 or .001 to reduce them.

CREATING A VERTICAL BAR GRAPH

Using another spreadsheet technique, you can create vertical bar graphs. This technique does not use the + and − number format; instead it uses a series of formulas to create bars out of spreadsheet cells. The graphs you saw in Figure 9.3 are examples that were created using the following steps. Try these out on the sample file.

1. Move the pointer to cell E8 and enter the values **2, 5, 10,** and **5** in cells E8..H8. These are the values we'll be graphing; you can change them at any time.

2. Move the pointer to cell C8 and enter the number **1.** This value represents the increment used for the vertical axis scale. You can change this value to get various increments of vertical axis values.

3. Move the pointer to cell C9, enter **10,** and press ←. This value represents the maximum value of the vertical axis and can be changed as desired.

4. Move the pointer to cell C10, enter the formula **+C9 − $C$8,** and press ←.

5. Copy the formula in cell C10 into the range C11..C19 using the F10, Worksheet, Copy command.

6. Move the pointer to cell E9.

7. Enter the formula **@IF($E$8>C9,"###","")** and press →.

8. Enter the formula **@IF($F$8>C9,"###","")** and press →.

9. Enter the formula **@IF($G$8>C9,"###","")** and press →.

10. Enter the formula **@IF($H$8>C9,"###","")** and press ←.

11. Enter the command F10 W C (Worksheet, Copy).

12. Specify the range E9..H9 as the range to copy *from*, and press ←.

13. Specify the range E10..H19 as the range to copy *to*, and press ←.

14. Refer to Figure 9.3 and enter the labels under the four bars that appear in that figure. Reduce the width of column D.

You can embellish the graph by adding labels for the vertical and horizontal axes and by using graphics characters. Try changing the values at the top of the graph, and watch the graph change. Also, you can change the maximum value of the vertical axis to match the values being graphed. There are many ways to expand this technique. For example, you can alternate the pattern used for the bars to show two comparative data ranges.

USING ASCII CHARACTERS WITH YOUR SPREADSHEETS

Enable lets you create graphs and enhance your spreadsheet by using any of the standard ASCII characters in your computer, plus the extended character set, consisting of ASCII values 128 through 255. While you might not be able to print all these characters (depending on your printer), they can be used to enhance the appearance of your spreadsheets on screen. Refer to your Enable documentation on spreadsheets and graphics (Appendix H) for a complete listing of ASCII characters available in the spreadsheet.

To display an ASCII character that does not appear on the keyboard, you must enter the character by typing its ASCII value directly. To do this, simply hold down the Alt key and enter the ASCII value of the character using the numeric keypad. For example, to create the character ■, move to the desired cell and hold down the Alt key while typing the ASCII code 219. Experiment with other characters for best results. The bar graph shown in Figure 9.3 uses the line graphics characters in the ASCII range 185 through 205 to produce a solid border around three sides of the graph.

PRINTING A SPREADSHEET

Enable offers several printing options for spreadsheets. Use the F10, Print command to display these options.

The *Execute* option actually begins printing. You can use this command at any time—but you will probably want to set up the printout and apply other options before printing. When you print, the options you have chosen up to that time are applied. Also, you will be asked if you want to print to a disk file or to the printer. If you choose a disk file, you are prompted to enter a file name. If you choose the printer, be sure the correct printer has been chosen using the Setup command.

View Options simply displays the setup you have chosen. Often, this is handy for quickly checking the options before printing.

The *Setup* option contains numerous options for controlling the print-out. In fact, Enable provides four screens full of options when you select the Setup command. You can move from screen to screen by pressing PgUp or PgDn. These screens are shown in Figures 9.4–9.7.

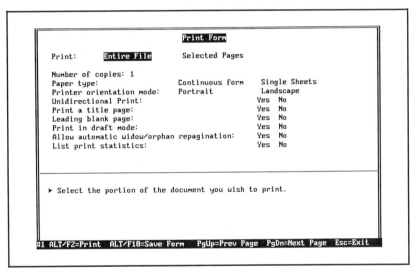

Figure 9.4: The first print-setup screen

If you have read the word processor section of this book, these four screens will look familiar; they are exactly like the print-setup screens in the word processor. And they affect the printout in the same way. See Table 3.1 in Chapter 3 for a list of the keys you can use to manipulate these screens.

When you use ◄─┘ or ↓ to move to the various prompts, Enable highlights the currently selected option for that prompt. Of course, when you change the options and save the changes, the new options will be highlighted the next time you view the screens. See Chapter 3

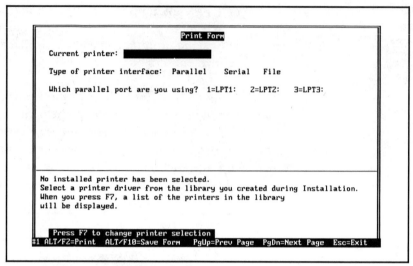

Figure 9.5: The second print-setup screen

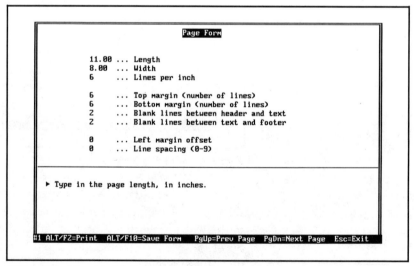

Figure 9.6: The third print-setup screen

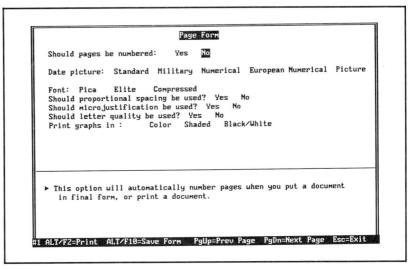

Figure 9.7: The fourth print-setup screen

for a complete description of each option on each of the print-setup screens.

SELECTING THE PRINT AREA

You don't have to print the entire spreadsheet each time you print. You can select a specific area for printing. This is done with the *Range* option. After you select this option, Enable asks you to enter the print range. This print range remains current until you quit the spreadsheet.

If you commonly print several different ranges in the same spreadsheet, try naming each print range using the Worksheet, Range, Name command. Then, when you use the Print, Range command, just enter one of the names you specified. This will be easier than entering a range reference.

If you print the entire spreadsheet by specifying *All* as the print range, Enable will fit as much data on each page as possible, then break to the next page. If the entire contents of a column cannot fit within the right margin of the page, the entire column is moved to the next page. Likewise, the number of rows that fit on each page is determined by the top and bottom margins. To fit more on each page, try printing the spreadsheet in Landscape mode with no top or bottom margins. These options are found in the print Setup command.

LIST FORMULAS: PRINTING SPREADSHEET FORMULAS

This option prints a list of the formula text in each cell of the spreadsheet. This is useful for examining the formulas for debugging. It is also helpful in describing a spreadsheet for others to build, since each cell and its contents is displayed.

CREATING HEADERS AND FOOTERS

Enable provides options for adding headers and footers to your spreadsheet printouts. The two options work identically, except that headers print information at the top of each page and footers print at the bottom.

To create a header, select F10, Print, Header. Enable asks if you want to specify a header or delete a header. Choose the *Specify* option and enter the header information you want printed on each page.

Headers and footers are ideal for printing the current date and page numbers on the pages. This can be accomplished with two special commands. To print the current date in a header or footer, just type %**DATE** where the date is to appear in the header. To print the current page number, type the # symbol where the page number is to appear.

PRINTING HEADINGS

While headers are handy for printing descriptive information at the top of each page, they do not help when it comes to printing headings. Instead, Enable provides the Borders command for establishing print headings.

Headings should align with the columns to which they apply—aligning these titles within a header would be difficult. You can print headings at the top of each page, the left side of each page, or both.

Usually, these headings come from the top or left side of the range you are printing, but they can come from any cells in a spreadsheet.

To specify this kind of heading, select F10, Print, Borders command. You are given three options; *Row-Borders* prints headings at the top of each page. The headings should come from a spreadsheet row. *Col-Borders* prints headings at the left side of each page. The headings should come from a spreadsheet column. *ID-Borders* prints the row headings (1, 2, 3, and so on) and column headings (A, B, C, and so on) on each page.

After specifying the desired option, Enable asks if you would like to *Set Border* or *Clear Border*. If you set a new border, you are then asked to specify the range of cells that contain the border information. The information in this range will print on every page. Of course, you are not asked to specify a range for the *ID-Borders* option.

Adding Power to Your Spreadsheet with Functions

THIS CHAPTER PROVIDES A BRIEF EXPLANATION OF the Enable spreadsheet functions. It lists the most common functions; for a complete listing, refer to the Enable *User Manual*. Each function is listed, briefly described, and its syntax shown. There are a lot of functions available, but you will probably use only a few in your applications. However, it's a good idea to be familiar with the capabilities offered in the spreadsheet. Once you've read through the function descriptions, you'll have a good idea of the functions you'll be using most often.

ARGUMENTS

Before listing the functions, let's review the types of arguments that can be used with functions. Remember, an argument is the portion of the function that provides the variable or constant values on which the function works. Not all functions require arguments, but those that do have arguments require that you enter them accurately. Following are the arguments used by the various functions.

Nexp stands for "*n*umeric *exp*ression" and indicates that the argument can be any numeric value or expression that results in a numeric value. An expression can include formulas, functions, or cell references. The following are all expressions (assuming that all cell references contain numbers):

```
A5
A5 + 100
A5 + 1/(B5 − 1)
@SUM(A1..A5)
B5 + @SUM(A1..A5)
```

When a function uses the nexp argument, it's indicated as in this example: @SQRT(*nexp*). This means that any numeric expression, such as those listed above, can be substituted for *nexp* when you use the function (for example, @SQRT(A5 + 100)).

Exp stands for "*exp*ression" and indicates that any expression, numeric or text, can be used as the argument to the function. Examples include all those listed above, plus any text expressions. This is rarely used as an argument.

Range indicates that a range of cells can be used as the argument. A range is indicated by entering the first and last cells in the range separated by two periods. A typical range looks like this: A1..A10. You can also use a valid range name wherever a range is required. Often, you can use an nlist argument (see below) where a range is required. The @SUM function is one that uses a range as its expression: @SUM(*range*).

The identifier *nlist* stands for "*n*umeric *list*" and indicates that a list of cells or numeric expressions can be used as the argument. If cells are used, they must contain numbers or numeric expressions. A list includes multiple cell addresses separated by commas. Besides allowing a range as its argument, the @SUM function allows a numeric list: @SUM(*nlist*). An example may look like this:

```
@SUM(A1,A4 + 100,B5,Z25)
```

where all the listed cells contain numeric values or numeric expressions. (Notice that the second item in the list is an expression.)

List is similar to the nlist argument but does not require the cells or expressions to be numeric. Any numeric or text expression is accepted.

Test or logical expression tests the relationship between two values, cells, or expressions. The result of the test can be either true or false. The @IF function uses a test as part of its expression:

@IF(*test,exp,exp,exp*)

An example is @IF(A1 = 50,F5,F6 + 2). In this example, the test evaluates to either true or false, and the function returns the first or second expression accordingly (see the exp argument). This argument is sometimes called a *conditional expression* or *condition*.

STATISTICAL FUNCTIONS

These functions perform basic statistical needs. This usually requires that the functions operate on many pieces of information (for example, a range of data). These functions include averaging values, finding maximum and minimum values, and more. Table 10.1 lists Enable's statistical functions.

Table 10.1: Statistical Functions and Their Uses

@AVG(*range*) or @AVG(*nlist*)	Calculates the average of the values in the range or list
@AVGPRD(*range*) or @AVGPRD(*nlist*)	Calculates the average of the sum of the products in the range or list
@COUNT(*range*) or @COUNT(*list*)	Counts the nonblank cells in the range or list
@MAX(*range*) or @MAX(*nlist*)	Finds the maximum value in the range or list
@MIN(*range*) or @MIN(*nlist*)	Finds the minimum value in the range or list
@PCT(*range,range*)	Calculates the percentage each value is to the total in the first range, and returns the percentage for each value to the second range

Table 10.1: Statistical Functions and Their Uses (continued)

@STD(*range*) or @STD(*nlist*)	Calculates the standard deviation of the values in the range or list
@SUM(*range*) or @SUM(*nlist*)	Calculates the sum of the values in the range or list
@SUMPRD(*range*) or @SUMPRD(*list*)	Calculates the sum of the products in the range or list
@CUMPCT(*range,range*)	Calculates the cumulative percentages of the values in the first range and places them in the second range
@CUMSUM(*range,range*)	Calculates the cumulative totals of a series of values and places them in the second range
@VAR(*range*) or @VAR(*nlist*)	Calculates the variance of a population represented by the range or list

CALCULATING AVERAGES

@AVG(*nlist*) or @AVG(*range*) returns the average of the values provided in the range or list provided. If a range is used, blank cells within the range are not used in the average calculation; however, labels that appear in the range are considered values of zero. If you use the nlist style, blank cells are considered values of zero. In the example

    @AVG(B1..B3)

cells B1, B2, and B3 contain 25, 50, and 60, which returns a value of 45.

@AVGPRD(*range*) or @AVGPRD(*nlist*) calculates the average over the products of number pairs. In the example

    @AVGPRD(2,2,3,3)

a value of 6.5 is returned—the average of 4 (2*2) and 9 (3*3). Of course, these values can be any numbers or numeric expressions.

COUNTING CELLS

@COUNT(*list*) or @COUNT(*range*) counts all nonblank cells in the list or range. Blank cells that appear in the range do not affect the total, but blank cells in a list argument do affect the total. In the example

@COUNT(A1..A10)

where all cells in the range contain text or numbers, this returns 10.

FINDING MAXIMUM AND MINIMUM VALUES

@MAX(*range*) and @MIN(*range*) return the maximum and minimum values in a range, respectively. The cells in the range must contain numbers or numeric expressions. Labels will be considered values of zero. These functions can also be used with nlist arguments. In the example

@MAX(E4..E8)

where the values of the cells in the range E4..E8 are 1, 5, 35, 34, and − 5, this function returns 35.

CALCULATING SUMS

@SUM(*range*) or @SUM(*nlist*) totals all the cells in the range or list. All cells must contain numbers or numeric expressions. Blank cells are ignored and text is treated as zero. In the example

@SUM(A1..A3)

where cells A1, A2, and A3 contain 5, 15, and 100, this function returns 120.

@SUMPRD(*range*) or @SUMPRD(*nlist*) calculates the sum of a set of values that are the results of product calculations. The first two numbers in the range or list are multiplied together, then added to the product of the next two values, and so on. All values must be numeric, and you should use an even number of arguments. The example

@SUMPRD(2,2,3,3)

returns 13—the sum of 4 (2*2) and 9 (3*3). Of course, these constant values can be cell references or numeric expressions. You can also use two ranges as the argument, as in the example

@SUMPRD(A1..A5,B1..B5)

This calculates (A1*B1) + (A2*B2) + (A3*B3), and so on.

FINDING THE PERCENTAGE OF A TOTAL

@PCT(*range,range*) requires two ranges to be entered with a comma between. The first range should contain numeric values and the second should be blank. The second range should contain the same number of cells as the first. First, the function calculates the total of the first range, then calculates the percentage each cell is of the total. The percentages of the total for the cells in the first range are entered into the second range. The function must be entered into a cell not included in either range. The example

@PCT(A1..A3,B1..B3)

returns the values shown in Figure 10.1.

CALCULATING THE STANDARD DEVIATION

@STD(*range*) or @STD(*nlist*) calculates the standard deviation of the values in the range or list. It's often useful to calculate the standard deviation of a group of graph values so you can add a deviation line. All values must be numeric. Blanks are ignored. Note that this calculates the "biased" deviation and not the "unbiased" (or sample) deviation. The example

@STD(A1..A5)

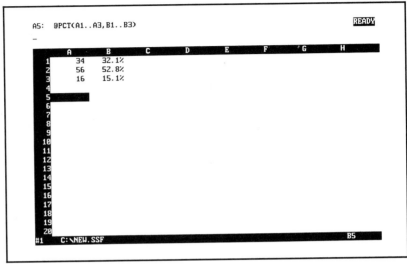

Figure 10.1: A calculation with the @PCT function

returns 31.00 when the values in the range are 45, 56, − 30, 30, and 3.

FINDING THE CUMULATIVE SUM AND PERCENTAGE

@CUMSUM(*range,range*) calculates the cumulative totals of a series of values. The first range should contain the values to total and the second range should be blank. Enable will place the cumulative totals in the second range. The second range does not have to be the same size as the first. This function is useful for check registers and other financial spreadsheets. In the example

> @CUMSUM(A1..A5,B1..B5)

where the first range contains 4,6,2,6,9, the second range will contain 4,10,12,18,27. Figure 10.2 shows this calculation using this function.

@CUMPCT(*range,range*) calculates the cumulative, or running, percentage of a series of numbers. The first range should contain the values for which you want to calculate a running percentage. The second range should be blank. The running percentage calculates the

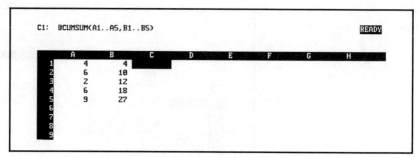

Figure 10.2: Example of the @CUMSUM function

percentage of the total of the entire range (the first range) for each running total in the range. In the example

@CUMPCT(A1..A10,B1..B10)

where each of the cells in the first range contains 10, the second range will contain 10%, 20%, 30%, 40%, 50%, 60%, 70%, 80%, 90%, 100%. This represents the percentage of the total represented by each cell when added to the preceding cells.

CALCULATING THE VARIANCE OF A POPULATION

@VAR(*range*) or @VAR(*nlist*) calculates the variance of a population represented by the range or list of values. The example

@VAR(3,5,6,2,9)

returns 6, the variance of this population.

MATHEMATICAL FUNCTIONS

These functions perform mathematical calculations. With them, you can find the absolute value of a number, calculate exponents, round numbers, and perform many other useful math tasks. Table 10.2 lists Enable's mathematical and trigonometric functions and their uses. (Trigonometric functions are discussed in the next section.)

Table 10.2: Mathematical and Trigonometric Functions and Their Uses

Mathematical Functions	
@ABS(*nexp*)	Produces the absolute value of any number or expression
@E	Returns the value *e*
@EXP(*nexp*)	Raises *e* to any power specified by *nexp*
@EXP10(*nexp*)	Raises 10 to the power specified by *nexp*
@INT(*nexp*)	Returns *nexp* as an integer
@MOD(*nexp,nexp*)	Calculates the modulus of two numbers: the first *nexp* divided by the second
@PI	Returns the value of pi
@RAND	Chooses a random number between 0 and 1
@ROUND(*nexp,nexp*)	Rounds first *nexp* to precision specified by second *nexp*
@SIGN(*nexp*)	Returns the sign of *nexp* (positive or negative status) as either 1 or − 1; if nexp = 0, returns 0
@TRUNC(*nexp,nexp*)	Truncates first *nexp* to the precision specified in second *nexp*
@SQRT(*nexp*)	Calculates the square root of *nexp*
Trigonometric Functions	
@ACOS(*nexp*)	Returns the arccosine of the numeric expression
@ASIN(*nexp*)	Returns the arcsine of the numeric expression
@ATAN(*nexp*)	Returns the arctangent of the numeric expression

Table 10.2: Mathematical and Trigonometric Functions (continued)

Trigonometric Functions (continued)	
@ATAN2(*nexp*,*nexp*)	Computes the angle whose tangent is equal to argument 2 divided by argument 1
@COS(*nexp*)	Returns the cosine of the numeric expression
@SIN(*nexp*)	Returns the sine of the numeric expression
@TAN(*nexp*)	Returns the tangent of the numeric expression

ABSOLUTE VALUE

@ABS(*nexp*) returns the absolute value of any number or expression. This is the number of places "away from zero" expressed in a positive number. In the example

@ABS(B6)

where cell B6 contains −5, this returns 5.

NATURAL NUMBER e

@E returns the value *e*, which is the value 2.7182818284590. The example

@E+50

returns 52.7182818284590.

EXPONENTIATION

@EXP(*nexp*) or @EXP10(*nexp*) raises values to the power specified in *nexp*. @EXP raises *e* to the specified power; @EXP10 raises 10 to the specified power. In the example

@EXP(4) and @EXP10(4)

the first expression results in 54.59815 (*e* to the power of 4). The second expression results in 10000 (10 to the power of 4).

INTEGERS

@INT(*nexp*) returns the integer portion of a number. This is the number without decimal values. This function performs no rounding; it simply drops the decimal portion of the number. In the example

@INT(B5)

where B5 contains 45.233, this returns 45. You can obtain the decimal portion of a number using the formula

+B5 – @INT(B5)

where B5 contains 45.233. This returns .233.

CALCULATING THE MODULUS

@MOD(*nexp,nexp*) calculates the modulus of two numbers. The modulus is the remaining value after the first number is divided by the second. Numbers that divide evenly produce a modulus of zero. The example

@MOD(10,3)

returns 1 because 3 goes into 10 three times with 1 remaining.

CALCULATIONS WITH PI

@PI uses no arguments. It returns the value of pi to a formula or cell. For accurate calculations using pi, use the @PI function. The example

@PI*D5**2

is a typical "pi times radius squared" formula, where D5 contains the radius and the operator ** calculates exponentiation.

RANDOM NUMBERS

@RAND is another function that has no argument. It provides a random number between 0 and 1. You can add numbers to this basic random number to increase the value. Use the following formula to specify the starting and ending number of the random numbers:

$$+ start + @INT(@RAND*(end - start) + .5)$$

Substitute the starting number for *start* and the ending number for *end* in this formula. The example

$$/ + @INT(@RAND*(10 - 1) + .5$$

calculates a random number between 1 and 10.

You can use the @RAND function with the @CHOOSE function to select values randomly from a predefined list. Use the formula

$$@CHOOSE(1 + @RAND*max - 1,value,value,value,...max)$$

The value of *max* should be equal to the number of items in the list. See @CHOOSE in the section "Choosing Values from a List" for more information.

ROUNDING NUMBERS

@ROUND(*nexp,nexp*) can round any number by a specified number of places. The first number or expression is the number to be rounded, the second is the number of places to round. If the value after the specified place is 5 or greater, @ROUND rounds it up to the next value. Note that @ROUND changes the value of the number for subsequent calculations. In other words, all calculations that include a rounded value use the rounded value and not the original value. In the example

$$@ROUND(B5,2)$$

where cell B5 contains 45.359, this returns 45.36. Although the second value can be a cell reference or expression, it is generally a constant value.

SIGN OF A NUMBER

@SIGN(*nexp*) returns the positive or negative status of a value. If the value specified is positive, @SIGN returns 1. If the value is negative, @SIGN returns − 1. If the value is zero, @SIGN returns 0. In the example

@SIGN(B5)

where cell B5 contains 47, this returns 1. If B5 contains − 389, this returns − 1.

TRUNCATING VALUES

@TRUNC(*nexp,nexp*) is identical to @ROUND except that the value is truncated at the specified decimal place rather than being rounded up or down. In the example

@TRUNC(B5,2)

where cell B5 contains 45.359, this returns 45.35.

CALCULATING THE SQUARE ROOT

@SQRT(*nexp*) calculates the square root of any value. Simply enter a value, cell reference, or expression as the argument, and the square root is returned. In the example

@SQRT(B5)

where B5 contains 9, this returns 3.

TRIGONOMETRIC FUNCTIONS

These functions calculate trigonometric values using an argument. Among their uses are computing the sine, cosine, and tangent. Table 10.2 lists Enable's trigonometric (and mathematical) functions and their uses.

ARCCOSINE

@ACOS(*nexp*) returns the arccosine of the numeric expression. Enter the cosine for the desired angle and this function will return the angle in radians for the cosine you entered. The cosine must be a value between −1 and 1. The example

> @ACOS(.17)

returns 1.3999 as the angle in radians.

ARCSINE

@ASIN(*nexp*) returns the arcsine of the numeric expression. Enter the sine for the desired angle and this function will return the angle in radians for the sine you entered. The sine must be a value between −1 and 1. The example

> @ASIN(.23)

returns .232 as the angle in radians.

ARCTANGENT

The function @ATAN(*nexp*) returns the arctangent of the numeric expression and @ATAN2(*nexp,nexp*) computes the angle whose tangent is equal to argument 2 divided by argument 1. The result is expressed in radians. The example

> @ATAN(1.2)

returns .876 as the angle in radians.

COSINE

@COS(*nexp*) returns the cosine of an angle expressed in radians. In the example

@COS(B5)

where cell B5 contains 45, this returns .53.

SINE

@SIN(*nexp*) returns the sine of an angle expressed in radians. In the example

@SIN(B5)

where cell B5 contains 45, this returns .85.

TANGENT

@TAN(*nexp*) returns the tangent of an angle expressed in radians. In the example

@TAN(B5)

where B5 contains 45, this returns 1.62.

FINANCIAL FUNCTIONS

These functions perform common calculations used in financial work. With them you can find interest rates, loan terms, value of an investment, and more. Table 10.3 lists Enable's financial functions and their uses.

Table 10.3: Financial Functions and Their Uses

@CTERM(*interest, future value, present value*)	Calculates the number of compounding terms required of an investment

Table 10.3: Financial Functions and Their Uses (continued)

@FV(*payment,interest,term*)	Calculates the future value of an investment
@IRR(*guess,range*)	Calculates the internal rate of return earned on a series of cash flows over time
@NPV(*nexp,range*)	Calculates the net present value of an investment given the interest rate and a series of cash flows
@PMT(*principal,interest,term*)	Calculates the periodic payment required of an investment given the principal, interest, and term
@PV(*payment,interest,term*)	Calculates the present value of an investment
@RATE(*future value,present value,term*)	Calculates the interest rate required of an investment given the future value, present value, and term
@TERM(*payment,interest,future value*)	Calculates the number of terms required in a loan based on the payment amount, periodic interest rate, and future value

TERMS REQUIRED IN A LOAN

@TERM(*payment,interest,future value*) calculates the number of terms required in a loan when you know the payment amount, the periodic interest rate, and the future value of the loan. You can use the annual interest rate and divide it by the number of periods in a year (for example, 12 months for a monthly period). In the example

@TERM(120,.12/12,5000)

120 represents the monthly payment, .12/12 represents a 12% annual interest rate divided by 12 months (this calculates the monthly interest rate), and 5000 is the total value of the loan. This returns 35.00453.

CALCULATING THE
INTEREST RATE OF AN INVESTMENT

@RATE(*future value, present value, term*) calculates the required interest rate of an investment when you know the desired future value after payments, the present loan value, and the term of the loan. Enable uses a compounded rate scenario. In the example

    @RATE(5000,3000,24)

where 5000 is the total value of the loan or investment, 3000 is the principal amount of the investment, and 24 is the number of periods (that is, two years) of the investment, this function returns the applicable interest rate: 0.021513 or 2.2%.

CALCULATING THE TERM OF AN INVESTMENT

@CTERM(*interest, future value, present value*) calculates the number of compounding terms of an investment based on the interest rate, future value, and initial value of the investment. The example

    @CTERM(.0215,5000,3000)

returns 24, the required term for a $3000 loan at 2.15% compounded interest to grow to $5000.

CALCULATING THE
PERIODIC PAYMENT AMOUNT

@PMT(*principal, interest, term*) calculates the payment required, given the principal of a loan, the interest rate, and the term. Note that the interest rate should be entered as the periodic rate, not the annual rate. The term should also be entered as the number of periods. The example

@PMT(3000,.015,36)

calculates a monthly payment of $108.46 on a $3000 loan at 0.015% monthly interest (or 18% annual interest) over 36 months. If you don't know the periodic rate, divide the annual rate by the number of periods per year (for example, divide by 12 for monthly).

CALCULATING PRESENT, NET PRESENT, AND FUTURE VALUES

@PV(*payment, interest, term*) calculates the present value of an investment based on the periodic payment amount, the periodic interest rate, and the number of periods (term). The example

@PV(120,.012,36)

represents an investment with monthly payments of $120 at 1.2% monthly interest over 36 months. The present value of this investment is $3491.19.

In @NPV(*nexp, range*), the net present value is the present value of an investment's cash flows minus the initial cash outlay. It is used to compare investments of equal risk, but with, perhaps, unequal interest rates and payment schedules (cash flows). The first parameter in the argument must be a numeric expression and represents the interest rate. The second parameter is the range of cells containing the cash flows. This can be any portion of a row or column containing positive (income) and negative (outflow) numbers. The example

@NPV(.015,A1..A12)

represents an investment paying 1.5% monthly interest rate (or 12.5% annual) with cash flows specified in cells A1..A12. Figure 10.3 shows a spreadsheet with this formula and the range of cash flows.

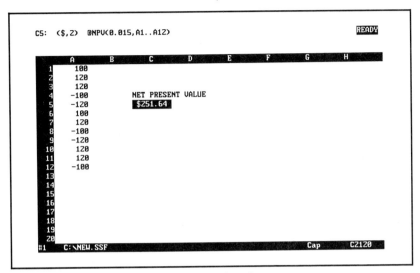

Figure 10.3: An example of the @NPV function

@FV(*payment,interest,term*) is identical to the @PV function, except that it returns the future value of the investment rather than the present value.

INTERNAL RATE OF RETURN

In @IRR(*guess,range*) the internal rate of return is the interest rate earned on a series of cash flows over time. This function uses your guess at the interest rate to calculate the correct rate. It performs 20 calculations to find the correct rate. The range should contain the series of cash flows, with the first cell being the amount of the loan entered as a negative. Income should be positive and payments negative in this range. Typically, a guess of .1 will produce a result. The example

@IRR(.1,A1..A10)

produces the result shown in Figure 10.4.

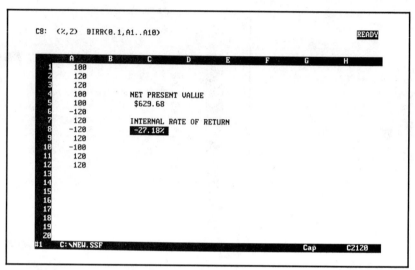

Figure 10.4: An example of the @IRR function

LOGICAL FUNCTIONS

Logical functions return a value of true or false, which is determined by the result of the arguments. Some of these functions are often used together. Logical functions are used for tasks such as error checking and decision making. See Table 10.4 for a list of logical functions.

RETURNING AN ERROR

@ERR returns the value of ERR (error) to a cell. This can be used with the @ISERR function to test for errors throughout the spreadsheet and to respond to them. Often @ERR is used with the @IF function to return ERR when no other acceptable value is possible. The example

@IF(A1 = 1,25,@ERR)

where cell A1 does not equal 1, returns ERR.

Table 10.4: Logical Functions and Their Uses

@ERR	Returns the value of ERR to a cell.
@ISERR(*cell*)	Tests whether the specified cell contains an error. Returns 1 if true and 0 if not.
@IF(*test,exp,exp*)	Tests whether a statement is true or false. Returns first *exp* if true, or second *exp* if false.
@ISBLANK(*cell*)	Tests if a cell is blank. Returns 1 if true, 0 if false.
@ISLABEL(*cell*)	Tests whether a cell is a label or a number. Returns 1 if a label (true), 0 if a number (false).
@ISNA(*cell*)	Works with @NA to handle unavailable values. Tests if a cell contains NA and returns 1 if so, 0 if not.
@ISNUM(*cell*)	Tests whether a cell is a label or number. Returns 1 if a number (true), 0 if a label (false).
@NA	Works with @ISNA to handle unavailable values. Returns NA to the cell.

CHECKING FOR ERRORS

@ISERR(*cell*) tests whether the specified cell contains an error (ERR). It returns a 1 (true) if the cell contains ERR and 0 (false) if it does not. This is primarily used for error trapping in a spreadsheet. *Error trapping* is the ability to anticipate errors and respond as desired. Error trapping uses the @IF function in conjunction with @ISERR. For example

@IF(@ISERR(B5) = 1,"Check Your Entry",B5)

checks whether cell B5 contains an error. If so, the statement "Check Your Entry" is printed; if not, then the value of B5 is returned. Of course, in this example, this function goes into any cell other than B5.

MAKING DECISIONS

@IF(*test,exp,exp*) tests whether a statement is true or false. If true, the first numeric expression is returned; if false, the second is returned. A logical operator must be used to express the test. Logical operators include =, >, = >, <, < =, and < >. The expressions returned do not have to be numbers or numeric expressions. If they are labels, they must be placed inside quotation marks. In the example

@IF(A1 = 1,B5,B6)

where A1 contains 1, B5 contains 5, and B6 contains 6, this function returns 5. If A1 contained anything but 1, this function would return 6. Cells B5 and B6 can also contain labels. However, to use labels inside the function, you must use quotation marks:

@IF(A1 = 1,"yes","no").

TESTING IF A CELL IS BLANK

@ISBLANK(*cell*) allows only a cell address as its argument. If the cell is blank, this function returns 1 (true); if the cell is not blank the statement returns 0 (false). This function is often used with the @IF function to act on the result of the test. Note that a blank cell must contain no value, formula, or label of any kind. In the example

@ISBLANK(B4)

where B4 is blank, this function returns 1.

The @IF function lends decision-making power to this logical function. Here's another example using the @IF function in conjunction with @ISBLANK:

@IF(@ISBLANK(B4) = 1,5,6)

This function returns 5 if cell B4 is blank and 6 if it's not.

TESTING IF A CELL IS A LABEL OR NUMBER

@ISLABEL(*cell*) and @ISNUM(*cell*) check whether a specified cell contains a label or number. You must enter a cell address as the argument. @ISLABEL returns 1 (true) if the cell is a label or expression resulting in a label, and 0 (false) if it's not a label. @ISNUM returns 1 (true) if the cell is a number or expression resulting in a number or expression resulting in a number, and 0 (false) if it's not a number. In the example

> @ISNUM(B5)

where B5 contains "January," this function returns 0. You can combine this function with the @IF function for decision-making capabilities:

> @IF(@ISNUM(B5) = 1,5,6)

This function returns 5 if cell B5 contains a number and 6 if it does not.

VALUE NOT AVAILABLE

@NA and @ISNA(*cell*) work together to handle unavailable values. If a formula depends on a particular value to be entered, it can test that the value has been entered before producing its result. Often these functions are used with @ISBLANK and @IF to act on the result. The function @NA simply returns the value NA to the cell. The function @ISNA tests if a cell contains NA and returns 1 if so and 0 if not.

Figure 10.5 shows an example of the functions @NA, @ISNA, @IF, and @ISBLANK. The cells contain these formulas:

> C1: @IF(@ISBLANK(A1) = 1,@NA,A1)
> C2: @IF(@ISNA(C1) = 1,"Value not Available",C1)

When cell A1 is blank, cell C2 produces the message "Value not Available." When A1 contains information, cell C2 contains that information.

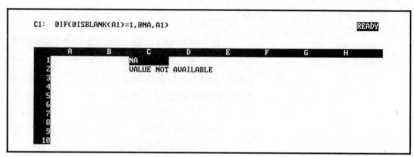

Figure 10.5: Example using @NA and @ISNA with @IF and @ISBLANK

STRING FUNCTIONS

These functions return strings and use strings to make calculations. Among the uses of string functions is to change from upper- to lowercase (and vice versa) and to insert and replace portions of a string. These functions are often used when working with mailing labels. Table 10.5 lists Enable's string functions.

CONVERTING BETWEEN LOWERCASE AND UPPERCASE

@LC(*string*) and @UC(*string*) convert text to and from lowercase letters. Normally, the argument of each function will be a cell reference. In the example

@LC(B5)

where cell B5 contains "LABEL," this function returns "label."

CONVERTING LABELS TO PROPER-NAME FORMAT

@PROPER(*string*) takes the specified string and converts it to proper-name format. This is a lowercase label with an initial capital letter. All words separated by spaces receive initial capital letters. In the example

@PROPER(B5)

Table 10.5: String Functions and Their Uses

@LC(*string*)	Converts a string to lowercase letters
@LEFT(*string,nexp*)	Returns the left portion of a string; the length returned is specified by *nexp*
@LEN(*string*)	Returns the length of a string
@NUM(*string*)	Converts a string value to a number
@PROPER(*string*)	Converts a string to proper-name format using an initial capital letter
@REPEAT(*string,nexp*)	Repeats a character or string *nexp* number of times
@REPLACE(*string,nexp, nexp,string*)	Removes number of characters in second *nexp* from first *string* at first *nexp* position, then places second *string* in first *string* at that position
@RIGHT(*string,nexp*)	Returns the right portion of a string; the length returned is specified by *nexp*
nexp number of times @STRING(*nexp*)	Converts *nexp* to a string value
@TRIM(*string*)	Removes extra spaces at the end of a string
@UC(*string*)	Converts a string to uppercase letters

where cell B5 contains the text "JANE DOE," this function returns "Jane Doe."

SPLITTING LABELS

@LEFT(*string,nexp*) and @RIGHT(*string,nexp*) return a specified portion of any label entry beginning from the left or right side of the label. The *string* argument will most likely be a reference to a cell containing a label. The *nexp* argument is the number of characters to return beginning from the left (@LEFT) or right (@RIGHT) edge of the label. In the example

@RIGHT(B5,5)

where cell B5 contains the label "San Diego, CA 92121," this function returns "92121," or five characters from the right of the label.

DETERMINING THE LENGTH OF A LABEL

@LEN(*string*) returns a number that represents the number of characters in the specified label (*string*). Spaces at the beginning of the string are counted; spaces at the end are not. In the example

@LEN(B5)

where cell B5 contains "John Doe," this function returns 8. Note that the space is counted as a character.

CONVERTING NUMBERS TO LABELS AND BACK

@NUM(*string*) and @STRING(*nexp*) are useful for making certain values conform to the rules of other functions. The @NUM function takes a number that has been entered as a label and converts it to a number. The @STRING function takes a number and converts it to a label. The @LEN, @LEFT, and @RIGHT functions, for example, work only with labels; to use these functions on numbers, you must first convert the number to a string. In the example

@STRING(B5)

where cell B5 contains the number 4392, this returns 4392 as a label entry.

REMOVING UNWANTED SPACES

The function @TRIM(*string*) removes unwanted spaces at the ends of labels. This is useful when you are using the @LEN, @LEFT, and @RIGHT functions to manipulate labels. This example

@TRIM("*Example* ")

returns "Example." Of course, the argument can be any string, string expression, or reference to a cell containing a string.

REPLACING AND INSERTING PORTIONS OF A STRING

@REPLACE(*string,nexp,nexp,string*) replaces a portion of a specified string with another string. It can also be used to insert one string into the middle of another. The first *string* represents the label upon which the function will act. The second *string* is the label to be inserted into the first *string*. The first *nexp* represents the location (from the left) of the insert point. The second *nexp* represents the number of characters (if any) of the first string that will be replaced by the second. If this number is 0, the second string will be inserted without replacing anything. In the example

@REPLACE(B5,11,10,"CA")

where cell B5 contains "San Diego, California 92121," this function returns "San Diego, CA 92121". (Count eleven characters from the left, then replace the next ten characters with "CA.") This function can be used to personalize a spreadsheet for others. In the example

@REPLACE(B5,10,0,A1&" ")

where cell B5 contains "I'm sorry that's the wrong answer!" and cell A1 contains the spreadsheet user's name (say, John), this returns "I'm sorry John that's the wrong answer." Notice that the expression A1&" " adds a space to the end of the name entered into cell A1. This is so the name does not run into the word "that's."

REPEATING AN ENTRY

@REPEAT(*string,nexp*) repeats the specified label (*string*) a specified number of times (*nexp*). This is useful for creating borders and other graphic effects. The example

@REPEAT(" = ",250)

creates a double line across the spreadsheet. Figure 10.6 shows some examples of the types of borders you could use with this function.

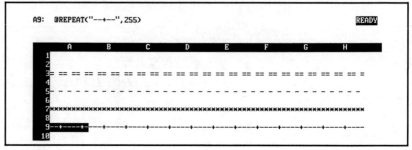

Figure 10.6: Creating borders with @REPEAT

DATE AND TIME FUNCTIONS

These functions calculate dates and times. You can convert dates and text (and vice versa), find the day of the week for any date, get the current date and time, and more. See Table 10.6 for a list of the date and time functions in Enable.

Table 10.6: Date and Time Functions

@ADDM(*nexp,nexp*)	Adds a month to any valid date
@DATE(*nexp*)	Converts serial date into a text string
@DATE(*year,month,day*)	Creates a serial date from three individual entries
@DAY(*date*)	Returns the day portion from a serial date
@END_MONTH(*date*)	Returns the value of the last day of the specified month
@HOUR(*time*)	Returns the hour portion of a time, and changes number of seconds to hours
@MINUTE(*time*)	Returns the minute portion from a serial time
@MONTH(*date*)	Returns the month portion of a date
@NOW	Returns the current time as seconds

Table 10.6: Date and Time Functions (continued)

@SECOND(*time*)	Returns the second portion from a serial time
@TIME(*hh,mm,ss*)	Creates a serial time value from three separate entries
@TIME(*nexp*)	Converts a serial time value into a text string
@TODAY	Returns the current serial date
@WEEKDAY$(*date*)	Returns the day from the week of any given serial date
@YEAR(*date*)	Returns the year portion from a serial date

ADDING MONTHS TO A DATE

Basic information about entering dates and Enable's use of date serial numbers is found in Chapter 7.

Using @ADDM(*nexp,nexp*) you can add a month to any given date. Enable will change the value of the date to include the extra month. This results in a particular number of days being added to the original date. The number of days depends on the month of the original date. Since Enable contains a perpetual calendar, it knows how many days are in each month of the year. In the example

@ADDM(B5,1)

where cell B5 contains the valid date formatted as January 5, 1991, this produces February 5, 1991.

CONVERTING DATES

"Valid date" here means a date serial number formatted to appear as a normal date.

@DATE(*year,month,day*) or @DATE(*nexp*) can be used to convert dates to text and back. The first syntax uses three numeric expressions representing the year, month, and day of a date. These three numbers will be converted to a date that Enable recognizes as a date serial number (that is, a valid date). The second syntax uses a date serial number and converts it to a text string equivalent of that date. This is useful for using the date in functions that require text as their arguments. The example

@DATE(91,5,30)

returns the date "33387," which can be formatted to 5/30/91. In the example

@DATE(B5)

if cell B5 contains the valid date 5/30/91, this function returns the text string "91/5/30." A variation of this function will produce a different date format as a text string:

@DATE$(B5)

where B5 contains the valid date 5/30/91, this function returns the text string "May 30, 1991."

BREAKING UP A DATE

@DAY(*date*) or @MONTH(*date*) or @YEAR(*date*) break up a date into its respective portions. This can be useful for returning only the year in a date entry—or only the month. The *date* argument must be a valid date serial number. In the examples

@DAY(B5)
@MONTH(B5)
@YEAR(B5)

where cell B5 contains the valid date 5/30/91, these functions return 5, 30, and 91 respectively.

These functions can be used with the @STRING function to produce a text string. Consider this example:

+ "This took place in the year 19" & @STRING(@YEAR(B5))

where B5 contains the date 5/30/91, this returns the text "This took place in the year 1991." The @STRING function converts the result of the @YEAR function to a text string. This text string is then concatenated with the rest of the sentence. You also can add a dollar sign to the @YEAR function so that it returns the four-digit year as a text string. This would read

+ "This took place in the year " & @STRING(@YEAR$(B5))

Likewise, you can add a dollar sign to the @MONTH function so it returns the month name instead of the month value.

FINDING THE LAST DAY OF A MONTH

Using @END_MONTH(*date*) with a reference to any valid date allows you to find the last day of a given month. The last day is calculated for the month and year of the referenced date. (The year is required because leap years change the number of days in the month of February.) In the example

@END_MONTH(B5)

where B5 contains 5/30/91, this returns the value 33388, which can be formatted to the date 5/31/91.

This function is also useful for calculating how many days remain in a month. This is done by subtracting the original date from the result of this function:

+ END_MONTH(B5) − B5

Where B5 contains 5/30/91, this returns 1.

DAY OF THE WEEK

@WEEKDAY$(*date*) returns the day of the week of any given date. In the example

@WEEKDAY$(B5)

where B5 contains the valid date 5/30/91, this returns "Thursday."

CURRENT DATE AND TIME

@TODAY and @NOW are used to get the current date and time from the internal clock in your PC. The functions return the date and time serial numbers, which then have to be formatted with an appropriate date and time format. The time serial number is the number of seconds that have passed since midnight.

BREAKING UP A TIME

@MINUTE(*time*) or @HOUR(*time*) or @SECOND(*time*) return the minute, hour, and second portion of a valid time. In the example

@MINUTE(B5)

where B5 contains the valid time 12:05:00 PM, this returns 5.

CONVERTING TIMES

With @TIME(*hh,mm,ss*) and @TIME(*time*) you can convert valid time entries to text and back again. This can be necessary when using times with text functions. The example

@TIME(11,45,05)

takes the three numbers and forms a valid time entry. The result is the time serial number 42305, which can be formatted to appear as "11:45:05 A."

In this example

@TIME(B5)

if B5 contains the valid time 42305 (or 11:45:05), this returns the text string "11:45:05." In another example, you could then turn a text string back into a valid time with the function @TIME(B6), where B6 contains the text string "11:45:05."

LOOKUP FUNCTIONS

Enable has two lookup functions that search for a given value in a column or row of values and return a value from the table. Table 10.7 lists these lookup functions (as well as some other special Enable functions that are discussed in the next section).

Table 10.7: Lookup and Other Special Functions and Their Uses

Lookup Functions	
@CHOOSE(*nexp,list*)	Chooses the *nexp* value from the *list*
@HLOOKUP(*nexp, table range,offset row*)	Searches the horizontal table range for the specified number and returns the value in the offset column
@VLOOKUP(*nexp, table range,offset column*)	Searches the vertical table range for the specified number and returns the value in the offset column
Special Functions	
@ALPHA(*string*)	Returns 1 if the string contains no numerals and 0 otherwise
@CURCOL	Returns the column position of a pointer as a numeric value
@CURPOS	Returns the address of the pointer as a text string
@CURROW	Returns the row position of the pointer as a numeric value
@NUMERIC(*string*)	Returns 1 if the string contains only numbers and 0 if the string contains any letters

TABLE LOOKUPS

@VLOOKUP(*nexp, table range, offset column*) or @HLOOKUP(*nexp, table range, offset column*) search for a given value (the *nexp* variable) in a column or row of values (the first column or row in the *table range*) and return a corresponding value from the table (the value in *offset column*).

With @VLOOKUP, the *nexp* value can be any number or numeric expression. The *table range* should be the range containing the entire table. The *offset column* is any value from 0 to the number of columns in the table, where 0 is the first column. This function always looks up the specified value in the first column of the table. The values in this column should be in ascending numerical order. If the lookup value (that is, *nexp*) cannot be found in this column, the function uses the closest value smaller than the lookup value. Hence, if the lookup value is larger than all the values in the column, Enable matches it with the last cell in the column; if the lookup value is smaller than all the values of the table, Enable returns an error.

For example, the table in Figure 10.7 is in the range A5..D12. The first column of the table is the lookup column. Cell B14 contains the value that you want to find in the table. Cells B15, B16, and B17 contain the corresponding value from each of the three columns in the table. These three cells use these formulas:

B15: @VLOOKUP(B14,A5..D12,1)
B16: @VLOOKUP(B14,A5..D12,2)
B17: @VLOOKUP(B14,A5..D12,3)

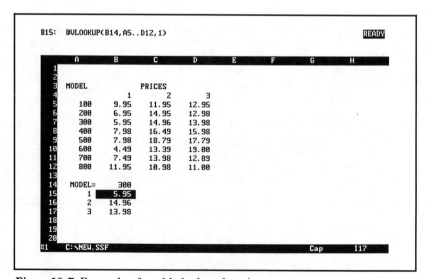

Figure 10.7: Example of a table lookup function

Notice that the lookup column is sorted in ascending order; this is essential for the lookup function to work properly. Enter any value into cell B14 and watch the lookup functions work. Note that you can use text in any column of the table except the lookup column.

The @HLOOKUP function is identical to @VLOOKUP except that it looks across the first row of a table and returns a value corresponding to the offset number of rows. The table must be row oriented rather than column oriented.

CHOOSING VALUES FROM A LIST

The @CHOOSE(*nexp,list*) function chooses a value from a list based on an input value. This is similar to the functions @VLOOKUP and @HLOOKUP, but the *nexp* value must be a number from 0 to the number of items in the list. If the value is 0, the first item is returned; if the value is 1, the second item is returned; and so on. This is sometimes more useful than the @LOOKUP functions since it does not require a table. But it can be used only in cases where the lookup value is sequential, beginning with 0 (for example, 0,1,2,3,4). In the example

@CHOOSE(B5,*"red","green","yellow"*)

where B5 is 0, this returns "red." Where B5 has a value of 2, this returns "yellow."

SPECIAL FUNCTIONS

This section describes some useful special functions. Among their uses is finding the location of the cell pointer and determining whether a cell contains numbers or text. See Table 10.7 for a list of these special functions.

POSITION OF THE CELL POINTER

@CURPOS, @CURCOL, and @CURROW determine the position of the cell pointer. The first, @CURPOS, returns the current cell address as a text string. @CURCOL returns the column position as a value. @CURROW returns the row position as a value. For example, if the pointer is in cell C5, @CURPOS returns the text string "C5," @CURCOL returns 3, and @CURROW returns 5.

NUMERIC OR ALPHABETIC TEXT

@ALPHA(*string*) or @NUMERIC(*string*) tests whether or not a text string contains numbers. @ALPHA returns a value of 1 if *string* is alphabetic only and 0 if *string* contains numbers. @NUMERIC returns 1 if *string* contains only numbers, 0 if *string* contains any alphabetic characters, and ERROR if the reference is not a text string. The table below shows you how @ALPHA is used with the example @ALPHA(B5):

WHERE B5 CONTAINS	THIS RETURNS
127	ERR
"12345"	0
"January"	1
"January 5"	0

This is how the example @NUMERIC(B5) is used:

WHERE B5 CONTAINS	THIS RETURNS
127	ERR
"12345"	1
"January"	0
"January 5"	0

Creating Graphs from Spreadsheet Data

THIS CHAPTER SHOWS YOU HOW TO USE ENABLE'S graphing commands and options in order to present spreadsheet data graphically. Using graphs in presentations helps your audience understand the point you are making with data. Graphs emphasize particular aspects of data and make your conclusions more memorable. It's a fact that information presented graphically is remembered longer than information presented numerically.

The chapter begins with an overview of the graphing process in a step-by-step guide. You can experiment with graphs after reading this brief overview, or you can continue with some of the details about creating basic graphs in Enable. You'll also learn the parts of a graph and how to manipulate these parts with Enable's commands, as well as several ways to customize a graph.

AN OVERVIEW OF GRAPHING

Graphing is pretty simple. You might find that this general overview is enough to get you started. If you need more detail, you can complete the exercise in the section "Creating a Bar Graph," in which you build a graph from the Expenses spreadsheet.

BASIC GRAPH BUILDING

Following are the steps to building a basic bar graph. Begin by specifying the group of data in the spreadsheet that you want to graph.

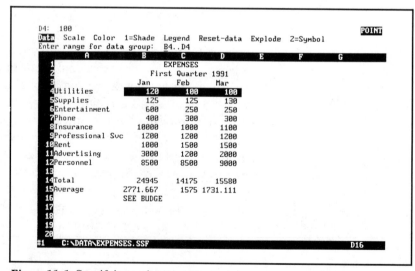

In this chapter, we use the slash (/) key in place of the F10 key to call up the Top Line menu. Either command is acceptable.

1. Choose the command /G S ◂──┘ O (F10, Graph, Select, Default, Options) to get to the Graph Options menu.

2. Select *Data Group 1* and press ◂──┘.

3. Select *Data* and press ◂──┘.

4. Enter the range of cells containing the values for the first item in the graph. If more than one cell is chosen, each cell represents a category of items. Do not include labels as part of this range (see the example in Figure 11.1). You can use the keyboard to specify the range if desired. Press ◂──┘ when finished.

```
D4:   100                                                              POINT
Data  Scale  Color  1=Shade  Legend  Reset-data  Explode  2=Symbol
Enter range for data group:  B4..D4
          A            B         C        D        E       F      G
 1                        EXPENSES
 2                     First Quarter 1991
 3                     Jan       Feb      Mar
 4Utilities            120       100      100
 5Supplies             125       125      130
 6Entertainment        600       250      250
 7Phone                400       300      300
 8Insurance          10000      1000     1100
 9Professional Svc    1200      1200     1200
10Rent                1000      1500     1500
11Advertising         3000      1200     2000
12Personnel           8500      8500     9000
13
14Total              24945     14175    15580
15Average          2771.667     1575 1731.111
16                  SEE BUDGE
17
18
19
20
#1    C:\DATA\EXPENSES.SSF                                              D16
```

Figure 11.1: Specifying a data group

Now enter the text that will be the graph legend.

5. Select the *Legend* option.

6. Enter the legend text that describes the data series you just specified. This will often correspond to labels on the spreadsheet (see Figure 11.2). Press ⏎ after typing the text.

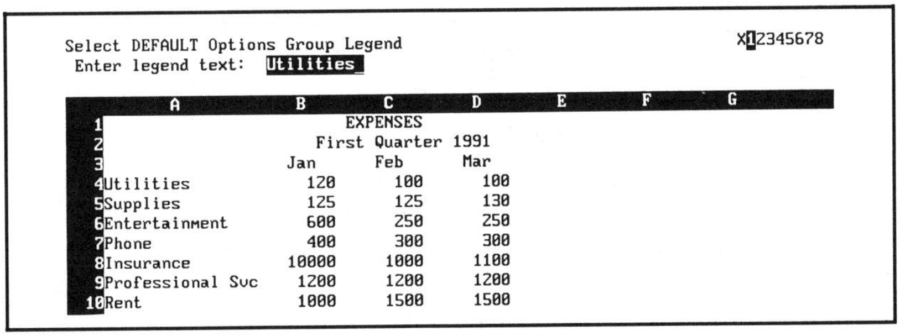

```
Select DEFAULT Options Group Legend                              X02345678
Enter legend text: Utilities

          A          B        C         D        E       F       G
    1                      EXPENSES
    2                First Quarter 1991
    3                 Jan       Feb       Mar
    4 Utilities       120       100       100
    5 Supplies        125       125       130
    6 Entertainment   600       250       250
    7 Phone           400       300       300
    8 Insurance     10000      1000      1100
    9 Professional Svc 1200     1200      1200
   10 Rent           1000      1500      1500
```

Figure 11.2: Entering legend text for a data group

7. Press Esc.

8. Repeat steps 2 through 6 for each data group in the graph. Enable will give each data group a different pattern in the graph.

Now enter the title for the graph.

9. Select the *Global* option.

10. Select the *Headings* option.

11. Select the *Main* option.

12. Enter the graph title and press ⏎.

13. Repeat the previous two steps for any other titles desired. These include the Headings options *Main Subtitle*, *X-Axis Title*, *Y-Axis Title*, *X-Axis Subtitle*, *Y-Axis Subtitle*, and *Legend Title*.

The x-axis is the horizontal axis; the y-axis is vertical.

Your graph is built. Now display it.

14. Press Esc three times, then select the *Display* command to display the graph.

You can now customize the graph if desired. This includes changing the colors and patterns used for the bars, changing the axis labels, adding grid lines, and changing the graph type.

NAMING GRAPHS

Enable lets you create an almost unlimited number of graphs per spreadsheet. You can, for example, graph different portions of a spreadsheet, or you can graph the same data in several different ways.

Each graph has a unique name; you enter the name before creating the graph. This is done by selecting the following commands—F10, Graph, Create—then entering the graph name and pressing ←⏎.

After you enter the name, the Graph menu appears, offering the following options: *Options*, *Display*, *Print*, *Plot*, and *Perspective*. This is the basic starting point for all graph commands whether you are creating a new graph or changing an existing one.

As you build the graph using these Graph options (described throughout this chapter), Enable stores the graphs under the name you entered in the previous steps. You can then return to any named graph using the following procedure:

- Return to the Ready mode by pressing Esc several times.
- Press F10.
- Press **G** for *Graph*.
- Press **S** for *Select*.
- Choose the name of the graph from the list provided.

You can change an existing graph by selecting the appropriate name. When you save the Enable spreadsheet, all named graphs are saved along with it. You can view any of the named graphs using the steps listed above.

This chapter will show the above commands as /G [*name*]. In this command, [*name*] represents the steps required to create and name the graph or to select an existing name. In short, all graphing commands described in this chapter require that you first create and name a new graph or select an existing graph: When you see the command /G [*name*], the [*name*] part of the command means "create and name a graph" or "select a name."

ENABLE'S DEFAULT GRAPH

Save time by setting up standard options for your new graphs, then customizing the graphs from there. If you do not change the default, it will contain the options established in the corresponding profile.

Keep in mind that Enable provides one graph name for you: all spreadsheets contain a graph named Default. This graph is like all other named graphs, except that it also acts as the default for all new graphs. In other words, when you create a new graph, Enable starts the graph with the definitions contained in the current Default graph. If you change the Default graph, all new graphs will change accordingly. The purpose of the Default graph, then, is to provide a shortcut to creating new graphs.

PARTS OF A GRAPH

Before you begin creating graphs, take a look at the graph shown in Figure 11.3. This figure shows the various parts of a graph. This

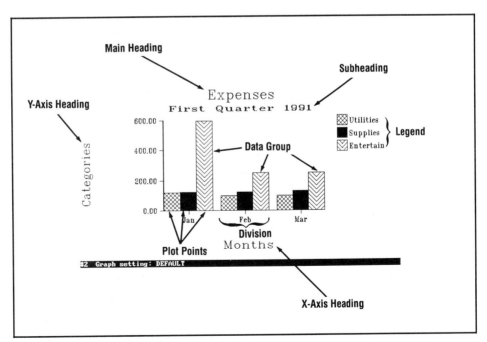

Figure 11.3: Parts of a graph

section discusses each of these graph elements and shows you how you can use them to customize graphs in Enable.

HEADINGS

Enable allows you to place three headings on a graph: the *main title*, the *y-axis title*, and the *x-axis title*. Each heading can have up to two lines (a main and a subheading), giving you a total of six headings. The commands used to create these titles are F10, Graph, [*name*], Options, Global, Headings (/G [*name*] O G H). You then can choose the type of heading or the legend:

OPTION	DESCRIPTION OF HEADING
Main	Text for the main title
Main-sub	Text for the main subtitle
X-Axis	Text for the x-axis title
X-Axis-sub	Text for the x-axis subtitle
Y-Axis	Text for the y-axis title
Y-Axis-sub	Text for the y-axis subtitle
Legend	Text for the legend's title

Enable lets you access a number of fonts for these titles. These fonts come with the Enable system and can be selected using the commands /G [*name*] O G F, then selecting one of the following options:

OPTION	DESCRIPTION OF FONT
Main Title	Sets the font for the main title
XY-Axis Titles	Sets the font for the x- and y-axis titles together. (You cannot use a different font for each axis title.)
Secondary Titles	Sets the font for all subtitles
Labels-and-Legends	Sets the font for nontitle labels. This includes the text used for the x-axis labels, y-axis scale labels, and the legend items.

PLOT POINTS, DATA GROUPS, AND DIVISIONS

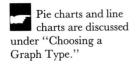 Pie charts and line charts are discussed under "Choosing a Graph Type."

Each value that you chart is called a *plot point*. Each bar on a bar chart, each wedge of a pie chart, and each marker point on a line chart represents a different value in the spreadsheet, and becomes a plot point on the graph. Plot points are often grouped together into two sets, called *divisions* and *data groups*. Think of a data group as a row in a spreadsheet and a division as a column. The more rows you include in a graph, the more data groups you will have. These data groups represent different items being charted. For example, apples and oranges would represent two data groups (perhaps apples would be in row 1 and oranges in row 2). Each different data group gets a different shade for its bar or pie wedge.

If you have two rows of data (say, apples and oranges) but only one column of values for each, the chart will contain only one bar for each data group. However, if you have two columns of data for each group, the graph will display two bars for apples and two bars for oranges. Hence, the graph has a total of four plot points—two using one pattern (representing apples) and two using another (representing oranges). Each added column of data represents a new division. Each division uses the same bar patterns as every other division, but represents a new column of values. Of course, all the graphs have at least one division.

For example, suppose you graph the sales of oranges over four quarters. Each quarter will contain a bar with the same pattern as the other bars. This is because the plot points come from a common data group: oranges. The quarters are the divisions. Figure 11.4 shows an example.

Now suppose you add a second data group. This data group must contain four plot points (that is, four quarters) to match the other group. The result might look like Figure 11.5.

If you graph only one column, or division, it can be confusing whether the bars represent four data groups over one division or one data group over four divisions. Just remember that each data group corresponds to a legend item. Therefore, if you want four legend items, treat the data as four different groups of one division each.

Enable allows up to eight data groups in a single graph (pie charts allow only one data group). (You can have more than eight data groups when you use Perspective—see Chapter 12.) Unless you

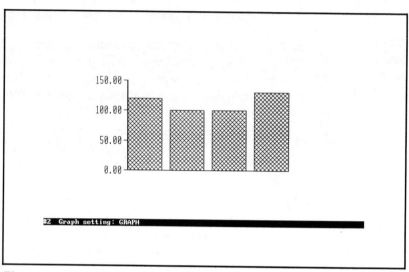

Figure 11.4: A graph with four divisions and one data group (containing four plot points)

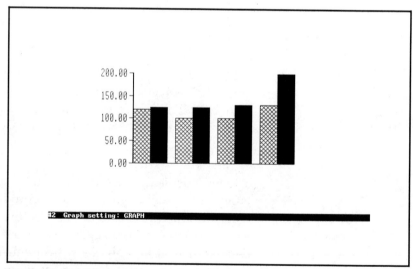

Figure 11.5: Adding a data group to the graph

See "Changing the Patterns of Data Groups" for more information on customizing graph patterns.

specify otherwise, Enable automatically assigns patterns and colors to these groups. All you have to do is tell Enable which data (cells) belongs in each group. This is done with the command /G [*name*] O [*n*] D (F10, Graph, [*name*], Options, Data Group [*n*], Data) where *n* represents the desired data group. After entering this command, specify the range containing the plot points for the data group. Repeat this command as many times as you have data groups, changing the value of *n* each time.

Remember that each data group will most probably contain the same number of cells. The number of cells in each group represents the number of divisions. And each group should have the same number of divisions.

X-AXIS

See "Changing the X-Axis" for more information about label designations.

The x-axis usually displays the various divisions in a graph. This is done by including titles below each division. The x-axis titles are set using the command /G [*name*] O G A 1 (F10, Graph, [*name*], Options, Axes, X-axis-data). After selecting this command, you can highlight the spreadsheet range that contains the desired division labels. Often, this will be column headings above the charted values.

XY charts use the x-axis differently: These charts consider the x-axis to be another value axis, and Enable takes care of choosing the values for the chart. For XY charts, the X-axis-data command does not choose labels for the value axis, but chooses additional plot points. See "XY Graphs" later in this chapter for more details.

Y-AXIS

The y-axis (the vertical axis) represents the value of the plot points in the graph. Enable automatically chooses the values used in the y-axis, based on the values of the plot points. However, you can customize the y-axis in two ways: you can change the scale of the values on the axis and you can change the format of those values (that is, the appearance of the numbers). See "Changing the Y-Axis" later in this chapter.

GRID

You can add a grid behind the chart's plot points if desired. A grid can enhance the appearance of the chart and emphasize the difference between bars or lines. Grid lines can be displayed both vertically and horizontally. Vertical grid lines show the different divisions in a graph, whereas horizontal grid lines show the values on the y-axis. The command used to add grid lines to a graph is /G [*name*] O G G (F10, Graph, [*name*], Options, Global, Grid). This command produces the options *Horizontal*, *Vertical*, and *Both*, which can be used to add grid lines in any combination you like, and *Neither*, which turns off grid lines.

LEGEND

The graph legend contains text that represents each data group in the graph. You may enter the legend label for each data group individually or leave the legend text empty. When you enter a legend label for a data group, its pattern and label appear in the legend. If you do not specify a legend label for any data groups, the graph will contain no legend. To specify a legend label, enter the command /G [*name*] O [*n*] L (F10, Graph, [*name*], Options, Data Group [*n*], Legend) where *n* is the number of the data group. Next, enter the legend text and press ←┘.

CREATING A BAR GRAPH

Following is a step-by-step exercise to build a bar graph from the Expenses spreadsheet data. Begin by bringing the Expenses worksheet into view. Now, use the following steps to create the graph. First you'll access the Graph Options menu:

1. Press F10, G, S (Graph, Select).

2. Select *Default* and press ←┘.

3. Press **O** for *Options*.

Now you'll select the first data group:

    4. Press **1** to begin data group 1.

    5. Press **D** for *Data*. Enter the range **B4..D4** and press ←.

Next, enter the legend for this data group:

    6. Select **L** for *Legend*:

    7. Enter **Utilities**, press ←, then press Esc.

Select the second data group and enter the legend:

    8. Press **2** for data group 2.

    9. Press **D** for *Data*. Enter the range **B5..D5** and press ←.

    10. Select **L** for *Legend*.

    11. Type **Supplies**, press ←, then press Esc.

Now enter the graph title:

    12. Press G, H, M (Global, Headings, Main).

    13. Type **Expenses Chart**, press ←, then press Esc.

Now select the titles for the x-axis:

    14. Press **A** for *Axis*.

    15. Select the option *X-Axis-Data*. Enter the range **A4..A6**, press ←, then press Esc three times to exit the Graph menu.

Your graph is completed. Now display it:

    16. Press **D** for *Display*. The chart should look like the one in Figure 11.6.

You can display both the graph and its worksheet at the same time by pressing Alt-F7 while the graph is in view. Press Alt-F7 again to view only the graph.

Enable provides several commands and options for changing graphs to your liking. Often, the default options will be sufficient for your needs. But if not, try some of the customization features

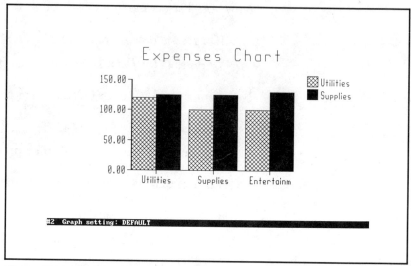

Figure 11.6: The Expenses bar graph

described in the next sections. For example, you can change a bar graph into another type of graph, change the layout, select different patterns, and customize the x- and y-axes.

CHOOSING A GRAPH TYPE

Bar graphs are useful for many business graphing needs. However, you'll undoubtedly find the need to use Enable's other graph types: 3-D, Stacked, Line, Pie, XY, and High-Low-Close. Within some of these types are more selections. First, create a graph using the default options—this will produce a standard bar graph. Now you can change the type using the command /G [*name*] O G T (F10, Graph, [*name*], Options, Global, Type).

3D AND STACKED BAR GRAPHS

Enable offers four types of bar graphs: 3-D-Standard, 2-D-Standard, 3-D-Stacked, and 2-D-Stacked. The stacked graphs combine all the data groups in each division as a single bar. The height of the bar represents the total value of the data groups in that division; each portion of the bar represents each data group's percentage of the total. Figure 11.7 shows an example of a stacked bar graph.

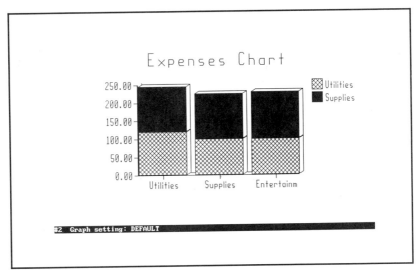

Figure 11.7: A stacked bar graph

Stacked bar graphs are useful for comparing the totals of several data groups, but not for comparing the data groups to one another. Consider using a stacked bar graph instead of several pie charts.

Enable's 3-D bar graphs are identical to the standard bar graphs, but they display the bars three-dimensionally. That is, each bar has a small amount of depth added. This is not quite the same as a true 3-D graph; a true 3-D graph is plotted differently than a 2-D graph. Enable includes true 3-D graphing in the Perspective program, which is discussed in Chapter 12.

PIE GRAPHS

When you create a pie chart, remember that each wedge of the pie comes from one cell of the chosen data groups. In other words, select as many data groups as you want wedges in the pie. Each data group should have only one cell in it, since pie charts show only one division of data. When you choose the Pie type for the graph, Enable presents the three options: *Type*, *Format*, and *Shade*.

The *Type* option offers the two pie chart types: standard and exploded. An exploded pie chart has one or more wedges set apart from the rest. But merely selecting this option does not explode a pie

wedge. After selecting the Exploded format, use the following procedure to select the desired wedges to explode:

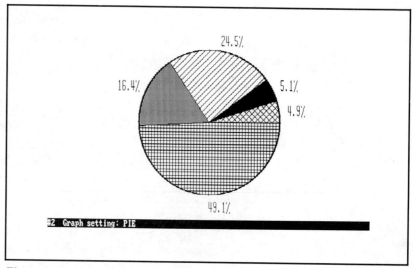

Repeat these steps
for any other wedge
you want to explode.

- Press Esc three times to return to the Options menu. The
  three options *Global, Data Group 1 2 3 4 5 6 7 8*, and *Device*
  appear.

- Select the data group (that is, pie wedge) that you want to
  explode from the rest by typing its number.

- Select *Explode*.

- Select Yes to explode the wedge or No to return an exploded
  wedge to normal.

- Press Esc.

Use the /G [*name*] O G T P F (F10, Graph, [*name*], Options,
Global, Type, Pie, Format) option to display or remove data labels
and legend text from the pie. The Data-Labels command displays
the value of each pie wedge as a percentage of the whole. This
command also displays the name of each wedge. These wedge
names come from the range you specify with the command /G [*name*]
O G A 1 (F10, Graph, [*name*], Options, Global, Axis, X-Axis-Data).
Figure 11.8 shows an example.

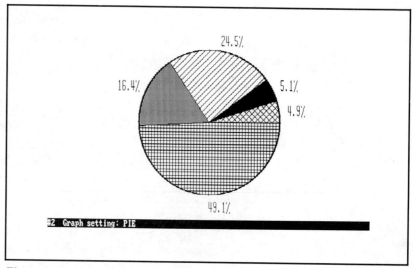

Figure 11.8: Displaying the data labels with the pie chart

The Legends command displays the pie chart along with the legend information that you entered for each data series. You cannot have both data labels and a legend active at the same time. For information about entering this legend data, see "Legend" earlier in this chapter. Figure 11.9 shows an example of a pie chart with the legend data displayed.

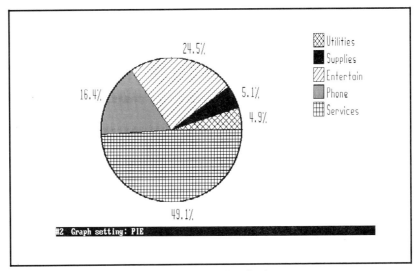

Figure 11.9: Displaying the legend with the pie chart

Use the /G [*name*] O G T P S (F10, Graph, [*name*], Options, Global, Type, Pie, Shade) command to control the shades used for the pie wedges. You can choose the *Enable* option to let Enable control the shades or the *User* option to control them yourself. If you choose the *User* option, you can then choose shades using the command /G [*name*] O [*n*] 1 [*m*] (F10, Global, [*name*], Options, Data Group [*n*], Shade) where *m* is the shade value 1 through 8. For more details about changing shades, see "Changing the Patterns of Data Groups" later in this chapter.

LINE GRAPHS

Enable's line charts display data points with lines connecting them. Actually, you can display a line chart in one of three ways. You can remove the lines and use symbols to represent the data points.

You can display lines without these symbols. And you can display both lines and symbols. To select one of these options, use the command /G [*name*] O G X (F10, Graph, [*name*], Options, Global, XYL-format). Then select from the options *Lines*, *Symbols*, or *Both*. Press Esc repeatedly to move back to the Display menu.

If you display symbols in the line chart (by selecting either *Symbols* or *Both* in the previous command), Enable chooses a unique symbol for each data group. However, you can select your own symbol if desired. Choose your own symbol using the following steps:

- Select /G [*name*] O [*n*] 2, where *n* is the desired data group number and 2 represents the command 2 = Symbol.

- Select *Keyboard* to choose a keyboard character for the symbol or *Special* to choose from Enable's special characters.

- If you selected *Keyboard* in the previous step, enter the keyboard character desired for the symbol, then press ◄┘. If you selected *Special*, choose one of the special characters presented and press ◄┘. You can use a special symbol for one data group and a keyboard character for another if desired.

XY GRAPHS

XY graphs plot data points in a grid. In an XY graph, the horizontal axis no longer contains division labels; it acts as another value axis for horizontal plotting of the points. Hence, the graph plots two values for each item: a vertical and a horizontal value. The vertical plot point comes from the data group range you select with the command /G [*name*] O 1, where 1 is data group 1. The horizontal plot point comes from the range entered for the x-axis values. This is done with the command /G [*name*] O G A 1 (F10, Graph, [*name*], Options, Global, Axes, X-axis-data). Enter a range consisting of the same number of cells specified for the data group.

Suppose you have a list of people's height and weight. The height values are in column B and the weight values are in column C. Figure 11.10 shows this spreadsheet.

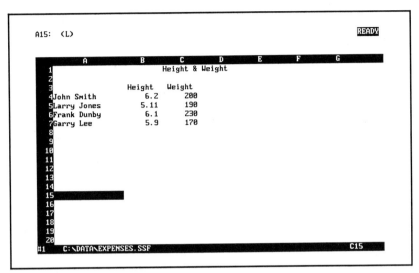

Figure 11.10: Example of XY data

Now suppose you want to create an XY chart that plots each person's height and weight on a grid. Following are the basic steps you would take to plot this data:

- Enter the command F10, Graph, Create, and then name the graph. Press ◄┘ after entering the name.
- Select *Options*.
- Select *Data Group 1*.
- Select *Data* and enter the range **B4..B7**.
- Press Esc once, then select *Global*.
- Select *Axis*.
- Select *X-axis-data* and enter the range **C4..C7**.
- Press Esc and select *Type*.
- Select *XY*.
- Select *Connect*.
- Press Esc two times, then press **D** to display the graph.

As with line graphs, your XY graph can display lines, symbols, or both. Refer to the commands under "Line Graphs" earlier in this section for details.

HIGH-LOW-CLOSE GRAPHS

High-low-close graphs represent three pieces of data for each plotted point. These graphs are most commonly used for tracking stock prices, where a high price, a low price, and a closing price is charted for each day. Just remember that three data groups are required for this type of graph. Unless you have a reason for doing otherwise, use data groups 1, 2, and 3. Make sure that each group contains the same number of cells. The first group represents the high, the second group represents the low, and the third group represents the close. Most commonly, you will have three columns of data representing the three groups. Each row you include in the group represents a new plot point in the chart.

SELECTING A GRAPH LAYOUT

You can change a graph's basic proportions to make it taller or wider than normal. This can be useful for emphasizing certain elements of a graph. For example, you can emphasize the difference in the bars of a bar graph by making the graph taller than normal. If you use a lot of plot points in a line graph, you might want the graph wider than normal.

To change the proportions, use the /G [*name*] O G L command. The four options are

1   Normal setting

2   Taller than normal

3   Wider than normal

4   Taller and wider than normal

Figure 11.11 shows the same graph printed using two different proportions.

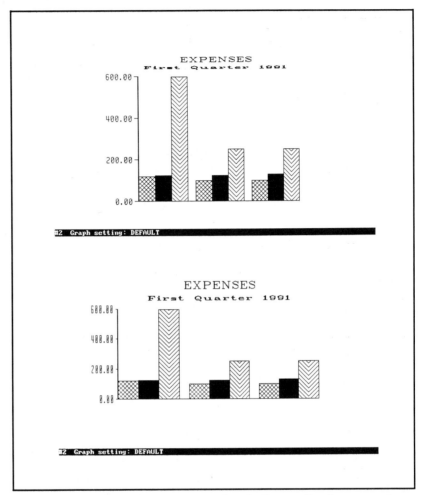

Figure 11.11: The graph on top was printed using a taller-than-normal setting; the one below was printed using a wider-than-normal
setting.

You also can change the size and shape of a graph using the F10 W
commands while the grpah is in view. This command lets you adjust
the graph's window proportions. Press E to expand the window, S to
shrink it, or M to move it. See Chapter 23 for details about changing
window size.

CHANGING THE PATTERNS OF DATA GROUPS

Enable gives you control over the pattern used for each data group in a graph. Selecting the pattern can be done as you define the data group—or you can change the patterns later. The procedure is as follows:

- Select the command /G [*name*] O [*n*], where *n* is the number of the data group whose pattern you want to change.

- Select the command 1 = Shade.

- Enter the number corresponding to the desired shade and press ◄┘. The shades and their numbers are displayed in Figure 11.12.

- Press Esc, then select the next data group you would like to change.

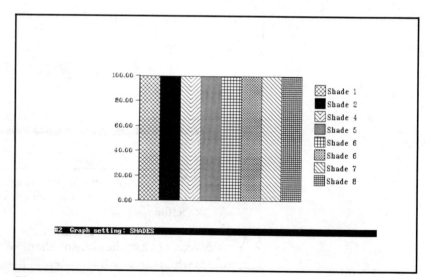

Figure 11.12: Enable's shades and their numbers

CHANGING THE AXES

All graphs except pie graphs have two axes for displaying data. The vertical axis, or y-axis, shows the value of each bar or plot point; the horizontal axis, or x-axis, shows the divisions of data. (XY graphs do not use horizontal axes in the same manner. See "XY Graphs" earlier in this chapter for details.) Following are some changes you can make to these axes.

CHANGING THE Y-AXIS

You can make two changes to the y-axis: You can change its scale (that is, the upper and lower values) and you can change the way the numbers are displayed. To change the scale of the axis values, use the command /G [*name*] O G S (F10, Graph, [*name*], Options, Global, Scale). Select the *User Specified* option to change the scale. Enable then asks you to enter the lowest value, the highest value, and the increment for the scale. These three settings work together to present the axis and the number of "tick marks" along the axis.

For details about these options, see "Number Formats" in Chapter 10.

You can control the way the y-axis values appear by using the command /G [*name*] O G A Y (F10, Graph, [*name*], Options, Global, Axis, Y-Axis-Format). Enable presents nine formatting options from which to choose. Figure 11.13 shows the same graph with two different y-axis formats.

CHANGING THE X-AXIS

You can designate the labels you want used for the divisions along the horizontal axis only. This is done by entering a range of cells in the spreadsheet that contain the desired division labels. Often this will be the top row of a block of data, such as month names or the names of quarters. To set the division labels, use the command /G [*name*] O G A 1 (F10, Graph, [*name*], Options, Global, Axis, X-Axis-Data). Next, enter the range of cells that contains the desired labels. These labels will appear along the x-axis as division labels; hence, the range you specify should have the same number of cells as there are divisions in the graph. (This is the same number of cells that are included in each data range.)

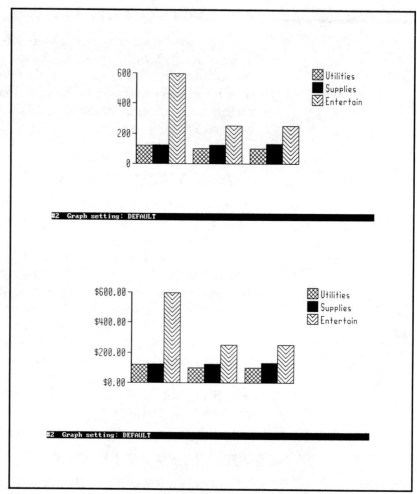

Figure 11.13: A graph showing two Y-axis label formats

If the division labels are numeric, you can format them using the familiar number formats. Do this with the command /G [*name*] O G A X.

PRINTING GRAPHS

Before printing a graph, you can set the density and format for the printout. This is done by selecting the command /G [*name*] O D P (F10, Graph, [*name*], Options, Device, Printer), then choosing the

Density or *Format* option. *Density* changes the quality of print for dot-matrix printers. It includes *Single*, *Double*, *Triple*, and *Quad*. Consult your printer manual for information about these options and other density options pertaining to your printer. The *Format* option includes *Landscape* and *Portrait*. Landscape prints the graph sideways on the paper—a useful format for extra-wide graphs.

Print a graph using the following procedure:

- Press F10.

- Press **G** for *Graph*.

- Press **S** for *Select*.

- Choose the desired graph from the list and press ←┘.

- Press **P** for *Print*.

Using Perspective for Graphs

IN THE PREVIOUS CHAPTER, YOU LEARNED ABOUT Enable's basic graphing features. These features are excellent for producing basic graphs quickly, but Enable includes more powerful graphing capabilities. You can use many more graph types, including several three-dimensional (3-D) graphs. You can also control the perspective of 3-D graphs. In addition to the extra graph types and 3-D options, Enable's extended graphing features let you graph more than eight data groups—you can add groups from 9 to 64.

The key to all this graphing power is a special segment of Enable called Perspective, which is a separate program that you can access from within the Enable spreadsheet module (from the Graph menu, in fact). Perspective has its own style of presenting options and commands—different from Enable's menus and keystroke commands, which is explained in detail in this chapter, along with information about Perspective's most useful commands and options.

While reading this chapter, you might try some of the exercises on your sample graph from the previous chapter. This will help you see the effects of each command.

BEFORE YOU START

Perspective is not an alternative way of creating graphs in Enable; it's an extension of the usual method. Before you can use Perspective to create a graph, you must first create a graph using the standard graphing commands in Enable. You can then enhance this graph with Perspective. Enhancements include selecting from several graph types not offered in Enable, making a graph three-dimensional, using various fonts, and adding data series beyond the Enable limit of eight.

Perspective does not use the same type of menu structure as Enable. There is no Top Line menu, nor are there F9 keystroke commands. Everything is accomplished with the function keys. As you perform different actions in Perspective, some function keys will change their functions. Then, pressing the same key again may perform a different action. At times, pressing a function key will display a special kind of selection screen. Since the function keys change frequently—depending on your actions—Perspective displays the current meaning of each important function key on the screen. This appears as a graphic representation of the keys, as shown in Figure 12.1. The display of horizontal function keys shows keys F1, F2, F3, F4, and F5. The display of vertical function keys shows keys F1, F3, F5, F7, and F9.

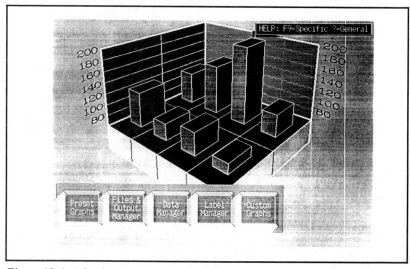

Figure 12.1: A horizontal function key display in Perspective

As you make key selections, the help display will change to reflect the new meanings of the keys. You can return to a previous set of function-key meanings by pressing the F10 key repeatedly.

You might find that this display gets in the way of viewing the graph. You can move the display by pressing the Arrow keys. This moves the key display around the screen. To completely remove the display, press the space bar. Press the space bar again to show the display.

STARTING PERSPECTIVE AND DISPLAYING A GRAPH

Once you have created and saved a graph for the spreadsheet, you are ready to start Perspective. The Perspective command is in the /Graph menu. After creating the graph, you can either return to the spreadsheet by pressing Esc repeatedly, or you can simply move back to the /Graph menu where the *E=Perspective* option appears. If you return to the spreadsheet, reenter the Graph options again by pressing /G S [*name*] to select the desired graph by name. Now follow these basic steps, using the graph you created in Chapter 11:

1. Select the *E=Perspective* option.

2. At this point you could select the *Set* option to set data groups 9 to 64—beyond those allowed by Enable. If you don't want more data groups, skip this option and select the *Display* option to display the graph in Perspective. Select *Display*.

When you display the graph using the *Display* option, Perspective automatically shows the graph as a 3-D bar chart. Besides selecting the chart type, Perspective automatically selects other layout elements, such as the rotation angle. A default graph using these settings is shown in Figure 12.2.

Graph types are discussed in the "Selecting a Graph Type" section in this chapter.

You now can enhance the graph, or change the settings using the *2-D*, *3-D*, or *3-D Stacked* option displayed on the screen. These options correspond to the function keys.

3. Press the function key that corresponds to the desired option.

Keep the graph on the screen—in a moment you'll save it.

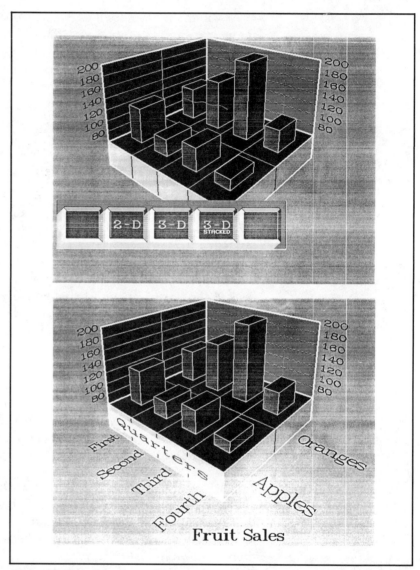

Figure 12.2: Displaying a graph in Perspective using the default options

LOOKING AT A BASIC 3-D GRAPH

A 3-D graph contains all the same information shown in a 2-D graph, but its orientation is different. First, its *category divisions* (the sets of bars along the category axis) appear along one of the 3-D axes (the 3-D category axis) with each division of bars behind the previous division (see Figure 12.3). On a 2-D graph, divisions are beside, not behind, one another.

The *data groups*, which correspond to the legend entries, appear along another axis of the graph, the *depth axis*. This is an entirely new axis that does not appear in 2-D graphs. Also, 3-D graphs contain two *vertical axes*, which are displayed against a backdrop (or *plot area*).

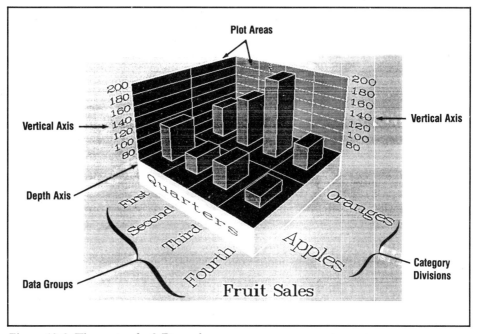

Figure 12.3: The parts of a 3-D graph

You can imagine a 3-D bar chart as a sideways picture of the spreadsheet (as if the sheet were laying flat on the ground). Each cell, instead of containing a number, contains a bar whose height corresponds to its value. The column and row orientation of the chart reflects the same orientation used in the spreadsheet.

SAVING THE GRAPH
AND QUITTING PERSPECTIVE

At any point, you can save your work and return to Enable. Save the graph on your screen:

1. Select the 2-D or 3-D function key. If the function key display does not show the 2-D, 3-D, and 3-D stacked options, press F10 repeatedly until they are displayed.

2. Select *Output* for the Files + Output Manager.

3. Select *Save Files*.

4. Select one of the save formats, as described below.

When you save a graph, Perspective offers several formats for the file. Following is a brief description of each.

Save Picture File .IMG   This option saves the graph as a GEM formatted file with the .IMG extension. These files can be transferred to many GEM programs.

Save Picture File .3PX   This option saves the graph in Perspective's format. This is a good option to use when you are using the file with Perspective only.

Save Picture File .SCR   This option saves the graph as a standard picture file with the .SCR extension. These files are compatible with many paint programs.

Save Look File   This option saves the formatting applied to your graph, but does not save the data, colors, or the graphical image. It is useful for graphing new data with previously set graphing options. Just enter Perspective with new graph data and load the Look file.

Save Color File   This option saves the color of a graph for use in other graphs. To use the color on a different graph, just enter Perspective with new graph data and load the Color file.

5. Enter the desired file name, including the DOS directory path. Do not enter an extension—if you do, Perspective will replace it with its own.

Once you have saved your graph, you can quit Perspective. You have three exit options. Following is a description of each.

Temp. Exit to DOS   Temporarily takes you to DOS so you can perform DOS commands. Perspective will remain in memory, and you can return at any time by entering **EXIT** at the DOS prompt. Your Perspective graph will be unchanged.

Exit Program   Returns you to Enable without saving your file. Remember to save before using this option.

Return to Program   Returns to Perspective.

6. Return to the *2-D*, *3-D*, or *3-D Stacked* option and press F10 to change the keys. Then select one of the options listed.

SELECTING A GRAPH TYPE

Perspective offers many graph types besides those offered by Enable's basic graphing features. To view the different selections for your graph, select one of the options *2-D*, *3-D*, or *3-D Stacked*, then select the Preset Graphs function key. Finally, choose the *Select 2D Graph Type*, *Select 3D Graph Type*, or *Select Stacked 3D Type* option. For example, to see the 3-D graph selections, use the following function keys in this order: *3-D*, *Preset Graphs*, *Select 3D Graph Type*. Perspective will now display the various graph types available. Figure 12.4 shows

Figure 12.4: 3-D graph types (This illustration was reprinted with permission from Three D Graphics and Enable Software, Inc. Perspective is a copyright of Three D Graphics 1987. All rights reserved.)

the 3-D selections. Figure 12.5 shows the 2-D selections. Figure 12.6 shows the 3-D Stacked selections.

The 2-D graph types are all labeled in the selection screen, but the 3-D types are not, and some of them may be unfamiliar. Many of

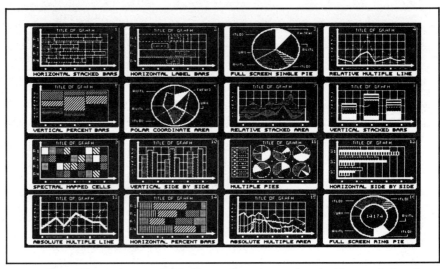

Figure 12.5: 2-D graph types (This illustration was reprinted with permission from Three D Graphics and Enable Software, Inc. Perspective is a copyright of Three D Graphics 1987. All rights reserved.)

the 3-D graph types are variations of bar graphs using different kinds of bars (also called *risers*). Some of the bars appear as pyramids, others as 3-D octagons.

To select from these screens, use the four Arrow keys to highlight the desired graph type (represented in miniature), and press F10. This procedure redraws the graph currently on the screen in the chosen type.

If you want to view your graph in various types to find the one that works best, you might consider using a shortcut to changing the graph type. This shortcut is especially useful for flipping through the different types to try them all. Select the following function keys:

3-D, 2-D, or 3-D Stacked

Preset Graphs

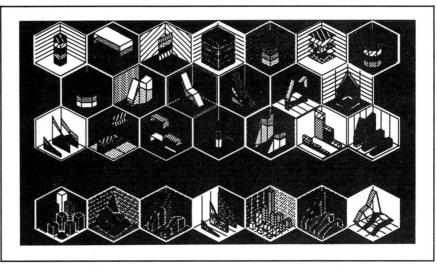

Figure 12.6: 3-D Stacked graph types (This illustration was reprinted with permission from Three D Graphics and Enable Software, Inc. Perspective is a copyright of Three D Graphics 1987. All rights reserved.)

Post Drawing Options

Cycle Graph Types

Now, to change the graph, just press the → and ← keys. The → key cycles forward through the different types, and ← cycles backward.

CHANGING AND CUSTOMIZING THE VIEWING ANGLE

When you use a 3-D graph type, Perspective draws the graph using a default viewing angle, or perspective. You can change this angle using one of Perspective's 16 preset viewing angles or by manually setting the angle.

USING A PRESET VIEWING ANGLE

To use one of the preset viewing angles, follow these steps:

1. Select the function key *3-D* or *3-D Stacked*.

2. Select *Preset Graphs*.

3. Press the *Select Viewing Angle* key. The screen shown in Figure 12.7 appears.

4. Use the four Arrow keys to select one of the angles.

5. Press F10 to redraw the graph with the chosen angle.

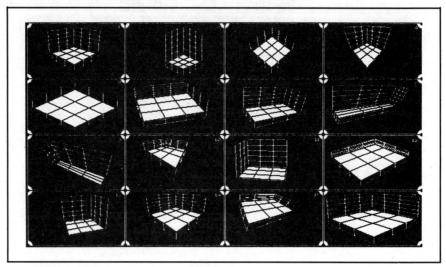

Figure 12.7: Preset viewing angles (This illustration was reprinted with permission from Three D Graphics and Enable Software, Inc. Perspective is a copyright of Three D Graphics 1987. All rights reserved.)

CUSTOMIZING THE VIEWING ANGLE

Besides selecting a viewing angle from the 16 preset angles, you can customize the angle by rotating the graph on three different axes. To use the manual method, follow these steps:

1. Select *3-D* or *3-D Stacked*.

2. Select *Custom Graphs*.

3. Select *Custom Viewing Angles*.

4. Use the five keys presented to change the angle. These are *Hide or Show Graph, Rotate in 3-D, Move in 3-D, Zoom Pan Distort*, and *Box Proportions*. Each of these options is described below.

The wire-frame outline is a simple representation of the real graph. This is used for manipulation to avoid using too much memory.

HIDE OR SHOW GRAPH This command toggles between two pictures of the graph: a wire-frame outline and a full graph. It is often used after each of the other options. Normally, Perspective shows you a wire-frame outline of the graph when you are manipulating its viewing angle; the program operates faster this way. If you want to view the entire graph at any time, however, select the *Hide or Show Graph* option. Select the option again to return to the wire-frame image.

ROTATE IN 3-D This option lets you rotate the graph, as well as the point of view, on three axes. The option has several keys available: *Sets of Axes*, *X-Rotate*, *Y-Rotate*, *Z-Rotate*, and *Stepping Options*.

The *Sets of Axes* option presents two more options: *Screen Axes* changes the point of view; this is like walking around the graph or stepping up on a ladder to view the graph. In other words, the graph does not change—your position does. *Box Axes* changes the rotation angle of the graph box itself; this is like reaching into the screen and flipping the graph by hand. In this case, your position does not change—the graph does.

X-Rotate, *Y-Rotate*, and *Z-Rotate* let you rotate the graph or the point of view (depending on your selection) on one or more axes. Just press the appropriate key for the desired axis, then press the ← and → keys to change directions. Press the space bar to stop rotation. After rotating on an axis, you can rotate on a different axis by pressing the appropriate key, then using the Arrow keys and space bar again. You can change the speed of rotation using the *Stepping Options*.

Stepping Options change the speed of rotation caused by the *X-Rotate*, *Y-Rotate*, and *Z-Rotate* commands. Select *Small*, *Medium*, or *Big* to change the size of the "jump" each time you rotate the graph or viewing angle. If you use the Manual Repeat mode key, the rotation will occur only when you press the Arrow keys. The Auto Repeat mode returns to the default, continuous movement. The Manual Repeat mode is useful for making small, controlled changes to the viewing angle.

When you are finished rotating the graph, press F10 to exit the viewing angle options and redisplay the graph at the new angle. When you exit this screen, Perspective displays three options: *Accept Look*, *Go Back & Edit More*, and *Revert to Old Look*. Use *Accept New Look* to complete your changes or *Revert to Old Look* to throw out the changes. Use *Go Back & Edit More* if you want to continue changing the viewing angle instead of exiting.

MOVE IN 3-D Moving a graph is similar to rotating a graph. In fact, its options are identical to those in the *Rotate in 3-D* option above: *Stepping Options, Sets of Axes, X-Move, Y-Move,* and *Z-Move*. Rather than rotating the graph or viewing angle, the *X-Move, Y-Move,* and *Z-Move* options change the position of the graph on the screen (more accurately, these options move the graph or viewing angle on the imaginary vertical, horizontal, or depth plane). For the effects of the *Stepping Options* and *Sets of Axes* keys, see "Rotate in 3-D."

ZOOM PAN DISTORT This command changes some basic ways of viewing the graph. After selecting *Zoom Pan Distort*, choose one of the five options presented: *Stepping Options, Zoom, Pan-X, Pan-Y,* or *Distort*.

Stepping Options is identical to the *Rotate in 3-D* stepping options, except that here they apply to zooming, panning, or distorting. See "Rotate in 3-D" for more details.

The *Zoom* option is used to move the graph closer or farther away, as if you were using a zoom lens on a camera. You can actually bring the graph into the frame (screen) so that it fills it up. Everything will be enlarged as it gets closer. After pressing the Zoom key, use the ← and → keys to move the image.

Pan-X and *Pan-Y* move the graph left/right and up/down, respectively. This is similar to moving the graph, but panning does not change the proportions or shape of the image. It is simply used to reposition the graph on the 2-D screen. After selecting the Pan-X or Pan-Y key, use the Arrow keys to move the graph.

Distort changes the perspective of the graph as if you were using a fish-eye lens. In Perspective terms, this moves the vertical or horizontal vanishing point closer or farther from the point of view. (See Figure 12.8.) After selecting this option, use the ← and → keys to make changes.

BOX PROPORTIONS The *Box Proportions* option changes the depth-to-width ratio of the graph's base or the depth/width-to-height ratio of the graph's background. Using this option you can make a

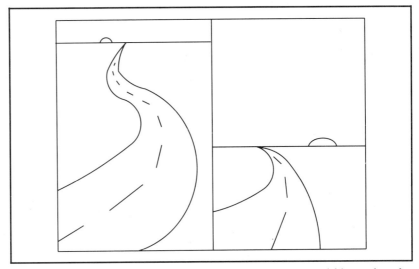

Figure 12.8: The drawing on the left illustrates a distant vanishing point; the one on the right shows a close vanishing point.

graph long and narrow, perfectly square, tall and narrow, and so on. After choosing the Box Proportions key, just select *X-Width* to change the width of the graph, *Y-Height* to change the height of the graph, or *Z-Depth* to change the depth of the graph. Then use the ← and → keys to control the growth or reduction of the chosen proportion.

The *Auto Square Cells* key makes the width and depth of the bars perfectly square. The *Stepping Options* key provides the same stepping options described under "Rotate in 3-D" earlier in this chapter.

CHANGING GRAPH ELEMENTS

Perspective has several options for changing the various graph elements. Using these options, you can change the height of the graph's base, the appearance of grid lines, and the space between the bars (or risers). This section describes how you can control the appearance of each of these elements.

CHANGING THE BASE HEIGHT

Each 3-D graph has a base on which the bars (or risers) are resting. This base displays the horizontal and depth axis titles. Perspective gives you control over the size of this base—you can make it thick or remove it entirely. (A height of 0 removes the base.) To change the base height, follow these steps:

1. Select *3-D* or *3-D Stacked*.

2. Select *Custom Graphs*.

3. Select *Custom Variable Param's*.

4. Select *Adjust Base Height*.

5. Adjust the height by pressing the ← and → keys. Use Ctrl-← and Ctrl-→ for faster results.

6. Press F10 when finished and again to view the new graph.

CHANGING GRID LINES

You can control the appearance of the grid lines on the graph using the *Grid Lines* option. Here are the steps:

1. Select *3-D* or *3-D Stacked*.

2. Select *Custom Graphs*.

3. Select *Custom Variable Param's*.

4. Choose *Select Grid Lines*.

5. Choose the key that corresponds to the desired graph wall. This will be F2, F3, or F4 on the horizontally displayed keys, or F3, F5, or F7 on the vertically displayed keys.

6. Press the key containing the horizontal arrow (F1) to add or remove horizontal grid lines, or press the key containing the vertical arrows (F5 for horizontal function keys or F9 for vertical keys) to add or remove vertical grid lines.

7. Press F10 when finished.

SPACE BETWEEN RISERS

Perspective gives you control over the space between the bars (or risers) in a graph. You can use this spacing in creative ways with other viewing options, such as Box Proportions. The space between cells actually controls the depth and width proportions of the risers—it does not change the proportions of the graph itself, which is done with the Box Proportions option. You can shrink the depth or width of the risers to the point that they appear two-dimensional. Follow these steps:

1. Select the *3-D* or *3-D Stacked* key.

2. Select *Custom Graphs*.

3. Select *Custom Variable Param's*.

4. Select *Adjust X Spacing* to change the width of the risers or *Adjust Z Spacing* to change the depth of the risers.

5. Use the ← and → keys to adjust the proportions.

6. Press F10 when finished and again to view the graph.

LABELS

Controlling the labels and titles on a graph is an important part of customization. Although each graph type has its own prescribed label formats, you might want to change those formats for special purposes. This can be done for all 3-D graphs using the Perspective Label Manager. Following are the basic steps:

1. Select *3-D*, or *3-D Stacked*.

2. Select *Label Manager*.

3. Select the desired label field or area that you want to change by choosing one of the five function keys that correspond to the area. The graph shown in Figure 12.9 illustrates these areas.

These are the function keys and the areas they control (vertical function keys are in parentheses):

F1 (F1)   Controls the titles (numbers) for the left vertical axis.

F2 (F3)   Controls the titles for the data groups. This is set using the legend text entered for the data groups, and often comes from the row headings in the spreadsheet.

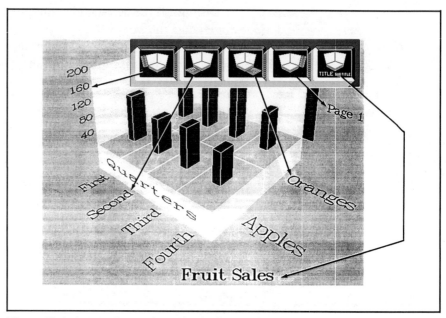

Figure 12.9: Areas of a graph are controlled by five function keys.

F3 (F5)   Controls the titles for the categories. This is set
             using the *X-Axis-Data* option in Enable, and often
             comes from the columns in the spreadsheet.

F4 (F7)   Controls the titles (numbers) for the right
             vertical axis.

F5 (F9)   Controls the title and subtitle text.

4. Choose one of the options listed below to change the selected
   labels:

   • *Size*   Changes the size of the text. When adjusting
     labels, use the → and ← keys to increase and decrease
     the size, then press F10. When adjusting the title or
     subtitle, use ← and → to change the width of the
     titles; use ↑ and ↓ to change the height and width
     together.

   • *Width*   Changes the character width of the selected
     labels. Use the → and ← keys to make the adjustments.

- *Fonts I*   Changes the font of the text. Select from the five different fonts provided. When you select the desired font using the function key, Perspective shows you the selection by changing the first character in the label range. Press F10 if you are satisfied.

- *Fonts II*   Changes the font of the text. Select from the four display fonts provided. These are best used for titles and subtitles. When you select the desired font using the function key, Perspective shows you the selection by changing the first character in the label range. Press F10 if you are satisfied.

- *Options*   Offers four additional font formatting options. *Spacing* controls the space between characters. *Bold X* adds boldness to a character's width; *Bold Y* adds boldness to a character's height. Use both options for extra boldface type. *Slant* slants the font in various ways. For each of these options, use the ← and → keys for control, then press F10 when finished.

Perspective offers many attractive options for graphing Enable's spreadsheet data. Feel free to experiment with the various function key options available. You cannot damage your spreadsheet data by using Perspective. At the worst, the graph may have to be started over in Perspective. Just remember that Perspective uses an entirely different command system than Enable. The first five function keys on your keyboard provide most of the functionality of Perspective.

PART

3

*The Database and Database
Reports*

<table>
<tr><td>

CHAPTER

13

</td><td>

Getting Started with the Database

</td></tr>
</table>

THIS CHAPTER DESCRIBES THE BASIC FEATURES OF the database module. It shows how to manipulate data and how to extract information to create a report. The chapter begins with an overview of database terminology and then shows the steps involved in building a simple database.

Building a database involves three basic elements: the database definition, the input form, and the report form. The database definition determines the information that will be contained in the database. The input form controls the appearance or layout of the database. The report form controls the way information is printed or viewed in summary reports. All three of these elements are needed for a database—but most important is the database definition.

DATABASE BASICS

Before you begin working with the database, you should become familiar with some basic terms and concepts of database management.

A *database* is a systematic way of keeping files. Except for the media used for storage (electronic or magnetic), these files are not very different from the paper files kept by your school, your dentist, or your government.

A database contains units of information called *records*. Generally these units of information are broken down by individual unit: student, patient, or taxpayer, or a single item of inventory, like a turbine rotor or fan belt. Each of these individuals or items would comprise a record.

Each record is further divided into elements called *fields*. A field is a piece of information, such as the student's name, the patient's allergy to a medication, a taxpayer's social security number, or a fan belt's manufacturer. Usually, you can get the maximum use of a database by breaking its records down into the maximum number of fields. You could, for instance, place a person's whole name in a single field. However, you will discover that it's much more efficient to break the name down into several fields, such as TITLE, FIRSTNAME, MIDDLENAME, LASTNAME, and SUFFIX (such as Jr. or II).

Databases can be used for a broad range of applications. If you have a Rolodex, you have a physical manifestation of a database. A telephone book, encyclopedia, and dictionary are all examples of databases. Currently, computer storage is just reaching the point where such massive databases can be used by personal computers, and so they are relatively rare. It is more likely that you would use a microcomputer database, like the database module of Enable, to keep a customer list, an inventory, a telephone list of clients and friends.

An Enable database can contain an unlimited number of records, and each record can contain as many as 254 fields. Each field can contain as many as 254 characters. This imposes a maximum of nearly 64K (64,517) per record, a generous amount. The only upper limit on the number of records per database is imposed by the storage medium rather than by Enable itself. You can have as many records as your storage medium can handle. If you are working with double-density floppy disks, you could have a database as large as 360K.

Each database can contain up to 10 indexes, consisting of up to 100 characters each. An *index* is a field on which the database can be sorted. for example, you might want to index a database on the customer's last name, zip code, company name, customer number, or some other piece of information. You would have different reasons for using the various indexes. Sorting on a zip code is useful for large mailings. Sorting by last names might be used for printing summary reports. Additionally, you can specify more than 20 editing and validation criteria per database. We'll discuss those in more detail in a later chapter.

One of the most powerful aspects of a database is its ability to search for and extract records based on your criteria. When a database contains thousands of records, automatic searching capabilities become essential. Using these capabilities, you can, for example, prepare a list of all customers who live in a particular zip code. Or you might print a list of all purchases from a particular vendor. But the search criteria can be much more complex—giving you the power to break out specific groups from within the database.

HOW TO CREATE A DATABASE DESIGN

As with any major task, a database requires a bit of planning before it is begun. Not only will you need to consider the immediate use of the database you are designing, you should think about other databases that may interact with the one you are designing. Another thing to think about is storage space. Enable allows generous amounts of storage, but making fields oversized is wasteful. Enlarging a field later is easy and will be covered in full.

STARTING A DATABASE

The first database you'll create will be a simple mailing list. This example database is probably simpler than working databases you will construct to accomplish actual tasks. In this example, at every point where you are given the option of a simple or a complex action, the simple action will be chosen. But don't think that such a database, made as quickly and simply as possible, is useless. You can construct powerful, useful databases very quickly and simply with Enable. But you are also given powers that rival dedicated database systems. Later, we will explore all the high-powered options Enable provides.

Here are the basic steps for starting a database:

- Get to the Main menu by starting Enable or by pressing Alt-Home from inside any module.

- Select the commands Use System, DBMS/Graphics, Design, Database Definition.

- Enter a name for the new database and press ←⎯. Confirm that this is a new database definition by selecting the *New File* option.

Nothing could be easier than to enter the database:

1. Go to the Enable Main menu by starting Enable or by pressing Alt-Home from within any module.

2. Choose the options *Use System* and *DBMS/Graphics*. You will see the screen shown in Figure 13.1.

3. Select *Design*, and from the next menu, select *Database-Definition*. You will see the Database Definition screen shown in Figure 13.2.

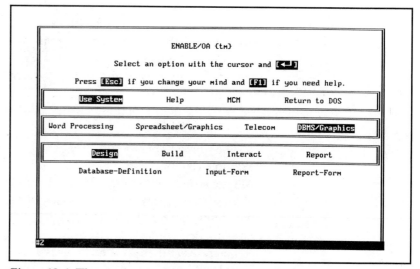

Figure 13.1: The starting database screen

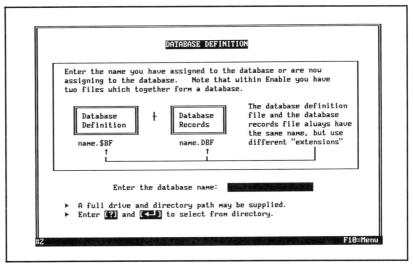

Figure 13.2: The first database definition screen

You can include DOS pathname along with the database name if desired.

4. If you were going to work with an existing database, you could call it up by typing in the name of the database at the "Enter the database name" prompt. Since you are creating a new database, enter the name **FORMLTR** for this database and press ◄—.

You will be informed that the file couldn't be found and you will be given these options: *New File, List Dir,* and *Re-enter.* The last two choices let you view a directory or try reentering the database name.

5. Since you are creating a new database, select *New File* and press ◄—. You will see the screen shown in Figure 13.3.

DEFINING FIELDS

Enable now asks for three pieces of information before letting you define the database itself. The first prompt asks for a *database description.* This is any word or phrase that reminds you of the purpose for the database. You can enter a description or skip this option by pressing ◄—. The *default input form* is the name of the input form that is automatically used for this database—unless you switch to another.

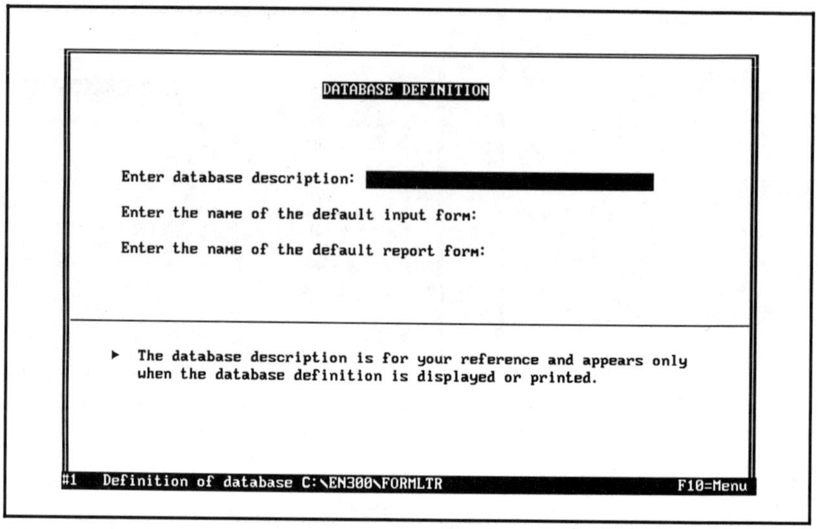

Figure 13.3: Database definition screen with three prompts

One input form must always be the default. (Remember, the input form is the visual appearance of the database and the screen that you will work with most often. You'll learn more about it later.) The *default report form* is the report form used automatically—unless you switch to a different form. (The report form is the layout of information for reports.) Since you can have multiple input and report forms, Enable requires that you specify one of each for the defaults.

1. Enter the description **FORMLETTER** for the first database description.

2. Enter the name **FORMLTR** for the default input form. This input form has not been created yet, but it's a good practice to make the default input form the same name as the database. We can, therefore, anticipate what the name of the form will be.

3. Enter the name **FORMLTR** for the default report form. When you press ◄──┘, the screen in Figure 13.4 appears.

You are now ready to define the fields in the database. You can have a virtually unending list of fields, but this particular example is designed to be as simple as possible, and requires only a few fields.

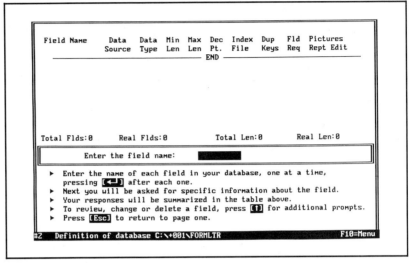

Figure 13.4: The field definition screen

You will begin by entering the name of the first field in the database. You should always use descriptive names for fields. Your field name can be as long as ten characters. It can contain letters, numbers, the underscore character, and the colon, but it must begin with a letter. Enter the first field name as follows:

4. Type **LASTNAME** and press ◄—┘. You'll see the screen shown in Figure 13.5.

Information about the *Detailed* option is given in Chapter 14.

5. Enable asks if you want to enter this field definition in a quick or a detailed manner. Since you are working on a simple database, select *Quick*. This will provide a bare-bones field definition.

You are now asked to choose an option to specify the type of data in the field. Fields can hold numbers (*Integer* and *Decimal*), text (*Text*), logical values (*Logical*), and lengthy memos (*Memo*). Let's take a closer look at each data type.

An *integer* is a numerical value without decimal places. The values 1, 200, and 2001 are integers. If you select integer, you will be prompted for field length.

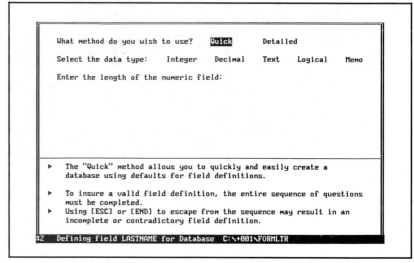

What method do you wish to use? `Quick`   Detailed

Select the data type: Integer   Decimal   Text   Logical   Memo

Enter the length of the numeric field:

▸ The "Quick" method allows you to quickly and easily create a
   database using defaults for field definitions.

▸ To insure a valid field definition, the entire sequence of questions
   must be completed.
▸ Using [ESC] or [END] to escape from the sequence may result in an
   incomplete or contradictory field definition.

#2   Defining field LASTNAME for Database C:\+001\FORMLTR

Figure 13.5: Choosing the Quick or Detailed definition method

A *decimal* value is a numerical value that may have decimal places. 1,200.1 and 3.141592 could be entered in a field designated as a decimal type. If you select *Decimal*, you will be prompted for the number of decimal places to use. You will also be prompted for field length.

Any combination of characters can be entered in a *text* field, up to 254 characters. Text can be sorted alphabetically. If you choose *Text*, you will be asked to enter the maximum length of the field entry.

Logical values are values that may contain only one of two values: T or F (true or false). You can also define the logical type to accept Y or N (yes or no). You can get creative with this field type to allow for choices like male/female, or any other information with two categories.

Memo information is similar to text information, but a memo field can contain an unlimited amount of information and it is stored separately from the database in its own file. This field is useful for narrative information, such as a catalog description or a paragraph of biographical data. The file containing the memo will have the same name as your database, but it will have the extension .DBT. This field cannot be used to sort a database.

6. Select the *Text* option for the LASTNAME field you are currently defining.

7. Enter a maximum length of **20** characters for the text field, then press ←┘. The screen in Figure 13.6 appears.

When you enter the maximum length, you have to make a judgment. On the one hand, you don't want the information space to be unnecessarily large (you won't specify 254 characters for a first name, for instance); and on the other, you don't want to have too little space. It's fairly easy to adjust the size of the field, but doing so leaves the path open for errors and loss of information. Logical and decimal values can be selected exactly, but text fields are more difficult. In a database, you should be conservative with space allocation. Placing ten extra spaces in a field can result in a significant amount of wasted space, if your database contains thousands of records.

Enable now displays the first field definitions and asks for the next field name. Note that the first field, along with the data type and maximum length, is displayed in the upper part of the screen. Certain defaults were entered for you because you selected the Quick method of defining the field: *Keyboard* was entered as the data source and 0 was entered as the minimum length. Now finish defining the fields for this database.

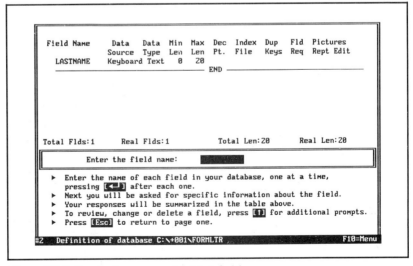

Figure 13.6: Ready for a second field definition

8. Repeat steps 4 through 7 to define the next three fields, using the options shown in Figure 13.7. Enter the appropriate field names, data types, and maximum lengths as shown in the figure.

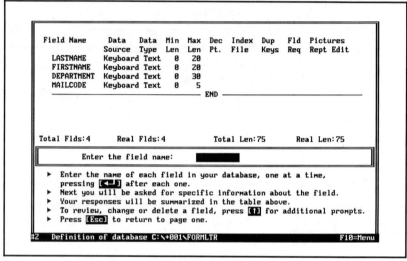

Figure 13.7: All fields in the sample database

SAVING THE DATABASE

Now that you have entered all this information, you won't want to lose it. You must save your changes. Here are the steps for saving the database.

1. Press F10 to see the Top Line menu.

2. Select *Save*. You will be asked if you want to save the database under its current name or under a new name. Save it under its current name (the name you entered on the first screen of the database definition). Enable will append the appropriate extension for you.

CHANGING A FIELD LENGTH

As you saw earlier, changing the field length is not difficult. This section will describe how to do it. Suppose you have a new employee named Helen Coopersmith-Littlehammersville. You would need to adjust the LASTNAME field to accommodate 30 characters instead of only 20. Here's how you would make this adjustment:

- Go to the database component of Enable. Select *Design* and then *Database-Definition*, then load the FORMLTR database and press ◄── three times to accept the same default description, input form, and report form.

- Press ↑ to highlight the LASTNAME field (or use the Arrow keys to highlight whatever field you want to edit), and press ◄── to begin editing.

- Move to the maximum length line and enter a new length of **30**. When you press ◄──, Enable will update the summary screen.

- Press F10 and select the *Save* command. Indicate that you want to save the file under its old name. This will replace the old database with the new definition. You will see the screen in Figure 13.8 if you had entered records in the database.

This screen warns you that your existing database is no longer compatible with the definitions you have made for it. If you had

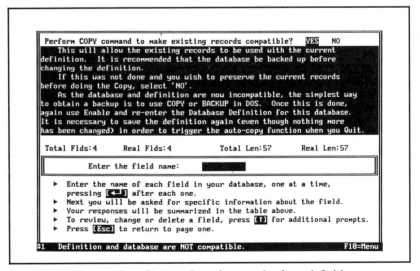

Figure 13.8: Converting old records to the new database definition

shortened rather than lengthened the field, you would stand to lose data at this point, and you would be wise to return to DOS and back up your information before proceeding. If you elect to change the definition without backing up your information, prepare yourself for a rude shock when you begin using your database: shortened fields will be truncated if necessary to make the data fit.

CREATING AND SAVING A DATABASE INPUT FORM

A database input form controls the way database fields are arranged on the screen during data entry. In essence, this is the appearance of the database for day-to-day use. You can use several input forms for a single database—each for a different purpose. However, Enable requires that one of the forms be the default. The default is the form that normally comes into view when you enter the database for data entry.

Creating an input form is even simpler than creating the database. The finished form can be saved as a separate file on the disk and is connected to the database definition via its name. You entered the name of this input form when you first defined the database.

1. Return to the Main menu.

2. Select the commands *Use System*, *DBMS/Graphics*, *Design*, *Input-Form*.

3. Enter the name **FORMLTR** when the next screen appears, then press ◄┘. This name corresponds to the name specified in the database definition, allowing the database definition to link to the input form.

4. Indicate that this is a new form by selecting *New File*.

5. Enable now asks for the name of the database to which this form is connected. Enter the name **FORMLTR** and press ◄┘. Respond to the prompt requesting a description. You'll see a screen of instructions for creating the form.

Use a DOS path name with the input form name if desired; however it's best to keep the input form and the database in the same directory.

Writing and revising the input form is done on a design screen on which you select where in the form an item of information should be placed. You will then be prompted for information. When the information has been entered, Enable returns to the input screen so you can enter the next item.

6. Press any key to move to the design screen.

7. Use any word processor commands to type text onto the design screen. Usually, this text will include field names and descriptive information. In this case, enter **First Name:**. Leave enough room after each text description to insert the corresponding field. The amount of space would be determined by the number of characters in the field as you defined it. Figure 13.9 shows the text for the first field in place.

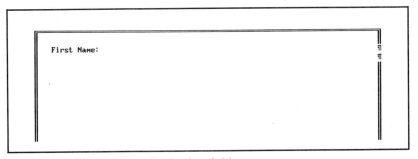

Figure 13.9: Entering text for the first field

8. When the text is entered, place the cursor where the information should be entered and press Shift-F9. That will call up the box shown in Figure 13.10.

9. Enter the name of the field you specified, then press ←⟶. If you misspell the name of the field, or if you enter a field name not in your selected database (FORMLTR), you will have to provide information on where the data can be found. Enable will prompt you for the path and filename.

10. Select No when prompted for special processing options.

For certain fields, you may elect to use special processing options. You could use such options for a STATE field, if it existed, to check the entry against a separate file containing the names or abbreviations for all the states in the nation. For instance, you could make

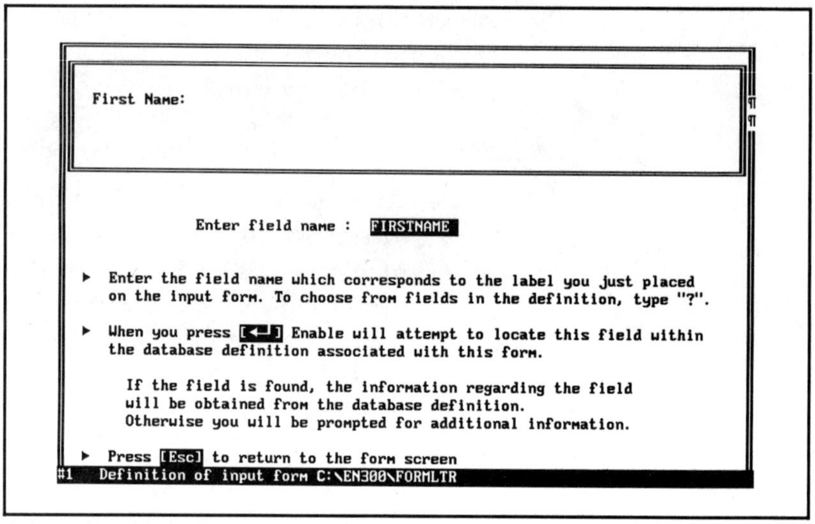

Figure 13.10: Inserting a field

sure that West Va. or Penna. could not be entered, but only WV and PA. There are other special processes, such as automatically entering a specific state in a STATE field— you can avoid some typing by having Enable enter common entries, such as state names. Since you are keeping this database as simple as possible, we have forgone the special processing options by selecting No in step 10.

As you enter each of the fields, a rectangle just long enough to contain the requested information appears on the input form screen. Your finished input form will appear as a set of highlighted rectangles and text on the screen. The rectangles represent fields and the text helps the user understand what the form is showing. Technically, you need not enter text to guide the user, but an input form would be useless without it.

11. Enter the remainder of the fields as shown in Figure 13.11, providing, when prompted, the name of the field and so on, as described in this section.

The database input form can be altered very easily. When you enter the fields on the input form, you are using a text editor. Simply

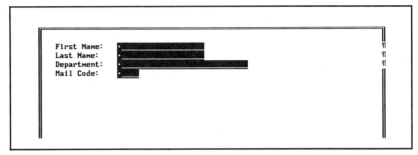

Figure 13.11: The completed input form for the FORMLTR database

call up the input form as if you were creating it. Specify the name of the form you want to alter. Create any new fields you need. Be sure to create these new fields in the database as well. If you place a field in the input form that doesn't exist in the database, Enable will ask from where it should take the information. Enable's database manager knows what fields are in the database. Unless you have an alternate place from which to pull the information in the requested field, you will be unable to place it in the input form. You may also relocate fields by deleting the old field, moving to a new location, and replacing it as if it were a new field.

When producing your database input form, remember that the full range of word processing features is available. Try to make the form's layout easy to understand by separating types of information and making the data entry task easier. Seemingly small details in an input form can result in large data-entry time savings.

Now save your input form:

1. Press F10.

2. Select *Form Design Options*, highlight the *Save* option, and press ◄───.

3. Select *Same name and disk*.

Remember that if you later establish new fields in the database definition, they are not automatically added to the input form. If you enlarge the amount of information contained in your database, you must go through the process of adding fields to your input form.

ENTERING RECORDS INTO THE DATABASE

After designing the database and input form, you're ready to enter data into the database. This is where you get to see how your design work has turned out.

1. Return to the Main menu and select *Build* under DBMS/ Graphics. In the screen that appears, enter the name of the database—**FORMLTR**. The input form will be entered automatically. You will see the screen in Figure 13.12. Press ◄─┘ to select the input form.

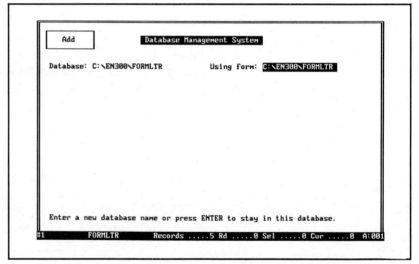

Figure 13.12: Getting ready to enter information into the database

The input form you designed will be in view with a blank record— ready to be filled out.

2. Type the information for the first record into the various fields (allowing for any restrictions you specified in the database setup).

In addition to the familiar editing keys such as Del, Ins, and Backspace, use the following keys to move around within the record:

Tab, ↵, or ↓	To next field
←	Left one space
→	Right one space
Shift-Tab or ↑	To previous field
Home	To top of record (first field)
End	To bottom of record (last field)

When you reach the end of a record, Enable displays some options on the status line. Figure 13.13 shows a sample record that has already been filled in with data.

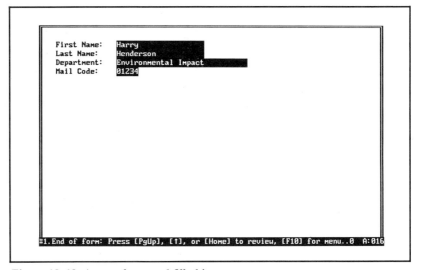

Figure 13.13: A sample record filled in

Note that the instructions at the bottom of the screen provide three different ways to return to the record and change the information entered there. If you wanted to return to this record and make changes, you'd press one of the keys—PgUp, ↑, or Home.

So how do you get a new record to fill out?

3. Press F10 to display the Top Line menu (see Figure 13.14). The options on the menu are *Next, Previous, Save, Ignore, 1 = Query, 2 = Index, Where,* and *Quit.* Select *Next* to get a new record. Making this selection will take you to the next blank record, in which you may enter the next person's information.

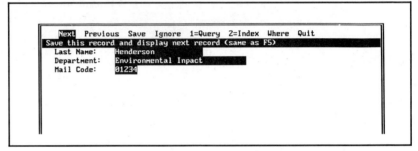

Figure 13.14: Database menu options on the Top Line menu

> You can insert a record into an existing database from the input form by clearing the input form (F10), selecting *Add* from the menu, entering data, and selecting *Save* from the Input Form menu.

When you enter large numbers of records, you should be sure to save your database periodically, by pressing F10 and selecting *Save* or pressing Alt-F10. You can make record entry much faster by pressing F5 to save the current record and advance to the next. F6 saves the current record and goes to the previous record.

Let's review the procedures for entering records in the database:

- Select the commands Use System, DBMS/Graphics, and Build from the Main menu.

- Enter the name of the database definition you want to use, then press ↵. Be sure to include any drive location and prefix needed to specify the file.

- Enter the name of the input form you want to use (or confirm Enable's selection), then press ↵.

- Begin typing the first record using Tab, Shift-Tab, ↑, ↓, Home, and ↵ to move between fields.

- Get another blank record by entering the command F10, Next or by pressing F5. (F10, Next will provide a new, blank record only when you reach the end of existing records. Otherwise it moves to the next existing record.)

- Repeat these steps for the new record.

EDITING EXISTING RECORDS

The options on the Top Line database menu in Figure 13.14 enable you to display and change records that have already been entered.

If you want to return to a previous record, select *Previous*. When you return to a previous record, you can change the information in it by simply typing over the information showing on the screen, then moving to a new record.

The *Ignore* option is used to throw away the record on screen. This is useful when you make changes to an existing record and decide to return the record to its original state. Just select F10, *Ignore*.

SEARCHING FOR RECORDS IN A DATABASE

Enable provides several ways to locate records in a database. All of these methods use options from the database Top Line menu (Figure 13.14): *Query*, *Index*, and *Where*. In this section you'll take a look at how each works.

QUERYING THE DATABASE

If going to *Next* and *Previous* were your only options when it came to moving around in the database, database management would be very tedious. Fortunately, Enable provides a record Query command. You can use Query to specify some aspect of the record. After selecting the command F10, Query, you will be returned to the input form. Enter any detail of the information for which you are looking.

Add returns to the previous screen, where you can add a new record; *Quit* returns to the screen where you specified the database and input form.

For example, suppose you want to find the record for Harry Henderson. You would enter the name Henderson in the LASTNAME field or both Harry and Henderson in the FIRSTNAME and LASTNAME fields. To begin the search after specifying the query information, press F10 again. The menu provides three options: *Find*, *Add*, and *Quit*. *Find* is the command you want to select for locating the record matching your query specification. Once you locate the record (if it exists) Enable displays it in the input form, where you can edit the information or simply review it.

Let's browse through existing records:

- Press F10, Next to save the current record and view the next. If no record exists past the current record, this will produce a new, blank record. Alternatively, you can press F5 to move to the next record. This command will produce a blank record when it reaches the end of the database.

- Press F10, Previous to view the previous record. Alternatively, you can press F6 to view the previous record.

- When you reach the desired record, you can edit its fields by typing over the information currently in the record. At that time, you can press F10, Ignore to ignore the changes you made and restore the original record, or press F10, Next to accept the changes.

To query the database for any information:

- Select the command F10, Query.

- Enter any information into the blank form provided. This specifies the information that you would like to match in the database.

- Select F10, Find. Enable will find any matching records.

PERFORMING INDEXED SEARCHES

The *Index* option on the database Top Line menu is only available if you have indexed one of your fields. If you use the Detailed method of defining fields (which is covered in Chapter 14), you will be given the option of creating an indexed field. (Since all the fields created so far were created using the Quick definition method, we have skipped over a discussion of the *Index* option.)

When a field is indexed, a separate DOS file is created for that field, and all the items in that field in the database will also be entered in the DOS file. The DOS file must have a unique name. The DOS file is then sorted. This lets you specify various kinds of searches for database subsets (groups of database records). For example, you can find records of employees whose names begin with A through M because all of these records are indexed alphabetically in the index file. You can index zip codes to generate mass mailings in zip-code order. Another strategy is to index date fields in order to locate orders before or after certain dates. All of these fields can be indexed in the same database, resulting in great flexibility in information retrieval.

To perform an index search, select the command F10, Index. A window appears at the bottom of the screen for your index information. Enter the name of the indexed field followed by an equal sign, followed by the information for the search. For example, you might look for a record created on 31 January 1990. In that case, you would enter

DATE = "90/01/31"

presuming the indexed field is named DATE, and that you used the recommended year, month, date format for entering date. You could enter a series of dates simply by separating them with commas. You can enter a range of values with the ".." command. For instance, to specify the range from 31 January 1990 to 28 February 1990, enter

DATE = "90/01/31".."90/02/28"

If you are searching an indexed record for text, you may use an additional item: the wildcard character $. To search an indexed record for Henderson, you might enter the index criteria

LASTNAME = "$enderso$"

and you would locate all names that contain that particular string of characters. If you are searching for everyone whose last name starts with S, you could use

LASTNAME = "S$"

All indexed searches are in ascending order (A to Z, 0 to 9), unless you specifically ask for a descending search. To take the date search shown above, the first record located will be one generated on 31 January, and the last will be one generated on 28 February. If the indexed search had been initiated with the command

DATE = "90/01/31".."90/02/28",d

the first date would have been 28 February, and the last, 31 January. This is because the command ",d" was added to the criteria.

USING THE WHERE OPTION

The final option in the menu accessed from the input form screen is *Where*. *Where* is an option that works with the Query command to provide more flexibility in queries. *Where* lists out the query you have specified in the Query command. Subsequently, you can edit the query. Let's look at an example: If you had performed the query earlier to locate Mr. Henderson's record, and subsequently selected *Where* from the input form menu, you would have seen the following text in the *Where* line:

Where LASTNAME = "$Henderson$"

Instead of using the Query command, you may specify your queries by typing onto the *Where* line the field name, an equal sign (or other operator, listed below), and the criteria text you are seeking. This would be done instead of entering the information in the fields themselves using the Query command. Alternatively, you can edit the Query information in the *Where* line to add more flexibility. What is the advantage to using the *Where* line? It lets you use operators to identify specific records. These operators include the following:

MEANING	OPERATOR	SYNONYM
Equal to	=	EQ
Not equal to	< >	NE
Greater than or equal to	>=	GE
Less than or equal to	<=	LE
Greater than	>	GT
Less than	<	LT
Concatenate	&	
Concatenate and add space between items	& +	
Concatenate and remove extra spaces	& –	

You can use in your database searches many of the same functions that are used with spreadsheets. No function that takes a range of cells as an argument will work—but that still provides dozens of functions for the database. See Chapter 10.

These operators allow you to locate a record with much more flexibility. You could locate all records created before 31 August 1990, for instance, with the *Where* instruction

Where DATE < "90/08/31" or Where DATE LT "90/08/31"

Another powerful tool is the logical operator. With it, you can select more than one criterion for a search. The logical operators are AND, OR, and NOT. AND is restrictive, and OR is inclusive. NOT inverts the search. If you specify

LASTNAME = "H$" AND DEPARTMENT = "E$"

you will only have access to the people whose names begin with "H" and who work in departments beginning with "E." This could be a very small group.

If you specify

LASTNAME = "H$" OR DEPARTMENT = "E$"

you will have access to a potentially larger group of people: all people, regardless of their department, whose names start with "H," as well as all members of all departments that begin with "E."

The NOT operator is a little more complicated. If you want a list of all orders after August 31, 1990, you would enter in the *Where* line

NOT (DATE LE "900831")

which would have the same effect as DATE GT "900831" The NOT operator means "is not equal to" when used with an equal sign, or "is not greater than" when used with the > sign, and so on.

Parentheses are used to group clauses on the *Where* line. Operations within parentheses will be evaluated first. If there are no parentheses, they will be evaluated in this order:

NOT, AND, and OR
left to right

You can use the wildcard ? with *Where* searches. It stands for any missing character. To locate all files generated in May of 1990, you can specify

DATE = "90/05/??"

Another powerful feature of the *Where* search is the truncation wildcard $, which you have seen used in searching text fields. This wildcard stands for any string of characters. Using the specification "H$" found all the records containing a name beginning with H. "H" would have found all records containing the letter "H" at any position within the field. You can also specify how many characters should be found on one side or the other of the specified string: "H$8" would have found Henderson and Haldemann, but would have skipped over Hammersmith and Hudson. Similarly, "4$h" would locate the names Smith and Marsh and any other five-letter names ending with "H." You can only specify up to nine missing characters this way.

CREATING A
SIMPLE DATABASE REPORT

In Chapter 15 you'll learn about more reporting features.

Let's pause a moment and take a look at where we are. So far you have learned how to put information into the database. But what good is it there? Data can be used for many purposes. You can create tables of data, for example, in which you pull out individual records with some aspect in common. A table might be made up to see which sales people were selling the most of a given product. Or you could construct a table that shows in what zip-code area a product was doing poorly, thus helping you to see better where your advertising dollars ought to be spent. In this section we will create a simple database report.

Until now, you have been working with a very simple data entry scheme. In this section, you will use data to create a simple data report. Earlier, when you created the FORMLTR database, you specified FORMLTR to be the default report form. Now you'll design your own version of this form. We are going to bring together a small amount of information from the database and create a form letter: the simplest form of a report.

1. From the Main menu select Use System, DBMS/Graphics, Design and select *Report-Form.* You will see the Report Form Definition screen. Note that this screen is the same as the screen you saw when you began to design your input form and your database.

2. Type in the report name: **FORMLTR.** Your screen will look like Figure 13.15. Enable looks for an existing report form called FORMLTR. Because there isn't one, it asks whether it should create the file.

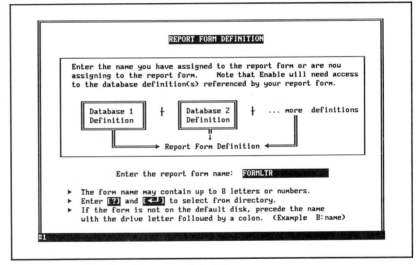

Figure 13.15: Starting the report definition screen

3. Press ← to create the file.

4. Enter the name of the associated database (**FORMLTR**) and a report description of your own devising. You will see the screen in Figure 13.16.

Essentially, creating a report form is very similar to creating an input form: you will locate the cursor in the word processing screen where the field should be displayed, then press Shift-F9 to place the field.

5. Press ← to leave the instruction screen. Type **To:** and use the cursor keys to move down a line. Type **From: Management** as shown in Figure 13.17.

You are now ready to revise or create your report form.

1. Lay out your report as you would have it appear on the screen or the printed page. All of Enable's word processing features are available to do this.

2. Position the cursor where you want database information to be shown. Press **[Shift]** and **[F9]** to tell Enable to "Put It Here".

3. Type a field name and answer the questions asked about the field.

4. Repeat the process for each field in your report form. If you wish to delete a field after you have positioned it on the screen, or if you wish to revise a field's options, press **[F10]** for a menu.

5. When you're finished, press **[F10]** to save the form using the Save options or to return to the Main Menu.

6. Press any key when you're ready to begin and Enable will display a blank screen or your previously-created report form.
   Note: If you wish to use headers and footers in your report, create a word processing document and use the Report Language.

#1   Definition of report form C:\EN300\FORMLTR   F10=Menu

Figure 13.16: The instruction screen

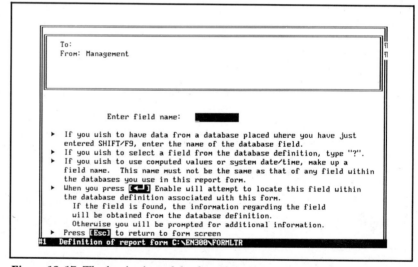

To:
From: Management

            Enter field name: ▮

▸ If you wish to have data from a database placed where you have just entered SHIFT/F9, enter the name of the database field.
▸ If you wish to select a field from the database definition, type "?".
▸ If you wish to use computed values or system date/time, make up a field name. This name must not be the same as that of any field within the databases you use in this report form.
▸ When you press **[◄─┘]** Enable will attempt to locate this field within the database definition associated with this form.
   If the field is found, the information regarding the field will be obtained from the database definition.
   Otherwise you will be prompted for additional information.
▸ Press **[Esc]** to return to form screen

#1   Definition of report form C:\EN300\FORMLTR

Figure 13.17: The beginning of the form letter

6. Move the cursor to the second space after *To:* and press Shift-F9. You will see the window shown in Figure 13.17. In this figure, the cursor is located on the same line as *To:* and just above the *M* in *Management.*

7. Enter the name of the field in the FORMLTR database: **FIRSTNAME**. You are prompted for the report picture.

A *report picture* tells Enable what kind of information to place in a position in a field. For example, in some kinds of fields, entering an N will cause Enable to reject anything but a number in that particular position. Recall that earlier we had the opportunity to create either detailed fields or quick fields. Since this chapter is just an introduction, we opted to work with quick fields. Creating a report picture is an option provided when defining a detailed field. Since there was no picture created when the field was created, the data picture is blank in Figure 13.18.

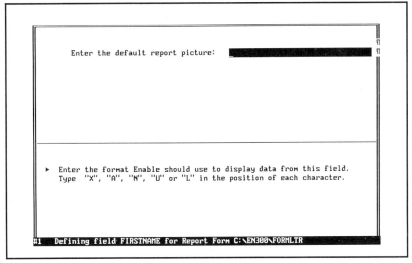

Figure 13.18: The blank report picture screen

If you were placing the field in a report at the beginning of a sentence, and if the field contained only lowercase letters, you would enter the picture U followed by 39 L's so that the first letter of the derived field would be capitalized.

However, you may, if you wish, enter a picture now. A picture for a telephone number might resemble

CC-AAA-NNN-NNNN/XXX

In this example, C stands for the country code, A for the area code, N for the phone number, and X for the phone extension. Using a series of Xs allows whatever is entered in the database to come through unaltered. U and L change the letters appearing in the positions where they appear to be shown in upper- (U) or lowercase (L) letters. For example, if the database field contained the data "animal rights" and the picture contained ULLLLLXULLLLL, the report would show "Animal Rights." These picture placeholders have other specialized uses, which will be discussed when we turn to the detailed field definition.

8. Press Esc to return to the word processor screen.

9. Use the Del key to remove the highlighted rectangle left there when you defined the position.

Some fields contain information that has been entered from the keyboard, and other fields will contain data that is derived from other sources. For example, if you had as fields in your database the weight of a piece of inventory, and you also had a field that contained its cost per pound, you would use a derived field to give its cost simply by multiplying the values in the other two fields. In this example, you are going to derive the full name of a customer from the fields that contain his or her first and last names.

If you used the FIRSTNAME field and then the LASTNAME field to place the recipient's name in the form letter, the first name would be padded with many spaces (recall that you left 20 spaces for the first name and so far only one of the first names has actually contained 20 spaces). Using a derived field allows you to take some information from one field and some from another and eliminate any extra spaces.

10. Once again, place the cursor where the recipient's name should be and press Shift-F9. You will again see the screen shown in Figure 13.17. Enter **NAME**. Since that field doesn't exist in the database, you will be prompted by the screen in Figure 13.19.

11. Select *Derived*. You will see a screen with several prompts. In the "Formula" prompt, type

    firstname & + lastname

    For "Result data type?" specify *Text*. Enter **40** for the derived field length. You can leave the report picture prompt blank. Your screen should now look like Figure 13.20.

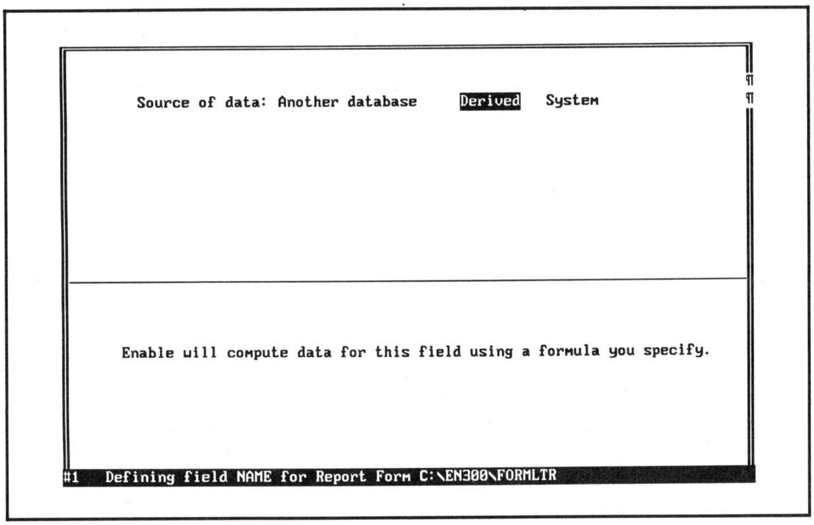

Figure 13.19: Electing to create a derived field

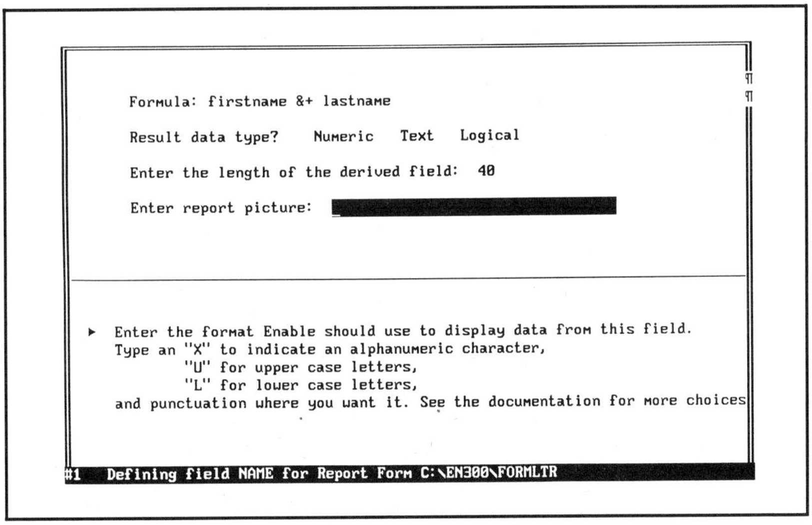

Figure 13.20: Concatenating FIRSTNAME with LASTNAME

Let's take a closer look at the formula line. The words FIRST-
NAME and LASTNAME, of course, refer to fields in the
FORMLTR database. The operator & + has an effect like that used
in the WHERE field discussed earlier. It concatenates the two fields
(attaches the second field to the end of the first field), removes all

extra spaces, and places a space between the field entries. Therefore, if the FIRSTNAME field contains "Ann" followed by 17 spaces, and LASTNAME contains "Pym" followed by 17 spaces, a printout without the &+ operator would contain 34 extraneous spaces. Using the &+ operator would trim the name to "Ann Pym," with no extra spaces.

The operators available are

MEANING	*OPERATOR*
Concatenate	&
Concatenate and trim	&–
Concatenate, trim, and place space between fields	&+
Add	+
Subtract	–
Multiply	*
Divide	/
Exponentiate	**

The AND, OR, and NOT operators are also available for use, as described earlier.

12. Continue creating the report, entering this memo to your employees:

> This is to inform you that there will be a sale open to all employees on all inventory from December 20 until December 24. This will be an excellent opportunity to stock up on the flexible couplings and tapered roller bearings that are so useful around the home, particularly at the holiday season. The inventory will be marked down 10 percent for the duration of the sale.

When you have finished the report, use the word processor menu to place a page break at the end of the memo (F10, Word Processor Options, Layout, Insert a page break), or all the printed reports will be printed as if they will appear on a single sheet of paper.

Now you're ready to issue the report, but before you proceed, you must save the report.

13. Press F10, select *Form Design Options, Save, Same Name and Disk*.

14. Press Alt-Home to return to the Main menu.

15. Select Use System, DBMS/Graphics, Report.

16. Once again, type in the database—**C:\EN300\FORMLTR**—and form—**C:\EN300\FORMLTR**. You also have the option of entering Index and Where search commands. You will see the Database Management System screen in Figure 13.21. Press ↩, and you see the first report. Since no Index or Where items were entered, the report will contain these two lines for every record in the database.

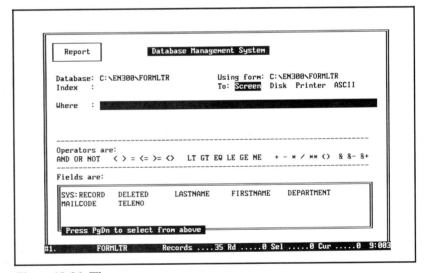

Figure 13.21: The report screen

Note that in Figure 13.21 you had the option of printing either to the screen, to disk, or on paper, through a printer. If you elect to print to disk, you will be prompted for a filename. If you are printing to disk or to a printer, you will see the first of the four print setup screens that are used to format the printout. (These screens are shown in Chapter 3, Figures 3.5 and 3.7–3.9.)

17. Press PgDn to go to the second screen, shown in Figure 13.22, where you will select a printer.

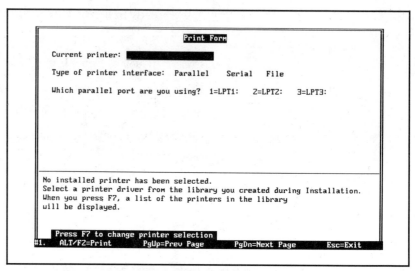

```
                              Print Form
Current printer: ███████████████████

Type of printer interface:  Parallel    Serial    File

Which parallel port are you using?  1=LPT1:    2=LPT2:    3=LPT3:




No installed printer has been selected.
Select a printer driver from the library you created during Installation.
When you press F7, a list of the printers in the library
will be displayed.


    Press F7 to change printer selection
#1.   ALT/F2=Print       PgUp=Prev Page       PgDn=Next Page       Esc=Exit
```

Figure 13.22: Second print form selection screen

18. Press F7 to see a menu of printers available.

19. When all the selections on this screen are made, press Alt-F2 to print the reports.

Now that you've created a database and a report, you can see how simple and straightforward this process can be. When you mention the word "database," most people go into a trance state. There is something very pallid and humdrum about databases that prevents people from seeing the power beneath the simplicity. In the next three chapters, you will learn about some more complex aspects of the database manager, and the power Enable places in your hands. All integrated packages have a star component, the component that outshines the others. In Enable, the database is a remarkable entity. Now that you are familiar with the basics, we can move into the power of database management.

Building Complex Databases

THIS CHAPTER SHOWS YOU HOW TO BUILD COMPLEX databases using Enable's *Detailed* option for defining fields. You can customize a database to your liking—and you can link two or more databases. After providing an overview of the Detailed field definition options, this chapter presents a step-by-step guide to building three interactive databases.

When you're finished with this chapter, you might want to experiment with building a few databases of your own. And remember, you can always go back and change a database's definitions as described in the previous chapter.

DEFINING FIELDS WITH THE DETAILED OPTION

As you read in the previous chapter, there is a simple way to define databases (using the *Quick* option) and a detailed way (using the *Detailed* option). One might instantly and irrevocably opt for the simple database definition, if the *Detailed* option were not so powerful.

You should be familiar with the initial steps for defining fields; these were covered in Chapter 13. This section deals with the options presented under the Detailed method of field definition in the Database Definition screen (DBMS/Graphics, Design, Database Definition).

Following is a summary of the most useful options for defining *Detailed* fields.

Do you wish to copy an existing field definition? This option lets you avoid going through the *Detailed* definitions when you want this field to be like a previously defined field. You can simply copy the definitions from a different field. If you choose Yes for this option, Enable asks for the name of the database and field you want to copy.

Is this an indexed field? Indexed fields are stored in alphabetical or numerical order. Also, you can display the database in sorted order according to these fields. If you answer Yes to this option, Enable asks for a file name. This should be any legal file name (including the directory path) for the index file. Enable takes care of applying the extension. You will not need to pay much attention to this file once it's on disk—it simply contains the indexed data separated from the rest of the database. Enable also asks if duplicates are allowed in the indexed field. If you answer No to this question, Enable will present a message whenever you enter two identical values in the indexed field to prevent you from duplicating information. This is useful for fields that contain unique data, such as customer numbers.

Is this a required field? A required field must be filled out by the data entry operator. Enable will not let the operator continue to fill out the record if a required field is not completed.

Source of data This option indicates from where the data for the field comes. *Keyboard* is the most common source—indicating that you will type the data. Other sources include *Another Database* (pulling information from a different database), *Derived* (calculating the information from other fields in this database), and *System* (filling the field with system-supplied information).

Select the data type This option also appears for the Quick method of defining fields. It controls the type of data that you can enter into the field. When you use this option in the Detailed method, Enable offers several additional options for specifying the type of information allowed:

- *Numeric* fields can include Integer values (no decimals), Decimal values, or Currency values (preformatted for currency with dollar signs, comma separators, and decimal point).

- *Text* fields can include Anything (all characters), Letters (alphabetic characters and specified punctuation only), Numbers + Letters (no special characters except specified punctuation), and Special (a user-defined format for text, based on a "picture").

- *Logical* fields can be displayed as True/False or Yes/No.

- *Other* fields are for special fields that require accurate values. These include Date, Time, State-Code, Zip-Code, and Phone-No. If a database contains one of these fields, specify it as the appropriate Other type. This causes Enable to "approve" the data as you enter it—making sure that it is a correct value.

- *Memo* fields are large fields for paragraphs of information.

What text is permitted? This option allows you to limit the kind of text the user inputs. You can specify that only letters, letters and numbers, anything, or only special characters are accepted.

Does field have minimum and maximum values? This option sets minimum and maximum values for a field. If the operator enters a value outside this range, Enable presents an error message and refuses the entry. This is most useful for numeric fields, but can also be used in text fields to specify alphabetical ranges.

Does field have a list of acceptable values? This option determines the acceptable values that can be entered into a field. When you select Yes at this prompt, Enable asks for the list of values. Enter the values separated by commas. If an operator enters anything other than one of these values, Enable presents an error message and refuses the entry. This option is only provided for text and numeric data types.

Enter the minimum length of field and *Enter the maximum length of field* determine the minimum and maximum length of an entry. The minimum can be 0 to indicate that the field can be left empty. These options are provided only for text and numeric data types.

Enter report picture   This option sets a "picture" of the data for this field—when displayed in the report form. If you leave this blank, the field will be unformatted. For example, a telephone number might use the picture CC-AAA-NNN-NNNN. In this case, the operator could enter 006195551212 and the number would automatically appear as 00-619-555-1212.

Columnar report heading   This option specifies the title used in a columnar report at the top of the column that corresponds to the field. If you do not enter a heading, Enable uses the field name.

Error msg   This field holds any message that you want printed if the operator enters an unacceptable value. The message can provide details about what type of value is expected.

CREATING THREE COMPLEX DATABASES

To design an effective database, consider your future needs. Which fields will you need? Which should be indexed? How many databases will you need? The answer to these questions is unique to each application. If you are operating a business database, the bare minimum will probably consist of a customer file, an inventory file, and an order file. You might consider creating separate databases for accounts receivable, accounts payable, and (if you have employees) a payroll file and a personnel file.

In this section you'll create three databases: one for customers, one for inventory, and one for orders. Of course, these databases are extremely simplified. There are several fields that you might want to add, such as the customer's fax number, back-ordered inventory, the date an order was received, and the ship date. A second customer address field (and even a third) might be wise in a real-world application to accommodate suite and department designations. You might want additional databases to cover the financial end of the transaction. To cover all the database possibilities would take a separate book all by itself. In this chapter, we will go over the most important things to take into consideration when creating a complex database.

THE CUSTOMER DATABASE

Begin by going to the Use System, DBMS/Graphics, Design, Database-Definition screen to create the customer database.

1. Enter **CUST** as the name of the database; select New File. Enter **Customer Information** as the database description. The input and output forms can be identified as **CUST** as well.

2. You now see the screen where you identify the names of the fields. Enter the field name **CUSTNAME** and press ←. You will see the first field definition screen. Use the → key to move the highlight to *Detailed* and you will see the field definition screen (Figure 14.1).

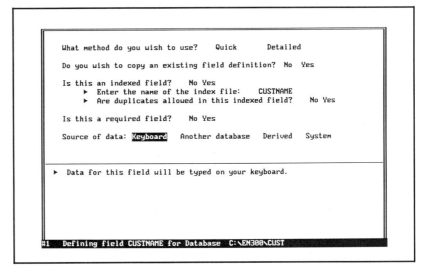

Figure 14.1: The first Detailed field definition screen

You will answer the prompts shown on this screen. Note the prompt asking whether you want to copy an existing field definition. In this case, you will not. But when it comes time to create the customer name field in the orders database, you will want to copy the field you are defining at this moment.

3. Respond No to the *Copy* prompt.

4. Respond Yes to the *Index* prompt. You will occasionally want to organize your customer records alphabetically, and indexing the field allows you to do this. You are then prompted for the name of the index file; type **CUSTNAME**. You are asked if the database should tolerate duplicates in the field. This is an important consideration. In this case, select No.

5. Respond Yes to the *Required* prompt.

Next you will tell Enable the source of your data. If you already had a database containing all your customer names, you could indicate that the source of data will be another database. You will probably be entering the customer names from the keyboard, however.

6. Specify *Keyboard* as the source. (When you create the ORDERS database, you will select *Another database* and indicate that the customer database is the source.) The screen should now change and you will go the second Detailed field definition screen. When this screen is filled in, it will look like Figure 14.2.

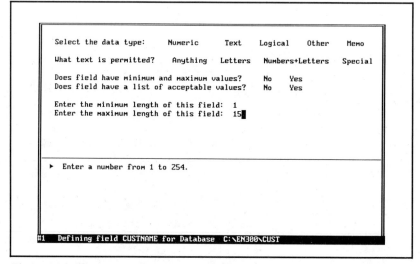

Figure 14.2: The second Detailed field definition screen

7. Choose *Text* as the data type.

8. You now are given the option of defining the kind of text that can be entered in CUSTNAME. Since customers are very creative in naming themselves, using unpredictable combinations of letters, numbers, and other characters, you should select *Anything*.

9. The field has no minimum or maximum values, so select No.

10. There is no list of acceptable values, so select No again.

11. Since this is a required field, the minimum acceptable length of the data in this field will be 1 character. You can determine your own maximum length, but, since this database will be lengthy, you should make the field only as long as the longest name that will be placed in it. If a longer name comes along, you can increase the length of the field as described in Chapter 13. For this example, enter **15**. Enable displays the third field definition screen. Figure 14.3 shows what this screen will look like when the information is filled in.

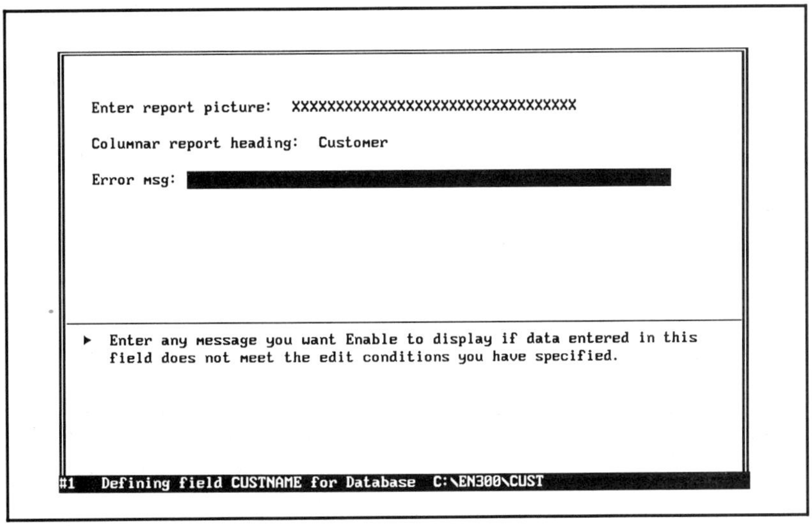

```
  Enter report picture:   XXXXXXXXXXXXXXXXXXXXXXXXXXXXXXXXX

  Columnar report heading:  Customer

  Error msg: ███████████████████████████████████████████




  ▶  Enter any message you want Enable to display if data entered in this
     field does not meet the edit conditions you have specified.




#1   Defining field CUSTNAME for Database   C:\EN300\CUST
```

Figure 14.3: The third Detailed field definition screen

12. Enter the report picture. This formats the field for any report you will create. Since you have no way to predict what will be placed in this field, you should create a report picture using Xs (X stands for any character) until the field is full.

13. When you create a report using Enable's built-in columnar format containing the data in this field, it will be headed by the title you place in the *Columnar report heading* prompt. Enter **Customer**.

14. The *Error msg* prompt is a block where you can enter a warning or reminder to enter only a specific kind of data. For instance, if this were a field containing only numbers, you could set it up to refuse alphabetic entries and to prompt the user with a message like, "Enter only numbers in this field." Since it is unlikely that crucial and detectable errors will appear in this field, leave the error message prompt blank.

As you can see, the Detailed field entry lives up to its name. By now you have all the information you need to enter the next fields for customer address and city—CUSTADD and CUSTCITY. These two fields should not be indexed.

15. Go ahead and define these two fields now.

The next fields—CUSTSTATE, CUSTZIP, and CUSTTELE— are fields that will contain special values. The CUSTSTATE field requires specific state abbreviations. For instance, an inexperienced worker might enter "PE" for Pennsylvania, rather than the correct "PA." The CUSTZIP field requires correct zip codes and the CUSTTELE field requires correct area codes. If this data is accidentally entered incorrectly, the record could be useless.

But Enable has a special capacity to deal with these potential entry errors. It contains listings of all acceptable values for these fields (that is, STATE fields, ZIP CODE fields, and PHONE fields). When the input form is used, it will rapidly compare the entry to the list of acceptable values to ensure that it is valid. To specify one of these special fields, choose the *Other* option when defining the data type. For example, in Figure 14.4, CUSTSTATE is being defined. Rather than making it a text field by selecting *Text* (as you might expect), *Other* was selected. As shown in the figure, the other types of fields include Date, Time, State-Code, Zip-Code, and Phone-No.

16. Define the CUSTSTATE, CUSTZIP, and CUSTTELE fields using the *Other* data type. CUSTSTATE should match the specifications in Figure 14.4. CUSTSTATE and CUST-ZIP should be indexed fields. Use the names CUSTST and CUSTELE for the names of the index fields. Figures 14.5 and 14.6 show the entries to make when defining the CUST-TELE field. Figures 14.7 and 14.8 show the entries to make when defining CUSTZIP. (Figure 14.7 covers a five-digit zip; Figure 14.8 covers a nine-digit zip.)

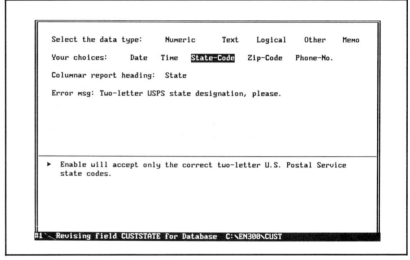

Figure 14.4: Selecting the *Other* data type option restricts input at the input form to applicable entries.

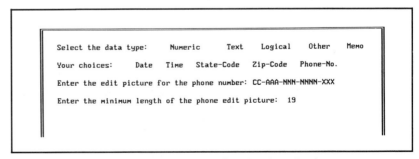

Figure 14.5: Defining the CUSTTELE field for the edit picture

Country codes are enormously more complicated than Enable allows. If you will be storing many overseas numbers, you would be wise to make this a Memo field.

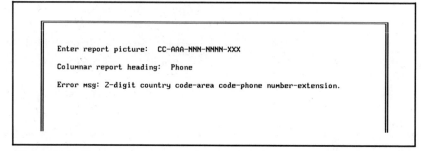

```
Enter report picture:  CC-AAA-NNN-NNNN-XXX

Columnar report heading:  Phone

Error msg: 2-digit country code-area code-phone number-extension.
```

Figure 14.6: The error message and report heading for the CUSTTELE field

```
Select the data type:      Numeric      Text      Logical      Other      Memo

Your choices:      Date    Time    State-Code    Zip-Code    Phone-No.

How many numbers in this zip code?    5    9

Columnar report heading:  Zip

Error msg: 5-digit zip, please. ███████████████████████
```

Figure 14.7: Defining the CUSTZIP field with a five-digit zip

```
Select the data type:      Numeric      Text      Logical      Other      Memo

Your choices:      Date    Time    State-Code    Zip-Code    Phone-No.

How many numbers in this zip code?    5    9

Columnar report heading:  Zip

Error msg: 9-digit zip, please. ███████████████████████
```

Figure 14.8: Defining CUSTZIP with a nine-digit zip

Figures 14.7 and 14.8 show you two options. In practice, you would use one or the other—not both.

If you need to change a field definition, don't worry. It is very easy to go back and edit a field definition. At the screen where you are prompted for the field name, press ↑ to place the cursor on the field names in the upper part of the screen. You can delete a field by pressing Del, or you can open a field definition for editing by pressing ↵.

Simply press ◀━┛ for each parameter that is still correct until you reach the one you want to change. Make your correction and press ◀━┛ until you return to the field-naming screen again.

Finally, you will want to enter CUSTCONT, the field containing the name of your contact. Many people like to keep more information than simply a name. You may want to keep the name, personal extension, title, number of children, birthday, type of relationship, and other important information that is difficult to classify. The kind of field ready-made for this sort of free-form data entry is the Memo field.

> 17. Create the CUSTCONT field just as before: name it CUST-CONT, select *Quick* and *Memo*. Essentially, you will have space for an unlimited amount of text.

That completes the entire customer database. Next, you'll create the inventory database. Be sure to save your database before moving on: F10, Save, Same Name, F10, Quit, Yes.

THE INVENTORY DATABASE

You'll place three fields in this database—product number, product description, and quantity on hand.

Create the database using the same procedures as for the customer database.

> 1. Enter **INVEN** for the database name. Select *New File*. Enter **Product Number** as the database description. The input form and report form can also be identified as **INVEN**.
>
> 2. When prompted for a field name, enter the product number field name, **PRODNO**, and press ◀━┛. Use the *Detailed* option for the field definition.
>
> 3. Respond No to the prompt asking whether you want to copy an existing field definition.
>
> 4. Index this field by pressing Yes to the index prompt. (Although the number used is meaningless now, it is important to index it so you can link it when you create the orders database in the next exercise.) Name the index file **PRODNO** and select No for the duplicates prompt.

5. Respond Yes to the required line prompt and select *Keyboard* as the source of data.

6. Specify *Numeric* and *Integer* as the data type.

7. Finish defining the PRODNO field by following steps 9–14 in the previous exercise. This time when you complete step 12 you must enter Ns instead of Xs for the report picture.

8. Define the quantity-on-hand field, PRODINV, and the product description field, PRODDESC, by following steps 2–7 of this exercise. When you define PRODDESC, however, specify the data type as either Text or Memo; there is no need to index this field. Also, when you define PRODINV, enter Ns not Xs.

You've completed the inventory database. Save the database definition and quit. In the next exercise you'll build the last complex database.

THE ORDERS DATABASE

The next challenge is to enter the orders database. This will pull a field from the customer database (CUSTNAME) and a field from the inventory database (PRODNO) and it will have a field of its own—ORDER—that will contain the number of units ordered.

1. Enter the word **ORDERS** for the database name, database description, input form, and report form.

2. When prompted for a field name, enter **CUSTNAME**. Elect to enter a detailed field definition. This time, elect to copy an existing field definition. You will be prompted for the name of the other database and field. Fill them in as shown in Figure 14.9. Instantly, all the database definition parameters are set to match the definition of CUSTNAME in the CUST database (see Figure 14.10). Press ↵ at each of the options to accept the automatic definition.

3. Perform a similar definition of the PRODNO field, specifying the INVEN database and the PRODNO field.

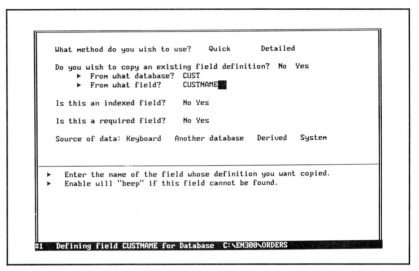

Figure 14.9: Copying the CUSTNAME field from the CUST database

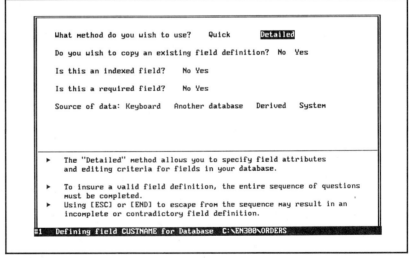

Figure 14.10: The CUSTNAME field takes on another field's definition

Finally, enter the ORDER field.

4. Specify the field name **ORDER**.

5. Select the options *Quick*, *Integer*, and specify six-digits.

That's all there is to the database. Save it now. Of course, you will want to go on to create many additional fields and other databases as mentioned at the beginning of the chapter, but for the purposes of demonstration, these will be enough.

CREATING THE
DATABASE INPUT FORMS

You will want to create input forms for each of the databases. You have already created some input forms in Chapter 13, so this process will be explained quickly.

1. Create a CUST input form by selecting Use System, DBMS/ Graphics, Design, Input-Form. Enter **CUST** as the name of the input form. Press any key after you've read the instruction screen. Press ←┘ to select New File and then enter **CUST** for the associated database and input form descriptions.

2. Place your cursor anywhere on the resulting screen. Type **Customer:** and press Shift-F9. You will be prompted for a field name. Enter **CUSTNAME**.

3. You will be asked if you want to select special processing options. You won't, so select No. You now see the input form screen; the new field will be placed for you.

4. Move to a new location and continue to enter the rest of the fields: CUSTADD, CUSTCITY, CUSTSTATE, CUST-ZIP, CUSTTELE, and CUSTCONT.

5. Save your work.

6. Now make a similar input form for INVEN, providing an input area for each of the fields involved.

The last step is to make the ORDERS input form.

7. Select Use System, DBMS/Graphics, Design, Input-Form. Enter **ORDERS** as the name of the input form, the associated database, and input form description. Create the form,

including areas to enter information for the CUSTNAME, PRODNO, and ORDER fields.

LINKING AN INPUT FORM TO A DATABASE

Next, you are going to link the ORDERS input form to the database.

1. Move the cursor down about two lines on the form and enter **Confirming Information**. Move down two more lines and enter **Customer Address**.

This will insert the address for the database, if it exists. If it doesn't exist, you are taking an order from a new customer, and you will be given the opportunity to enter the address.

2. Press Shift-F9 to place the field, and enter **CUSTADD**.

Enable instantly recognizes that CUSTADD is not a field in the orders database, and it prompts you for information on where it is to find this information. It gives you the option of pulling in the information from another database, deriving it from other fields, and other options.

3. Select *Another Database*. You will see the screen necessary for specifying this information. In Figure 14.11, these specifications are filled in. This screen asks from which database the information should be taken, the name of the field to look up, the indexed field that links the databases, the linking field, and whether this field can be keyed over. Respond with the entries shown in Figure 14.11.

4. You now are asked if you want special processing features. You don't, so answer No.

5. Enter all the other fields in the customer database just as you entered CUSTADD. At the "From what database?"

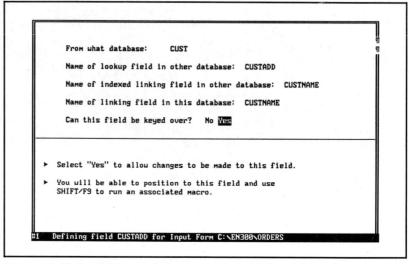

Figure 14.11: Establishing a look up, indexed, linking field

prompt, enter **CUST**. Enter the name of the field you are currently requesting (each field in the CUST database, one by
one) at the next prompt. Enter **CUSTNAME** as both the
name of the indexed linking field in the other database and
the name of the linking field in this database. Answer Yes
to the prompt "Can this field be keyed over?" Refer to Figure 14.12 if you need help. Notice that the CUSTNAME
field is the linking field in this database (ORDERS) and in
the CUST database. The field appears in both databases and
links all other fields.

6. Move the cursor to another, discrete location, and enter the
PRODINV field in the inventory database. Substitute **INVEN**
when prompted "From what database?", **PRODINV** as the
Lookup field, and **PRODNO** when prompted "Name of
indexed linking field in other database" and "Name of linking
field in this database" (Figure 14.11). Your screen should
resemble Figure 14.12.

After linking these
databases, you may
only need the orders
database for data entry.

Now, whenever you enter a customer name into the orders database that doesn't already exist in the customer database, it will be
entered in both the orders database and the customer database.
All the customer information can be entered on the orders database

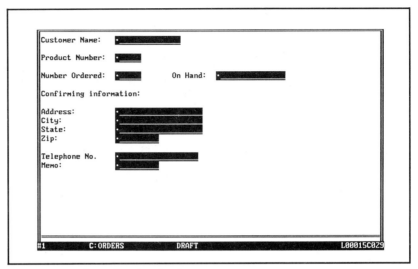

```
┌──────────────────────────────────────────────────────────────┐
│┌────────────────────────────────────────────────────────────┐│
││Customer Name:    ▪▬▬▬▬▬▬▬▬▬                                  ││
││                                                              ││
││Product Number:   ▪▬▬▬▬                                       ││
││                                                              ││
││Number Ordered:   ▪▬▬▬▬        On Hand:  ▪▬▬▬▬▬▬▬▬▬▬          ││
││                                                              ││
││Confirming information:                                       ││
││                                                              ││
││Address:          ▪▬▬▬▬▬▬▬▬▬▬▬                                ││
││City:             ▪▬▬▬▬▬▬▬▬▬▬▬                                ││
││State:            ▪▬▬▬▬▬▬▬▬▬▬▬                                ││
││Zip:              ▪▬▬▬▬▬▬▬▬▬▬▬                                ││
││                                                              ││
││Telephone No.     ▪▬▬▬▬▬▬▬▬▬▬                                 ││
││Memo:             ▪▬▬▬▬▬▬                                     ││
││                                                              ││
││                                                              ││
││                                                              ││
││                                                              ││
│└──────────────────────────────────────────────────────────────┘│
│#1        C:ORDERS          DRAFT                    L00015C029 │
└──────────────────────────────────────────────────────────────┘
```

Figure 14.12: Completed order form

from the orders input form (Figure 14.13). Furthermore, if the customer name exists, all the corresponding customer information will be entered into the orders input form instantaneously, as soon as you enter the name into the orders database.

```
┌──────────────────────────────────────────────────────────────┐
│┌────────────────────────────────────────────────────────────┐│
││Customer Name:    Gimbal Computer                             ││
││                                                              ││
││Product Number:   111111                                      ││
││                                                              ││
││Number Ordered:   1            On Hand:  11                   ││
││                                                              ││
││Confirming information:                                       ││
││                                                              ││
││Address:          1212 32nd Street                            ││
││City:             Baldwin                                     ││
││State:            MI                                          ││
││Zip:              48840                                       ││
││                                                              ││
││Telephone No.     00-616-222-2222-222                         ││
││Memo:             MEMO ALT/M                                  ││
││                                                              ││
││                                                              ││
││                                                              ││
││                                                              ││
│└────────────────────────────────────────────────────────────┘│
│#1.End of form: Press [PgUp], [↑], or [Home] to review, [F10] for menu..0  A:016│
└──────────────────────────────────────────────────────────────┘
```

Figure 14.13: The order form filled with data

Similarly, as soon as you enter the product number, if it is a product that already exists in the inventory, the quantity on hand will appear on screen. Admittedly, this is just a skeleton of a database. You will want to make significant changes and additions, but, now that you understand the structure, those changes and additions will be easier.

Now that you have seen how to structure a database, it is time to move on to creative uses for the information you will enter. In the upcoming chapters, you will see the value of intelligent database design.

CHAPTER

15

Creating Reports from Database Information

ONE OF THE MAIN FUNCTIONS OF A DATABASE IS TO present information in a report. These reports are useful for statistical analysis, updated listings, and many other purposes. This chapter deals with creating database reports.

In the previous chapter you have seen one of the methods for creating a report: the Use System, DBMS/Graphics, Design, Report Form options. This procedure resembles the database definition and input-form definition procedure.

Enable provides two other options for creating reports: creating a columnar report and using the dot commands in the procedural language. This chapter will cover both of these reporting procedures and provide examples for creating them.

ORGANIZING YOUR RECORDS BY SORTING

Your information is useful only to the extent that it is organized. One way to organize your data is to select the field that determines the order in which information is be listed, or sorted. Using the CUST database you created earlier as an example, if you are creating a report listing which customers are active with your company, you would select the CUSTNAME field as the key field. This means that the database is sorted by customer names. If, on the other hand, you were interested in who ordered the largest amount of a product, you would sort on the ORDER field in the ORDERS database. In other words, each case is different; you will select a key field that results in a report organized in the most useful way.

In this section you'll use the ORDERS database you created earlier to make a report based on zip codes. Before you begin, though, you'll add some information to the inventory database. If you are not currently at the Main Enable menu, press Alt-Home to begin there.

1. Select Use System, DBMS/Graphics, Interact. You will be taken to the Database Management System screen.

2. Cursor to the *Add* option and press ◄┘.

3. Enter **INVEN** as the database. "INVEN" will automatically be entered as the form. Press ◄┘ to accept it.

4. Enter the data for the Product Number (PRODNO) field and the On Hand (PRODINV) field for the six records shown in step 9.

5. Select F10, Save and return to the Main menu.

6. Select Use System, DBMS/Graphics, Interact. You will be taken to the Database Management System screen.

7. Cursor to the *Add* option and press ◄┘.

8. Enter **ORDERS** as the database. ORDERS will automatically be entered as the form. Delete this and enter **ORDERS** as the form.

Notice that when you enter the product number, the inventory automatically appears. After entering these records, try retyping one of them—all data will reappear as soon as you retype the name.

9. Enter the following 6 records in the resulting data entry form:

Customer Name: Able Computers
Product Number: 102126
Number Ordered: 92
On Hand: 3145
Address: 2323 Highland
City: Detroit
State: MI
Zip: 48818
Telephone No.   00-313-222-1111-111

Customer Name: Arentson
Product Number: 102127
Number Ordered: 90
On Hand: 12143
Address: 333 Grand River
City: Detroit
State: MI
Zip: 48801
Telephone No.   00-313-222-2222-222

Customer Name: Terra Nova, Inc
Product Number: 102128
Number Ordered: 100
On Hand: 102
Address: 3113 Grand River
City: Lansing
State: MI
Zip: 48588
Telephone No.   00-517-3333-333

Customer Name: Alwin Computers
Product Number: 102129
Number Ordered: 10
On Hand: 1534
Address: 3223 Belding Way
City: Greenville
State: MI
Zip: 48121
Telephone No.   00-616-222-2222-222

Customer Name:	Gimbal Computer
Product Number:	120130
Number Ordered:	15
On Hand:	255
Address:	1212 32nd Street
City:	Baldwin
State:	MI
Zip:	49940
Telephone No.	00-616-222-2222-222

Customer Name:	Gimbal Pianos
Product Number:	120131
Number Ordered:	14
On Hand:	141
Address:	1212 Amberhill
City:	Los Angeles
State:	CA
Zip:	90010
Telephone No.	00-213-222-2222-222

Following are the steps involved in sorting database records. You'll use the CUST database you created earlier.

1. From the Main menu, select *Use System*, *DBMS/Graphics*, *Interact*.

2. From the resulting array of options (the DBMS Command Chart), select *Report* and enter the database name (**CUST**).

3. Press Esc to return to the DBMS Command Chart and select the *Sort* option. You will be taken to the screen shown in Figure 15.1.

4. Enter the necessary information in the lines on this screen: The name of the database to sort, the index (if it exists), and any information in the Where field (if you want to use a subset of the records), and then enter the sort fields followed by **,A** for ascending (A to Z and 0 to 9) or **,D** for descending sort (Z to A and 9 to 0). Figure 15.2 shows the CUST database set up for a sort based on zip codes.

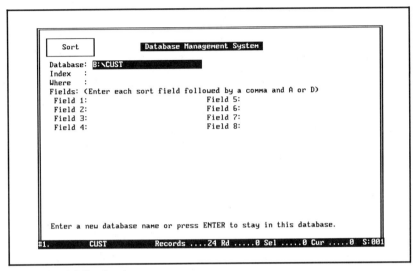

Figure 15.1: The database sort screen

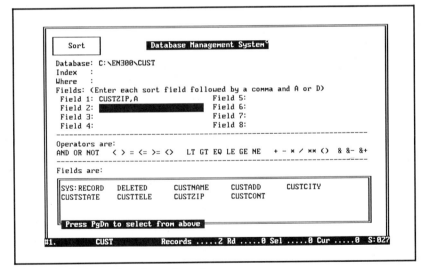

Figure 15.2: A sort based on zip codes

5. When you have entered all the fields on which to sort, press ←┘ on an empty field and the sort will commence, creating and saving (to disk) a special sorted database called CUST.SS.

6. Press Esc to return to the DBMS Command Chart, and select *Report* again. CUST.SS will already be entered in the

Database line. Press ◀── to select this as the database that will serve as the basis for the new report.

7. If there is a form entered in the *Using Form* line, delete it with the Del key or Alt-F3. You won't want to use a form; Enable will create its own form to fit the information contained in the database.

8. Enter the Index information, if the database has an index, and if it is to be used.

9. Now you must decide whether the resulting report should be directed to the screen, the disk, or the printer. It's a good practice to direct all reports to the screen first, in order to save paper, so select *Screen*. You may discover, for instance, that the data should be sorted on a different field, or that your Index and Where selections have allowed too many records or too few to come through in the report. You can also enter a title.

If you select *Disk*, you will be prompted for a file name. If you select *Disk* or *Printer*, you will be led through a series of screens used to define the printer format. These are the same four printer definition screens you've seen previously in the word processing and spreadsheet chapters.

10. When everything is entered to your satisfaction, press ◀── through all of the prompts, the last one being *Title*. Enable then displays the report.

You may discover that only the first few columns are visible on the screen. You can see the remaining columns by using the → key to move to the right. Move the cursor back to the left side of the report with the ← key. You can see the finished report with a list of six customers in Figure 15.3.

CREATING SUBGROUPS

As you may have noticed in the Report screen in the previous exercise, you can insert a title into the report. Other enhancements include *breaks*, or blank lines each time a change occurs in the field.

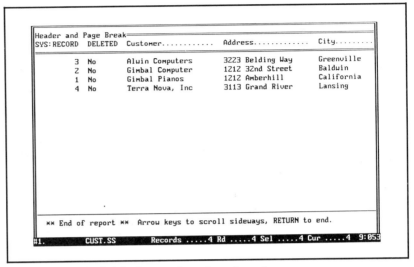

```
┌─────────────────────────────────────────────────────────────────────────┐
│ Header and Page Break                                                     │
│ SYS:RECORD   DELETED   Customer..........   Address............  City...... │
│                                                                           │
│           3   No        Aluin Computers     3223 Belding Way    Greenville │
│           2   No        Gimbal Computer      1212 32nd Street    Balduin   │
│           1   No        Gimbal Pianos        1212 Amberhill      California │
│           4   No        Terra Nova, Inc      3113 Grand River    Lansing   │
│                                                                           │
│                                                                           │
│                                                                           │
│                                                                           │
│                                                                           │
│                                                                           │
│                                                                           │
│     ** End of report **   Arrow keys to scroll sideways, RETURN to end.   │
│ #1.        CUST.SS        Records .....4 Rd .....4 Sel .....4 Cur .....4  9:053 │
└─────────────────────────────────────────────────────────────────────────┘
```

Figure 15.3: The finished report based on zip codes

You can specify a break simply by entering the name of a field, followed by a letter code and a number in curly braces. For example, if you wanted a break in the report between state names, you would enter CUSTSTATE{B1} at the Fields prompt on the Report screen. (B stands for *break*, and the 1 indicates the hierarchy of the break.) That would cause the report to be broken and to skip a line each time a new state name was encountered. Naturally, you would want to plan your database organization carefully with this in mind: If your database contains entries from every state in the union and you have sorted on CUSTNAME, your state codes would be randomly distributed. Therefore, you would probably end up with many times the number of breaks you would expect, with only one or two entries following each break. In short, make sure you sort the database by the field on which you are breaking.

The report will print all your fields unless you specify otherwise in the Fields line in the Report screen. You can control the size of the report, allowing only relevant data through, by specifying fields.

You also can include codes for certain computations in your report. For example, CUSTSTATE{T,C,B1} uses the T, C, and B codes to specify the number of records since the last break in the report (called a tally) and the number of different states, and it would provide a break based on the state. The codes are as follows:

CODE	MEANING
{A}	Average
{C}	Count
{S}	Sum
{H}	Maximum value (highest)
{L}	Minimum value (lowest)
{T}	Tally
{B}	Break

Normally, the computations are printed at the end of the report, but you can arrange to have them printed at the break simply by entering the level of break. For example, the entry

CUSTSTATE{T1,C1,B1}

would place a tally and count subtotal at each break (of that level or lower), along with a tally and count total at the end. Therefore, if this database had included fields for counties and municipalities, and if they were broken out with commands like COUNTY{B5}, each of these breaks would have featured a subtotal of tally and count.

THE DATABASE PROGRAMMING LANGUAGE

Enable's database has powers that go far beyond the simple reporting features described thus far. You can build reports that include any information you like from any database you like, and you can format these reports in any way. The source of all this power lies in Enable's database procedural language. The *procedural language* is a simple programming language that controls your databases and reports. But don't let the word *language* scare you off; the procedural language is easier to use than a true programming language such as Pascal or C.

Like complex languages, the procedural language consists of commands that you can combine in particular ways to perform actions. These commands form the basis of the language and are called *dot commands*. A complete explanation of dot commands is contained in Chapter 16. In this chapter, the commands are grouped according to their functions.

Each dot command is preceded by a period (for example, .add). You can combine them into a command set, or *program*, by typing them into a procedural language file. A *procedural language file* is merely a word processor document containing dot commands entered in a specific way. Like any language, the procedural language has a syntax. In other words, you must follow certain rigidly defined rules when writing a procedural language program. Failure to follow these rules will result in a useless program, and hence a useless database report. In extreme cases, this could even lead to loss of data or a system crash.

Before we dive into an explanation of building programs, let's cover some basics about how your procedural language program should look on screen. First, the commands are entered into a word processor document. Each command should appear on a line by itself, and data relating to the command should be indented below the command:

```
.do case
  .case [custname] = "A$"
.endcase
```

Often, a command requires you to specify a field or a database name on which the command operates. The program assumes that the specified field is part of the current database—that is, the open database. If you are pulling a field from another database (a linked database), its name must be entered as follows:

DATABASE.FIELD

You must include the database name and the field name desired. Be sure to include the entire path name for the database (unless it's the current default path). For example, to pull the CUSTNAME field from the CUST database, which is located in the \DATA\ directory, you would enter

```
C:\DATA\CUST.CUSTNAME
```

CREATING
A SIMPLE REPORT PROGRAM

Entering a program is no different than typing a letter in the word processor except that the text of the document is limited to the procedural language commands.

When creating a program, keep in mind the two types of commands: section commands and processing commands. *Section commands* are used to begin parts of the program that contain processing commands. Hence, a program is divided into parts. Each part (beginning with a section command) must be present for a complete report. The section commands must include the following:

> ◄ To be sure you don't skip one of these section commands, use a macro to automatically enter these commands into your new word processor file. Macros are discussed in Chapter 19.

```
.report division
.definitions
.map section
.intro
.body
.conclusion
```

If the program includes *subroutines* (short programs set off by themselves, containing code that is called repeatedly from various routines within the program), you will need an additional section command:

```
.subroutines
```

Suppose you want to create a simple report that lists only those customers whose names begin with A and whose businesses are in the 313 area code. (These two conditions could be replaced by any other conditions, of course.) You'll use these two conditions to create a report program from the CUST database. Here's how to start.

1. Enter the word processor with a new document. Use the commands *Use System, Word Processing, Create* to create a new

file. Enter the name **PROG1.RPT** as the name of this new document.

2. Press ← to accept suggested margins and tabs.

3. Enter the following section commands in order (remember to include the dots and to press ← after each command so it begins a new line):

```
.report division
.definitions
.map section
.intro
.body
.conclusion
```

You have begun the structure of the report. Now, fill out the introduction section as follows:

4. Move the cursor to the line containing the command *.intro* and press F3 to insert a line.

5. On the inserted blank line, type this introductory phrase:

This report consists of all customers in southeast Michigan whose businesses begin with A.

This line will appear at the top of the report. (If the text doesn't wrap to the next line, press F9 O A R to turn on the automatic reformat feature.) Now you are ready to type the procedure that chooses the desired records from the database.

6. Move the cursor to the command *.body* and press F3 seven times to insert seven blank lines.

7. Type the following commands on the seven new lines. Be sure to indent as shown (the first command—*.do case*—should not be indented):

```
.do case
  .case [custname] = "A$"
  .do case
    .case [custtele] = "00-313$"
[custname] [custcity]    [custtele]    [custstate]    [custzip]
    .endcase
.endcase
```

8. Add a conclusion to the report by inserting a blank line under the *.conclusion* command and typing the following on the new line:

    This is the end of the brief report.

You are now ready to generate this simple report. Here are the steps:

9. Save the program file using the command F9 S Home. This takes you to the Main menu.

10. Enter the database using the *Use System*, *DBMS/Graphics*, and *Report* options.

11. Enter the database name **CUST** in the space provided, then press ←⎯.

12. Enter the form name **PROG1.RPT** as the form name. Remove any existing form name if Enable presents one.

13. Skip the index prompt by pressing ←⎯. (You could use this option to specify an indexed field for the report.)

14. Specify that you want to print the report to the screen.

15. Skip the Where line by pressing ←⎯. The report will be generated; it should look like the one in Figure 15.4.

You can insert all the instructions you need to make the report as detailed as necessary. For example, suppose you want a listing of all your customers, broken down by state and with breaks between states. You could use the following program to create this:

```
.report division
.definitions
.break 01 procedure
.break on [custstate]
.break heading
[custstate]
Customer            Telephone
.break summary
[custname{t}]
```

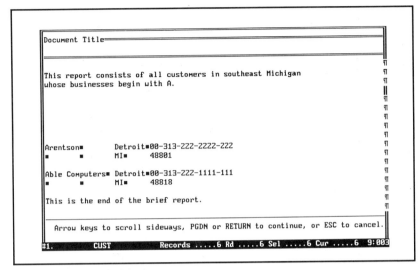

Figure 15.4: The finished report

```
.break end
.map section
.intro
Customers broken down by state.
.body
[custname]          [custtele]
.conclusion
```

By now, you should have no trouble reading this program. Basically, it creates a break that lists the state and provides the column headings for two columns: customer names and telephone numbers. When all the customers in a given state are listed (by name and telephone number), the tally number, or the number of customers in that state, is listed.

You could add commands to this basic program to create a listing broken down by state, and then by city (the lines in boldface type are new lines).

```
.report division
.definitions
.break 01 procedure
.break on [custstate]
```

```
.break heading
[custstate]
.break end
.break 02 procedure
.break on [custcity]
.break heading
[custcity], [custstate]
Customer        Telephone        City
.break summary
[custname{t}]

.break end
.map section
.intro
Customers broken down by state.
.body
[custname]         [custtele]        [custcity]
.conclusion
```

SOME TIPS FOR
USING PROCEDURAL LANGUAGE

Following are some special features that will make entering your procedural language programs easier. First, use *comments* to remind yourself of the action caused by a section of the program. Comments are preceded by a double semicolon. Each comment line must have the double semicolon in it, even if it is a continuation from a line above. In the following example, the first three lines are the comment lines:

```
;;Following creates a break on the
;;custcity field and adds a heading and
;;summary.
.break 02 procedure
.break on [custcity]
.break heading
[custcity], [custstate]
Customer        Telephone        City
.break summary
[custname{t}]
.break end
```

Another handy feature is the use of *system fields* provided by Enable, which contain special data. You can use them anywhere you would normally use a database field. Often, they are used in summaries and headings. These are the four system fields:

sys:record	Provides the number of the current record.
sys:lchar	Provides the scan code of the last key typed. (Details about this field are found in Chapter 16 under "Getting and Placing Information.")
sys:date	Provides the current date in year, month, day format.
sys:time	Provides the current time in 24-hour format.

The sys:record field is a useful feature that deserves a closer look. Each time a record is added to the database, it is issued a serial number known as the sys:record. This is an indexed field provided by Enable for each database that you can use with any database. It is sequential throughout the database, and you can use it in linking as an alternative to an indexed field. If you do not use an indexed field, you save disk space, because each indexed field has an accompanying disk file in which all entries are kept in sorted order.

Let's look at another time-saver. It's easy enough to recall the contents of a field in the current record by entering its name in brackets in the text file, especially when the example database contains only half a dozen fields. But what will you do when you can't remember a field name when creating a complex report? To list fields in any database while working in the word processor, enter the command F10, DBMS. Then position the cursor, press ←⏎, and type the name of the desired database. Enable presents a list of the fields in the specified database (use PgUp and PgDn to flip through multiple screens). Use the cursor keys to highlight the desired field, then press ←⏎ to see the contents of the field (see Figure 15.5).

KEYBOARD DATABASE COMMANDS

As you become more familiar with the database, you may want to use some of the keyboard equivalent commands for your actions. Table 15.1 lists the keyboard commands available for the database.

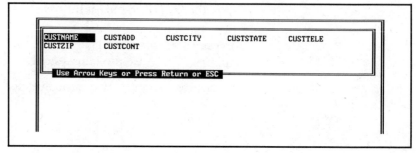

Figure 15.5: Using F10, DBMS to list database fields while in the word processor module

Table 15.1: Keyboard Database Commands

KEY/S	DESCRIPTION
F1	Accesses help
Shift-F1	Switches to Query mode
Alt-F2	Prints
Ctrl-F2	Cancels printing
Alt-F3	Erases an entry
F4	Edits a field (in Display mode)
F5	Saves current record and advances to next record
Ctrl-F5	Switches from Edit to Add mode
Shift-F5	Adds an Index statement
F6	Saves current record and returns to previous record
Alt-F6	Ignores record entry
Shift-F6	Adds a Where statement
F7	Marks a block (press at beginning and end)
F8	Copies information between Add and Edit modes; also makes masked entries visible in VERIFY.
Alt-F9\[*key*]	Begins the macro recorder

Table 15.1: Keyboard Database Commands (continued)

KEY/S	DESCRIPTION
Alt-F9 End	Turns the macro recorder off
Alt-F9 [*key*]	Begins the specified macro
Shift-F9	Places a field entry area in the report or input form design screen
F10	Displays the Top Line menu
Alt-F10	Saves the form
Ctrl-F10 [*key*]	Brings up the user-defined menu named with [*key*]
Shift-F10	Brings up the default user-defined menu

The key to programming success is experimentation. For example, enter a database of friends' addresses and telephone numbers and use the basic report form created here to display the data in many different ways. A good database like Enable's database module can set you free to organize information in almost infinite varieties of ways.

Using the Procedural Programming Language

This chapter deals with *dot commands*, which make up a special command language called the *procedural language.* In Chapter 15, you saw how procedural language files are created and some of the purposes they serve. Now that you are familiar with the basics of procedural language files, you're ready to learn some details about the actual commands and how to use them. Refer to this chapter as you build procedural language files for your applications. Table 16.1 summarizes the dot commands and their syntax.

Table 16.1: Enable Procedural Language Commands

COMMAND NAME	DESCRIPTION
.add	Creates a new record containing the totals of numeric fields (those you specify to be totaled).
.body	Begins a section of the program that controls the body of the report.

Table 16.1: Enable Procedural Language Commands (continued)

COMMAND NAME	DESCRIPTION
.break end	Used to mark the end of a .break *xx procedure*.
.break on	Used after .break *xx procedure* to actually break the report on a specified command or piece of information. For example, .break on CUSTNAME would tell Enable that the 01-level break specified in .break 01 procedure should occur whenever the customer name changes.
.break *xx procedure*	Begins a section of the program that produces a break in the report. Commonly used to split groups of similar records onto their own pages or to start a new page with a new heading. For example, .break 01 *procedure* would prepare Enable to create a break.
.case	Used to specify multiple conditions with the .do case command.
.checkkey	Used with linking procedures to check which databases are linked to the current one.
.close	Closes a database that was opened with the .open command.
.conclusion	Begins a section of the program that applies to the end of the report.
.define	Creates new fields that do not appear in the database. These fields apply to the report only.
.define using	Creates a picture for printing out the contents of a variable.
.definitions	Begins a section of the program that contains definitions. You specify these definitions with the .define command.

Table 16.1: Enable Procedural Language Commands (continued)

COMMAND NAME	DESCRIPTION
.do case	Begins a section of the program that performs a specific action based on a specific occasion. Also called a *do loop*.
.else	Branches to an alternative sequence of commands after an .if procedure.
.elseif	Branches to an alternative sequence of commands after an .if procedure.
.endcase	Used to mark the end of .do case.
.endif	Concludes an .if procedure.
.endwhile	Concludes a .while procedure.
.escape off	Deactivates the Esc key during reporting.
.escape on	Activates the Esc key during reporting.
.exit	Exits from the report before the actual conclusion. Often used with an .if procedure to exit only under certain circumstances.
.getchar	Pauses the report until any key is pressed.
.gosub	Branches to a specified .subroutine procedure.
.goto *heading*	Branches to a section of commands containing a specified *heading*.
.if	Begins a section of the program that tests for a condition in the report. If the condition is met, one action can be taken; if the condition is not met, a different action can be taken. Also called an *.if procedure*.
.input	Pauses the program and asks for a piece of information to be input.
.intro	Begins a section of the program that controls the introduction of the report.

Table 16.1: Enable Procedural Language Commands (continued)

COMMAND NAME	DESCRIPTION
.label	Provides a label to be used with the .goto and .gosub commands.
.let *value*	Defines a *value*.
.macro	Begins a section of the program that defines a macro sequence.
.map	Begins a section of the program that defines the layout (or map) of the report.
.maxscreen	Accesses the entire screen without the status line. Useful in a .map procedure.
.open	Opens a database for use in linking.
.otherwise	Used with .do case to determine the action to be taken if none of the cases are met.
.passthru off	Deactivates the linking feature, which links fields from one database to another.
.passthru on	Activates the linking feature, which links fields from one database to another.
.perform	Runs a different program file from inside the current program.
.position	Controls the location of the pointer in a report.
.read	Accesses and reads a record from an external (linked) database.
.reformat off	Deactivates the automatic reformat feature, which formats each report record according to its data. Useful for business forms and mailing labels that use a common ''form'' regardless of the data.
.reformat on	Activates the automatic reformat feature.
.report division	Begins the procedural language program.
.return	Returns the program flow to its normal progression after a subroutine.

Table 16.1: Enable Procedural Language Commands (continued)

COMMAND NAME	DESCRIPTION
.status	Displays a named field each time the field changes.
.subroutines	Begins a section of the program that contains a subroutine. (See also the .gosub command.)
.update	Passes information to another database.
.while	Begins a section of the program that performs an action while another action is taking place (also called a *.while procedure*).

REPEATING ACTIONS WITH LOOPS

The ability to use loops within a program is one of the most vital and troublesome aspects of programming. A *loop* repeats an action or series of actions until a given condition exists. For example, a new recruit in boot camp must make and remake his bunk until a quarter can bounce on the sheet. When the condition is met (when the quarter bounces), the loop is finished, and the recruit can proceed to the next set of instructions (probably KP).

Enable's procedural language provides a looping option in the form of the command *.while*. After you enter the command, you state the condition under which the loop continues. Following this command, on separate lines, are the actions that take place during the loop. The loop is ended with the *.endwhile* command. When Enable encounters the .while command, it performs the commands in the loop until the condition is no longer met. Then Enable jumps to the command following the .endwhile command. Here's an example:

```
.while Y < 10
.read ORDERS.ORDER next
.let Y = ORDERS.ORDER
.endwhile
```

The fourth line determines the value of the variable Y by setting the value of *Y* to the value contained in the ORDER field of the ORDERS database. If this value is less than 10, the program will read the next order, then the next, until it reaches an order equal to or greater than 10. The first three lines of the program say, "While the value of Y (the ORDER) is less than 10, read the next ORDER field (the next record). Then continue until you reach a value equal to or greater than 10."

CHANGING THE PROGRAM'S FLOW WITH BRANCHING

Enable usually reads a procedural language file from top to bottom and performs the commands as they are listed, but you can change this natural flow using a *branching* command. You generally change the program's flow when a certain condition is met by having the program jump to a new set of commands. Since a program has so many decisions, Enable provides several ways for the program to branch.

CONDITIONAL BRANCHING

Conditional branches make the decision to branch based on a condition, which may change over several records. The most common branching command is the *.if* command. The .if command is usually accompanied by *.else* and *.elseif*, and it must be paired with an *.endif* command. These commands are used as follows:

COMMAND	DESCRIPTION
.if	Tests whether a statement is true. If it isn't, processing jumps to the .endif, .else, or .elseif statement.
.else	If there are only two choices, .if is used to specify one and .else is used to specify the other. For example, a coin toss could be seen as

```
.if tails
    (you win)
.else
    (you lose)
.endif
```

The procedure to follow in each case is enclosed in parentheses here.

.elseif   If there are several choices, a series of .elseif statements may follow the .if statement. If you are picking out ice cream, for example, you might have a series of statements like this:

```
.if vanilla
    (get a chocolate dip)
.elseif chocolate
    (sprinkle with nuts)
.elseif strawberry
    (smother in strawberry syrup)
.endif
```

You can also use the .else command for the last .elseif option, to indicate what to do if all preceding options fail.

.endif   This command simply tells the Enable program interpreter that the .if statements are at an end.

Another branching command is the *.do case* command. Its function is similar to the .elseif command. You might think of it as a substitute for multiple .elseif commands. You begin by typing .do case on a line by itself, and then follow it with however many options you need, each indented and preceded by the command *.case*. When you have completed all the .case options, use the *.otherwise* command. This determines the actions taken if none of the cases are met. Finally, use *.endcase* to tell the processor that you are through specifying cases:

```
.do case
    .case income < 10000
        .let class = "lower"
    .case income >50000
        .let class = "upper"
```

```
            .otherwise
             .let class = "middle"
          .endcase
```

UNCONDITIONAL BRANCHING

Unconditional branches result in a change of program flow whatever the current condition. The commands involved are .goto and .gosub, two commands familiar to BASIC programmers.

The *.goto* command takes you to a position elsewhere in the program identified with the .label command. The syntax for this command is

```
   .goto label
```

where *label* is the specified label at the point of reentry. Labels are defined using the *.label* command. For example, you might use the branching statement

```
   .goto special
```

which requires that somewhere in the program, the command

```
   .label special
```

is found. Labels can contain uppercase or lowercase alphabetic characters and may contain no spaces or other punctuation.

The *.gosub* command (its name derives from "go to subroutine") also branches to a label. It differs from .goto in that the program flow should eventually return from a .gosub, whereas a .goto may conclude after branching. In other words, use a .gosub when you want to return to the point where the program branched off.

If you find yourself writing the same set of programming lines again and again, you can enter the lines beneath a label and use .gosub to jump to those lines temporarily (that is, jump to the label). At the end of the subroutine, you should have a *.return* command, which returns the program flow to the point where it branched. Here is an example:

```
.gosub warning
(rest of program)
...
.subroutines
.label warning
   LOOKOUT!!!
.return
```

All subroutines must be in a section headed with the *.subroutines* command. Each subroutine begins with a .label command and ends with a .return command.

Whenever the program interpreter encounters the line ".gosub warning," it will print "LOOKOUT!!!" on the screen and then return to the main program at the .return command. It then proceeds to the next command after the .gosub warning command identified in the example as (*rest of program*). Naturally, subroutines are usually far more complicated than this example.

Similar to .gosub is the *.perform* command. Essentially, .perform calls another program file and executes it. This is a more powerful command than .gosub because it allows what is essentially an external program to be accessed by any active program.

You can pass up to nine parameters to the program called by .perform by including them in a DOS-like parameter scheme. For instance, within your procedure, you might have a command to open a file and then perform some action on its contents. Say you are writing a perform file called ORGANIZE. Inside ORGANIZE, you could have the command .open %1. Then, when you call ORGANIZE to straighten out your CUST file, you would use the command

.perform organize CUST

This places CUST in the position occupied by %1 and would result in CUST being opened. The command .perform can be followed by nine parameters, identified within the perform file as %1, %2, %3, and so on, up to %9.

Another way to divert the program flow is with *.exit*. This command simply stops the program. It is normally used with an .if command to indicate an error is encountered, as in

```
.if ORDER > PRODINV
* * * *out of stock* * * *
.exit
.endif
```

FORMATTING

You have seen some of these commands in use in Chapter 15. Though their form was different, you will instantly recognize the effect of the commands.

The *.map section* command is used to begin the section of a program that formats, or designs, the report itself. This part of the report will follow the *.define* statements and will contain the commands .intro, .body, and .conclusion. In other words, when you're ready to design the report using a procedural language file, you must include the following sections:

```
.map section
    .intro
    .body
    .conclusion
```

Specific formatting commands are placed within each of these sections; each section controls a different part of the report. Several commands are used specifically for formatting output.

THE INTRODUCTION

The *.intro* command controls the format of the report's introduction. The .intro section is also where you will define values used globally through the program. For example, you might want to insert a heading explaining what will be contained in the report. Breaks such as .break 01 CUSTNAME also naturally fit into the .intro section.

THE BODY

The *.body* command tells Enable how and where each record will be printed for the body of the report. Simply place .body at the left margin and follow it with field names in brackets. If you were printing the CUST database, the .body section of your file might look like this:

```
.body
[custname]        [custtele]
[custadd]
[custcity]
[custstate]
[custzip]
```

This program places the information on the page as indicated (see Figures 16.1 through 16.3). Figure 16.1 shows the simple program DOTFILR.WPF written in the word processor module. Figure 16.2 illustrates how you can place the program name in the report form at the "Using from:" prompt. Figure 16.3 is the actual screen display of a record as a result of using the program.

The calculations and breaks for summarizing reports at crucial points mentioned in Chapter 15 can be placed in the program as well. Simply follow the syntax in Table 16.1 and enclose the curly braces

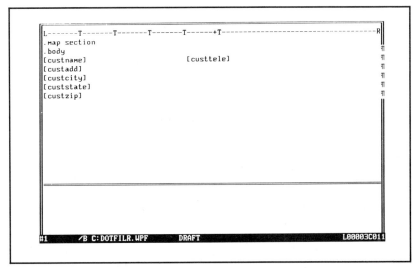

Figure 16.1: The procedural language program DOTFILR.WPF

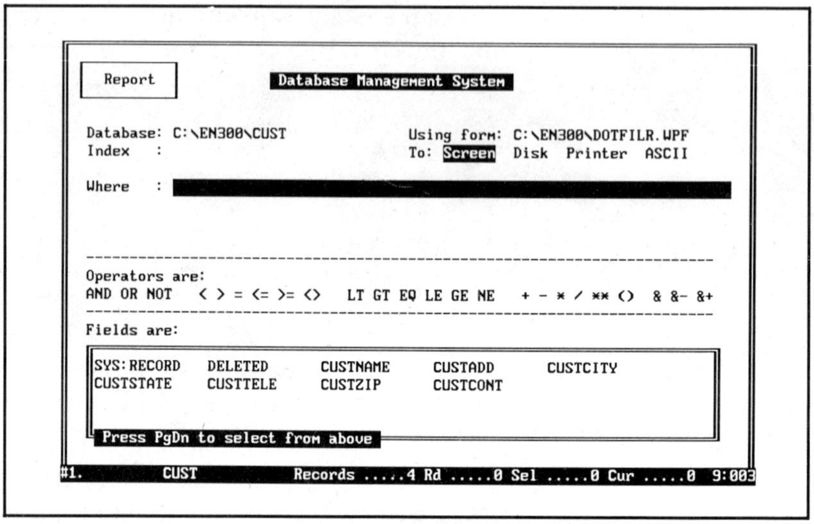

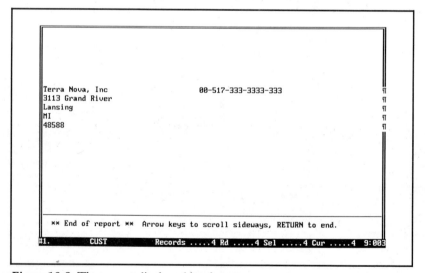

Figure 16.2: Accessing the program to print a report

Figure 16.3: The report displayed by the program

within brackets. For example, if you use

[custname{t}]

you will get only the number representing the tally of customer names. If you want to see both the number and the contents of the field, enter

[custname{t}]. [custname]

This will format the output to look like Figure 16.4. Note that each customer's name is preceded by a number. This is generated by the [custname{t}] code.

Another formatting option is to align the text in the field. Normally, numerical values are right-aligned and text entries are left-aligned. By inserting one of the following codes in the field description, you can change this:

Center   {^}

Flush left   {<}

Flush right   {>}

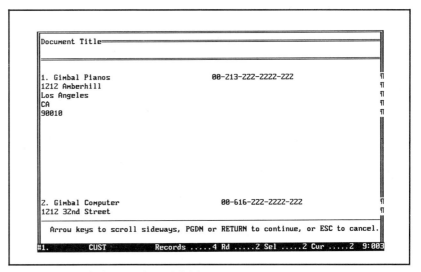

Figure 16.4: Printing totals and fields

You may recall using breaks in the report generator. You can also specify breaks in your dot-command program file. A break creates an open space in a document, like pressing the carriage return key twice on an electronic typewriter. But it is more powerful than this. Rather than a simple blank line, a break procedure can insert information. In each report, you are allowed up to 16 break procedures.

Breaks are inserted whenever a condition in the report changes. When breaks were discussed earlier, the example used created breaks with tallies and subtotals that were entered when the state or the county changed. Recall that for this procedure to work properly, the file had to be sorted ahead of time on the fields that would contain breaks.

The command used to produce a break is *.break xx procedure*. The first level would be identified as

.break 01 procedure

Under this you would type

.break on

followed by the list of conditions necessary to trigger a break. For example, to break on the state field in the CUST database, you would enter

.break on CUSTSTATE.

The next command is

.break heading

which will define the information that should precede the break (that is, heading information). The next item is

.break summary

followed by the computations to perform. For example, you might want a simple tally of the number of customers you are serving. In that case, you would enter

```
.break summary
    [custname{T}]
```

At the end of the procedure, you would type

```
.break end
```

to tell the processor that the break is ended.

THE CONCLUSION

You can insert text and calculations for the conclusion portion of the report by using the *.conclusion* command. Enter any concluding statement you wish to make and any summary calculations you want to provide.

ASSIGNING VALUES

The *.let* command assigns a value to a variable or the value of an expression to a field. You can use this command to change a variable's value or to set it in the first place. Here's an example:

```
.let middle = 10000
```

This command allows you to use the word *middle* as if it were the value 10000. Thus, you can easily change a value throughout a program simply by altering its .let statement or by calculating it with other values.

PRELIMINARY COMMANDS

In every programming language some commands deal with setting up the computer or the software to make sense of the program that follows. These preliminaries are dealt with at the beginning of the program in a series of lines following the .definitions command.

You can use the *.let* command in the first section of the program to define the contents of variables in advance of their use.

The .*define* command is used to create variables. Enable considers these to be local fields because they don't exist in any database. There are three kinds of variables that can be defined: derived variables, variables that take their value from existing fields in other databases, and variables containing values supplied within the procedure. For example, you can derive a field from other fields:

.define ARREARS = OWED - PAID

where OWED and PAID are fields that exist in the current database, and ARREARS is a local field (a field made up for use only with the program).

Another use of .define is to obtain information from another database, as in

.define CUSTID = CUSTTELE in CUST link CUSTNAME = NAME

In this example, CUSTID is a local field used to identify the customer based on the customer's telephone number in the CUST database. The field CUSTTELE is the field to be brought in from the other database (the telephone number field in the CUST database). CUST is the name of the other database. CUSTNAME is the indexed field in the other database. NAME is the link field in the current database.

The general form is

.define FIELDNAME = LOOKUPFIELD in DATABASE2 link INDEX2 = LINKNAME

where FIELDNAME is the locally defined field, LOOKUPFIELD is the name of the field to be looked up in the other database, DATABASE2 is the other database, and INDEX2 is the indexed link field in the other database. The last part, = LINKNAME in the general form and = NAME in the example, is only necessary when the link field has a different name in the two databases.

A third .define option is to prepare fields that will then be used in the .map section of the program. For example, you might define TODAY as the DATE field with

.define TODAY as DATE

This makes TODAY a date-type field for use in the procedure.

Finally, you can use *.define using* to create a picture for printing out the contents of a variable. A dollar value might use the following definition:

.define INCOME as DECIMAL using "$nn,nnn.nn"

You can use a few other commands at the beginning of the program. The command *.escape off* disables the Esc key while the program is running, so that you can interrupt the report. The *.escape on* command turns the Esc key back on. The *.maxscreen* command uses the entire screen for the report, eliminating the status line at the bottom.

The *.passthru on* and *.passthru off* commands turn on and off the ability to write to an outside file. In the ORDER input form, you could enter a customer name, telephone number, and address, for instance, although the telephone number and address were actually stored in an external database (CUST). The same effect can be obtained with .passthru on. (See .updatekey and .checkkey in the section "Getting and Placing Information.")

The commands *.reformat on* and *.reformat off* allow fields to adjust themselves to the length of output. For example, if you have made your CUSTNAME field 20 characters long, but your customers' names vary from three to twenty letters, .reformat on causes the output to act as if the field were only as long as the text it contains. Therefore, when your report is printed, you will have eliminated all the extra spaces that would be printed if all fields were assumed to be a uniform length.

GETTING AND PLACING INFORMATION

Several commands provide access to information from other databases. These commands enable you to perform such tasks as open and close a second database, prompt the user for information, tell the user where information is located, and pass information to another database.

.OPEN AND .CLOSE

The *.open* command allows you to specify a second database to work with. The *.close* command closes that database. Here is the format for .open:

.open *NAME*

Enter the desired database name in the *NAME* location. You must use the .open command before you can use .write or .read commands on a second database. Here is a variation on the command:

.open CUST index CUSTNAME

This command opens the second database to be accessed in indexed order via its indexed field (in this case, CUSTNAME).

.READ

While the database is open, it can be read and written to with the commands .read and .write. (The .write command is discussed later in this chapter.) The *.read* command is accompanied by three modifiers: first, next, and prior. These result in reading the first record, the next record, and the previous record, respectively.

Now .read becomes a little more complicated: The first, next, and previous records can be connected to conditions. The command

.read CUST first CUSTCITY = "Boston"

would take you to the first customer in the database who lives in Boston. The command

.read CUST next CUSTCITY = "Boston"

would take you to the next customer in Boston. Presuming that you are using a database containing a field called SALESCITY (perhaps where one of your franchise locations can be found), the following command will locate the first customer in a franchised city:

.read CUST first where CUSTCITY = SALESCITY

You can only read one record at a time. If multiple records are likely to match your specification, you should place the .read command in a loop that continues until SYS:RECORD = 0 (indicating the end of the database) is reached. Another .read statement option is to read based on an index entry:

.read CUST index CUSTNAME = "Bal$"

This locates the first record in CUST where the CUSTNAME field begins with "Bal." Using the index lets you locate a field containing a value greater than a specified amount, such as the following, which will locate the first record with a zip code greater than 5000:

.read CUST index CUSTZIP > "50000"

You should use the .read command only on databases other than the current database, since you can access the current database more directly by simply calling for a field name.

.INPUT

The *.input* command prompts the user for information, which is then placed in the field you indicate in the current database. You could use

.input "Enter customer name" CUSTNAME

to tell the user to type in the customer's name.

.STATUS

The *.status* command is similar to .input. It displays a named field each time it changes. For instance, if you had a team of sales representatives, you could see a notation on the screen stating which sales representative's report was being processed by including the command

.status Salesrep: [*SALESREP*]

In this case, "Salesrep:" is the text that will be printed on the screen, and "[*SALESREP*]" represents the name of the sales representative as called from the field of that name.

.GETCHAR

The .*getchar* command pauses the program for keyboard input. Use .getchar to enable the user to make a choice among courses of action. The scan code for the key pressed is stored in a system variable called sys:lchar. The program below halts the printing of the report until a key is pressed, then it checks the sys:lchar variable. If you have pressed the Q key, the program will quit. If not, you will be prompted for the next customer name. Scan code 4177 represents the Q key. (See Appendix F in the Enable database user manual for a list of scan codes.)

```
.getchar
.if sys:lchar = 4177
.exit
.else
.input "Enter customer name" CUSTNAME
.endif
```

.POSITION

The .*position* command is a powerful way to specify where in a database a piece of information can be found. To identify the tenth record in the CUST database, for instance, you would enter

```
.position CUST seq sys:record = 10
```

You can follow this command by a .read command, which would send it to the first, next, or previous record and read it. You could read any number of records in database order by using the .read command again and again, but database order is not always useful. Databases are stored in the order they were entered—often chronological order—and that order could have little relevance to the order you need. Rather, you will probably want to position the pointer somewhere in an index file and take, for example, the third record alphabetically. In that case, you would use a slightly more complicated .position syntax:

.position CUST index = CUSTNAME sys:record = *VARIABLE*

This command allows you to locate a record based on the value in *VARIABLE*. If it is 1, you can have access to the first record in the file in alphabetical order. By incrementing the value in *VARIABLE*, you can position your report at each record in the file in alphabetical order.

.UPDATEKEY

You use the .*updatekey* command to pass information to another database, if it isn't already there. For example, if you entered a new customer name, .updatekey would determine that the customer name doesn't exist in the second database and would create a new record for him or her in the second database. The .*update* command is similar, but it doesn't add a new record.

.ADD

The .*add* command (which has the syntax .add*DATABASE*) appends the fields of the specified database to the end of the current database.

.WRITE

The .*write* command checks to see whether the sys:record equals 0, indicating an unsuccessful search of the database for an existing record that matches the current specification. If sys:record does equal 0, a new record is added. If it doesn't equal 0, Enable assumes that the current record is the one to which the information applies, and it will update that record to contain the current information.

.CHECKKEY

The .*checkkey* command is used to look for data in another database that is linked to the current database by their sys:record fields. It can be used only if .passthru off has been used.

PART

4

Telecommunications

Telecommunication Basics

THIS CHAPTER DESCRIBES THE BASIC OPERATION OF the telecommunications module in Enable. Telecommunicating is simple, once you have set the proper hardware specifications and have given Enable the proper settings. To determine the proper settings, you must consult your hardware manuals and the protocol used by the services to which you are connecting. Once you have established that information, this chapter will show you how to begin a communications session, specify the hardware information for the session, and control various options during the session.

This chapter also describes each menu command in the Telecommunications module and provides a step-by-step tutorial for connecting to the Enable corporate bulletin board.

AN INTRODUCTION TO THE TELECOMMUNICATIONS SETUP

Before you can begin telecommunicating, you must tell Enable about your specific telecommunications setup. This includes information about your hardware and specifics about the various "remote" locations you will be calling, such as their phone numbers. You tell Enable about this information by defining a "setup." The setup controls the basics of making calls and signing on to remote stations.

Since your computer might have more than one modem connected, and since you can call numerous remote locations, Enable lets you create numerous setups (256, to be exact). Each different setup can specify the modem to use, the COMM port to which that modem is connected, the name of the remote station, its phone number, and many more specifics. You can store these setups on disk for repeated use. For example, if you have a subscription to an online database service, you can create a custom setup that contains the service's phone number, sign-on instructions, passwords, and other data. Then, when you telecommunicate, simply choose the custom setup you defined and Enable takes care of calling, signing-on, and so on. Each service or remote computer you call can have its own setup. In Chapter 18, you'll learn the details about each setup option and how to create a custom setup.

USING QUICK-CONNECT

Using a setup is the easiest way to connect with a service that you use regularly, but you don't have to use a setup to telecommunicate. Enable lets you type connect commands, passwords, and other instructions directly to the modem. This is called the Quick-Connect method, and it's handy for connecting to seldom-used remote locations or for overriding the setups. Using the Quick-Connect method avoids a lengthy setup procedure and gets you connected right away.

Here are the basic steps to using the Quick-Connect method:

- From the Enable Main menu, select *Use System*, *Telecom*, *Communicate*, and *Quick-Connect*.
- Specify the baud rate of your modem.
- Select one of the four settings for parity, word size, and stop bits.
- Select *Half* or *Full* duplex.

- Select the COMM port to which your modem is connected.

- If you wish to capture the data that comes to the screen, enter the desired file name including the prefix and path name.

- Press ↵ at the screen displaying a progress message.

At any time during the session, you can use Enable's menu options by pressing F10 to see the Top Line menu.

Now try making a Quick-Connect connection. Since telecommunicating relies heavily on your hardware setup and communications protocol, you might encounter problems during this lesson. Before you begin, check your system and hardware configuration for the correct settings. In this example, we'll call up the Enable corporate bulletin board for information. This may be a toll call from your area.

1. From the Main menu, enter the commands *Use System, Telecom, Communicate, Quick-Connect*. You see the screen in Figure 17.1.

2. Make the appropriate selections for the baud rate and parity options (the first two options on the screen).

3. Select *Full* at the "Select type of duplex" prompt.

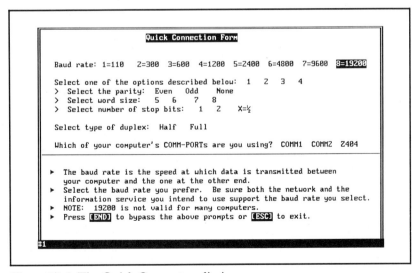

Figure 17.1: The Quick-Connect preliminary screen

4. Select the appropriate COMM port and press ◄┘. You see the screen in Figure 17.2.

Enable now asks if you want to capture all the data that appears on the screen in an Enable word processor file. This lets you review the data at another time. If you enter a file name, Enable uses this name to store the captured data, starting at the beginning of the session. If you do not enter a file name, however, you can still capture data by using one of the menu commands in the Telecommunications module. The difference is that you will not be capturing data from the beginning of the session when you use the menu command—only from the time the command is used.

See "Capture" in the next section for details about capturing screens.

5. Press ◄┘ at the "Enter file name" prompt to forgo the screen capture feature for this session.

At this point, Enable will show you its progress in the modem setup. If all goes well, Enable presents the message shown in Figure 17.3.

6. Press ◄┘ at the message screen (if you wait long enough, the message goes away).

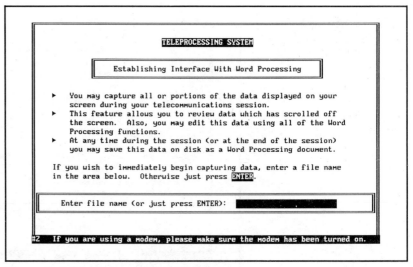

Figure 17.2: The Teleprocessing System screen

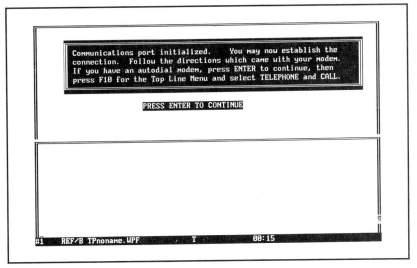

Figure 17.3: Ready to telecommunicate

You should see a blank screen with a status line at the bottom. From here you can send commands directly to your modem. You'll need to check your modem's manual for instructions at this point.

7. Enter your modem's "dial" command along with the phone number 1–518–887–6316. Then press ◄─┘. Alternatively, press F10 T C and enter the phone number. Then press ◄─┘.

In a moment, you will be connected to the Enable corporate bulletin board. Follow the instructions presented on the screen to use this board. This board contains customer service information about Enable and may be useful for future reference. When you're ready to quit, use this step:

8. Enter the command F10 D to disconnect. Then choose Yes at the verification prompt and No when asked to save the captured data. Enable returns to the Main menu.

TELECOMMUNICATIONS MENUS

Telecommunicating is relatively simple. The commands for telecommunications offered by Enable in the Top Line menu perform basic operations for your connection. Following is a discussion of these commands and their functions. Note that many of the Top Line menus do not have options—the menu name is also the option.

BREAK

The Break command sends a break to the remote station or service. Telecommunication services often require a break to activate or deactivate some function. When you are requested to enter a break (sometimes shown as Ctrl-C or Ctrl-Break), use this command. The effect of the break varies, depending on the service you are using.

CAPTURE

The Capture command starts or stops the screen capture feature. You use it to send all incoming information to a word processor file for future reference. If you entered a file name during the startup process, Enable is already sending the screen information to the specified file, and you can use a Capture option to insert a pause. The Capture options are as follows:

Word Processing ON/OFF	Opens and closes a word processing file for the captured data and begins or stops capturing. This file will not be on disk until you save it using word processing commands. This option toggles between opening and closing the file.
Active File ON/OFF	This command starts or stops capturing data to the file you opened with the Open command below. First open the disk file, then use this command to begin capturing. Use this command again to stop, then close the file.

These last three options are alternatives to the *Word Processing ON/OFF* option, since they send data directly to a disk file rather than to a word processor file.

Open	Opens a new file on disk for captured information.
Close	Closes the current disk file for captured data.

DISCONNECT

The Disconnect command simply disconnects the phone, concluding your communication. (It's a good practice to sign off the remote system before disconnecting.) After confirming your choice, Enable asks if you want to save the captured data. This is not necessary if you are capturing information on disk—only if you used the Word Processing ON/OFF option. This command takes you to the Enable Main menu when finished.

FILES

The Files command lets you transmit or receive files during the communication session. To transmit a file, follow these steps:

- Select *Files, Transmit.*
- Select the desired file protocol, which determines how the file is read at the other end.
- Enter the file name to transmit. Include the directory path and the file extension. Press ←┘ to begin transmission. Enable displays the screen shown in Figure 17.4.

To receive a file, follow the same procedure, but select *Files, Receive* and enter the name of the file to be received (as you would like it to be stored on your disk) instead of the transmitted file.

MCM

This MCM command is the same as the MCM commands in the other Enable modules. It lets you control windows, files, and screen display elements while you are using the Telecommunications module. See Chapter 23 for details about using the MCM options.

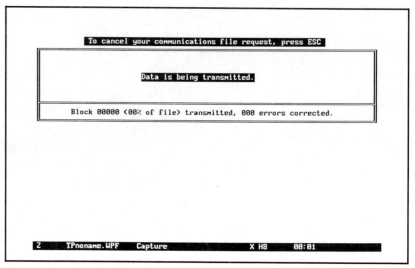

Figure 17.4: Transmitting files

OTHER

The Other command controls several special features. These are listed below. Many of these options, when activated, display messages or "indicators" at the bottom of the screen.

FEATURE	DESCRIPTION
Cost	Toggles the cost display on or off, which is useful for subscription services.
Duplex	Toggles between Full and Half duplex. Duplex is determined by the remote location you are calling. If you see double characters on the screen, change the duplex setting.
LF	Sends or suppresses a line feed after each line of data.
Pause	Pauses after each line of data is sent to the remote station. This option is useful when transmitting data to systems that cannot handle the transmission speed.

Set Break	Sets the length of the "break" signal. This option is used only for remote stations that require nonstandard break lengths. If you use the Break command and nothing happens, try changing the Set Break length.
Time	Displays or removes the elapsed time from the status line. This is the length of the call or "connect time."
Xon/Xoff	Toggles the Xon/Xoff option on or off. Consult the remote location's protocol for the proper setting.
Emulation	Sets the terminal emulation type. You can switch types in the middle of a communication session if desired.
Map	Activates or deactivates a keyboard mapping table.

PRINT

The Print command turns the printer on and off for the session. You can send all screen information to the printer as it is received, if desired. This command also lets you select the appropriate printer port.

TELE

The Tele command lets you answer a call, make a call, and hang up modems. If you select the Call option, Enable will disconnect any calls currently in progress on the same line. You will then be prompted for the phone number to call. Use this feature for autodial modems to begin your connection.

WP

The WP command displays the word processor Top Line menu for use with the captured information. You can then save and edit the data using standard word processing commands. When you quit this menu, Enable returns to the Main menu.

Using More Telecommunications Features

TELECOMMUNICATIONS SETUPS ARE DISCUSSED IN this chapter. As you learned in Chapter 17, a setup is a set of instructions that controls a communication session. Setups hold information such as the telephone number of the service or computer you are calling, information about the modem, transmission specifications, terminal emulation specifications, and more. You can create a unique setup for each online service or remote station you call—up to 256 setups. Using a setup is the easiest way to make a connection because it contains all the information needed to connect.

When you define the specifications within a particular setup, you can save that setup under a unique name. Then you can go on to create other setups, if desired. When you are ready to make a connection, simply choose the desired setup from the list you've saved. All saved setups are stored by Enable in a single file on disk (even though the file contains several setups). This file is called TPSETUP.$TP, and Enable refers to it whenever you ask for a list of setups.

Finally, you can change any of the setups you've previously defined. You must change a setup when a telephone number changes or if you change your hardware, for example. To make a change, call up the existing setup and repeat the setup process to update the various settings.

CREATING A CUSTOM SETUP

To begin a setup, use the following commands from the Main menu: *Use System*, *Telecom*, *Setup*. You will have to close all other windows before entering the setup procedure. Enable displays the screen shown in Figure 18.1. Read this screen, then press any key to display the setup listing screen (see Figure 18.2). This screen contains all the available setups.

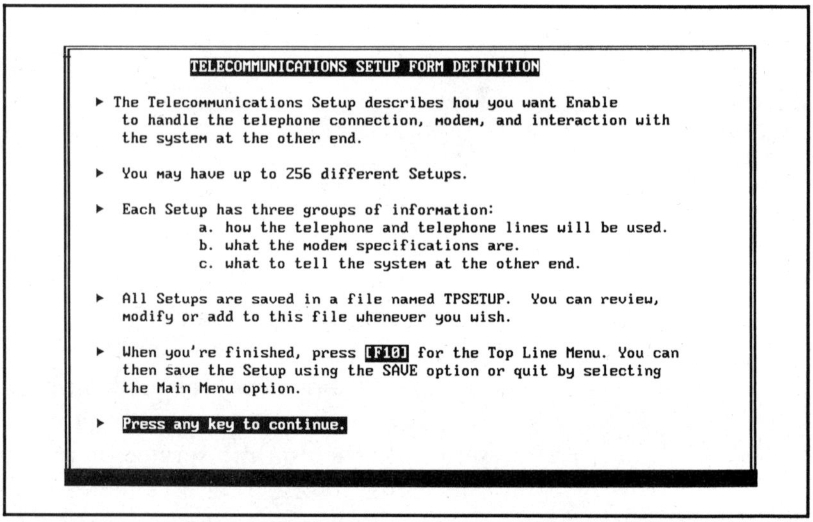

```
        TELECOMMUNICATIONS SETUP FORM DEFINITION

 ► The Telecommunications Setup describes how you want Enable
   to handle the telephone connection, modem, and interaction with
   the system at the other end.

 ► You may have up to 256 different Setups.

 ► Each Setup has three groups of information:
              a. how the telephone and telephone lines will be used.
              b. what the modem specifications are.
              c. what to tell the system at the other end.

 ► All Setups are saved in a file named TPSETUP.  You can review,
   modify or add to this file whenever you wish.

 ► When you're finished, press [F10] for the Top Line Menu. You can
   then save the Setup using the SAVE option or quit by selecting
   the Main Menu option.

 ► Press any key to continue.
```

Figure 18.1: The telecommunications setup introduction screen

Notice that Enable comes with a few setups already established. These include a few of the most popular online services available. (These services are not free, of course; they require payment over and above the cost of the call.) The screen also shows you a summary of the settings in each setup, including the Setup Name, Connect Method, Phone Number, Auto Dial status, Baud Rate, and more.

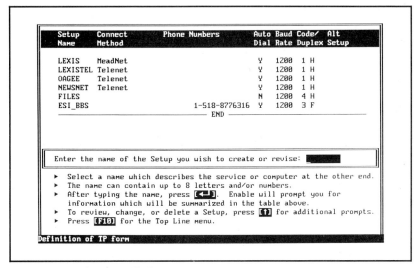

Figure 18.2: The setup listing screen

Following is a summary of the existing setups:

LEXIS   A legal information service developed by
                 Mead Data Central, on the MeadNet
                 network. Contains legal documents that can
                 be referenced on line.

LEXISTEL   Identical to LEXIS, but accesses the Lexis
                 and Nexis services through Telenet instead of
                 MeadNet.

OAGEE   A travel-related service, called Official
                 Airline Guide Electronic Edition. It provides
                 information about airline flights for travel
                 agents and others.

NEWSNET   A service that provides business articles and
                 newsletters for review.

NEXIS   A news service on the MeadNet network,
                 developed by Mead Data Central.

FILES   A setup useful for connecting to other
                 computers for file transfer.

ESI_BBS   A setup that connects to Enable's customer
                 bulletin board, which contains information
                 about Enable.

Though Enable provides these setups, most have no phone numbers; this is so you can find the local number for the service and enter
it yourself. If you subscribe to any of the services listed, you probably
have special sign-on codes and passwords that are required for connection. You can add these to the existing setup simply by modifying
the setup, as described later in this chapter.

ADDING A NEW SETUP

You can enter the name of a setup in the space provided in the
setup listing screen, then press ⟵. Enable will then display
the various specifications you can set. (These are described in the
"Setup Options" section.) When you are finished, Enable will add
the new setup (under the name you entered) to the list. At that point,
you can either save the setup permanently using the F10, Save command, or quit the setup procedure without saving your setup. These
options are described next.

QUITTING AND SAVING

You quit and save the setup by first displaying the Top Line menu.
When you press F10, only two options appear on the Top Line menu
in the communications setup screens: *Save* and *Quit*. The *Save* option
lets you save all the setup changes you've made (such as adding a new
setup, changing an existing setup, and so on). This option updates
the TPSETUP.$TP file on disk and makes all new or changed setups
available in the future.

Alternatively, you can quit without saving by using the F10, Quit
command. When the Top Line menu is showing, pressing the Esc
key returns you to the list screen.

CHANGING AN EXISTING SETUP

You can make changes to an existing setup if desired. This includes
renaming the setup, changing specific settings, or completely removing

it. You might want to add your password and the local phone number to one of the existing setups, for example. The complete way to revise a setup is to first enter its name in the space provided. This takes you into the detailed setup screens where you can modify the current settings (these options are discussed in the next section). When you are finished, be sure to use the F10, Save command to store the new data permanently.

A simpler way to change an existing setup is to modify only the information showing on the list screen, such as the setup's name, connect method, phone number, and so on. You can do this as follows:

- Press the ↑ key.

- Highlight the setup you would like to change by using the ↑ and ↓ keys.

- Press the → or ← key to move to the column you want to modify (for example, Phone Numbers). Continue to press → or ← until the desired column is highlighted.

- Press the space bar to edit the information in the chosen column.

- Change the option as desired, then press ←—.

- When finished, press Esc to return to the setup listing, where your new setup will be showing.

DELETING OR RENAMING A SETUP

You can completely remove a setup or change its name. This is done with the following procedure:

- Press the ↑ key.

- Highlight the setup you would like to change by using the ↑ and ↓ keys.

- Press **D** to delete the setup entirely (Enable confirms this choice). Press **R** to rename the setup (Enable then asks for the new name).

THE SETUP OPTIONS

Whether you start a new setup or revise an existing one, the setup options are the same. This section describes each prompt you encounter in the setup screens.

As described earlier, the detailed setup screens come to view when you enter a new or existing setup name in the setup listing screen. As soon as you enter a name and press ⏎, the first setup screen appears (Figure 18.3).

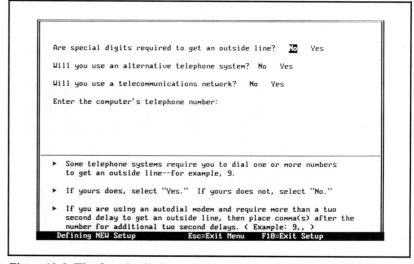

Figure 18.3: The first detailed setup screen

Note that you cannot "flip" through these screens without answering the prompts. You must use the ↓ and ⏎ keys to move from option to option, selecting as you go. When you get to the bottom of one screen, the next will appear when you press ↓ or ⏎.

ENTERING SPECIAL DIGITS

Answer Yes to the first prompt if you must enter special digits to reach an outside line on your phone system. For example, some phone systems require you to enter the digit 9 prior to entering a phone number. If you select Yes, Enable asks you to enter the required digits. When connecting to the remote computer, Enable waits two seconds after sending this digit before sending the phone number. If your system needs more time to reach the outside line, enter commas after the digits. Each comma tells Enable to wait an additional two seconds.

USING OTHER PHONE SERVICES

If your long-distance service requires that you enter a special code for outside calls, select Yes at the prompt "Will you use an alternative telephone system?" This option lets you enter the code numbers that will be issued prior to the phone number. Enter commas after the digits to tell Enable to pause before issuing the phone number. Each comma pauses for two seconds.

If your system requires a code *after* the phone number is issued, you must enter both the phone number and the code on this line. Again, use commas for pauses. You may use hyphens between numbers.

USING A NETWORK

If your computer is linked to a telecommunications network, enter Yes at the prompt "Will you use a telecommunications network?" If you select Yes, Enable asks you to specify the network, enter the remote telephone number, and specify other network requirements. If you select No, Enable prompts you for the computer's telephone number. This is the main number of the remote location you are establishing in this setup. Enter the area code and telephone number. Use hyphens if desired. If you entered the number in the prompt "Will you use an alternative telephone system?," then do not enter the number here.

USING AN AUTODIAL MODEM

Enter Yes to the prompt "Will you use an autodial modem?" if you are using an autodial modem with your system. This is a modem that dials the telephone number itself (when issued from the computer). Acoustic modems and older-style modems are not autodial modems and will require that you type the phone number during the communication link. If you enter Yes, Enable will ask if you are using a tone or pulse telephone line. Consult the modem's documentation and your phone system for these specifications.

SPECIFYING THE BAUD RATE

At the "Baud rate" prompt, enter the baud rate at which your modem is sending and receiving data. Modems at both ends of the connection must be set to the same baud rate, though most newer modems adjust automatically. Consult your hardware manuals for specifications. Also, determine the baud rate of the remote computer. Usually, the slowest (lowest) baud rate is the one you must use for the connection. However, some modems automatically shift from 2400 to 1200 when necessary.

CHOOSING THE PARITY, WORD SIZE, AND STOP BIT OPTIONS

At the the prompt "Select one of the options described below," you will see four digits, each representing a set of options for setting the parity, word size, and stop bits for the setup. Consult the requirements of the remote computer for details about these options. If you choose option 4, Enable lets you set the parity, word size, and stop bits individually.

ENTERING THE DUPLEX MODE

At the "Select type of duplex" prompt, select *Half* or *Full,* depending on the requirements of the remote computer. Full duplex lets the computers on each end of the connection send and receive data at the same time. If both computers are using Enable, use Half duplex.

SETTING THE TRANSMISSION DELAY

Some remote computers may not be able to receive data as fast as you can send it. You can slow down the transmission of data by selecting one of the "Inter-character transmission delay" settings.

The setting 0 causes no slowing and should be used unless you are sure a slower setting is required. A setting of 5 is the slowest transmission speed.

SELECTING XON/XOFF

At the prompt "Does the system at the other end support Xon/Xoff?," select Yes if the remote computer supports Xon/Xoff. This is a feature that remote systems use to tell each other when to start and stop sending data. Most online services, as well as Enable, support this feature. If the remote computer is using Enable, select Yes.

If you enter No, Enable prompts for another setting: "Does the system at the other end require turnaround character(s)?" These are characters that indicate whose turn it is to send data. For example, you may have to wait until you see the character] before entering data. This is a turnaround character for systems that do not use Xon/Xoff. Other systems may use a different character. When you select Yes, Enable asks you to enter the character(s) used for turnaround. If the system does not use a turnaround character, select No at this prompt. This presents a selection of pause times for turnaround (from 0 to 4 seconds). Use 0 if you do not require a pause before sending each line of data from your system.

If the turnaround character sequence requires the Ctrl key, as in Ctrl-S, use the circumflex, or caret character (^) in place of Ctrl. For example, ^S represents Ctrl-S.

ENTERING A PASSWORD

Most online database systems require you to enter a password before getting onto the system. You have two lines for entering initial responses to the system. Enter the first response after the prompt "Enter the password or first response" and the second at the next prompt. The actual password may be the second response, depending on the sign-in procedure required by the remote system.

DISPLAYING THE ONLINE COST

At the prompt "Do you wish to see the approximate cost on the Status Line?," specify Yes if you want Enable to display the accumulating cost of the online time at the bottom of the screen. If you select Yes, Enable asks you to enter the cost per hour of the system time.

DISPLAYING THE CONNECT TIME

At the prompt "Do you wish to see the approximate time of the connection?," enter Yes if you want Enable to display the accumulating online length of your calls to this remote location. This elapsed time is displayed at the bottom of the screen.

SPECIFYING THE PORT

To respond to the prompt "Which of your computer's COMM ports are you using?," consult your computer hardware setup. Of course, if your computer has only one COMM port, select COMM1.

REPEATING THE SETUP

If a connection is not made on the first try, you can use the "Enter number of times to retry this setup" option to retry the procedure. Usually, only two or three tries are required to make the connection. If the connection is not made after that, the problem is probably elsewhere. Enter 0 or leave this option blank if you don't want the setup to repeat at all.

SPECIFYING ANOTHER SETUP

Enable lets you switch to a different setup if the current one fails. First Enable tries the current setup as many times as you specified in the previous option. Then it tries the alternative setup. Your alternative setup can contain different settings for different situations. If that setup has an alternative setup specified, Enable will use it if necessary. Enable waits 60 seconds for the remote computer to answer before using the alternative setup specified. Leave the "Enter name of Setup to try if this one fails" option blank to cancel after a failure.

SPECIFYING TERMINAL EMULATION

At the "Terminal emulation" prompt, enter the type of terminal emulation required by the remote system (if any). This option lets your computer act as a terminal for a mainframe system.

SPECIFYING ADVANCED OPTIONS

At the prompt "Do you wish to select any of the options listed below?," Enable offers some specialized options for the communication setup. Most simple connections will not require these options. Consult the Enable manual for details about each of these.

As you telecommunicate more and more, you'll appreciate these Enable setups—they take much of the repetition out of going online. But remember, you can always use the Quick-Connect method described in the previous chapter for new or seldom used services. Using telecommunications effectively relies to a great degree on your hardware and your knowledge of it. If you have trouble connecting, consult your hardware manuals for details about the settings you should be using. Then, modify your setups accordingly.

PART

5

Customizing Enable

Getting Started With Macros

THIS CHAPTER DEALS WITH ONE OF THE MOST important shortcuts available to Enable users: the macro. Macros will save you time and trouble when using Enable by automating complex or repetitious tasks. This chapter explains how you can use macros in Enable to make your work easier. You'll then discover how to build a basic macro and how to make it work in your application. When you finish this chapter, you'll be ready to start creating your own macros to take over the tedious work you currently do by hand.

MACRO BASICS

In simplest terms, a macro is a small program that controls your application. Most macros duplicate the kind of input that you would type into the computer, but they offer the advantages of speed and accuracy. Few typists would be able to make entries as rapidly as a macro, and macros eliminate the possibility of typos in repeated procedures. Macro operation is easy; it consists of the following process:

- Enter a macro (this chapter will show you how).
- Give it a name.
- Press Alt-F9 when you're ready to use the macro.
- Type in the name of the macro.

You can store virtually unlimited amounts of typing—both text and command entries—in a macro. If you write many letters for your business, for instance, you can write a macro to enter the heading. If many of your letters have stock paragraphs, you can create a macro to enter these paragraphs and save an enormous amount of typing. Similarly, you can create macros to prepare a spreadsheet worksheet to contain your monthly accounts, or to set up your database. You can even write macros that interact with you. If you want the macro to pause while you make an entry in a spreadsheet cell, for example, you can easily program this action.

Enable provides three ways to create a macro:

- You can set up Enable as if it were a tape recorder, and go about your work while the recorder carefully notes all the actions you are taking and saves them for replay.
- You can record your keystrokes without having them affect what is on the screen while the recorder is operating.
- You can write your macro with the word processor, using command names, as if you were writing a program in BASIC or some other computer language.

RECORDING A MACRO

The easiest way to create a macro is to let Enable record it for you. This involves simply going through the steps you want to "program" into the macro while the recorder is on. The macro then repeats those steps at any time. Here's how to begin:

- Press Alt-F9.

- Press the backslash key (\) to tell Enable you want to record your keystrokes.

- Press a key that will be the name of the macro.

Macro names can consist of any key on the keyboard except \, – , = , End, PgUp, PgDn, →, ←, ↑, or ↓. The Shift, Alt, and Ctrl keys have no effect when used in combination with the keys on the normal keyboard to name a macro (Shift-M is the same as M, when you are naming a macro). You can use these three keys in combination with the function keys, however, if you want to give a macro a function-key name. For example, you can use the name Alt-F6 for a macro. Remember that you cannot use Alt-F9 or Ctrl-F2 as macro names because these are reserved for Enable. Here are the next steps:

- Run through the procedure the macro is intended to run for you. Remember that Enable is recording everything you do at this point.

- When you are through recording your macro, press Alt-F9 again, and then press the End key. The macro will be stored on the default disk and directory.

To play back your macro, follow these steps:

- Press Alt-F9.

- Press the key or keys that represent the macro name.

Enable begins recording as soon as you press Alt-F9 and \ (back-slash) followed by the macro name. If you are at the Main menu when you do this, and then move into the word processor, Enable records this in the macro. When you run the macro, Enable will issue these commands exactly as you typed them. Hence, you should run the macro only when you are at the Main menu. For this reason, you should consider the specific occasions in which you will use the macro once it's recorded. For example, if your macro is intended only for word processor documents, you might begin the macro when you are inside the word processor, and run it only when you are inside the word processor.

You have a couple of additional options. When you replay your macro, you can press Alt-F9, then the minus key (on the numeric keypad), then the macro's name to "step" through your macro. When you use this option, the macro will pause after each macro command and wait for you to press a key before proceeding. If you don't press a key, it will wait indefinitely. You can use this feature to locate programming errors in a macro.

While you are actually recording a macro, you can press the Ctrl key with the hyphen key to insert a "wait" command in the macro. When replayed, the macro will pause where you entered the Ctrl-Hyphen command and wait for you to press a key before continuing. This will be an actual part of the macro, unlike the "step" command described above.

Another useful command is accessed through the Ctrl-I key combination. If you press Ctrl-I when the macro is recording, this will cause the macro, when it is replayed, to pause for input from the keyboard. When you press the ← key, the macro will continue. The keystrokes you enter during the pause (prior to pressing ←) are passed directly to Enable.

Let's record a sample macro. This macro will open a new word processor document and create a heading. Here are the steps to take:

1. Go to the Enable Main menu.

2. Press Alt-F9 and then press backslash (\).

3. Press **L** (or any other key—L was chosen because we are creating a letter). "MAC" appears on the status line to show you are recording.

4. Press ← five times. This will take you to a blank word processor document called NONAME.WPF.

5. Type your address. Press ← twice and type **Dear Sir:**. If you make a typographical error, simply backspace over it and continue typing as usual. If you want to perform some additional formatting, use the menus as you would normally. Enable will record all your actions.

6. Press ←— two more times.

7. Press Alt-F9 and End to end recording. Your macro will be stored on the default drive and directory. Notice that "MAC" is no longer displayed at the bottom of the screen.

See "A Word Processor Macro" for another time-saving macro that saves and prints a document.

Now you have a macro that will open a word processor file and create a heading and greeting, ready for you to write a letter. Let's play it back.

1. Return to the first Enable screen by pressing F10 Q Y.

2. Run the macro by pressing Alt-F9 L.

In practically no time (usually fewer than two seconds), you are in the word processor with your address typed in the document and your greeting in place. If you included formatting commands, they will also be entered.

Next, let's create a spreadsheet macro.

1. Go to the spreadsheet by selecting *Use System, Spreadsheet/ Graphics, Create.* You will be prompted for a spreadsheet name. Use any name that comes to mind, or just call it **SPREAD** and press ←—.

2. Press Alt-F9 \ S. "MAC" appears on the status line to show that you are now recording.

3. Move the pointer to cell A4 (use the ↓ key) and type **Office Supplies.** Move the pointer to cell A6 and type **Pens.** Move the pointer to cell A7 and type **Paper.** Move the pointer to cell B6 and type **.25** (the cost of a pen) and then in B7 type **3.50** (the cost of a ream of paper). Format both of these cells with the currency number format by pressing F10 W R F $ ←—, then type **B6..B7** and press ←—.

4. Enter **0** in cells C6 and C7, and format both of these cells as integers with the key sequence F10 W R F I, then type **C6..C7** and press ←—.

5. Move to cell D6, and enter the formula **(B6*C6).** Move to cell D7 and enter **(B7*C7).** Move to cell C6.

6. Press Alt-F9, End.

Your macro is ready to use. If you wanted to use it, you would start a new spreadsheet from the Main menu (or erase this one with F10 W E Y), then press Alt-F9 S to enter a duplicate of the spreadsheet.

Let's clarify something: although the first macro created took you to the word processor and created a letter, it was in fact an MCM macro because it began from the Main menu. The other macro you created was a spreadsheet macro, because it was created within the spreadsheet. This may seem like a picky distinction, but it can be important to your macro programming, as you will see in Chapter 20.

EDITING MACROS

Now it's time to take a look at a macro in its native form. When you examine your macros, you can also change them. This is done by editing the commands that Enable has recorded. Of course, a working knowledge of the macro language is helpful.

Here is how to examine a macro:

- Go back to the Main menu screen.

- Select *MCM, Macros, Revise, MCM*. Enable asks you to select the application where the macro was recorded. This is where the macro was begun. If you began at the Main menu, select MCM.

- You will be prompted for the key associated with the macro. Press **L**, and you will be taken to the macro (Figure 19.1).

As you might suspect, Enable doesn't literally record your actions like a tape recorder. Instead, it translates your actions in a series of commands resembling a programming language such as BASIC.

Let's take a look at the macro in Figure 19.1. The first line reads "{5X}~," which indicates that you pressed ↵ five times (the tilde represents a carriage return). The next line, "Willy's Wheelwells ~," is the name of a business, followed by a carriage return. The next line, "2323 Industria;{Bs}," indicates that an error was corrected with a backspace ({Bs}). The next line indicates

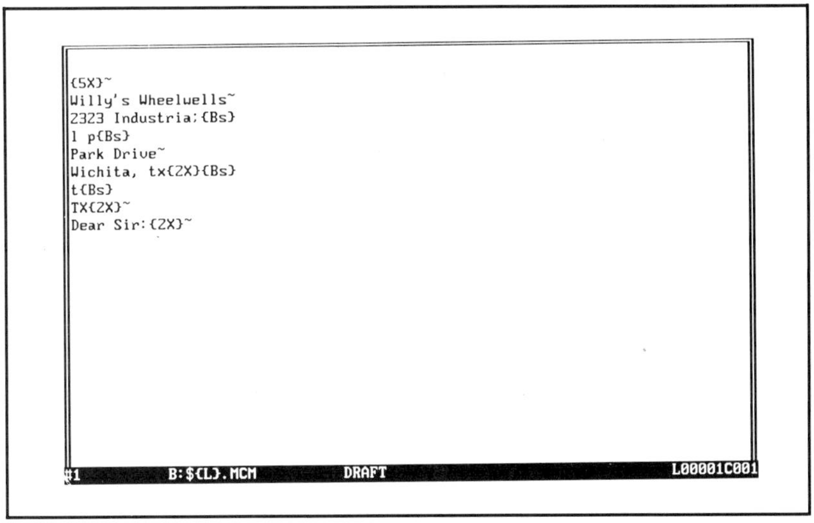

```
{5X}~
Willy's Wheelwells~
2323 Industria;{Bs}
1 p{Bs}
Park Drive~
Wichita, tx{2X}{Bs}
t{Bs}
TX{2X}~
Dear Sir:{2X}~
```
```
#1        B:$(L).MCM        DRAFT                    L00001C001
```

Figure 19.1: Contents of a macro

that the correct letter, "l," was typed, followed by another error: "p{Bs}"—a lowercase "p" was entered rather than uppercase "P." The next line shows where the correct letter was typed in, followed by the remainder of the line and a carriage return: "Park Drive ˜ ."

The next line shows the name of the city and state: "Wichita, tx." The state abbreviation, tx, should be uppercase, of course, so Backspace was pressed twice ({2X}{Bs}), followed by yet another error: another lowercase "t," followed by a backspace, followed at last by the correct abbreviation for Texas: "TX." Then come two carriage returns, followed by the greeting "Dear Sir:" and two more carriage returns.

With such terrible typing, it's clear that this macro will save a great deal of time. Let's edit the macro. After all, it's more efficient to have the macro simply enter the correct address and greeting than to make and correct each of your typing errors—even if it makes the corrections in the blink of an eye.

- Use the word processor features to remove all the errors and {Bs} commands. The result will look like Figure 19.2.
- Save your changes—F10, S, ←.

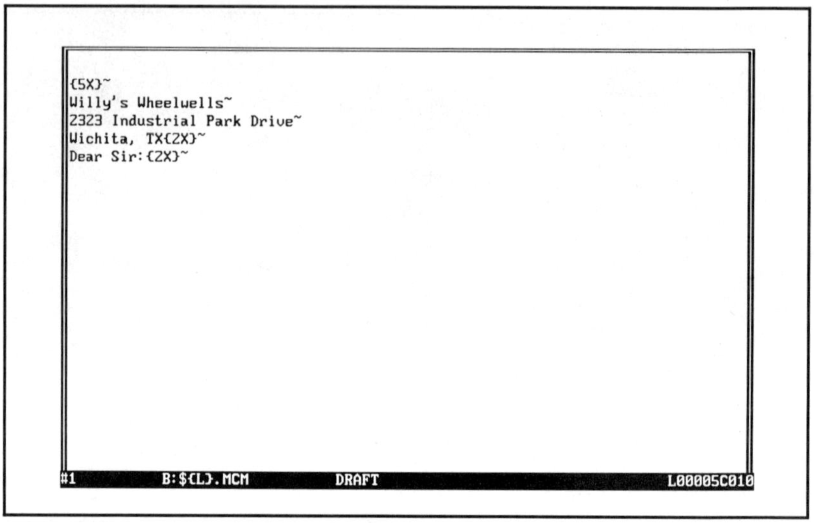

```
{5X}~
Willy's Wheelwells~
2323 Industrial Park Drive~
Wichita, TX{2X}~
Dear Sir:{2X}~




                                                                      
#1            B:$(L).MCM          DRAFT                    L00005C010
```

Figure 19.2: The macro in Figure 19.1 with corrections

RECORDING A MACRO WITHOUT PERFORMING COMMANDS

You can enter a macro through the recorder without actually executing each of the commands you are entering. In other words, you can turn Enable off temporarily, yet still record a macro. To do so, simply substitute the equal sign for the backslash key when telling Enable to record. Here are the steps:

- Press Alt-F9 and the equal sign (=).
- Press any key except \, – , = , End, PgUp, PgDn, →, ←, ↑, or ↓ to name a macro. You will be recording.
- Type in your macro, including command keys and text.
- End the recording by pressing Alt-F9, End.

Execute the macro in exactly the same way as a macro created with the backslash key.

WRITING A MACRO

Another way to create a macro is to simply write it out using the MCM, Macro, Create options. You will be prompted to enter the type of macro you want to create (word processing, spreadsheet, and so on) and the key press associated with the macro. You will then go to a word processor screen, where you can simply type in the actions you want the macro to perform. Table 19.1 provides the keystrokes you would make in the macro to simulate keyboard entry. Table 19.2 lists the macro commands that are available when writing a macro.

Table 19.1: Macro Keystrokes

MACRO KEYSTROKES	KEYBOARD EQUIVALENT
{F1}–{F10}	F1–F10
{Esc}	Esc
{Tab}	Tab
{Home}	Home
{Up}	↑
{Down}	↓
{Right}	→
{Left}	←
{Pgup}	PgUp
{Pgdn}	PgDn
{End}	End
{Ins}	Ins
{Del}	Del
{Bs}	Backspace
~	↵
{Lf}	Ctrl-↵
{{}	{
{}}	}

Table 19.1: Macro Keystrokes (continued)

MACRO KEYSTROKES	KEYBOARD EQUIVALENT
{ ~ }	~
{&*x*}	Alt-*x*, where *x* is any key
{^*x*}	Ctrl-*x*, where *x* is any key
{!*x*}	Shift-*x*, where *x* is any key
{PrevW}	Alt-↑ (Previous Window)
{NextW}	Alt-↓ (Next Window)
{CloseW}	Alt-End (Close Window)
{OpenW}	Alt-Home (Open Window)

Table 19.2: Macro Commands

MACRO KEYSTROKES	KEYBOARD EQUIVALENT
{If Error}*command*	If an error is detected, execute *command*
{Else}*command*	If no error is detected, execute *command*
{Endif}	End of If Error statement
{Do Menu}*name*~	Display user-defined menu designated by *name*
{Menu}*name*~	Make user-defined menu specified by *name* the default
{Do Macro}*name*~	Perform macro designated by *name*
{*n*X}	Repeat the following command, where *n* is the number of repeats
{Beep}	Make a beeping sound
{Send} (S) *message*~	Send *message* to the status line
{Send} (R)	Restore status line
{Pause}	Pause about one second
{Voff}	Video off (freeze display)

Table 19.2: Macro Commands (continued)

MACRO KEYSTROKES	KEYBOARD EQUIVALENT
{Von}	Video on (restore display)
{?}	Await input
{^F9}*key*	Wait for the specified key
{Wait}	Wait for any keystroke
{GotoW}*name*˜	Go to window designated by *name*
{Wname} *new name*˜	Name the window as *new name*

Whatever action you want Enable to take can be indicated by the related macro command. To display the macro entry screen, go to the Enable Main menu (on the initial screen that provides access to Use System, Help, MCM, and Return to DOS). Select *MCM, Macros, Create, Word Processing* (or whatever module will be using the macro), and then press the key that will be associated with the macro to name the macro.

Suppose you want to create a macro for deleting a line of text. Follow these steps:

1. At the Main menu, select *MCM, Macros, Create, Word Processing.*

2. Press the key that will be associated with the macro (in this case, press Del).

3. When the text-editing screen appears, press F10, select the EditOpts menu, and press C to turn reformatting on.

4. Type in the macro **{F10}D1**˜ .

This macro is fairly straightforward. The {F10} brings up the menu at the top of the screen, D selects the Delete menu, and 1 selects the first option on that menu: *Line at the cursor.*

Suppose you wanted to delete several lines at once, but you aren't sure when you write the macro how many lines you will want to delete. You will have to ask the user for some keyboard input. Here's how you would get around the problem: Use the {Send} command to place a message on the bottom of the screen telling the user to move the cursor to the end of the block. Then, when the user presses ◄─┘, the block indicated will be removed. This procedure eliminates several keystrokes. The macro is as follows:

```
{F7}
{Send} (S) Move cursor to end of block and press ◄─┘
{?}
{F7}
{F10}D2
```

To use the macro, place the cursor on the first character of the block to be deleted. Press Alt-F9 and Del (the key was used again, thus eliminating the original macro). The status line at the bottom of the screen will prompt you to move the cursor to the end of the block. Do so and press ◄─┘. Instantly, the block will be removed.

USING SPECIAL COMMANDS IN YOUR MACRO

Several commands that you can use when creating a macro deserve special mention here. These commands have enormous power, and their use is not as obvious as the macro cursor commands.

VIDEO COMMANDS

Activating the screen display during macro execution isn't always desirable because a new user, seeing the cursor flashing around on the screen deleting text or inserting boilerplate paragraphs as if the computer had a mind of its own, might become confused. If you want to freeze the video display for any reason, use {Voff} in your macro. When you are through with the macro, be sure to use {Von} to restore the display. Be sure to turn the screen display back on again at the appropriate point in the macro.

MENU COMMANDS

The menu commands don't refer to the Enable menus, but to menus you create for your own use (this is covered in Chapter 21). A user-created menu will be in a special file with the extension .MNU.

When you use a menu command to call up a menu you created, use the entire name of the menu:

{Do Menu} USER.MNU ˜

will call up the menu USER.MNU.

{Menu} USER.MNU ˜

will make USER.MNU the default menu.

CALLING MACROS

Macros are so flexible that they can call other macros. Thus, you can use a macro with a name longer than a single character for use within other macros. The only problem you will encounter with {Do Macro} is that Enable won't let you call ordinary one-letter macros with this command. Therefore, to record a macro for use in another macro, you must create the macro with a single-key name, rename it, and then use its new name in your {Do Macro} calls. Use the F9 S N command to save the macro under a different name. To edit a macro with a longer name, use the command M M L A from the Main menu, then select the macro from the list.

Actually, the one-key files you have been using have four characters (or more) in their file names. The block-delete macro is identified on disk as ${DEL}.WPM. WPM identifies a word processor macro. To rename this file for use from other macros, copy or rename it as BLOCKDEL.MAC. Then you can write a macro and include the following command to access the block-delete macro:

{Do Macro} BLOCKDEL.MAC ˜

When the block-delete macro is through with its business, control will return to the calling macro.

You can use the DOS RENAME command to rename a macro file.

ERROR-TRAPPING COMMANDS

Your computer can tell when an error occurs, as most users are painfully aware. Fortunately, you can use this information in your macro. Any error message that appears on the status line can be trapped by the macro. To trap an error, identify any action that might result in an error, and then use the error-checking commands:

```
{If Error} command ~ 1
{Else} command ~ 2
{Endif}
```

The macro would run command 1 only if there were an error. Otherwise, command 2 would be run. The {Endif} command lets Enable know the error-checking routine is finished.

WINDOW COMMANDS

Enable's macro facility features two window commands. To use these commands, follow these steps:

- Use whatever commands are necessary to go to a given window.

- Give the window a name with

    {Wname}*new name* ~

- Subsequently, whenever you want to go to the window *name*, you can use

    {GotoW}*name* ~

    to transport the program to that window from wherever you are.

WAIT COMMANDS

Enable has four wait commands: {Pause}, {?}, {^F9}, and {Wait}. The {Pause} command simply waits about a second and then moves on. If you want your macro to proceed after a longer time, simply specify how many seconds to wait by inserting a repeat command. For example, to wait one minute (60 seconds), use

    {60X}{Pause}

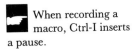 When recording a macro, Ctrl-I inserts a pause.

To wait for input of unknown length (say, to fill in a dialog box), use {?} when writing a macro. It will put macro operation on hold until a ⏎ is pressed.

To wait for a single specified key press, use {^F9} followed by the specified key press. For example, if the user is to type u, w, c (to create a word processor file from Enable's Main menu screen), use

```
{^F9}u
{^F9}w
{^F9}c
```

Note that this command is case-sensitive. If your user enters UWC rather than the expected uwc, he or she will make no progress. Enable will still be waiting for a lowercase u. If you use this command, be sure to prompt the user for the exact response you expect.

The fourth wait command is simply {Wait}. It waits for a user to press any key. If you are prompting the user to change a disk and then press a key, use {Wait}.

REPEAT COMMAND

You have already seen the repeat command (X) earlier in this chapter. It's used to repeat any command or keystroke a given number of times. Use the following syntax for the command:

{*n*X}*command*

In this example, *n* is any number representing the number of repeats you want and *command* is the action you want repeated. The "X" stands for "times" and should be entered literally. The command {5X}A repeats a press of the A key five times.

TONE COMMAND

If you have a particularly long macro that will take several seconds (or minutes) to complete, you should use the {Beep} comand to produce a beep tone to inform the user when a response is needed, and to let the user know the macro has ended. Enter this command anywhere in a macro.

VIEWING AND EDITING MACROS

You can view a listing of macros by selecting *MCM, Macros, List*. Then select the type of macro you want to see (word processing, spreadsheet, and so on). This will open up a directory screen listing all available macros on the default disk. If you want to look at a particular macro, highlight it with the cursor keys and press ← to view and edit the macro.

You could also select *MCM, Macros, Revise*. You will be prompted for the type of macro to revise and then for the one-key entry that invokes the macro. When you press the key, the macro will appear on the screen for editing.

A WORD PROCESSOR MACRO

What follows is a sample word processor macro that saves your document, prints it, and then returns to the Main menu:

```
{F10} SA
{F10} PE ˜ CPNNNNNN ˜
{18X}
{Down}
{&F2}
{F10} QY
```

Each of the entries responds to a prompt within the chain of commands necessary to perform these functions. This macro assumes that your printer has already been selected. Here's what each macro command means:

COMMAND	FUNCTION
{F10}	Calls the Main menu.
SA{F10}	Saves the current file, accepting all the defaults, then calls the Main menu again.
PE ˜	Selects Print, then responds to the first two options in the succeeding dialog boxes: *Entire document, 1 copy* (← selects the default).

COMMAND	*FUNCTION*
CPNNNNNN ~	Selects *Continuous form, Portrait orientation, No* to all the following options, ⬅ to select default printer.
{18X}{Down}	Reviews 18 default settings and retains them.
{&F2}{F10}	Alt-F2 begins the printing process, F10 calls up the Main word processing menu.
QY	Selects *Quit* and responds *Yes* to the Enable fail-safe prompt, thus returning operation to the Enable Main menu.

In this chapter you learned how macros can be used to automate tasks in Enable. You can record a macro by pressing Alt-F9 [*n*] and running through the commands you want to record. Then, use Alt-F9, End to end the recording session. These macros can be replayed using the command Alt-F9 [*n*] again. You can edit a macro using the command MCM, Macros, Revise and then selecting the module in which the macro was created and specifying the macro's name.

Remember that macros are stored in individual files on the root directory of your disk drive and appear in the form ${A}.MCM. If you rename a macro using a longer name, you can then run the macro from within a different macro. The next chapter shows you some of the special things you can accomplish with spreadsheet macros.

Using Spreadsheet Macros

CHAPTER 19 SHOWED YOU HOW TO CREATE MACROS that control many operations in Enable. As an example, you created a simple macro that entered and formatted data in the spreadsheet. The spreadsheet offers additional macro commands and features that are not available in other modules. These macro commands are useful for simplifying your spreadsheets, making them easier to use by others in your organization.

This chapter shows you how to enter and run spreadsheet macros using a host of special spreadsheet macro commands. It provides some simple examples that demonstrate particular commands. You'll also discover how to integrate a nonspreadsheet macro (such as those you learned in Chapter 19) with a spreadsheet macro.

SPREADSHEET MACRO BASICS

Spreadsheet macros are entered into spreadsheet cells. Each command is entered into a separate cell and the commands are listed, in order, down a column. Besides all the general macro commands listed in Chapter 19, here you have a set of extra spreadsheet commands. These are all preceded by the slash mark (/). When spreadsheet macro commands are the first thing entered in a cell, you should precede them by an alignment indicator (<, >, or ^), as in ^/XCL1. This simply prepares Enable for the slash character that normally activates the TopLine menu. Table 20.1 lists the spreadsheet macro commands. Detailed explanations are found later in this chapter.

Table 20.1: Spreadsheet Macro Commands

COMMAND	ACTION
/XC*cell*˜	Executes a subroutine that begins at the specified *cell* (/XR ends the subroutine and returns to the original cell)
/XE*expression* ˜ *cell* ˜	Evaluates the *expression* and places the result in the indicated *cell*
/XG*cell* ˜	Goes to specified *cell* and executes macro keystrokes found there
/XI(*condition*) ˜ *action*	Provides for an if-then branch (*condition*) or optional command (*action*)
/XL*message* ˜ *cell* ˜	Macro pauses, displays *message*, and awaits user entry of label in the named *cell*
/XM*cell* ˜	Macro pauses to process the user-created menu at the named *cell*
/XN*message* ˜ *cell* ˜	Macro pauses, displays *message*, and awaits user entry of numeric data into the named *cell*
/XQ	Quits execution of macro
/XR	Returns from subroutine (subroutines are accessed by /XC)

CREATING AND RUNNING
A SPREADSHEET MACRO

To create a spreadsheet macro, you must first enter the spreadsheet in which the macro will operate. As you know, macros are used to automate tasks that you perform manually. Spreadsheet macros are no different, except that they apply only to spreadsheets. Often, a spreadsheet macro will be useful only in one spreadsheet—the spreadsheet in which you enter it—but some will be useful in many different spreadsheets. You can either copy these macros from the original spreadsheet into each spreadsheet you like, or you can tell subsequent spreadsheets to use a macro located in the original spreadsheet.

Follow the basic steps below to create a spreadsheet macro:

- Enter the desired spreadsheet.

- In a blank column (or portion of a column), enter the macro commands in the appropriate order. You may use any of the macro commands listed in Table 19.1, plus the additional spreadsheet commands listed in Table 20.1.

- Select F10 W R N C (F10, *Worksheet, Range, Name, Create*). This command creates a name for your macro, since all macros must be named. To have Enable treat your range as a macro, begin the name with a backslash character (\) and enter a single-character identifier. For example, you enter \B for a macro range name. Press ← when finished.

- You will be prompted for a range. The range must be a single column of cells or a portion of a column. Enable will read the column from top to bottom, until it encounters an empty cell or is redirected by a macro command such as a branch.

- Move the highlight to the first cell of your macro range. Press the period key to make this the beginning of your range. Move the cursor to the other end of the range and press ← to mark the end of the range.

- When prompted for another range to name, simply press Esc to exit from the Range Name command.

- To run the macro, press Shift-F9 and then press the key used
  to name the macro. For example, to run the macro named
  \B, press Shift-F9 B.

Let's create a macro using this basic procedure. This macro will
save the current spreadsheet and exit from the spreadsheet. Begin by
creating a new spreadsheet file from the Main menu.

1. Enter the following commands in the indicated cells:

   A1: {F10}s ˜
   A2: {?}
   A3: {Right} ˜
   A4: {F10}qy

2. Select F10 W R N C and type \Q to indicate the one-key
   entry to run the macro. Press ←⏎.

3. Move the cursor to the first cell of your macro, A1. Press the
   period key and move down to the last cell in the macro (it's all
   right to overestimate the bottom of the macro range or even
   underestimate it, as long as the first cell is included). Then
   press ←⏎ and Esc.

Before running this sample macro, let's take a careful look at each
of its entries.

{F10} brings up the Top Line menu, as if you had pressed the F10
key. The s ˜ entry selects *Save* from the Top Line menu, as if you had
pressed the S key. The ˜ character, which is the equivalent to pressing ←⏎, selects the *Accept Options* option in the Save menu.

{?} anticipates the prompt for a file name by pausing the macro so
you can enter the name. Basically, the {?} command lets you make a
selection instead of the macro making it. When you run the macro,
you can enter a new file name for the spreadsheet or press ←⏎ to
accept the current name. If you enter a new name, the macro will
simply save the spreadsheet under the new name and exit from the
spreadsheet module.

If you press ←⏎ to accept the existing file name, Enable presents
the two standard options: *Cancel* and *Replace*. Here, you could have
inserted another {?} command so you could answer this Enable

prompt, but instead a {Right} ˜ command was used at this point in the macro. This tells the macro to use the Replace option (as if you had pressed the → key).

Finally, {F10}qy brings up the Top Line menu again and selects the Quit command. Although you will not see it, Enable presents the standard No/Yes prompt to make sure you want to quit at this point. The macro will answer Yes automatically—probably faster than the screen prompt can be displayed.

Once you have entered and named your macro, you are ready to run it. Remember that the spreadsheet macro takes effect in the spreadsheet in which it's entered. Sometimes, the position of the pointer can have an effect on the results. To run your macro:

1. Press Shift-F9 (not Alt-F9).

2. Press the one-key range name that identifies the range containing the macro: Q.

USING SPREADSHEET MACRO COMMANDS

Following are brief descriptions of some spreadsheet macro commands. See Table 20.1 earlier in this chapter for the syntax for these commands.

/XC AND /XR

The /XC and /XR commands are used with macro subroutines. A *subroutine* is a macro that performs a function independently of the main macro. Subroutines often perform routine operations for a macro. To avoid repeating the commands over and over—each time the operation is required in the macro—the subroutine is used. You can branch to a subroutine from any point in a macro and then return to the macro when the operation is complete. For example, if you had a macro in column G and a subroutine starting at location L1, you would insert ^/XCL1 ˜ into your column-G macro. You can also use a range name instead of the reference. At the end of the macro that begins at L1, you would insert /XR to indicate that the subroutine has completed and to return to the cell immediately following the /XC command.

/XE

The /XE command evaluates whatever expression follows and places the resulting value in the indicated cell. For example, suppose your macro contained the command

    ^/XE12*F2 ~ F1

If F2 contains 9, this command would place 108 in cell F1. Notice that the destination cell follows the ~ symbol. You can use any spreadsheet cell or range name as the destination.

/XG, /XI, AND /XQ

The command /XG*cell* ~ is similar to /XC, but complete control of the macro is turned over to the new routine. Unless there is a specific instruction in the new routine that sends the program flow back to the original macro, it won't return. Here's an example:

    E1: ^/XE12*F1 ~ F1
    F1: 1
    E2: ^/XIF1 < 1000000 ~ /XG E1
    E3: ^/XQ

The first two lines of this simple macro will place the smallest power of 12 larger than a million in cell F1. The command

    /XI(condition) ~ action

is shown in the next line example. If the value in cell F1 is less than 1,000,000, /XI uses /XG to send execution back to E1. As soon as the value in F1 reaches 2,985,984, the if-then statement fails and the macro quits with an /XQ command.

/XM

The /XM command opens a custom menu you have created ahead of time. Custom menus are discussed in Chapter 21.

/XL AND /XN

The /XL and /XN commands perform similar functions. The first uses the syntax

/XL*message* ~ *cell* ~

and displays a message. It then waits for the user to enter a text string and to press ◄┘. The label entered is placed in the cell indicated by ~ *cell*. For example, you might enter

^/XLEnter Label for Income Column ~ A1

This command pauses the macro and waits for your entry. When you press ◄┘, the label you enter is placed in cell A1.

The command /XN, which has the syntax

/XN*message* ~ *cell* ~

is identical to /XL, but requires a numeric entry instead of a text entry. The value entered is placed in the indicated cell. For example, you might enter

^/XNEnter Value for Employee's Income ~ A2

to place an entry in cell A2 after the prompt.

PUTTING MACRO COMMANDS TOGETHER

Let's create one more simple example to show some of the special spreadsheet commands in action. Suppose you have your current inventory of pens and paper in cells F2 and F3, respectively. The macro will inform you how many of each item to reorder. You want to have a minimum of 50 pens and 25 reams of paper on hand. When the quantity falls below these set points, your spreadsheet will prompt you to order enough to return the quantity on hand to 50 pens and 25 reams of paper.

Type the following commands into cells A13–A17, B13–B16, C12, and D13–D14 in a spreadsheet:

CELL	ENTRY
A13	^/XIF2<50~/XCB13
A14	^/XIF2 = >50~/XE0~C13
A15	^/XIF3<25~/XCB15
A16	^/XIF3 = >25~/XE0~C14
A17	^/XQ
B13	^/XE(50 − F2) +50~C13
B14	^/XR
B15	^/XE(25 − F3) +25~C14
B16	^/XR
C12	Order
D13	Pens
D14	Reams of Paper

To turn the text in the cells into a macro, place the cell cursor on A13, select F10 W R N C, and then type \R to indicate a single-key macro (use another letter, if you wish). You will be prompted for a range. Press the period key and press ↓, then ◀─┘, to name the range in such a way that Enable will know it is a macro. Press Esc to exit the range name command.

To run the macro, enter any value in cells F2 and F3, then press Shift-F9 and R. The macro will look over your inventory and determine how much you should order.

FINDING AND LINKING
MACROS WITH @MACRO

If you've been using Enable for a while, you may already have created several useful macros. When it comes time to use them in a new spreadsheet, you won't want to retype all those commands. Or, perhaps you have several macros that work with any spreadsheet, so you don't want to limit them to a particular spreadsheet, but want them available to all. The answer is to store your macros in a special spreadsheet file, called a *macro library file*, that contains only macros, and "link" your other spreadsheets to that file using the @MACRO command. Here's how.

First, create your spreadsheet macros in the usual way. You might combine several on the same sheet. Then save the spreadsheet under a unique name containing the .LIB extension (for example, MACROS.LIB). This is a macro library file. You can create and save as many of them as you like. The macros in this file are available to any other spreadsheet.

When you are ready to access a macro contained in a library file, simply use the command @MACRO inside the new spreadsheet. Its syntax is as follows:

@MACRO(#*filename*.LIB,"*display cell, execute cell*")

To enter a label with the backslash character, first type an alignment character and a space, as in ˆ \Q. Otherwise, beginning a label with the backslash character causes an automatic "repeat" of the information, filling the cell.

This command finds and "links" the specified macro to the spreadsheet containing this command. The macro can then be used (that is, run) from that sheet. The #*filename*.LIB entry is the name of the library file containing the desired macro. (The # symbol is required to indicate that this is an external file.) *Display cell* is a reference to the cell containing the name of the macro. This would be a label entry, such as "\Q." If you have not entered the name of the macro into a cell of the library file, then enter the first cell of the macro range. (It's common practice to enter the macro name into a cell adjacent to the macro's first cell.) The *execute cell* entry is a reference to the first cell of the macro range. This is the beginning of the macro commands.

An example would look like this:

@MACRO(#C:\data\MACROS.LIB,"A1,B1")

This would locate the macro that begins at cell B1 on the library file MACROS.LIB. Notice that the DOS path to that file is included, and that cell A1 is listed as the cell containing the macro name. The spreadsheet containing this macro would look like Figure 20.1.

The @MACRO function returns the *display cell* label to its cell. This label reminds you of the macro's purpose on the worksheet.

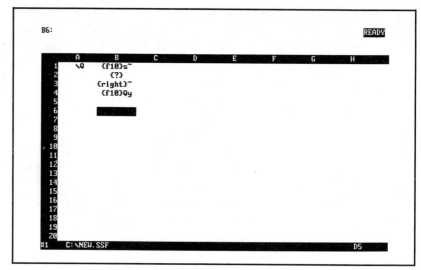

Figure 20.1: A sample macro library file

The final step is to enter a macro name for the cell containing the @MACRO function (which is now displaying the macro's name from the library file). In short, you have to rename the macro in the new sheet; it makes sense to use the same name as the original. Use the command F10 W R N C and enter a one-character name preceded by a backslash character.

This chapter described how to create macros for use specifically in the spreadsheet. By combining the general Enable macro commands with some special spreadsheet macro commands, you can accomplish many important tasks via macros in the spreadsheet. And since spreadsheet macros are entered into the spreadsheets themselves, they are saved along with the spreadsheets to which they apply. The exception to this is when you create a macro library file. A macro library file contains macros that can be accessed from any spreadsheet.

Customizing Enable with Macros and Menus

IF YOU HAVE BEEN USING ENABLE AND FOLLOWING the examples in this book, you are familiar with Enable's menus. They contain options organized in a hierarchy. A custom menu is like a standard Enable menu except that it contains custom commands, which are usually performed by macros. Hence, you can select and run a macro via a custom menu that you've designed. This chapter will show you how to create and use custom menus in Enable. You'll learn how to specify the options used in a menu and how to make those options perform desired actions.

With all the menus available in Enable, you may be wondering why you would need to create more. You don't. The menu feature is a convenience, designed for people who want to make their work smoother and more efficient. For example, you could have a subdirectory containing a dozen different kinds of form letters, such as a letter to a customer with a complaint, a letter to a customer who wrote in praise of your product or service, a letter to a debtor who is behind in his payments, a letter to a creditor who is demanding payment in full, and so on.

As you begin using Enable, you might want to go instantly to one of these boilerplate letters. Without a custom menu you would open the word processor, pull down the appropriate menu, go to the subdirectory with the letters and locate the appropriate one, then load it. Alternatively, you could create a custom menu, accessed by pressing Alt-10 L, that lists all these letters. Each option on the menu could call a macro that loads the letter by name. You could save an enormous amount of time.

In the menu you will design in this chapter, you will provide choices to open the word processor and insert some text, go to the order form in the CUST database created in Chapter 13, and open a budget spreadsheet. You can use menus to call macros, giving your custom features a professional look.

AN OVERVIEW OF CUSTOM MENU DESIGN

To create and use custom menus, the first step is to decide what commands or actions you want to put into a menu. Perhaps you already have macros that you would like to access via a menu. In any case, determine whether the actions taken by the menu options should be available to all modules or just one module. Later, you'll see why this is important. Here are the basic steps to creating custom menus:

- Enter the MCM module.

- Use the *Tools, Menu, Create* options to start the designing process.

- Lay out the options on the menu design form.

- Describe the action of each menu item. This is also done on the menu design form, and it often involves a reference to a macro.

- Customize your menu by selecting colors (assuming you have a color system).

Once you have created a menu, you can activate it in the appropriate module(s), as described later in the chapter. The next few sections provide details about the menu design procedure.

CREATING A CUSTOM MENU

Let's create a menu that will give you the following options:

- Enter an order from the database
- Create a letter named BILLING with the word processor
- Open a worksheet named BUDGET from the spreadsheet

These options could begin any typical business operation. You can add more, if you wish, simply by repeating the steps outlined here and creating your own macros.

Begin at the Enable Main menu.

1. Select *MCM, Tools, Menus, Create*. You will be prompted for a file name for the menu.

Here you have four choices for entering a file name. The file name lets Enable store your menu for future use. If you're creating a menu that can be called up in any module (except graphics), provide a single-letter file name (A or L, for example) with no extension. Enable will attach the extension .MNV.

If you're creating a menu to be used in only one module, enter a single-letter file name and provide a two-character extension to tell Enable in which module the menu will be used, as follows:

FILE NAME	*MODULE*
filename.WP	Word processor
filename.SM	Spreadsheet
filename.TP	Telecommunications
filename.DB	Database
filename.MC	MCM

These menus can be activated within their designated modules by pressing Ctrl-F10 and the letter associated with the menu.

You can also design a menu that pops up when you press Shift-F10. These are special menus that require the names listed below.

Only one of each can be used. Respond to the prompt for a file name by entering one of the following names:

FILE NAME	*MODULE*
WP	Word processor
SS	Spreadsheet
DB	Database
MCM	MCM

The advantage to these menus is that they appear without your having to remember their names. For example, when you're in the word processor and press Shift-F10, Enable searches for the menu file that you named as WP.

Your fourth option is to give your menu a file name up to eight characters long. If you select this option, you won't have direct access to the menu unless you use the {Menu} macro command to make this menu the default. Normally, you enter a full name only for menus that are accessed by other macros. In other words, you can "call up" a menu from a macro.

2. Enter **A.MC** as the name of the menu. This makes the menu (named A) available only in the MCM module. You will see the screen in Figure 21.1.

3. Read the screen, then press any key. You will see the screen shown in Figure 21.2.

4. Once again, press any key. You will be taken to the menu definition screen (Figure 21.3).

The menu definition screen appears to be completely blank. In fact, it is an empty menu that fills the entire screen. As the prompts along the status line on the bottom of the screen indicate, you can shrink the screen with the cursor keys. Since the menu will have three simple options, you need not have a menu much larger than 5 lines long and about 15 columns wide.

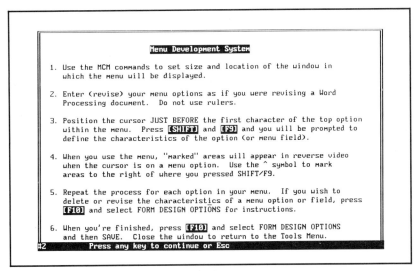

Figure 21.1: The Menu Development System screen

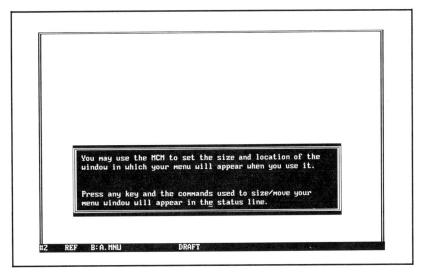

Figure 21.2: The second screen of instructions

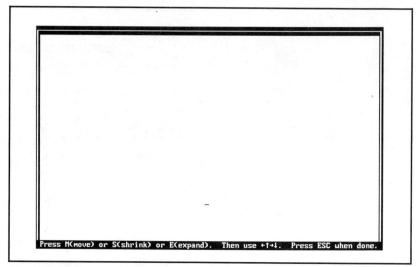

Press M(move) or S(shrink) or E(expand).   Then use ←↑→↓.   Press ESC when done.

Figure 21.3: The menu definition screen

5. Press **S** and use ↑ and ← to shrink the menu down to about 5 lines by 15 columns. To make further changes to the size and position of the menu, press F9 W L, then S to shrink, M to move, or E to expand.

Now move the menu to the position on the screen where it is to appear when in use.

6. Press F9 W L M. Use → to move the window and press ↵ when finished. The actual location isn't important, but for the sake of this example, move it to the position shown in Figure 21.4.

Now you are ready to design the menu itself. This involves entering the option names and indicating their functions. In this exercise, you will design a menu that will allow you to go directly to the word processor and begin a billing letter, to the database to start a order entry, or to the spreadsheet to a worksheet named BUDGET.

To enter the menu options, you are going to use an Enable feature that looks just like the word processor, although it has a few enhancements for menu design. To see all the word processing options, enter F10 W. Select the desired option or press Esc to return to the menu.

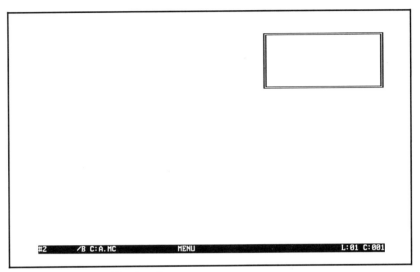

Figure 21.4: Repositioning the menu

You can have a maximum of 240 items per menu.

7. Enter the following lines. (Don't press ◄━┘, or paragraph return marks will appear in the right border of your menu. Rather, use the cursor keys to move down and enter the next item.)

    1. Order
    2. Billing
    3. Budget

Your menu will look like Figure 21.5.

You have probably noted that some menu options in the Enable modules are accessed by pressing a number key, and others are accessed by pressing the first letter in the option name. Since two of our menu items have the same first letter, this menu will use numbers as the "action keys" that call the menu item with a key press. That is why you placed numbers before the option names. This is an important feature of menu design, as you will see when you develop the menu further.

The next step is to delimit your menu items with carets—the carets inform Enable where menu items begin and end.

8. Enter carets, as shown in Figure 21.6, by moving the cursor
to the position of the caret and pressing Shift-6. (Note that
you will have to switch to the insert cursor by pressing the
Ins key.)

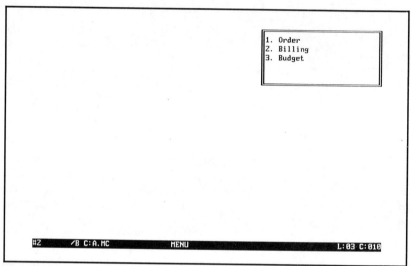

Figure 21.5: The custom menu so far

Figure 21.6: Delimiting the menu options

You can also display your menu horizontally, with the items in a single line across the screen. To create the A.MC menu as a horizontal menu, you would create a menu box about 3 lines high and 40 characters wide and enter the menu items like this:

^1. Order^ ^2. Billing^ ^3. Budget^

DEFINING
CUSTOM MENU OPTIONS

As you have probably suspected, there is far more to menu design and creation than simply creating a list of items. You must explain to Enable what to do when you select an item in the menu, and you must create any macros that are called by the menu options. These macros will actually perform the prescribed actions. Fortunately, Enable has created a friendly and efficient way to explain your intent when a menu item is selected.

To call a macro, you have to indicate to Enable what sort of input it should look for. That is, you need to tell Enable that when the user presses the number 1, it should go to the database order input form, and so on. Here is how:

1. With the menu shown in Figure 21.6 on your screen, place the cursor to the left of the 1 in the first line of the menu and press Shift-F9 to tell Enable which item you are defining. You will be taken to the screen in Figure 21.7.

2. Enable calls its menu options "fields." In the field name entry screen, enter **ORDER** as the unique field name.

It's simpler to name the field after the menu option, but this isn't always possible. You can enter any field name you desire (up to eight characters), and the name can contain any number or letter characters, so long as it begins with a letter.

3. Press ←⏎, and you will see the screen in Figure 21.8.

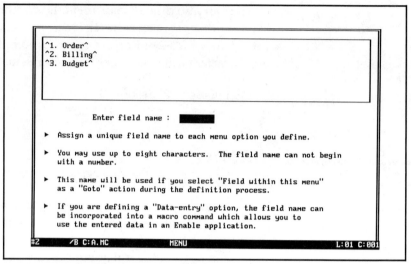

Figure 21.7: The field name entry screen

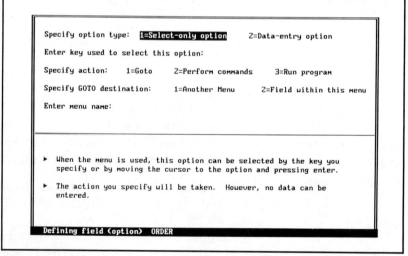

Figure 21.8: The field definition screen

Enable displays five prompts. The first asks you to specify the option
type for the indicated menu option. There are two types of custom
menu options you can use. A Select-only option simply performs
actions when you select it; a Data-entry option prompts the user to
enter information after selecting the option. This information can be

used by the menu's actions, or you can reference the entered text from some other menu option or macro.

4. Highlight *1-Select-only option* and press ←┘.

5. At the next prompt, you will enter the key used to make the selection. Type **1** to indicate the item number 1 and press ←┘.

Your options in the third prompt are *Goto, Perform commands*, or *Run program*. *Goto* will send the operation to another menu or another part of this menu. This is useful for using submenus where many subordinate options are connected with a higher-level option. For example, you might have an option that selects the word processor, then a submenu giving you the choice of opening a boilerplate letter or creating a new letter. Selecting the boilerplate option might call yet another menu containing the list of available form letters. Using this command, you can "link" the menus together by name.

The *Perform commands* option requires that you create a macro containing the commands performed by this option. You will use this option in the example.

The third option, *Run program*, requires you to enter the name of the program or batch file the menu option will put into action. This brings all the power of DOS into the Enable framework, allowing you to call, for example, a small batch file to alphabetize a file on disk before loading it. To use this option, you must start Enable with a parameter limiting its use of RAM. Enable ordinarily uses all available RAM. You must provide enough RAM for your batch file or application to operate with the memory options (as in ENABLE 448, which would free 64K for DOS operations, but limit the amount of RAM Enable itself could use).

6. Select *Perform commands*.

The next prompt is to select whether to display the Enable screen, your menu, or a message screen during the operation of the menu's actions. The message screen would be appropriate if the action of the macro is complex and time consuming. For example, it could warn your user to ignore the computer for a specified period of time while the menu action takes place.

7. Select *Standard* to display the Enable screen. There is no reason to hide what will happen during the example.

The final option is to place the macro commands within the menu or in another file. If you elect to place the macro program within the menu, you will be given a generous amount of program space to create the macro (about 400 characters in all). If you place your program in another file, you will be prompted for the name of the other file containing the macro that the menu selection should run. This would be a standard macro name.

8. Select *Another file*, and enter **ORDER** as the macro name—make a note of the name, because we will create the necessary macro file a little later.

9. The next screen asks whether informational and help messages should be displayed when the option is highlighted and where. Select *None* twice to place no message on the screen.

Note that a block of a contrasting color appears when the menu item is completely defined. These blocks won't be visible when the menu appears on the screen.

10. Repeat the procedure in the above steps to define the other two menu items. For *Billing*, provide the unique field name **BILLING**, the 2 key to call the item, and a command file named **BILLING**. For *Budget*, the unique field name is **BUDGET**, the calling key is 3, and the command file should be named **BUDGET**. Your screen will look like Figure 21.9.

Now let's save the menu.

11. Press F10 to call up the Top Line menu. You can select *Word Processing Options* or *Form (Menu) Design Options*.

12. Select *Form (Menu) Design Options*; you will see another menu, giving you more standard selections: *Color, Save, Delete field, Revise field, Mark field,* and *Quit*.

The *Color* option, which allows you to define colors for your menu, is impressive, but unnecessary for this menu. The action to take now is to save the current menu.

13. Highlight *Save* and press ⏎.

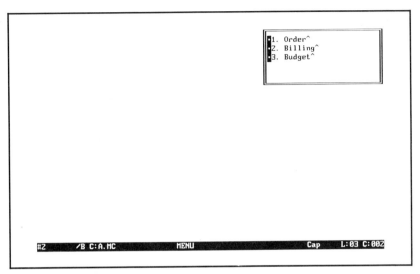

Figure 21.9: The finished menu

14. You will be asked whether to save the menu under the same name or a new name. Save it under the same name.

If you wanted to create a nearly identical menu, you could call this menu into the menu-definition module, edit it to suit your tastes, and then save it under another name to create a new menu.

15. Use the command F10 F Q to quit the menu design screen. Press **Q** again to return to the Enable Main menu.

In the next section, you will use your skill in writing macros to perform the actual tasks Enable should perform when the menu options are selected.

USING MACROS WITH CUSTOM MENUS

To add macros to your custom menu, simply go to the Enable Main menu and begin recording the macro:

1. Go to the Enable Main menu.

2. Press Alt-F9 and type \B to start macro recording.

3. Press U D B (*Use System, DBMS/Graphics, Build*).

4. In the resulting screen, enter **ORDERS** as the database and **ORDERS** as the input form. That will take you to the order form created in the database chapters.

5. Press Alt-F9 End to end the recording.

Now you will change the name of the macro to ORDER.

6. Go to the Enable Main menu and select M F A (*MCM, Files, All*).

7. Highlight the file called *${B}.MCM* (do not press ⏎). This is the name of the macro you just created; all one-key macros have similar names.

8. Press R to rename the file. You will be prompted for a directory and then for the new file name. Press ⏎ to keep the same direction; then type **ORDER** as the new file name and press ⏎.

To test your menu so far, return to the Enable Main menu by pressing Esc, and press Ctrl-F10. The status line will prompt you for the key associated with the menu. Press **A**. The menu will appear in the position you specified during the definition process (Figure 21.10). Press **1** to select *Order*, and your macro program will take you rapidly to the order form.

9. Create the other macros in the same manner. BILLING should take you to the word processor to revise an existing file called BILLING.WPF. The BUDGET macro should take you to the spreadsheet and create a worksheet you define in the macro, or call up a predefined worksheet containing your budget.

Creating menus for use within the individual modules is no different from creating a menu like A.MC (the menu you just created).

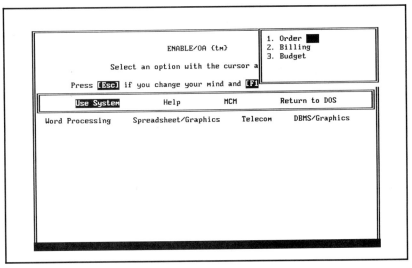

```
                                                    1. Order  █
                              ENABLE/OA {tm}         2. Billing
                                                    3. Budget
                    Select an option with the cursor a

             Press [Esc] if you change your mind and [F1]
           ┌──────────────────────────────────────────────────┐
           │  Use System        Help         MCM      Return to DOS │
           └──────────────────────────────────────────────────┘
           Word Processing    Spreadsheet/Graphics   Telecom   DBMS/Graphics
```

Figure 21.10: Display the custom menu

ADVANCED MENU TECHNIQUES

You can do far more than invoke program files with a menu. You can call another menu and provide data to a macro. You can also provide a message or tutorial to the user by simply typing the needed information into the menu at the time of definition.

CALLING ANOTHER MENU

To have an option in one menu call up another menu requires that you design two menus. The first menu will have an item that calls up the second using the *Goto* menu definition option. You can specify any single-character menu name to call up—or you can enter a larger name, such as "SUBMENU" for the second menu.

In the following exercise you'll create Menu B, which you'll call Menu A.

1. From the Main menu, select *MCM, Tools, Menus, Create* to begin a new menu.

2. Enter the menu name **B.MC** and press ←┘.

3. Press ◄─┘ two times to get to the menu definition screen.

4. Press **S** and use the ← and ↑ keys to shrink the window down to about 2 lines by 15 characters. Press ◄─┘ when finished.

5. Type the command name **^Get Menu A^** on line 1 (include the caret marks). The screen should look like Figure 21.11.

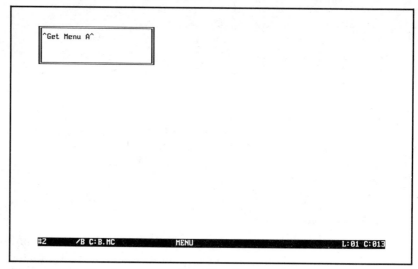

Figure 21.11: Creating a menu that will call up another

Now you're ready to define the menu item. Remember, this is done using the Shift-F9 command and responding to various prompts on the definition screen. Here are the next steps:

6. Using the ← key, move the cursor back to the first caret mark in the menu item, then press Shift-F9.

7. Type the field name **CALL** and press ◄─┘.

8. Choose *Select-only option* as the menu type.

9. Enter **G** as the key used to select this menu.

10. Choose *Goto* as the action for this menu.

11. Choose *Another Menu* as the Goto destination.

12. Type the menu name **A.MC**, then press ◄─┘ three times to complete the option definition.

The menu is now complete—of course, it has only one command, where a practical example would probably contain many. Remember that some menu commands can call up other menus, while other commands on the same menu can simply perform actions.

Save the menu and return to the Enable Main menu:

13. Press F10 F S S to save the new menu under the name B.MC on disk.

14. Press F10 F Q Q to return to the Main menu.

The next step is to try out the new menu:

15. Press Ctrl-F10 from the Main menu, then enter **B** as the menu to bring up. The menu, containing only the option "Get Menu A" appears.

16. Press ← to select the option, and menu A comes up on the other side of the screen. Figure 21.12 shows the result of calling up the second menu from the first.

Now you can select any option from menu A or press Esc to return to menu B.

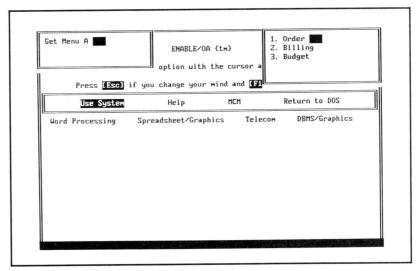

Figure 21.12: Menu A appears on the right, having been called by menu B on the left.

PROVIDING DATA TO A MACRO

Another power-user feature of menus is passing data to a macro. To try it out, first create yet another menu and call it C.MC. Once again, this menu will only have one item, so size the menu appropriately and place it where you please. When you've done that, follow these steps:

1. Type the menu option **^Open DB^** in the new menu. That's the only option you need.

2. Place the cursor *below* the option and press Shift-F9. The position of the cursor when you press Shift-F9 will be the beginning of the input field.

3. Give the field the name **INPUT**. Press ◄─┘ when finished. Select *Data-entry option*, then *Text* as the type of data and *Anything* as the text type. Enter **1** for the minimum length and **100** for the maximum length.

4. You see the screen shown in Figure 21.13.

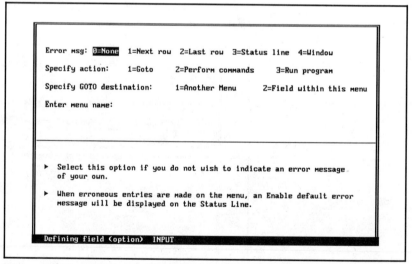

Figure 21.13: Defining field options for an information-retrieving menu selection

5. Opt to use no error message (*0 = None*) and select *2 = Perform commands*. The screen display should be *Standard Enable* and the location of the commands will be *Within Menu* this time. (You could as easily place them in another file as you did before.) You will see the screen in Figure 21.14.

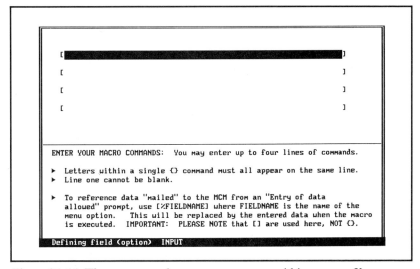

```
       [                                                 ]
       [                                                 ]
       [                                                 ]
       [                                                 ]

 ENTER YOUR MACRO COMMANDS:  You may enter up to four lines of commands.

 ▸  Letters within a single {} command must all appear on the same line.
 ▸  Line one cannot be blank.

 ▸  To reference data "mailed" to the MCM from an "Entry of data
    allowed" prompt, use [%FIELDNAME] where FIELDNAME is the name of the
    menu option.   This will be replaced by the entered data when the macro
    is executed.  IMPORTANT:  PLEASE NOTE that [] are used here, NOT {}.

 Defining field (option)   INPUT
```

Figure 21.14: The screen used to enter a program within a menu file

For this example, we used INPUT as a field name. Therefore, anywhere in the macro program where you want to use the data entered, you can insert [%INPUT] and Enable will expand this definition to the data entered in response to the prompt.

Let's write a menu program that opens a database for building. The name of the database and input form will be taken from the menu program.

1. Type this macro:

udb[%input] ˜ [%input] ˜

Note that you don't have to use the {?} macro command to await user input. Since Enable is aware that you intend to wait for input, it will wait until the user has typed in some information and has pressed ←.

2. Press ← to move to the next screen. You will be prompted for messages and help information. Opt for neither of these by pressing ← twice.

3. Save your menu with the command F10 F S S.

To use the database, go back to the Enable Main menu and press Ctrl-F10 C to call up the menu you just defined. The program will prompt you with a highlighted field for your input. Simply type in the name of your database (which also has to be the name of your input form for this scheme to work). Enable will take all the intervening steps, and you will find yourself in your input form awaiting an order.

You could go back and revise your first menu to call this menu, if you like. To revise a menu, follow these steps.

1. At the Enable Main menu, select *MCM, Tools, Menus, Revise*.

2. Enter the name of the menu, press ← twice, and place the cursor on the spot where you defined the field before (the highlighted rectangle). Press Shift-F9 and you will return to the definition screens, where you can make any necessary editing changes.

As you have seen, menus allow for a great deal of power, flexibility, and personalization. Create menus to make Enable behave the way you feel it should behave. Since you can call any menu from any other menu, or from within the macros driven by the menus, you can customize Enable almost endlessly.

Creating and Using Profiles

THIS CHAPTER SHOWS YOU HOW TO CREATE OR revise an Enable profile so you can customize your system's defaults. Throughout this book, we've pointed out how particular defaults can be altered via a profile. In the word processor, for example, you can change the appearance of the default ruler that appears at the top of all new documents. In all aspects of the program, Enable uses default settings from time to time. These settings come from the profile currently in use for the system. By changing the profile (that is, selecting a new one), you can effectively change the defaults used throughout the program.

So far, you've been using the Default profile throughout this book. This is a profile setting that Enable provides for you. You have no doubt already found some defaults that you would like to change, particularly in the word processor.

This chapter shows you how to create a new, custom profile using the various profile screens. You will be able to change default options in up to nine different aspects of Enable, including the four modules, the print options screens, and more. If desired, you can also change one of the existing profiles (such as the Default profile) to match your personal choices.

CREATING A PROFILE

There are two ways to begin customizing a profile. You use the first method when you first start up the Enable program from the DOS prompt; the other is used when you are already in Enable.

When you begin Enable from the DOS prompt, you see the familiar startup screen asking you for the date and time. The third prompt on this screen is "Do you use profiles?" By answering No to this prompt, you instruct Enable to use the Default profile. Answering Yes lets you select an existing profile from those you have created. When you answer Yes, you are asked to enter the name of the desired profile. Entering a question mark provides a list of available profiles. Pressing F1 displays the Help for Profiles screen shown in Figure 22.1.

Here, again, you can choose from the existing profiles by selecting the *Use Profile* option. You will be given a list from which you can choose the desired profile. Most likely, however, you'll want to select the *Create or Revise Profile* option. Using this option, you can begin a new profile. The screen shown in Figure 22.2 appears.

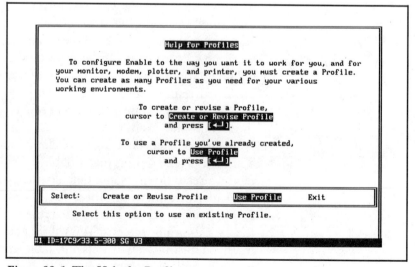

Figure 22.1: The Help for Profiles screen

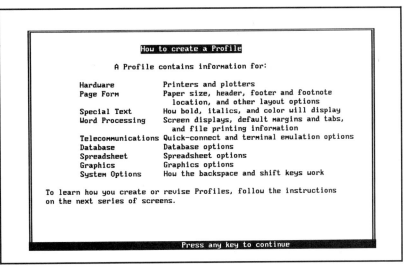

Figure 22.2: The How to Create a Profile screen

The second way to create a new profile is to select *MCM, Profile* from the Enable Main menu. (Of course, if you're at the Main menu, you have already chosen a profile for this session of Enable. But you can still create a new one. However, to use the new profile requires that you restart Enable.) After you select *MCM, Profile*, Enable displays the screen shown in Figure 22.2.

At the screen shown in Figure 22.2, press ◄─┘ to see Enable's list of available profiles (Figure 22.3). Notice that two profiles exist already: the Default profile and the Color profile. These are identical, except that the Color profile includes settings for color systems.

To edit one of the profiles listed, enter its name and press ◄─┘. You will be taken to the Categories screen shown in Figure 22.4.

As you can see, each profile has many different settings, any of which you can alter simply by moving the cursor down to the name of the setting and pressing ◄─┘. If you select Word Processing, for example, you will be led through eight screens of options, such as formatting, orientation of paper in printer, location of footnotes, and numbering convention. When you are through with the eighth word processing profile screen, you will return to the first. To return to the Categories screen, press Esc. The settings in the other categories

You can create a new profile by typing a new name into the space provided on the List of Profiles screen. This also takes you to the Categories screen.

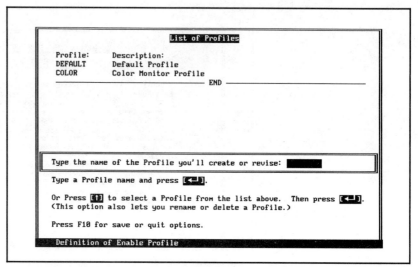

Figure 22.3: List of available profiles

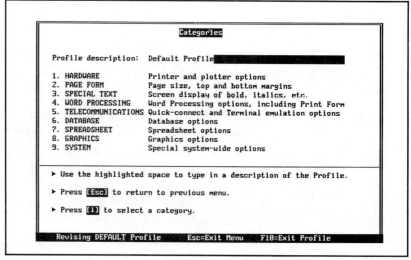

Figure 22.4: Categories screen

work approximately the same way, though they have different options. These are all covered in detail in the next section.

When you are through setting all the options, press Esc to return to the List of Profiles screen (Figure 22.3). You can leave this screen by pressing Esc. You then have two options: *Save* and *Quit*. *Save* adds the new profile or saves the changes made to the existing profile. *Quit* performs one of two actions. If you entered the profile screen from the Enable Main menu, *Quit* takes you back to the Main menu. If you entered the profiles screen from the Enable startup screen, you will return to the screen shown in Figure 22.1. From here, you can select your new profile for the current session, using the *Use Profile* option.

THE DEFAULT PROFILE SETTINGS

This section lists the settings in your default profile. The margin notes contain some suggested changes to the default settings, as well as other useful information.

HARDWARE

Use the Hardware setting to select your printer. This is important. If you fail to select your printer using this option, you will have to reselect your printer the first time you print from within Enable each time Enable is run.

The alternate Hardware screen allows you to select a plotter, if you have one.

PAGE FORM

The Page Form category describes the settings used by your printer. If you are using legal size paper, for instance, your page dimensions will be different. The defaults are shown in Table 22.1.

Table 22.1: Page Form Defaults

DEFAULT NAME	SETTING
Length	11 (paper length in inches; from 1–655)
Width	8.0 (paper width in inches; from 1–655)
Lines per inch	6 (from 0–99)
Top margin	6 (6 lines from text to top of page; from 0–99)
Bottom margin	6 (6 lines from text to bottom of page; from 0–99)
Blank lines between header and text	2 (from 0–99)
Blank lines between footer and text	2
Left Margin offset	0 (prints text at the specified number of columns from left margin; from 0–99)
Line spacing	0 (single spacing—can also be set within program; from 0–99.)
Should pages be numbered?	No
Date picture	Standard (This format appears as *January 16, 1991*. Other formats include Military (*16 January 1991*), Numerical (*1/16/91*), European Numerical (*16/1/91*), and Picture.
Font	PICA (Other options are Elite and Compressed for default print mode.)

The *Left Margin offset* setting is useful for continuous-feed paper, to avoid tractor feed holes.

Picture lets you specify your own format using year, month, and day symbols. Numerical and European Numerical let you choose whether slashes, hyphens, or dots separate the numerical portions of the dates.

Table 22.1: Page Form Defaults (continued)

DEFAULT NAME	SETTING
Should proportional spacing be used?	No (Proportional spacing allots less space for narrower letters and more space for wider letters.)
Should microjustification be used?	No (Justifies by adding full character spaces between words, which can cause broad spaces between words.)
Should letter quality be used?	No
Print graphs in:	Black/White (Other options include Color and Shaded for graphics systems.)

Some printers allow microjustification, which allows lines to be "padded" with small amounts of white space between characters to justify lines.

SPECIAL TEXT

The Special Text category sets the appearance of the special formatting options (such as italic or boldface) on the word processing screen. If you are operating a color system, you can specify any color.

WORD PROCESSING

The word processor's profile options are the most extensive, covering eight screens of choices. If you use the word processor frequently, you'll find these profile options quite helpful. Most users want to change at least a few options for their system. Turning automatic reformat on is, perhaps, the most common change. The word processor options and their defaults are listed in Table 22.2.

Table 22.2: Word Processing Defaults

Screen Display

These options determine whether particular screen elements should be displayed initially. You can always use the word processor Display *and* Hide *options (see Chapter 5) to display or hide the elements regardless of the profile settings.*

OPTION	SETTING
Display document title	Yes
Display ruler at top of screen	No
Display ruler at bottom of screen	No
Display ruler within body of text	Yes
Display headers	Yes
Display footers	Yes
Display comments	Yes
Display footnotes	Yes
Display table of contents entries	Yes
Display index entries	Yes
Display paper clips	Yes
Display page breaks	Yes
Display line spacing entries	Yes
Display shorthand entries	Yes
Display table of authority entries	No

Reformatting

Automatic text reformat	No (Refers to the end-of-line word wrap that occurs when you activate automatic reformat.)

Table 22.2: Word Processing Defaults (continued)

Reformatting	
Leading blanks retained during reformat	Yes (Refers to blank spaces that begin paragraphs. No removes the spaces when the paragraph is reformatted.)
Prompts	
Document title prompt in new document	Yes
Do you wish to be prompted to verify text deletion	Yes
Backups	
Back up existing files when saving	No
Tabs	
Display tab characters in document	Yes
Save ASCII files with tabs	No
Footnote Placement	
Location of footnotes	Bottom of each page
Blank lines between divider line and footnotes	1
Blank lines between footnotes	1
Minimum number of text lines per page	15

It's a good idea to change *Back up existing files when saving* to Yes to protect your files. Enable names the backup word processor file as *name*.WP@.

Table 22.2: Word Processing Defaults (continued)

Footnote Divider Line	
Divider line between text and footnote	* * * * (Determines the appearance of line following the text and preceding the footnotes on a page. The line can be any character and can be up to 30 characters long.)
Repeat count	2 (Number of times the divider line is repeated. Maximum is 99.)
Starting column	6 (distance from the left margin offset to begin the divider line)
Footnote Symbols	
Footnote symbol style	Numeric (Determines the type of footnote symbol. *Numbers* can restart at each page or continue through the document. *Character* lets you specify the characters used for footnote symbols.)
Footnote symbol position	L (for left margin; you can specify L $+n$ or L $-n$, where n stands for the number of characters from the left margin to the right (+) or left (−).)
Footnote symbol justification	Left

Table 22.2: Word Processing Defaults (continued)

Footnote Symbols	
Footnote symbol placement style	1 (Symbols are superscripted in text and footnote; 2 causes footnote symbols to be underscored and followed by slash; 3 causes footnote symbols to be superscripted in text and punctuated by a period in the footnote.)
Resequence draft footnote reference numbers in final form	No (Causes footnotes to be numbered in the order they were created rather than in sequence throughout the chapter.)
Footnote Continuation Messages *When a footnote must be continued on the following page, a message will alert the reader that the footnote continues.*	
Footnote continuation message	*footnote continues on next page* (maximum of 127 characters)
Position of continuation message	L (for left margin; you can specify L + n or L – n, where n stands for the number of characters from the left margin to the right (+) or left (–). Enter **C** to place the continuation relative to center, or **R** to place continuation relative to the right margin.)
Message justification	Left

Change *Resequence draft footnote...* to Yes so that your footnotes will be numbered sequentially in your final draft.

Table 22.2: Word Processing Defaults (continued)

Continued Footnote Messages	
Message at start of continued footnote	*continued footnote* (maximum is 127 characters)
Place message	Above the footnote
Position of continuation message	L (same options as for footnote continuation message: L + *n*, L − *n*, R, C.)
Message justification	Left
Default Ruler	
Left Margin on Default Ruler	1
Right Margin on Default Ruler	78
Distance between tabs on Default Ruler	8
Number of tab settings on Default Ruler	5
Should the default right margin be justified	No
Cursor Movement Options	
Should F2/Right position cursor to space after last character	No (places the cursor on the last character in the line when you press F2 →. Otherwise, F2 → places the cursor in the space after the last character in the line.)

A justified right margin is even, which makes a printout look more formal and professional. This option is best used with micro-justification.

Table 22.2: Word Processing Defaults (continued)

Cursor Movement Options	
Number of keystrokes between automatic document saves	[blank] (If a value is entered in this line, the document will be saved each time you reach the specified number of keystrokes.)
Print Setup Options	
Number of copies	1
Paper type	Continuous form
Printer orientation	Portrait (*Landscape* refers to a sheet of paper held "sideways"—wider than it is tall. *Portrait* refers to a sheet of paper taller than it is wide.)
Unidirectional Print	No
Print a title page	Yes
Leading blank page	No
Print in draft mode	No (Draft mode prints faster than NLQ mode, but NLQ is higher quality.)
Allow automatic widow/orphan repagination	No (Change to Yes to have Enable move a line to eliminate widows or break a page before a paragraph where an orphan would appear.)
List print statistics	No

Dot-matrix printers can improve the resolution of a printout by printing in only one direction.

Orphans are single first lines of paragraphs at the end of a page; widows are single last lines of paragraphs at the top of the page.

Table 22.2: Word Processing Defaults (continued)

Table of Contents	
Should Table of Contents entries be copied to text	No
Should Table of Contents entries have sequence numbers	No
Select style of Unit numbers	1
Select style of Chapter numbers	1
Select style of Section numbers	1
Select style of Minor section numbers	1
Optional outline style; end mark only	No (Entries will have "cascading" elements.)
Dictionary	
Select master dictionary	Standard (Enable can also use a Legal or Medical dictionary.)
Enter user dictionary path	(Enter the path to your personal dictionary.)

"Cascading" elements would format an entry in section 2 of chapter 3 of unit 1 as "1.3.2. Vampire Bats." The other option is to have only the lowest element associated with the table of contents entry: "2. Vampire Bats."

TELECOMMUNICATIONS

The Telecommunications profile options shown in Table 22.3 duplicate many of the items you can set within the telecommunications module. Setting options here simply changes the defaults when you create a new setup. You can, of course, override these choices within the setup screens. For details about each of these options, see Chapter 18.

Table 22.3: Telecommunications Defaults

Baud rate	1200
Select one of the options described below	3 (represents parity none, word size, 7 bits, 1 stop bit. The other options appear at the bottom of the screen.)
Select type of duplex	Full
Which of your computer's COMM-PORTs are you using?	COMM1
Terminal emulation	No (Enable can emulate VT100, VT52, and ATT4410.)
Transmission type	Polled
Modem table choice	ACOM
Filtered disk capture	Yes
Prompt for Quick-connect background capture file	Yes
Key to stop script	Esc

If you select VT100, you will be given the additional option of generating a Delete or Backspace when the Backspace key is pressed.

DATABASE

The Database profile options shown in Table 22.4 control some miscellaneous aspects of the database. These are mostly convenience options, including file formats, automatic save options, and others.

Table 22.4: Database Defaults

Database creation format	1 = Enable/OA|dBASE III (The other option— *2 = Enable 2.0|dBASE II*—makes the new version of Enable compatible with your old database file formats.)
Pass thru	Yes

With pass thru, you can correct or add to the information in one database while working in another.

Table 22.4: Database Defaults (continued)

Numeric fields in ADD/EDIT should be:	Left justified
Number of transactions between flushing files to disk	[blank] (turns off automatic backup)
Stop on all database errors	No (If this is set to Yes, you will have to press ↵ each time an error is encountered. With No, you can bypass this requirement on minor errors.)
DISPLAY record option	Full page (Enable waits until a screenful of records has been retrieved before displaying them. The *Immediate* option displays the records as they are found.)
REPORT print option	Immediate Spool report (prints immediately; all other operations cease until the report is finished printing.)

Computers can *spool print*, which places the printout on the disk and then moves it to the printer "in the background" while you are involved in other tasks.

SPREADSHEET

The Spreadsheet profile options in Table 22.5 are like the database options—they control miscellaneous aspects of the module. Only six options appear for this module since there are few defaults in the spreadsheet.

Table 22.5: Spreadsheet Defaults

Protect all cells in spreadsheet?	No (Selecting Global Protection within the spreadsheet will protect only those cells protected with a range command.)
Convert Lotus 1-2-3 macros	Yes

With this option set to *Yes*, selecting Global Protection within the spreadsheet will protect all cells except those specifically unprotected with a range command.

Table 22.5: Spreadsheet Defaults (continued)

Display zero values in cells	Yes (If set to *No*, cells containing zeros will display as blank cells.)
Do you wish to indicate pointer location in borders?	No
Recalculation options	2 (Recalculates only formulas that depend on values that have changed when F5 is pressed; the 1 option recalculates all formulas.)
Back up existing spreadsheet files when saving?	No

GRAPHICS

The graphics module contains only one profile option:

Function keys are arranged   Vertically (This tells Enable whether your function keys (for Perspective) are arranged vertically or horizontally.)

This is not so much a default setting as a permanent computer setting. It's unlikely that you will be changing this setting once you have established it (unless your hardware changes).

SYSTEM

System defaults (Table 22.6) control simple actions that occur throughout the Enable program, such as the effects of certain keys. You might find these options handy.

Table 22.6: System Defaults

What action should occur when the Backspace key is pressed?	3 (blanks the character to left of cursor)
What effect should Shift key have when in Caps Lock?	1 (letters remain uppercase)
What effect should Enter have in Insert mode?	1 (split the line and start a new paragraph)
Do you want to use the system print queue?	No
Use Q to exit the extended directory screen?	No

This chapter showed you how to access the profile settings and how to set new profile options for the nine different categories available. Though most of the profile options can be overridden by commands used in the various modules, it is time consuming to issue the same commands over and over to override the defaults. Hence, the profiles are useful for customizing Enable to suit your needs.

PART

6

Using Enable's Integration Power

Integrating the Enable Modules

YOU HAVE READ ABOUT THE INDIVIDUAL FEATURES of Enable: the spreadsheet, word processor, database, graphics, and telecommunications. One area of Enable makes all these features greater than their sum. You may have purchased Enable because it provided all the software an individual or small business would require. If so, you received more than you bargained for. Enable is *integrated* software. Integration means that anything created in one part of Enable is usable in other parts of Enable. You can create a spreadsheet and send the information from the spreadsheet to the database or the word processor. Or you can create a graph with the spreadsheet/graphics module and use it with the word processor to create a report.

Other options are windowing and multitasking. You can get your money's worth out of the package without ever using these features, but they're worth a look. *Windowing* is the ability to shrink, expand, or move a document window, or to jump from one window to another. As you may already know, a document window is the screen view of each document you use in Enable. In other words, when you view any word processor document, spreadsheet worksheet, or database, you are looking at the information within the confines of a window. You might not have known it, but you can change the size, shape, and position of that window—and you can open more than one at a time. *Multitasking* lets Enable work on complex calculations and procedures while you do something else. It's the ability to do two things at once, provided the computer can do one of them. This is commonly used for complex spreadsheet calculations and database reports. You'll see how it works in this chapter.

Windows, multitasking, and integration all fall under the general heading of MCM, the module that oversees the operations of Enable. MCM stands for *Master Control Module*. The Main menu options on the MCM menu are *Windows*, *Files*, *Macros*, *Profile*, *Screen*, *Tools*, and *DOS*. You have seen *Macros* and *Tools* in the course of creating macros and menus. We'll examine the other options in this chapter. First, let's take a look at the Windows feature.

USING WINDOWS

As mentioned earlier, a window is a screen view of each document you use in Enable. Whenever you open a new or existing document, it appears in a window. This is simply a box around the data that contains it. The following section will show you how to manipulate windows in Enable.

OPENING A WINDOW

Let's open some windows.

1. Go to the Main menu and start the word processor. Select *Use System*, *Word Processing*, *Create* and enter any name. Then press ⟵ to accept the default ruler. Call this word processor session **WP1**.

From within any module, you can press Alt-Home to open a new window.

2. In the word processor, press F10 M to select *MCM*. From the resulting menu, select *Windows*. From the next menu, select *Open a window*. You will find yourself back at the Enable Main menu, which has *#2* displayed in the status line.

3. Now open a spreadsheet: Select *Use System*, *Spreadsheet/Graphics*, *Create*. Call your spreadsheet **SS1.**

4. In the spreadsheet, press F10 M O O (F10, MCM, Other Windows, Open). You again will find yourself back at the Enable Main menu, which is now *#3* on the status line.

5. Open a database: Select *Use System*, *DBMS/Graphics*, *Interact*. From the resulting menu, select *Add*.

6. With the prompt for the database and database input form on the screen, type **CUST**, then press F10 M 1 1 (F10, MCM Windows, Open a window). And, of course, you will find yourself back at the Enable Main menu, ready to start another application.

Keep the Main menu on your screen; in a moment you'll look at the options available when you use windows. When you're finished, press F9 W C to close the current window. If the window contains any new information, Enable will pause to make sure you really want to stop the application and lose all data entered since the last save.

Speed-key options are also available for opening and closing windows. Press F9 W O to open a new window (you will be taken to the Enable Main menu). Alternatively, press Alt-Home to open a new window.

THE WINDOW SUMMARY OPTIONS

You could continue opening windows until you have eight (you may wish to do so, just to see it done), but let's take a moment to look at the Window Summary Options screen (Figure 23.1). This screen is displayed by starting from the Main menu and selecting *MCM*, *Windows*, *Display window summary*.

From the summary screen, you can use the arrow keys to highlight the name of the window you want to see and press ← to go to that window. Pause for a moment to look at the kinds of information available in the Window Summary screen. The columns along the top of the list of windows read Type, Status Line, State, and File Path.

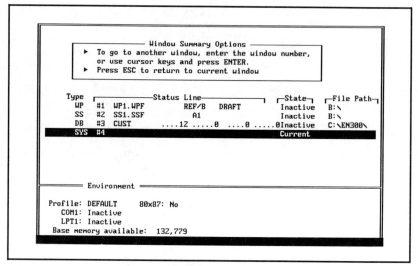

Figure 23.1: Window Summary Options screen

Type, of course, tells you what sort of application is running in the window. Status Line tells you the information that is normally available along the bottom of the screen in the module you are using. This information includes the window number and certain settings. State indicates what window is current, and what windows are active (multitasking) and inactive. The last column, File Path, tells where the file is located. The file path column will be blank if the document in the window has not been saved yet.

The Environment box at the bottom of this screen contains the name of your profile, whether the floating-point math coprocessor is available, the status of the communications ports, and available memory. Watch your available memory carefully. Multitasking and multiple applications take up considerable amounts of memory. If you push Enable too far, you may find yourself unable to open more windows or unable to add to documents because of a shortage of available memory.

RESIZING WINDOWS

Resizing and moving windows lets you organize your document on screen. By shrinking some windows and moving others, you can effectively view several documents at one time. This can be an important feature when the documents are related. And as you'll see in the next chapter, viewing two or more windows at one time is useful when copying information between them. This section will show you how to adjust a window's size and position.

From the window summary, go to the word processor window by highlighting window #1 and pressing ↵. Select F10 M 1 2 to resize or reposition the current window. You will see the options you saw when adjusting the size and position of a user-defined menu: press M to move, E to expand, or S to shrink (shrinking is your only option with a full-screen window), and then use the cursor keys to adjust the screen (the cursor keys correspond to the four sides of the window). When the window is the size and shape you require, press Esc. Figure 23.2 shows the word processor window resized to about a quarter of the screen. In the background, you can see a previous screen: the database module.

Try typing in the word processor window. You will note that as you reach the right side of the window, the window adjusts itself so your typing is always on the screen.

If you want to return the window to full size, select F10 M 1 5. Return to the window summary screen (F10 M 1 3) and go to the

The Expert command for changing a window is F9 W L.

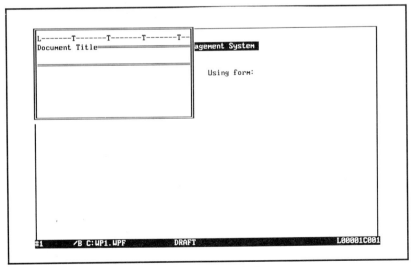

Figure 23.2: Shrinking the word processor window

spreadsheet by highlighting its line and pressing ↵. Within the spreadsheet, press F10 M. The menu in the spreadsheet is somewhat different from that in the word processor. Select *This Window*, *Modify Size* or *Location*. Figure 23.3 shows the shrunken and repositioned spreadsheet sharing the screen with the database and word processor. The spreadsheet is at its lower-right corner to illustrate that the entire spreadsheet, with its thousands of cells and all of its functions, is still available, despite the window's small size.

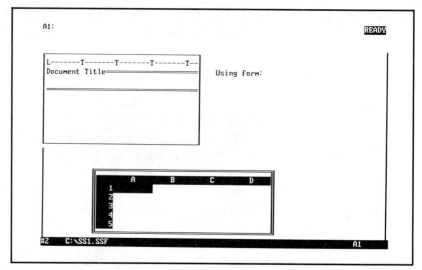

Figure 23.3: Adding the spreadsheet window

SWITCHING TO ANOTHER WINDOW

One way to move to a different window is to use the F10 MCM command from within the module. In the database and word processor, use the commands F10 M 1, then option 3 or 4. Option 3 moves you to the window summary screen where you can specify another window. Option 4 takes you to the next window number. In the spreadsheet, use the command F10 M O. This lets you specify the window number to which you would like to move.

Another way to move from window to window is to enter the expert command F9 W A from within any window. This advances to the next window. The command F9 W B goes back to the previous window. You can also enter Alt-↑ to move to the next window and Alt-↓ to move to the previous window. To move to a specific window, enter F9 W followed by the number of the window (each window is assigned a number corresponding to its order in the opening sequence). Finally, press G to go to the specified window.

WINDOW CONTROL WITH THE FUNCTION KEYS

Table 23.1 shows the important window-control keys.

Table 23.1: Window-Control Keys

FUNCTION	COMMAND
Advance to next window	Alt-↑ or F9 W A
Back to previous window	Alt-↓ or F9 W B
Clear split (unsplit) window	F9 W X (spreadsheet only)
Resize and move a window	Alt-5
Close a window	Alt-End or F9 W C
Go to specified window	F9 W [*window number*] G
Go to window summary	F9 W ? or F9 W G
Horizontally split window	F9 W H (spreadsheet only)
Open a window	Alt-Home or F9 W O
Return window to previous size	F9 W P (all modules except database)
Size and move window	F9 W L (all modules except database)
Synchronize scrolling	F9 W S (spreadsheet only)
Unsynchronize scrolling	F9 W U (spreadsheet only)
Vertically split window	F9 W V (spreadsheet only)
Zoom window to full screen	F9 W Z (all modules except database)

MULTITASKING

One of the principal attractions of OS/2 and UNIX is their ability to perform tasks *in the background*—that is, on their own and out of view—while you continue with other operations.

Enable's Master Control Module also offers multitasking. This means, for example, that if you have a spreadsheet that will require a great deal of time to calculate, you can leave it in the midst of its calculation and use another module. All you have to do is press Alt-Tab to escape from the calculating spreadsheet and go to the Window Summary screen. Unfortunately, after you press Alt-Tab, the recalculating spreadsheet is unavailable until the calculation is completed. This means that if you accidentally create an endless loop, it will continue recalculating until the computer is rebooted.

The only limit on multitasking is the number of available windows and the amount of available memory.

> If you wish to place in the background a screen containing a graph, you must press the space bar before pressing Alt-Tab.

OTHER MCM FEATURES

The MCM command from the Main menu provides a few other options worth noting. The *Files* option leads to a series of powerful file management commands. Using this command, you can view all the files for a particular module on any disk or directory. Plus, you can use special commands to manipulate those files, such as changing their names. After selecting *MCM*, *Files*, choose the type of files you would like to view by selecting the appropriate module. You will see the files for only the module you select. Choose *All* to see all files on a disk or directory. The screen will look like Figure 23.4.

As you see from the command listing at the bottom of the screen, you can use this screen to copy, delete, and rename files, among other things. Press A to change the DOS pathname and display files in a different directory. Use the Arrow keys, PgDn, PgUp, Home, and End keys to highlight files in the list. (Highlighting a file and pressing ⏎ opens it.) Press X to see a list of extended commands as shown in Figure 23.5.

Here you can perform the same copying, deleting, and renaming activities, but to a set of marked files. This lets you perform the actions to a large "batch" of files at one time. You can use various

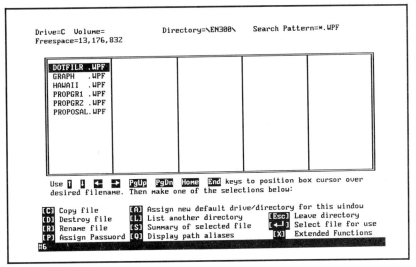

Figure 23.4: *MCM,* Files *listing and commands*

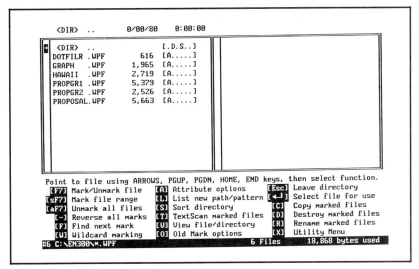

Figure 23.5: *MCM,* Files *listing and extended commands*

options for marking files. Pressing X again provides still more commands, as shown in Figure 23.6.

Here you can select default directories for various files used by Enable. You can also perform a series of DOS-like operations, such as removing a directory and making a new directory.

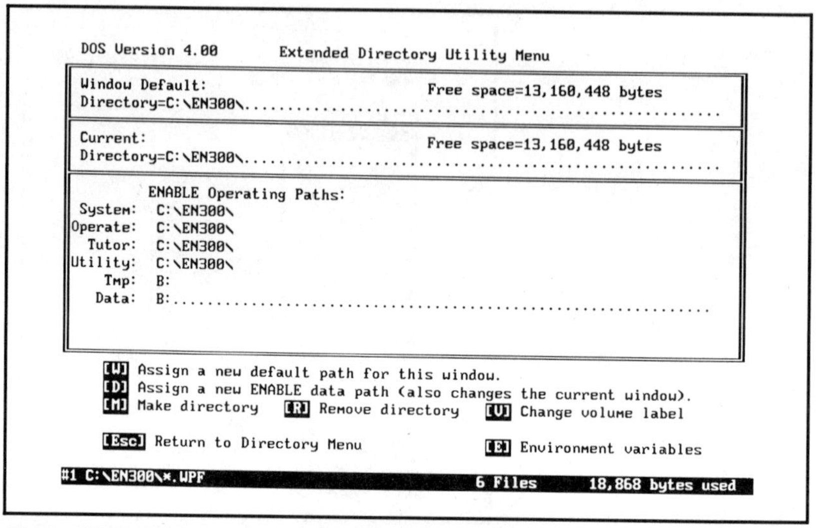

```
    DOS Version 4.88        Extended Directory Utility Menu

   ┌─────────────────────────────────────────────────────────────────┐
   │ Window Default:                                                   │
   │ Directory=C:\EN300\.................     Free space=13,160,448 bytes │
   ├─────────────────────────────────────────────────────────────────┤
   │ Current:                                                          │
   │ Directory=C:\EN300\.................     Free space=13,160,448 bytes │
   ├─────────────────────────────────────────────────────────────────┤
   │       ENABLE Operating Paths:                                     │
   │ System:   C:\EN300\                                               │
   │ Operate:  C:\EN300\                                               │
   │  Tutor:   C:\EN300\                                               │
   │ Utility:  C:\EN300\                                               │
   │    Tmp:   B:                                                      │
   │   Data:   B:.................................................     │
   │                                                                   │
   │                                                                   │
   └─────────────────────────────────────────────────────────────────┘
      [W] Assign a new default path for this window.
      [D] Assign a new ENABLE data path (also changes the current window).
      [M] Make directory   [R] Remove directory   [V] Change volume label

      [Esc] Return to Directory Menu          [E] Environment variables
    #1 C:\EN300\*.WPF                          6 Files      18,868 bytes used
```

Figure 23.6: MCM, Files listing and utilities options

The *Profile* option on the MCM menu provides the same options as electing to edit the profile upon starting the Enable program. These options are discussed in Chapter 22.

The *Screen* option lets you select your screen type. The options are *Mono* (monochrome text), *CO80* (color text, 80 characters per screen line), *BW80* (single color text, 80 characters per screen line), and *Graphics*. Graphics mode is barely discernible from normal color text mode, until you want to display both graphics and text; you can do so, but at some expense of processing time.

The *DOS* option is simply explained: If you want to use a DOS command from within Enable, simply select *MCM, DOS* and type in the DOS command you want to use. You will be unable to use this option unless you started Enable with a memory allocation parameter assigning a certain amount of memory to Enable and leaving the remainder to DOS. For example, to leave 128K available to DOS on a 640K system, you would start Enable with the command ENABLE 512. (Your system may vary, depending on the DOS version and memory-resident programs running.)

When the DOS window is available, you can treat it like any other Enable window. Press F10 to see the DOS window menu. Press Alt-5

(5 on the numeric keypad) to resize and move the DOS window. The rest of the options are listed in Table 23.1.

Having numerous windows open would be nothing more than an interesting trick if you had no way to convey information from window to window. You can cut information from one window, switch to the other window with the Window Summary screen, and copy the information there. The windows need not be visible on the screen at the same time. Sharing information among modules is the subject of the next chapter.

<table>
<tr><td>CHAPTER
24</td><td>Sharing Information
among Modules</td></tr>
</table>

THIS CHAPTER COMPLETES YOUR BASIC EDUCATION in Enable/OA. By now, you should have a good understanding of all the Enable modules, and you should be comfortable with the commands used to move between modules and between various windows in Enable. Using some basic features of macros and custom menus, you have learned how to add special "automatic" operations to Enable and to your applications.

This final chapter describes how to move information between modules in Enable. Moving between windows is useful, but sharing information between windows (that is, between different documents and different modules) can save you much time and effort.

The most common way to share data is to move database or spreadsheet information into the word processor for printing with your reports and memos. You might, for instance, want to include a graph or table of spreadsheet data in a report, or copy information between the spreadsheet and database. These processes are explained in this chapter.

COPYING WITHIN THE SAME MODULE

One of the simplest forms of sharing information is to copy data from one window to another within the same module. You might, for example, need to copy information from one spreadsheet into another. Or perhaps you want to use a paragraph from one word processor document in a different document.

COPYING BETWEEN WORD PROCESSOR DOCUMENTS

Copying between word processor windows was discussed briefly in the word processing section of this book. Here are the steps again:

- Open both word processor documents so that two windows are active. If desired, you can shrink the windows so that both can be seen at the same time, but this is not necessary.

- Using Alt-↑, move to the window containing the information to be copied (the "source" document).

- Highlight the block to be copied by pressing F7 at the beginning and end of the block.

- Using Alt-↑, go to the window into which you want to move the data (the "target" window).

- Move the cursor into the position in the document where the copied information will appear.

- Press F10 C 1 C B O (F10, Copy, Copy, Change Options, Block, Other Window). Enable moves to the Window Summary screen, where you can choose one of the other open windows.

- Using the ↑ key, highlight the name of the document containing the highlighted block (the block of text to be copied). Press ↵ when finished.

- Press Alt-F5.

If desired, you can alter the order of these steps slightly. Rather than highlighting the data to be copied first, you can enter the copy command F10 C 1 C B O, move to the source document window, and *then* highlight the desired block using the F7 block commands, pressing Alt-F5 to finish. Enable remains in the Copy Pending mode, as indicated at the bottom of the screen.

You can copy an entire unopened word processor file into an open word processor document. This requires a small variation of the procedure:

- Move the cursor into the position in the open document where the copied document will appear.

- Press F10 C 1 C F (F10, Copy, Copy, Change Options, File).

- Enter the name of the document you want to copy (include the entire path name), then press ⬅️.

This technique, called *boilerplating*, can be useful for compiling documents from several separate sources of data. It is often used for contract or proposal writing.

COPYING BETWEEN SPREADSHEETS

Copying between two spreadsheet documents is also simple. Figure 24.1 shows a screen displaying two spreadsheets. The window sizes have been changed so both can be seen at once. The window "underneath" (April) contains the data to be copied into the top (First Quarter 1991). Here are the steps:

- Activate the spreadsheet into which the data will be copied. This is window #2 in the example. Then press F10 C C W (F10, Combine, Copy, Window) to go to the familiar window display screen.

- Using the ↑ key, highlight the spreadsheet document containing the information to be copied. Press ⬅️ when finished. The screen should look like Figure 24.2.

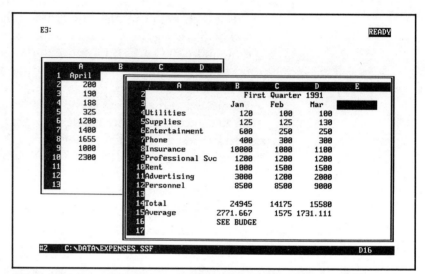

Figure 24.1: Two spreadsheet windows ready for copying

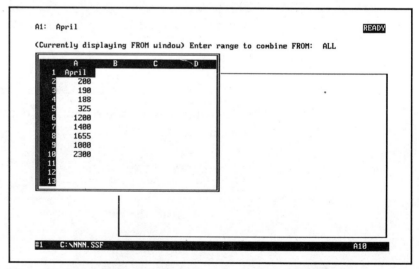

Figure 24.2: Copying information from the source worksheet

- Enter the range containing the data you want to copy. You can type the range as a range reference (for example, A1..B8) or as a range name (for example, SALES), or you can "point" to the range using the keyboard commands. When finished, press ◄─┘. Enable takes you back to the originating spreadsheet.

- Move the pointer to the desired location in the document. This is where the copied data will appear. Press ◄─┘ when finished. The document will soon contain the data from the other spreadsheet. Figure 24.3 shows the finished transfer of the example documents.

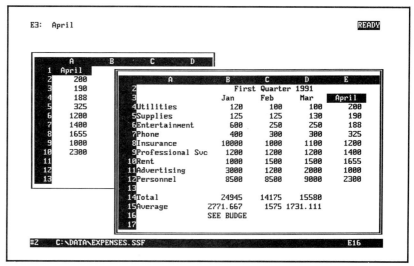

Figure 24.3: April data transferred into First Quarter spreadsheet

If you do not remember the range reference that you want to copy from the disk file, you can open the spreadsheet file and use the procedure for copying between open windows.

You can also copy spreadsheet data from an unopened worksheet file into an opened worksheet. The procedure is similar to the one for copying between open worksheets. As before, begin with the pointer in the worksheet that will contain the copied information. The other worksheet (the one containing the data to be copied) does not have to be open. Next, use the command F10 C C D (F10, Combine, Copy, Disk-File). Enter the name of the source spreadsheet file in the space provided, including the entire path to the file. When you press ◄─┘, Enable asks for the range of cells you want to copy. Enter the desired range, or enter **ALL** to copy the entire file. Finally, move the cell pointer into position or enter a range, then press ◄─┘.

CONSOLIDATING WORKSHEETS

If you use your spreadsheet to keep regular weekly or monthly records, you might find that you use an identical worksheet each week or month, but with new data in it. By saving your work under a new name each time, you can save previous records while continuing to create new ones. In short, you end up with several worksheets, each representing a different week or month.

Suppose you want to create a worksheet that totals each of 12 monthly worksheets and presents a grand total of the values. The easiest way to do this is to consolidate the spreadsheets using the Combine command. The procedure is similar to copying data from a closed worksheet file into an open file (described at the end of the preceding section). Just activate the last worksheet in the series. (If you have 12 monthly sheets, activate the sheet for December.) The rest of the sheets can remain unopened.

Next, use the command F10 C A D (F10, Combine, Add, Disk-File). This prepares Enable to copy the contents of a spreadsheet file on disk and add the values to the current spreadsheet. The next step is to specify the name of the first file on disk (this would be the spreadsheet representing the first month, January). After entering the spreadsheet name, specify the range of cells in the spreadsheet that you want to combine with the current sheet. If the spreadsheets use identical formats, you can use the open sheet as a guide for the range to copy. After entering this range, specify the range into which you want this information copied. This should be the corresponding range in the currently open sheet.

Because you specified the *Add* option in the Combine command, Enable does not replace the existing data with the copied data, but adds the two sets of values to produce the sum. Simply repeat this process for the remaining sheets in the series. The result will be the grand total of the copied cells. Since you used one of the 12 monthly sheets as a starting sheet, be sure to change the name of the consolidated file when saving. This leaves all 12 monthly files intact.

COPYING DATA FROM
SPREADSHEET TO WORD PROCESSOR —

You cannot copy information from the word processor into a spreadsheet—only from a spreadsheet into the word processor.

Copying from the spreadsheet into the word processor involves two different procedures: one for data and one for graphs. Copying data from a spreadsheet to a word processor document is similar to copying between two word processor documents. In the following steps, the two documents you created in previous chapters are used: the word processor file DEMOMEMO and the EXPENSES spreadsheet. If desired, follow along with your copies of these two documents.

1. Open both documents so that two windows are active. If desired, you can shrink the windows so that you can see both at the same time, but this is not necessary. Figure 24.4 shows the DEMOMEMO and EXPENSES documents in view.

2. Start out in the word processor document and position the cursor at the location in the document where you want the inserted information to appear.

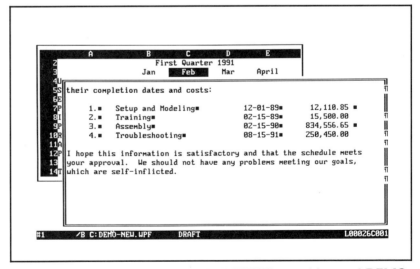

Figure 24.4: Windows open for the EXPENSES spreadsheet and DEMO-MEMO word processor document

3. Press F10 C 1 C B O (F10, Copy, Copy, Change Options, Block, Other Window). Enable moves to the Window Summary screen, where you can choose one of the other open windows.

4. Using the ↑ or ↓ key, select the EXPENSES spreadsheet from the list. Press ⏎ when finished. The spreadsheet will now be in view, as shown in Figure 24.5.

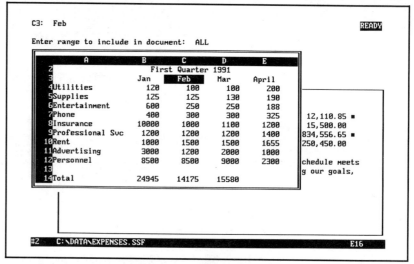

Figure 24.5: Specifying the spreadsheet block to copy

5. Enter the range reference to copy. You can type the reference or use the keyboard commands to enter the reference. In this case, enter **A2..C12** and press ⏎. Enable now moves you back to the word processor document where the data has already been entered. Figure 24.6 shows the result.

Note that the inserted spreadsheet data adheres to the appropriate ruler in the document (that is, the ruler controlling the area into which the data was inserted). You can add a ruler or change the existing one to alter the format of the spreadsheet data.

Use the same procedure to copy a graph from the spreadsheet into the word processor, but be sure to first display the graph in the spreadsheet window. You display the graph with the command F10, Graph, Select [*name*], Display (where [*name*] is the name of the graph you want to copy into the word processor). Also, you should change

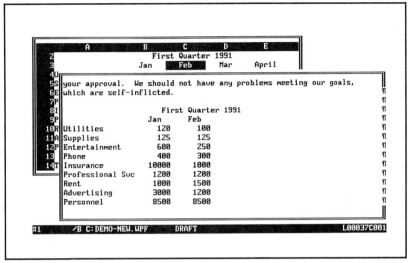

Figure 24.6: The spreadsheet data copied into the word processor document

the size and shape of the graph as desired before you move it into the word processor. With the graph in view, use the command F10, Modify to make these changes.

After returning to the word processor document, use the command F10 C 1 C B O (F10, Copy, Copy, Change Options, Block, Other Window), then specify the graph window in the list. Before copying the chosen graph, Enable displays the graph and asks that you confirm the selection by pressing Alt-F5. Enable then copies the graph into the word processor. Above the graph, Enable inserts a comment entry space for your comments. Figure 24.7 shows an example.

Notice that the graph is displayed as a shaded block. This block is a placeholder showing the graph's size and shape. When you print the document, the actual graph will appear on the page. To view the graph on the screen, you must switch to the graphics screen display with the command F10 M 3 4 (F10, MCM, Screen, Graphics). Your particular hardware setup controls the result of the graphics display.

Once the graph is inside the word processor, you can manipulate it using standard word processing commands. You can move it, copy it, delete it, and so on. You can also type text into the graph.

If the spreadsheet graph has a title, that title will appear in the comment area.

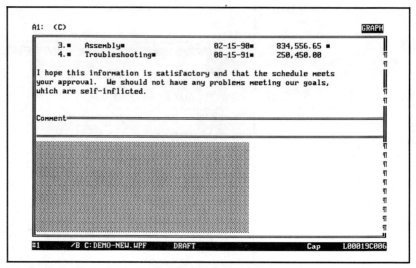

Figure 24.7: Inserting a graph into the word processor

COPYING FROM DATABASE TO SPREADSHEET

Copying information from the database to the spreadsheet can be useful for inserting database records into financial analyses, budgets, projections, and so on. You can thereby avoid a great deal of retyping. Follow these steps to copy data from a database into the spreadsheet.

- Activate the desired database from the Main menu (*Use System*, *DBMS/Graphics*, *Interact*).

- Use the *Display* option to display records in columnar format, then enter the database name and press ◄── to skip the Index and Where prompts. The screen should look like Figure 24.8. (When displaying the database, you can establish view criteria to limit the records that appear. See the database chapters for more details.)

- With the database in columnar format, return to the Main menu using the command Alt-Home.

- Activate the desired spreadsheet file (or create a new one) from the Main menu.

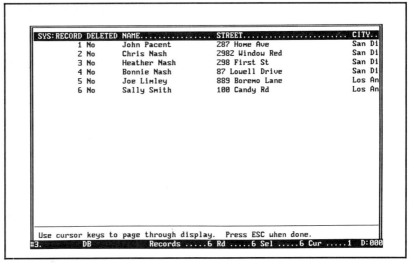

Figure 24.8: Database records displayed in columnar format

- Enter the command F10, DBMS from the spreadsheet. This takes you to the window listing, where you can select the database window. Alternatively, you can press Alt-F5 to view the open windows.

- Using the Arrow keys, highlight the database window and press ← to go to the database.

- Mark the records you want to copy into the spreadsheet. Use the ↑ and ↓ keys to move to the desired records and Alt-M to mark the records. Use the command Alt-N to "unmark" a marked record. If you want to mark a block of records, press F7 on the first and last records in the block. Figure 24.9 shows an example of marked records.

- When finished marking records, press Alt-F5.

- Press ← to pass up the "Fields to copy" screen prompt—or, if you're familiar with selecting fields, you can make changes at this point to control which fields are copied into the spreadsheet.

- Choose *Insert* or *Overlay* for adding the data to the spreadsheet. *Insert* will move existing information down, and *Overlay* will replace any information at the insert location of the data.

- Move the cell pointer to the starting location for the inserted data, where the data will appear in the spreadsheet. Press ←┘ to complete the transfer. Figure 24.10 shows an example of copied data from the database in Figure 24.9.

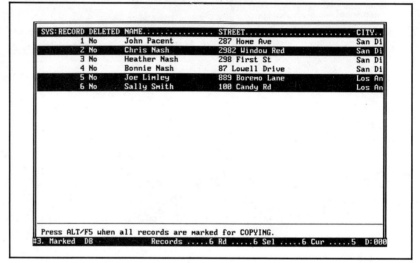

Figure 24.9: Marked records ready to be copied

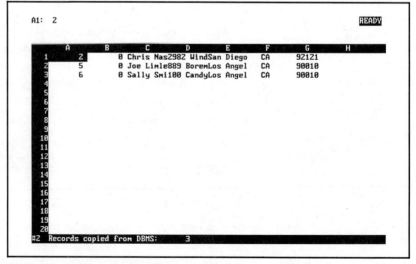

Figure 24.10: Data successfully copied into the spreadsheet

Notice that the database information appears in the same columnar format as displayed in the database. Each field occupies a cell in the spreadsheet.

COPYING FROM DATABASE TO WORD PROCESSOR

Copying information from the database into the word processor is similar to copying from the database to the spreadsheet. Prepare both documents as described in the preceding section. Then, within the word processor document, position the cursor where you want to insert the database records. Next, press Alt-F5 and select the database window. Mark the database records using Alt-M or the F7 block commands, and press Alt-F5 again when finished. Finally, press ←┘ or enter the fields to copy. The database data will appear in the word processor document.

COPYING FROM SPREADSHEET OR DATABASE TO DATABASE

The final copy procedure is to copy data from a spreadsheet or another database into the database. Enable provides many ways to import and export data with the database. In this section, you'll update an existing database file by adding new records from another database or from a spreadsheet. The example database file we'll use is the simple name and address file shown in Figure 24.11. Create this file if you want to work through this procedure.

If you want to update this database (we'll call this the master) with another database, be sure that the second database contains the same fields. You can add or remove fields by modifying the database definitions.

If you want to add records from a spreadsheet file, first prepare the spreadsheet as follows:

1. Enter the first field name in cell A1 (corresponding to one of the fields in the master database). Continue to enter all field names across row 1. Do not skip any columns.

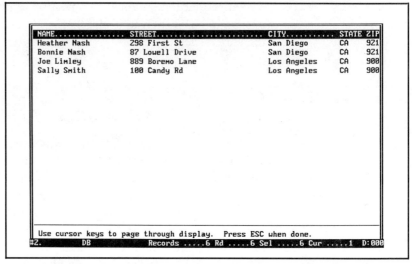

Figure 24.11: Example database

2. Under each field name (in row 2), enter a C if the field contains text or numeric characters, an N if the field contains a numeric value (to be used in calculations), or an L if the field contains a logical value.

3. Under each field type (in row 3) enter the field length, representing the number of characters allowed in the field. If the field is numeric, the maximum is 16. If desired, you can use a decimal value to indicate where the decimal should appear in the database field. For example, typing 5.5 requests 10 characters—5 on each side of the decimal point.

4. Under the field length indicator (in row 4) enter the first record. Be sure each piece of data appears under its respective heading. Remaining records should follow in row 5. Do not skip rows. Figure 24.12 shows an example to match the database in Figure 24.11.

5. Save the spreadsheet as a normal spreadsheet file. Do not include an extension when saving this file; you must let Enable use the standard .SSF extension. The example uses the name NEW.

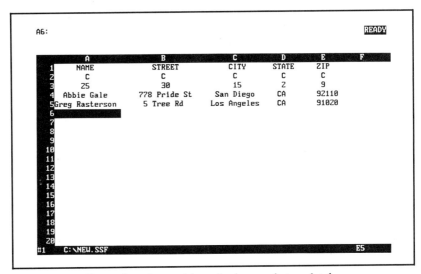

Figure 24.12: Preparing a spreadsheet for import into a database

With the spreadsheet or second database prepared, you can enter the database module and update the existing database. Here are the steps:

1. Enter the database module from the Main menu with the commands *Use System*, *DBMS/Graphics*, *Interact*.

2. At the command chart, select the *Update* command. The screen will look like Figure 24.13.

3. Under the "Master" heading, enter the name of the master database. Include the entire path name. Press ◄─┘ to continue.

4. At the "Link Field" prompt, press PgDn and then ◄─┘ to select the SYS:RECORD field. This should be the only field offered. Press ◄─┘ to continue.

5. Under the "Transaction" heading, select the *Database* option.

6. Enter the name of the matching database or the spreadsheet file you saved in the previous steps. Be sure to include the .SSF extension. The example uses the name **C:NEW.SSF**. Press ◄─┘ to continue.

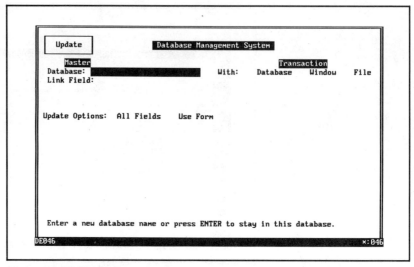

Figure 24.13: Updating a database

7. Press ↵ at the "Index" and "Where" prompts.

8. At the "Link Field" prompt, press PgDn and highlight the SYS:RECORD field from the list provided. Then press ↵. The screen should look like Figure 24.14.

9. Press ↵ again and indicate that you want *All Fields*. When you select the *All Fields* option, Enable updates the master database with the records contained in the spreadsheet file.

10. To examine the new records, select F10 D D (F10, Display-Opts, Display records in this database). Next, enter the name of the master database and press ↵ at the following prompts. The new records should appear in the database listing, as shown in Figure 24.15.

This procedure should give you an idea of the importing and merging powers of the Enable database. When using information from other database programs, first determine if Enable can read the database in its original format. If not, you might try the update procedure described here. Enable can read dBASE II, dBASE III, and other formats. Check the Enable documentation for a complete listing.

Update
Database Management System
Master
Transaction
Database: C:\DATA\DB
With: Database Window File
Link Field: SYS:RECORD
Database: C:\NEW.SSF
Index :
Where :
Link Field: SYS:RECORD
Update Options: All Fields Use Form
Operators are:
AND OR NOT < > = <= >= <> LT GT EQ LE GE NE + - * / ** () & &- &+
Fields are:
SYS:RECORD DELETED NAME STREET CITY
STATE ZIP
Press PgDn to select from above
#2. NEW.SSF Records ...... Rd .....0 Sel .....0 Cur 0 U:058

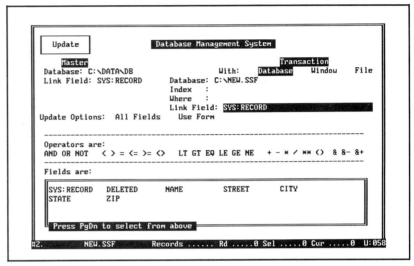

Figure 24.14: Update information completed

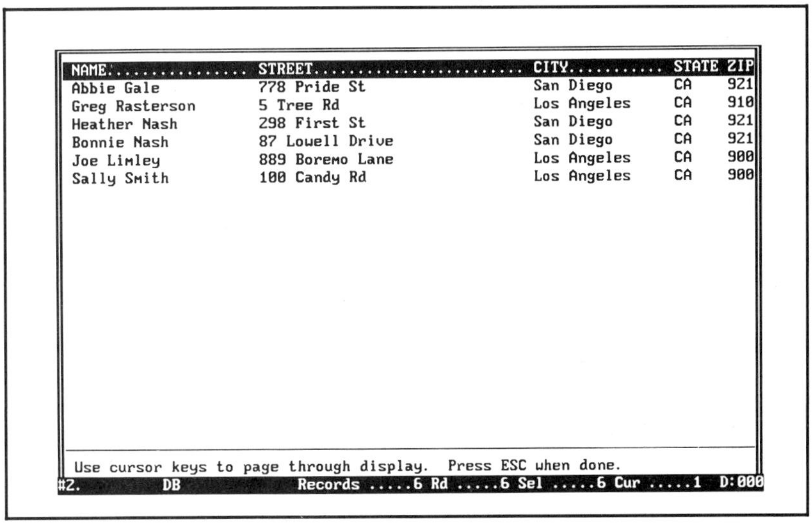

NAME................ STREET...................... CITY.......... STATE ZIP
Abbie Gale 778 Pride St San Diego CA 921
Greg Rasterson 5 Tree Rd Los Angeles CA 910
Heather Nash 298 First St San Diego CA 921
Bonnie Nash 87 Lowell Drive San Diego CA 921
Joe Limley 889 Boremo Lane Los Angeles CA 900
Sally Smith 100 Candy Rd Los Angeles CA 900
Use cursor keys to page through display. Press ESC when done.
#2. DB Records .....6 Rd .....6 Sel .....6 Cur 1 D:000

Figure 24.15: Completed database update

APPENDIX

Installing Enable

| APPENDIX |

Installing Enable

BEFORE ENABLE CAN BE RUN, IT MUST BE INSTALLED. although it is technically possible to use Enable without a hard disk, it would be a practical fiasco because there are so many different disks; even the most intrepid user would soon grow tired of changing disks—a condition known as "swap-happy." Since the hard disk is a practical necessity, the installation described here assumes a hard-disk installation. Likewise, since most Enable installations will be from 5¼-inch disks, this is the method described. Installation from 3½-inch disks will not vary greatly from the described installation.

COPYING THE ENABLE DISKS

Begin by copying each of your Enable disks to a new floppy disk. You'll need 24 5¼-inch double-density disks or 12 3½-inch 720K disks. Copy the disks and install Enable from the copies, not the originals.

Follow the instructions in your DOS manual that describe the DISKCOPY command to copy the disks. Be sure to label each of the copies exactly the same as the original. When you are finished making the copies, place the original disks in a waterproof plastic bag and store them in a safe place separate from the copies. A disaster may befall the originals or the copies, but probably not both.

INSTALLATION

Installing Enable is very simple.

1. Boot your system and go to the root directory by typing **CD** and pressing ↵ at the DOS or OS/2 prompt.

2. Insert the INSTALL 1 disk in drive A.

3. On the command line, type **A:** and press ↵, and then type **INSTALL** and press ↵.

From this point, you need only follow the instructions you see on the screen. The following information will be important as you respond to the prompts:

- This book presumes a complete installation.

- If you have a hard disk, press **H** when asked to indicate the type of installation.

- *Installing Perspective*   A screen will appear informing you of the kind of equipment you will need to use Enable's Perspective II Three Dimensional Graphics feature: an IBM PC or compatible with 640K RAM, DOS 2.0 or higher, and a hard disk with at least 1.9Mb of free disk space. You will need a CGA, EGA, VGA, or Hercules adapter, or an AT&T 6300 or Toshiba T3100 adapter. If your system meets the requirements, you may elect whether to install the graphics portion of the program.

- *Upgrading to a New Version*   If you are upgrading, you should pay attention to the screen that warns you that reinstallation of Perspective will result in the loss of all data that may already exist in a Perspective directory called \3D. If you are upgrading or reinstalling for any reason, take a moment to determine whether you have graphics files you want to save. If not, go ahead and install the graphics program. Otherwise, halt the installation program with the Esc key, protect your files by moving them to another subdirectory, and start over again.

- *Using Enable on a LAN*   You will be asked whether you are installing Enable on a hard disk to be used as a LAN server. If you are, you will be asked a series of questions to determine the kind of installation to make.

- *Installing on an OS/2 System*   You will be asked whether this installation is to a machine with the OS/2 operating system.

- *Installing Graphics Adapter Drivers*   If you have more than one graphics adapter, you can install drivers for all graphics adapters and then choose among them with a switch at the time you invoke Enable at the operating system prompt. If you have multiple graphics adapters and you are likely to use them, elect to install all of the video drivers at the next screen.

- *Installing Hypertext Documentation*   You will be asked whether you want to install Hypertext online documentation. In effect this will be like having an electronic version of the manual available at all times. If you have plenty of disk space, elect to install Hypertext.

- *Tutorial Lessons*   You can install tutorial lessons now or later. Install them now, on the hard disk.

- *Specifying a Subdirectory for Enable*   You will be asked to enter the subdirectory where Enable should be placed. Enable will place the program in a subdirectory called C:\EN300 unless you specify otherwise. Press ↵ if this is acceptable. If not, fill in your own preference. Enable will double check that you want to install the files in the named subdirectory.

Enable now checks your hard disk to determine whether you have enough space for the files. If not, you will be informed. If you

APPENDIX

have enough space, Enable will begin to install itself. Follow these steps to continue with the installation:

4. The first disk will install uneventfully. You then are prompted to remove the INSTALL 1 disk and insert the INSTALL 2 disk. Enable will pause to ask what sort of graphics adapter you will want for the default. Select the answer closest to your equipment. If you elected to install all drivers, it will install your main driver first, and then install the rest.

The installation program will prompt you to change disks.

5. Remove the INSTALL 2 disk and insert the INSTALL 3A disk.

Enable will pause for you to enter the printers you want installed.

6. Press **1** to install a printer. The upper half of the screen splits vertically. The names of printer manufacturers will appear on the left. Cursor down to the manufacturer of your printer. As you cursor through the list, printer models will appear in the right half of the screen.

7. When you reach your printer manufacturer, press ◄┘ and the highlight will skip to the other side of the split screen. Cursor to your printer model and press ◄┘ again. As you cursor, important information about the printer will be displayed in the lower third of the screen.

8. Press Esc twice to leave this screen and return to the printer driver installation screen. Your options are to select another printer (1), display a list of printers available (2), or install the drivers (3). Make the appropriate selection.

9. When you are finished selecting printers, press **3** and Enable will install the drivers necessary. You may have to swap disks several times, particularly if you have chosen more than one printer.

10. When you are finished installing the driver and its library from the installation disks 3A and 3B, press Esc. You will be

told that the printer installation was successful and to press any key.

11. Place the INSTALL 4 disk in drive A and press a key.

Installation is now a simple matter of changing disks in response to the prompts that appear on the screen. Before your installation is complete, however, you must prepare your profile. Please turn to Chapter 22 for instructions.

That's all there is to the installation of Enable OA. Before you begin using Enable, there are a couple of things you should do first.

CREATING THE DATA SUBDIRECTORY

In order to perform certain tasks in this book, you will need a sub-directory called DATA off the root directory. When Enable is completely installed, create this subdirectory by entering this command at the DOS prompt:

```
MKDIR \DATA ↵
```

ALTERING YOUR BOOT FILES

To run Enable with DOS 3.0 or later, you will need to have the following statement in your CONFIG.SYS file: FILES=40. Here's how to check if it's in your file:

1. Display the contents of the CONFIG.SYS file by typing this command:

```
TYPE \CONFIG.SYS
```

If the FILES statement isn't in the file, you can use an ASCII word processor to alter it, or you may follow this procedure:

2. Use the following commands to copy the CONFIG.SYS file and then change its name:

COPY CONFIG.SYS CONFI.OLD
REN CONFIG.SYS ANYTHING.SYS

Now use the following commands to make an appendable file:

3. First type

COPY CON CONFI.NEW

This will allow you to create an ASCII file from the command line. Your cursor will appear on a blank line.

4. Type

FILES=40

and press ◄─┘.

You will also have to add a BUFFERS statement.

5. If you are operating an XT compatible, enter

BUFFERS = 20

and press ◄─┘. If you are operating an AT compatible, enter

BUFFERS = 40

and press ◄─┘.

6. Finally, press F6. That will tell the operating system to close the file.

Now issue the last command to bind the two files together:

7. Type

COPY CONFI.* CONFIG.SYS

8. Display the CONFIG.SYS file again (see step 1) to make sure the FILES=40 line follows any other FILES statement in the CONFIG.SYS file.

Now each time you boot your computer, it will set itself up to run Enable (and a lot of other software) more efficiently.

Reboot your computer before running Enable.

INDEX

Selections from
The SYBEX Library

SPREADSHEETS AND INTEGRATED SOFTWARE

The ABC's of 1-2-3
(Second Edition)
Chris Gilbert/Laurie Williams
245pp. Ref. 355-4

Online Today recommends it as "an easy and comfortable way to get started with the program." An essential tutorial for novices, it will remain on your desk as a valuable source of ongoing reference and support. For Release 2.

The ABC's of 1-2-3 Release 2.2
Chris Gilbert/Laurie Williams
340pp. Ref. 623-5

New Lotus 1-2-3 users delight in this book's step-by-step approach to building trouble-free spreadsheets, displaying graphs, and efficiently building databases. The authors cover the ins and outs of the latest version including easier calculations, file linking, and better graphic presentation.

The ABC's of 1-2-3 Release 3
Judd Robbins
290pp. Ref. 519-0

The ideal book for beginners who are new to Lotus or new to Release 3. This step-by-step approach to the 1-2-3 spreadsheet software gets the reader up and running with spreadsheet, database, graphics, and macro functions.

The ABC's of Excel
on the IBM PC
Douglas Hergert
326pp. Ref. 567-0

This book is a brisk and friendly introduction to the most important features of

Microsoft Excel for PC's. This beginner's book discusses worksheets, charts, database operations, and macros, all with hands-on examples. Written for all versions through Version 2.

The ABC's of Quattro
Alan Simpson/Douglas J. Wolf
286pp. Ref. 560-3

Especially for users new to spreadsheets, this is an introduction to the basic concepts and a guide to instant productivity through editing and using spreadsheet formulas and functions. Includes how to print out graphs and data for presentation. For Quattro 1.1.

Advanced Techniques
in Lotus 1-2-3
Peter Antoniak/E. Michael Lunsford
367pp. Ref. 556-5

This guide for experienced users focuses on advanced functions, and techniques for designing menu-driven applications using macros and the Release 2 command language. Interfacing techniques and add-on products are also considered.

The Complete Lotus 1-2-3
Release 2.2 Handbook
Greg Harvey
750pp. Ref. 625-1

This comprehensive handbook discusses every 1-2-3 operating with clear instructions and practical tips. This volume especially emphasizes the new improved graphics, high-speed recalculation techniques, and spreadsheet linking available with Release 2.2.

The Complete Lotus 1-2-3
Release 3 Handbook
Greg Harvey
700pp. Ref. 600-6

Everything you ever wanted to know about 1-2-3 is in this definitive handbook.

As a Release 3 guide, it features the design and use of 3D worksheets, and improved graphics, along with using Lotus under DOS or OS/2. Problems, exercises, and helpful insights are included.

Excel Instant Reference
SYBEX Prompter Series
William J. Orvis
368pp. Ref. 577-8, 4 ¾" × 8"
This pocket-sized reference book contains all of Excel's menu commands, math operations, and macro functions. Quick and easy access to command syntax, usage, arguments, and examples make this Instant Reference a must. Through Version 1.5.

Lotus 1-2-3 Instant Reference
Release 2.2
SYBEX Prompter Series
Greg Harvey/Kay Yarborough Nelson
254pp. Ref. 635-9, 4 ¾" × 8"
The reader gets quick and easy access to any operation in 1-2-3 Version 2.2 in this handy pocket-sized encyclopedia. Organized by menu function, each command and function has a summary description, the exact key sequence, and a discussion of the options.

Lotus 1-2-3 Desktop Companion
SYBEX Ready Reference Series
Greg Harvey
976pp. Ref. 501-8
A full-time consultant, right on your desk. Hundreds of self-contained entries cover every 1-2-3 feature, organized by topic, indexed and cross-referenced, and supplemented by tips, macros and working examples. For Release 2.

Lotus 1-2-3 Tips and Tricks
(2nd edition)
Gene Weisskopf
425pp. Ref. 668-5
This outstanding collection of tips, shortcuts and cautions for longtime Lotus users is in an expanded new edition covering Release 2.2. Topics include macros, range names, spreadsheet design, hardware and operating system tips, data

analysis, printing, data interchange, applications development, and more.

Mastering 1-2-3
(Second Edition)
Carolyn Jorgensen
702pp. Ref. 528-X
Get the most from 1-2-3 Release 2.01 with this step-by-step guide emphasizing advanced features and practical uses. Topics include data sharing, macros, spreadsheet security, expanded memory, and graphics enhancements.

Mastering 1-2-3 Release 3
Carolyn Jorgensen
682pp. Ref. 517-4
For new Release 3 and experienced Release 2 users, "Mastering" starts with a basic spreadsheet, then introduces spreadsheet and database commands, functions, and macros, and then tells how to analyze 3D spreadsheets and make high-impact reports and graphs. Lotus add-ons are discussed and Fast Tracks are included.

Mastering Enable
Keith D. Bishop
517pp. Ref. 440-2
A comprehensive, practical, hands-on guide to Enable 2.0—integrated word processing, spreadsheet, database management, graphics, and communications—from basic concepts to custom menus, macros and the Enable Procedural Language.

Mastering Excel on the IBM PC
Carl Townsend
628pp. Ref. 403-8
A complete Excel handbook with step-by-step tutorials, sample applications and an extensive reference section. Topics include worksheet fundamentals, formulas and windows, graphics, database techniques, special features, macros and more.

Mastering Framework III
Douglas Hergert/Jonathan Kamin
613pp. Ref. 513-1
Thorough, hands-on treatment of the latest Framework release. An outstanding

introduction to integrated software applications, with examples for outlining, spreadsheets, word processing, databases, and more; plus an introduction to FRED programming.

Mastering Quattro
Alan Simpson
576pp. Ref. 514-X
This tutorial covers not only all of Quattro's classic spreadsheet features, but also its added capabilities including extended graphing, modifiable menus, and the macro debugging environment. Simpson brings out how to use all of Quattro's new-generation-spreadsheet capabilities.

Mastering SuperCalc5
Greg Harvey/Mary Beth Andrasak
500pp. Ref. 624-3
This book offers a complete and unintimidating guided tour through each feature. With step-by-step lessons, readers learn about the full capabilities of spreadsheet, graphics, and data management functions. Multiple spreadsheets, linked spreadsheets, 3D graphics, and macros are also discussed.

Mastering Symphony (Fourth Edition)
Douglas Cobb
857pp. Ref. 494-1
Thoroughly revised to cover all aspects of the major upgrade of Symphony Version 2, this Fourth Edition of Doug Cobb's classic is still "the Symphony bible" to this complex but even more powerful package. All the new features are discussed and placed in context with prior versions so that both new and previous users will benefit from Cobb's insights.

Teach Yourself Lotus 1-2-3 Release 2.2
Jeff Woodward
250pp. Ref. 641-3
Readers match what they see on the screen with the book's screen-by-screen action sequences. For new Lotus users, topics include computer fundamentals, opening and editing a worksheet, using

graphs, macros, and printing typeset-quality reports. For Release 2.2.

Understanding PFS: First Choice
Gerry Litton
489pp. Ref. 568-9
From basic commands to complex features, this complete guide to the popular integrated package is loaded with step-by-step instructions. Lessons cover creating attractive documents, setting up easy-to-use databases, working with spreadsheets and graphics, and smoothly integrating tasks from different First Choice modules. For Version 3.0.

DATABASES

The ABC's of dBASE III PLUS
Robert Cowart
264pp. Ref. 379-1
The most efficient way to get beginners up and running with dBASE. Every 'how' and 'why' of database management is demonstrated through tutorials and practical dBASE III PLUS applications.

The ABC's of dBASE IV
Robert Cowart
338pp. Ref. 531-X
This superb tutorial introduces beginners to the concept of databases and practical dBASE IV applications featuring the new menu-driven interface, the new report writer, and Query by Example.

The ABC's of Paradox
Charles Siegel
300pp. Ref. 573-5
Easy to understand and use, this introduction is written so that the computer novice can create, edit, and manage complex Paradox databases. This primer is filled with examples of the Paradox 3.0 menu structure.

Advanced Techniques in dBASE III PLUS
Alan Simpson
454pp. Ref. 369-4
A full course in database design and structured programming, with routines for

inventory control, accounts receivable, system management, and integrated databases.

dBASE Instant Reference
SYBEX Prompter Series
Alan Simpson

471pp. Ref. 484-4; 4 ¾" × 8"

Comprehensive information at a glance: a brief explanation of syntax and usage for every dBASE command, with step-by-step instructions and exact keystroke sequences. Commands are grouped by function in twenty precise categories.

dBASE IV Programmer's
Instant Reference
SYBEX Prompter Series
Alan Simpson

544pp. Ref. 538-7, 4 ¾" × 8"

This comprehensive reference to every dBASE command and function has everything for the dBASE programmer in a compact, pocket-sized book. Fast and easy access to adding data, sorting, performing calculations, managing multiple databases, memory variables and arrays, windows and menus, networking, and much more. Version 1.1.

dBASE III PLUS Programmer's
Reference Guide
SYBEX Ready Reference Series
Alan Simpson

1056pp. Ref. 508-5

Programmers will save untold hours and effort using this comprehensive, well-organized dBASE encyclopedia. Complete technical details on commands and functions, plus scores of often-needed algorithms.

dBASE IV User's
Desktop Companion
SYBEX Ready Reference Series
Alan Simpson

950pp. Ref. 523-9

This easy-to-use reference provides an exhaustive resource guide to taking full advantage of the powerful non-programming features of the dBASE IV Control Center. This book discusses query by example, custom reports and data entry screens, macros, the application generator, and the dBASE command and programming language.

dBASE IV User's
Instant Reference
SYBEX Prompter Series
Alan Simpson

349pp. Ref. 605-7, 4 ¾" × 8"

This handy pocket-sized reference book gives every new dBASE IV user fast and easy access to any dBASE command. Arranged alphabetically and by function, each entry includes a description, exact syntax, an example, and special tips from Alan Simpson.

Mastering dBASE III PLUS:
A Structured Approach
Carl Townsend

342pp. Ref. 372-4

In-depth treatment of structured programming for custom dBASE solutions. An ideal study and reference guide for applications developers, new and experienced users with an interest in efficient programming.

Mastering dBASE IV
Programming
Carl Townsend

496pp. Ref. 540-9

This task-oriented book introduces structured dBASE IV programming and commands by setting up a general ledger system, an invoice system, and a quotation management system. The author carefully explores the unique character of dBASE IV based on his in-depth understanding of the program.

Mastering Q & A
(Second Edition)
Greg Harvey

540pp. Ref. 452-6

This hands-on tutorial explores the Q & A Write, File, and Report modules, and the Intelligent Assistant. English-language command processor, macro creation, interfacing with other software, and more, using practical business examples.

Mastering Paradox
(Fourth Edition)
Alan Simpson
636pp. Ref. 612-X

Best selling author Alan Simpson simplifies all aspects of Paradox for the beginning to intermediate user. The book starts with database basics, covers multiple tables, graphics, custom applications with PAL, and the Personal Programmer. For Version 3.0.

Power User's Guide to R:BASE
Alan Simpson/Cheryl Currid/Craig Gillett
446pp. Ref. 354-6

Supercharge your R:BASE applications with this straightforward tutorial that covers system design, structured programming, managing multiple data tables, and more. Sample applications include ready-to-run mailing, inventory and accounts receivable systems. Through Version 2.11.

Quick Guide to dBASE:
The Visual Approach
David Kolodney
382pp. Ref. 596-4

This illustrated tutorial provides the beginner with a working knowledge of all the basic functions of dBASE IV. Images of each successive dBASE screen tell how to create and modify a database, add, edit, sort and select records, and print custom labels and reports.

Simpson's dBASE Tips and
Tricks (For dBASE III PLUS)
Alan Simpson
420pp. Ref. 383-X

A unique library of techniques and programs shows how creative use of built-in features can solve all your needs—without expensive add-on products or external languages. Spreadsheet functions, graphics, and much more.

Understanding dBASE III
Alan Simpson
300pp. Ref. 267-1

dBASE commands and concepts are illustrated throughout with practical, business oriented examples—for mailing list handling, accounts receivable, and inventory design. Contains scores of tips and techniques for maximizing efficiency and meeting special needs.

Understanding dBASE III PLUS
Alan Simpson
415pp. Ref. 349-X

A solid sourcebook of training and ongoing support. Everything from creating a first database to command file programming is presented in working examples, with tips and techniques you won't find anywhere else.

Understanding dBASE IV
(Special Edition)
Alan Simpson
880pp. Ref. 509-3

This Special Edition is the best introduction to dBASE IV, written by 1 million-reader-strong dBASE expert Alan Simpson. First it gives basic skills for creating and manipulating efficient databases. Then the author explains how to make reports, manage multiple databases, and build applications. Includes Fast Track speed notes.

Understanding R:BASE
Alan Simpson/Karen Watterson
609pp. Ref. 503-4

This is the definitive R:BASE tutorial, for use with either OS/2 or DOS. Hands-on lessons cover every aspect of the software, from creating and using a database, to custom systems. Includes Fast Track speed notes.

Understanding Oracle
James T. Perry/Joseph G. Lateer
634pp. Ref. 534-4

A comprehensive guide to the Oracle database management system for administrators, users, and applications developers. Covers everything in Version 5 from database basics to multi-user systems, performance, and development tools including SQL*Forms, SQL*Report, and SQL*Calc. Includes Fast Track speed notes.

Understanding SQL
Martin Gruber
400pp. Ref. 644-8

This comprehensive tutorial in Structured Query Language (SQL) is suitable for beginners, and for SQL users wishing to increase their skills. From basic principles to complex SQL applications, the text builds fluency and confidence using concise hands-on lessons and easy-to-follow examples.

Up & Running with Q&A
Ranier Bartel
140pp. Ref. 645-6

Obtain practical results with Q&A in the shortest possible time. Learn to design and program forms, use macros, format text, use utilities, and more. Or use the book to help you decide whether to purchase the program.

WORD PROCESSING

The ABC's of Microsoft Word (Third Edition)
Alan R. Neibauer
461pp. Ref. 604-9

This is for the novice WORD user who wants to begin producing documents in the shortest time possible. Each chapter has short, easy-to-follow lessons for both keyboard and mouse, including all the basic editing, formatting and printing functions. Version 5.0.

The ABC's of WordPerfect
Alan R. Neibauer
239pp. Ref. 425-9

This basic introduction to WordPefect consists of short, step-by-step lessons—for new users who want to get going fast. Topics range from simple editing and formatting, to merging, sorting, macros, and more. Includes version 4.2

The ABC's of WordPerfect 5
Alan R. Neibauer
283pp. Ref. 504-2

This introduction explains the basics of desktop publishing with WordPerfect 5: editing, layout, formatting, printing, sorting, merging, and more. Readers are shown how to use WordPerfect 5's new features to produce great-looking reports.

Advanced Techniques in Microsoft Word (Second Edition)
Alan R. Neibauer
462pp. Ref. 615-4

This highly acclaimed guide to WORD is an excellent tutorial for intermediate to advanced users. Topics include word processing fundamentals, desktop publishing with graphics, data management, and working in a multiuser environment. For Versions 4 and 5.

Advanced Techniques in MultiMate
Chris Gilbert
275pp. Ref. 412-7

A textbook on efficient use of MultiMate for business applications, in a series of self-contained lessons on such topics as multiple columns, high-speed merging, mailing-list printing and Key Procedures.

Advanced Techniques in WordPerfect 5
Kay Yarborough Nelson
586pp. Ref. 511-5

Now updated for Version 5, this invaluable guide to the advanced features of WordPerfect provides step-by-step instructions and practical examples covering those specialized techniques which have most perplexed users—indexing, outlining, foreign-language typing, mathematical functions, and more.

The Complete Guide to MultiMate
Carol Holcomb Dreger
208pp. Ref. 229-9

This step-by-step tutorial is also an excellent reference guide to MultiMate features and uses. Topics include search/replace, library and merge functions, repagination, document defaults and more.

Introduction to WordStar
Arthur Naiman
208pp. Ref. 134-9

This all time bestseller is an engaging first-time introduction to word processing as

TO JOIN THE SYBEX MAILING LIST OR ORDER BOOKS
PLEASE COMPLETE THIS FORM

NAME _____ COMPANY _____

STREET _____ CITY _____

STATE _____ ZIP _____

☐ PLEASE MAIL ME MORE INFORMATION ABOUT **SYBEX** TITLES

ORDER FORM (There is no obligation to order)

PLEASE SEND ME THE FOLLOWING:

TITLE	QTY	PRICE
_____	____	____
_____	____	____
_____	____	____
_____	____	____

TOTAL BOOK ORDER ____ $____

CUSTOMER SIGNATURE _____

SHIPPING AND HANDLING PLEASE ADD $2.00 PER BOOK VIA UPS ____

FOR OVERSEAS SURFACE ADD $5.25 PER BOOK PLUS $4.40 REGISTRATION FEE ____

FOR OVERSEAS AIRMAIL ADD $18.25 PER BOOK PLUS $4.40 REGISTRATION FEE ____

CALIFORNIA RESIDENTS PLEASE ADD APPLICABLE SALES TAX ____

TOTAL AMOUNT PAYABLE ____

☐ CHECK ENCLOSED ☐ VISA
☐ MASTERCARD ☐ AMERICAN EXPRESS

ACCOUNT NUMBER _____

EXPIR. DATE _____ DAYTIME PHONE _____

CHECK AREA OF COMPUTER INTEREST:

☐ BUSINESS SOFTWARE

☐ TECHNICAL PROGRAMMING

☐ OTHER: _____

THE FACTOR THAT WAS MOST IMPORTANT IN YOUR SELECTION:

☐ THE SYBEX NAME

☐ QUALITY

☐ PRICE

☐ EXTRA FEATURES

☐ COMPREHENSIVENESS

☐ CLEAR WRITING

☐ OTHER _____

OTHER COMPUTER TITLES YOU WOULD LIKE TO SEE IN PRINT:

_____

_____

OCCUPATION

☐ PROGRAMMER   ☐ TEACHER

☐ SENIOR EXECUTIVE   ☐ HOMEMAKER

☐ COMPUTER CONSULTANT   ☐ RETIRED

☐ SUPERVISOR   ☐ STUDENT

☐ MIDDLE MANAGEMENT   ☐ OTHER:

☐ ENGINEER/TECHNICAL   _____

☐ CLERICAL/SERVICE

☐ BUSINESS OWNER/SELF EMPLOYED

CHECK YOUR LEVEL OF COMPUTER USE

☐ NEW TO COMPUTERS

☐ INFREQUENT COMPUTER USER

☐ FREQUENT USER OF ONE SOFTWARE

   PACKAGE:

   NAME _____

☐ FREQUENT USER OF MANY SOFTWARE

   PACKAGES

☐ PROFESSIONAL PROGRAMMER

OTHER COMMENTS:

_____

_____

_____

_____

_____

_____

_____

PLEASE FOLD, SEAL, AND MAIL TO SYBEX

- -

SYBEX, INC.
2021 CHALLENGER DR. #100
ALAMEDA, CALIFORNIA USA
                94501

SEAL

SYBEX Computer Books are different.

Here is why . . .

At SYBEX, each book is designed with you in mind. Every manuscript is carefully selected and supervised by our editors, who are themselves computer experts. We publish the best authors, whose technical expertise is matched by an ability to write clearly and to communicate effectively. Programs are thoroughly tested for accuracy by our technical staff. Our computerized production department goes to great lengths to make sure that each book is well-designed.

In the pursuit of timeliness, SYBEX has achieved many publishing firsts. SYBEX was among the first to integrate personal computers used by authors and staff into the publishing process. SYBEX was the first to publish books on the CP/M operating system, microprocessor interfacing techniques, word processing, and many more topics.

Expertise in computers and dedication to the highest quality product have made SYBEX a world leader in computer book publishing. Translated into fourteen languages, SYBEX books have helped millions of people around the world to get the most from their computers. We hope we have helped you, too.

For a complete catalog of our publications:

SYBEX, Inc. 2021 Challenger Drive, #100, Alameda, CA 94501
Tel: (415) 523-8233/(800) 227-2346   Telex: 336311
Fax: (415) 523-2373

DATABASE MENU OPTIONS

INTERACT AND REPORT OPTIONS

DisplayOpts
Find (Build a database subset) {F9 C F}
Display records in this database {F9 C D}
Browse an Index to this database {F9 C B}
Graph selected fields {F9 C G}
Sort (Build sorted subset) {F9 C S}
Report (Produce a report) {F9 C 9}

EditOpts
Add records to database {F9 C A}
Edit selected records {F9 C E}
Verify selected records {F9 C V}
Replace selected records {F9 C R}
1 = Delete {F9 C 1}
2 = Undelete {F9 C 2}

BatchOpts
Update from transaction file {F9 C U}
Copy to another database {F9 C C}
Merge similar databases {F9 C M}
Sort (Build sorted subset) {F9 C S}
Index (Create new index) {F9 C I}

CmndChart
Select command chart option

MCM
Windows
  Open a window {Alt-Home} {F9 W O}
  Modify size or location {F9 W L}
  Go to another window {F9 W [n] G}
  Go to the next window {Alt-↑} {F9 W A}
  Zoom to full screen size {F9 W Z}
  Resume previous size {F9 W P}
  Display window status lines {F9 W ?}
  Close current window {F9 W C}
Files
Screen
  Mono
  Bw80
  Co80
  Graphics

Quit

BUILD OPTIONS

Next {F5}

Previous {F6}

Save {Alt-F10}

Ignore {Alt-F6}

Add (Find mode only) {Ctrl-F5}

1 = Query {Shift-F1}
  Find (Switch to Find mode)
  Add (Switch to Add mode)
  Quit

2 = Index {Shift-F5}
  Enter index

Where {Shift-F6}
  Enter location

Quit

DESIGN OPTIONS

Save
Same name
New name

Print

Delete

Quit
No
Yes

TELECOMMUNICATIONS MENU OPTIONS

Break

Capture
Word Processing (ON/OFF) {F9 T C} {F7}
Active File (ON/OFF)
Open
   Enter file name
Close

Disconnect
No
Yes {F9 T D}

Files
Receive
  Select protocol: None, Enable, Xmodem,
     Kermit, 1 = Kerm:Logout,
      2 = Kerm:Finish
  Enter target file name
Transmit
  Select protocol: None, Enable, Xmodem,
     Kermit, 1 = Kerm:Logout,
      2 = Kerm:Finish
  Enter target file name
Unattended
  Enter transfer table name
Auto timeout: 1 = Receive
  Select protocol: None, Enable, Xmodem,
     Kermit, 1 = Kerm:Logout,
      2 = Kerm:Finish
  Enter target file name
Auto timeout: 2 = Transmit
  Select protocol: None, Enable, Xmodem,
     Kermit, 1 = Kerm:Logout,
      2 = Kerm:Finish
  Enter target file name

MCM
Windows
  Open a window {Alt-Home} {F9 W O}
  Modify size or location {F9 W L}
  Go to another window {F9 W [n] G}
  Go to the next window {Alt-↑}
  Zoom to full screen size {F9 W Z}
  Resume previous size {F9 W P}
  Display window status lines {F9 W ?}
  Close current window {Alt-End}
    {F9 W C}
Files {F9 D}
  Select from listed files or use commands
Screen
  Mono
  Bw80
  Co80
  Graphics

Other
Cost
  On/Off
  Set
Duplex
LF (added line feed)
  No
  Yes
Pause
  Select pause time
Set Break
  Enter value
Time
Xon/Xoff
Emulation
  Off
  Resume
  1 = VT100
  2 = VT52
  3 = ATT4410
Map
  Use keymap table
  Cancel
  Resume

Print
On/Off
1 = COM1
2 = COM2
3 = LPT1
4 = LPT2

Tele
Answer-mode
Call
  Enter telephone number
Hang-up

WP
[*see Word Processor Menu Options*]